Praise for the First Edition

The closest thing I've seen to a class in a book. Contains tons of useful exercises that instill PowerShell prowess by hands-on learning.

—Chuck Durfee
Sr. Software Engineer, Graebel Companies

From beginners to intermediate—this is THE only book you need. Don Jones is a PowerShell superstar and in this book you will see why.

—David Moravec
SCCM Administrator, PowerShell.cz

The seminal guide to learning Powershell—highly recommended.

—Ray Booysen
Developer, BNP Paribas

The book I wish I'd had when I started PowerShell!

—Richard Siddaway
IT Architect and PowerShell MVP

This book not only teaches you PowerShell, it also teaches you to become an expert in PowerShell.

—Nikander Bruggeman and Margriet Bruggeman,
.NET consultants, Lois & Clark IT Services

Learn Windows PowerShell 3
in a Month of Lunches

SECOND EDITION

DON JONES
JEFFERY HICKS

MANNING
SHELTER ISLAND

Manning Publications Co.
20 Baldwin Road
PO Box 261
Shelter Island, NY 11964

Development editor: Cynthia Kane
Technical Proofreaders: James Berkenbile, Trent Whiteley
Copyeditor: Andy Carroll
Proofreader: Maureen Spencer
Typesetter: Dottie Marsico
Cover designer: Marija Tudor

ISBN 9781617291081
Printed in the United States of America
1 2 3 4 5 6 7 8 9 10 – MAL – 17 16 15 14 13 12

brief contents

contents

15 Multitasking with background jobs   182

16 Working with many objects, one at a time   196

17 Security alert!   211

preface

We've been teaching and writing about Windows PowerShell for a long time. When Don began contemplating the first edition of this book, he realized that most Power-Shell writers and teachers—including himself—were forcing our students to approach the shell as a kind of programming language. Most PowerShell books are into "scripting" by the third or fourth chapter, yet more and more PowerShell students were backing away from that programming-oriented approach. Those students wanted to use the shell as a shell, at least at first, and we simply weren't delivering a learning experience that matched that desire.

So he decided to take a swing at it. A blog post on WindowsITPro.com proposed a table of contents for this book, and ample feedback from the blog's readers fine-tuned it into the book you're about to read. He wanted to keep each chapter short, focused, and easy to cover in a short period of time—because we know administrators don't have a lot of free time, and often have to learn on the fly. When Power-Shell v3 came out, it was obviously a good time to update the book, and Don turned to long-time collaborator Jeffery Hicks to help out.

We both wanted a book that would focus on PowerShell itself, and not on the myriad technologies that PowerShell touches, like Exchange Server, SQL Server, System Center, and so on. We truly feel that by learning to use the shell properly, you can teach yourself to administer all of those "PowerShell-ed" server products. So this book tries to focus on the core of using PowerShell. Even if you're also using a "cookbook" style of book, which provides ready-to-use answers for specific administrative tasks, this book will help you understand what those examples are doing. That understanding will make it easier to modify those examples for other purposes, and eventually to construct your own commands and scripts from scratch.

We hope this book won't be the only PowerShell education that you pursue. In fact, this book's companion website, MoreLunches.com, is designed to help you continue that education in small chunks. It offers free videos that correspond to this book's chapters, letting you see and hear our demonstrations of key techniques. We've also co-authored *Learn PowerShell Toolmaking in a Month of Lunches*, which offers the same day-at-a-time approach to learning PowerShell's scripting and tool-creation capabilities.

If you need any further help, we encourage you to log on to www.PowerShell.org. We both answer questions in several of the discussion forums there, and we'd be happy to try and get you out of whatever you're stuck on. The site is also a great portal into the robust and active PowerShell community—you can learn about the annual Scripting Games, the in-person PowerShell Summit, and about all of the regional and local user groups and PowerShell-related events that happen throughout the year. Get involved—it's a great way to make PowerShell a more powerful part of your career.

Enjoy—and good luck with the shell.

about this book

Most of what you'll need to know about this book is covered in chapter 1, but there are a few things that we should mention up front.

First of all, if you plan to follow along with our examples and complete the hands-on exercises, you'll need a virtual machine or computer running Windows 8 or Windows Server 2012. We cover that in more detail in chapter 1. You can get by with Windows 7, but you'll miss out on a few of the hands-on labs.

Second, be prepared to read this book from start to finish, covering each chapter in order. Again, this is something we'll explain in more detail in chapter 1, but the idea is that each chapter introduces a few new things that you will need in subsequent chapters. You really shouldn't try to push through the whole book – stick with the one chapter per day approach. The human brain can only absorb so much information at once, and by taking on PowerShell in small chunks, you'll actually learn it a lot faster and more thoroughly.

Third, this book contains a lot of code snippets. Most of them are quite short, so you should be able to type them quite easily. In fact, we recommend that you do type them, since doing so will help reinforce an essential PowerShell skill: accurate typing! Longer code snippets are given in listings and are available for download at http://Morelunches.com (just click on this book's cover image and look for the "Downloads" section), as well as from the publisher's website at www.manning.com/LearnWindowsPowerShell3inaMonthofLunchesSecondEdition.

That said, there are a few conventions that you should be aware of. Code will always appear in a special font, just like this example:

```
Get-WmiObject –class Win32_OperatingSystem
➥ –computerName SERVER-R2
```

That example also illustrates the line-continuation character used in this book. It indicates that those two lines should actually be typed as a single line in PowerShell. In other words, don't hit Enter or Return after Win32_OperatingSystem—keep right on typing. PowerShell allows for very long lines, but the pages of this book can only hold so much.

Sometimes, you'll also see that code font within the text itself, such as when we write `Get-Command`. That just lets you know that you're looking at a command, parameter, or other element that you would actually type within the shell.

Fourth is a tricky topic that we'll bring up again in several chapters: the backtick character (`` ` ``). Here's an example:

```
Invoke-Command -scriptblock { Dir } `
-computerName SERVER-R2,localhost
```

The character at the end of the first line isn't a stray bit of ink—it's a real character that you would type. On a U.S. keyboard, the backtick (or grave accent) is usually near the upper left, under the Escape key, on the same key as the tilde character (~). When you see the backtick in a code listing, type it exactly as is. Furthermore, when it appears at the end of a line—as in the preceding example—make sure that it's the very last character on that line. If you allow any spaces or tabs to appear after it, the backtick won't work correctly, and neither will the code example.

Finally, we'll occasionally direct you to Internet resources. Where those URLs are particularly long and difficult to type, we've replaced them with Manning-based shortened URLs that look like http://mng.bz/S085 (you'll see that one in chapter 1).

Author Online

The purchase of *Learn Windows PowerShell 3 in a Month of Lunches, Second Edition* includes access to a private forum run by Manning Publications where you can make comments about the book, ask technical questions, and receive help from the authors and other users. To access and subscribe to the forum, point your browser to www.manning.com/LearnWindowsPowerShell3inaMonthofLunchesSecondEdition or to www.manning.com/jones3 and click the Author Online link. This page provides information on how to get on the forum once you are registered, what kind of help is available, and the rules of conduct in the forum.

Manning's commitment to our readers is to provide a venue where a meaningful dialogue between individual readers and between readers and the authors can take place. It's not a commitment to any specific amount of participation on the part of the authors, whose contribution to the book's forum remains voluntary (and unpaid). We suggest you try asking the authors some challenging questions, lest their interest stray!

The Author Online forum and the archives of previous discussions will be accessible from the publisher's website as long as the book is in print.

about the authors

DON JONES is a multiple-year recipient of Microsoft's prestigious Most Valuable Professional (MVP) Award for his work with Windows PowerShell. He writes the Windows PowerShell column for *Microsoft TechNet Magazine,* blogs at PowerShell.org, and authors the "Decision Maker" column and blog for *Redmond Magazine.* Don is a prolific technology author and has published more than a dozen print books since 2001. He is also is a Senior Partner and Principal Technologist for Concentrated Technology (ConcentratedTech.com), an IT education and strategic consulting firm. Don's first Windows scripting language was KiXtart, going back all the way to the mid-1990s. He quickly graduated to VBScript in 1995 and was one of the first IT pros to start using early releases of a new Microsoft product code-named "Monad"—which later became Windows PowerShell. Don lives in Las Vegas and travels all over the world delivering IT training (especially in PowerShell) and speaking at IT conferences.

JEFFERY HICKS is a multi-year Microsoft MVP in Windows PowerShell, a Microsoft Certified Trainer, and an IT veteran with 20 years of experience, much of it spent as an IT consultant specializing in Microsoft server technologies. He works today as an independent author, trainer, and consultant with clients all over the world. Jeff writes the popular Prof. PowerShell column for MPCMag.com and is a regular contributor to the Petri IT Knowledgebase. If he isn't writing books then he's most likely recording training videos for companies like TrainSignal or helping out in discussion forums. You can keep up with Jeff at his blog, http://jdhitsolutions.com/blog.

acknowledgments

Books simply don't write, edit, and publish themselves. Don would like to thank everyone at Manning Publications who decided to take a chance on a very different kind of book for Windows PowerShell, and who worked so hard to make the first edition of this book happen. Jeff would like to thank Don for inviting him along for the ride, and all the PowerShell community for their enthusiasm and support. Don and Jeff are both grateful to Manning for allowing them to continue the "Month of Lunches" series with this second edition.

Thanks also to the following peer reviewers who read the manuscript during its development and provided feedback: Bennett Scharf, Dave Pawson, David Moravec, Keith Hill, and Rajesh Attaluri; also to James Berkenbile and Trent Whiteley for their technical review of the manuscript and code during production.

Before you begin

We've been teaching Windows PowerShell since version 1 was released in 2006. Back then, most of the folks using the shell were experienced VBScript users, and they were eager to apply their VBScript skills to learning PowerShell. As a result, we and the other folks who taught the shell, wrote books and articles, and so forth, all adopted a teaching style that takes advantage of prior programming or scripting skills.

But since late 2009, a shift has occurred. More and more administrators who *don't* have prior VBScript experience have started trying to learn the shell. All of a sudden, our old teaching patterns didn't work as well, because we had focused on scripting and programming. That's when we realized that PowerShell isn't a scripting language. It's a command-line shell where you run command-line utilities. Like all good shells, it has scripting capabilities, but you don't have to use them, and you certainly don't have to *start* with them. We started changing our teaching patterns, beginning with the many conferences we speak at each year. Don also implemented these changes into his instructor-led training courseware.

This book is the result of that process, and it's the best that we've yet devised to teach PowerShell to someone who might not have a scripting background (although it certainly doesn't hurt if you do). But before we jump into the instruction, let's set the stage for you.

1.1   Why you can't afford to ignore PowerShell

Batch. KiXtart. VBScript. Let's face it, Windows PowerShell isn't exactly Microsoft's (or anyone else's) first effort at providing automation capabilities to Windows

1

administrators. We think it's valuable to understand why you should care about Power-Shell, because when you do, you'll feel comfortable that the time you commit to learning PowerShell will pay off. Let's start by considering what life was like before PowerShell came along, and look at some of the advantages of using this shell.

LIFE WITHOUT POWERSHELL

Windows administrators have always been happy to click around in the graphical user interface (GUI) to accomplish their chores. After all, the GUI is largely the whole point of Windows—the operating system isn't called "Text," after all. GUIs are great because they enable you to discover what you can do. Don remembers the first time he opened Active Directory Users and Computers. He hovered over icons and read tooltips, pulled down menus, and right-clicked on things, all to see what was available. GUIs make learning a tool easier. Unfortunately, GUIs have zero return on that investment. If it takes you five minutes to create a new user in Active Directory (and assuming you're filling in a lot of the fields, that's a reasonable estimate), you'll never get any faster than that. One hundred users will take five hundred minutes—there's no way, short of learning to type and click faster, to make the process go any quicker.

Microsoft has tried to deal with that problem a bit haphazardly, and VBScript was probably its most successful attempt. It might have taken you an hour to write a VBScript that could import new users from a CSV file, but once you'd invested that hour, creating users in the future would take only a few seconds. The problem with VBScript is that Microsoft didn't make a wholehearted effort in supporting it. Microsoft had to remember to make things VBScript-accessible, and when developers forgot (or didn't have time), you were stuck. Want to change the IP address of a network adapter using VBScript? OK, you can. Want to check its link speed? You can't, because nobody remembered to hook that up in a way that VBScript could get to. Sorry. Jeffrey Snover, the architect of Windows PowerShell, calls this "the last mile." You can do a lot with VBScript (and other, similar technologies), but it tends to let you down at some point, never getting you through that "last mile" to the finish line.

Windows PowerShell is an express attempt on Microsoft's part to do a better job, and to get you through the last mile.

LIFE WITH POWERSHELL

Microsoft's goal for Windows PowerShell is to build 100 % of a product's administrative functionality in the shell. Microsoft continues to build GUI consoles, but those consoles are executing PowerShell commands behind the scenes. That approach forces the company to make sure that every possible thing you can do with the product is accessible through the shell. If you need to automate a repetitive task or create a process that the GUI doesn't enable well, you can drop into the shell and take full control for yourself.

A number of Microsoft products have already adopted this approach, including Exchange Server 2007 and 2010, SharePoint Server 2010, many of the System Center products, and many components of Windows itself. Going forward, more and more products and Windows components will follow this pattern. The latest version of Windows Server, which is where PowerShell v3 was introduced, is almost completely managed from PowerShell—or by a GUI sitting atop PowerShell. That's why you can't afford to ignore PowerShell—over the next few years, it'll become the basis for more and more administration.

Ask yourself this question: If you were in charge of a team of IT administrators (and perhaps you are), who would you want in your senior, higher-paying positions? Administrators who need several minutes to click their way through a GUI each time they need to perform a task, or ones who can perform tasks in a few seconds after automating them? We already know the answer from almost every other part of the IT world. Ask a Cisco administrator, or an AS/400 operator, or a Unix administrator. The answer is, "I'd rather have the person who can run things more efficiently from the command line." Going forward, the Windows world will start to split into two groups: administrators who can use PowerShell, and those who can't. As Don famously said at Microsoft's TechEd 2010 conference, "your choice is 'learn PowerShell,' or 'would you like fries with that?'"

We're glad *you've* decided to learn PowerShell.

1.2 Is this book for you?

This book doesn't try to be all things to all people. In fact, Microsoft's PowerShell team loosely defines three audiences who use PowerShell:

- Administrators who primarily run commands and consume tools written by others
- Administrators who combine commands and tools into more complex processes, and perhaps package those as tools that less-experienced administrators can use
- Administrators and developers who create reusable tools and applications

This book is designed primarily for the first audience. We think it's valuable for anyone, even a developer, to understand how the shell is used to run commands. After all, if you're going to create your own tools and commands, you should know the patterns that the shell uses, as they allow you to make tools and commands that work as well as they can within the shell.

If you're interested in creating scripts to automate complex processes, such as new user provisioning, then you'll absolutely see how to do that by the end of this book. You'll even see how to get started on creating your own commands that other administrators can use. But this book won't plumb the depths of everything that PowerShell can possibly do. Our goal is to get you using the shell and being effective with it in a production environment.

We'll also show you a couple of ways to use PowerShell to connect to external management technologies—Windows Management Instrumentation (WMI) and regular expressions are the two examples that come quickly to mind. For the most part, we're going to introduce only those technologies and focus on how PowerShell connects to them. Those topics deserve their own books (and have them; we'll provide recommendations when we get there); we'll concentrate solely on the PowerShell side of things. We'll provide suggestions for further exploration if you'd like to pursue those technologies further on your own.

1.3   *How to use this book*

The idea behind this book is that you'll read one chapter each day. You don't have to read it during lunch, but each chapter should take you only about 40 minutes to read, giving you an extra 20 minutes to gobble down the rest of your sandwich and practice what the chapter showed you.

THE MAIN CHAPTERS

Of the chapters in this book, chapters 2 through 25 contain the main content, giving you 24 days' worth of lunches to look forward to. This means you can expect to complete the main content of the book in about a month. Try to stick with that schedule as much as possible, and don't feel the need to read extra chapters in a given day. It's more important that you spend some time practicing what each chapter shows you, because using the shell will help cement what you've learned. Not every chapter will require a full hour, so sometimes you'll be able to spend some additional time practicing (and eating lunch) before you have to get back to work.

HANDS-ON LABS

Most of the main content chapters include a short lab for you to complete. You'll be given instructions, and perhaps a hint or two, but you won't find any answers in the book. The answers are online, at MoreLunches.com, but try your best to complete each lab without looking at the online answers.

SUPPLEMENTARY MATERIALS

The MoreLunches.com website also contains additional supplementary content, including extra chapters, companion videos, and so forth. In fact, each chapter has at least one companion video, which means you can *see* what the chapter is trying to show you. Each video is only five minutes or so in length, which gives you time to watch them when you're done reading the chapters. You'll also find a collection of videos from this book's previous edition, all of which still apply to PowerShell v3. And they're all free.

FURTHER EXPLORATION

A few chapters in this book only skim the surface of some cool technologies, and we'll end those chapters with suggestions for how you might explore those technologies on your own. We'll point out additional resources, including free stuff that you can use to expand your skill set as the need arises.

ABOVE AND BEYOND

As we learned PowerShell, there were often times when we wanted to go off on a tangent and explore why something worked the way it did. We didn't learn a lot of extra practical skills that way, but we did gain a deeper understanding of what the shell is and how it works. We've included some of that tangential information throughout the book in sections labeled "Above and beyond." None of those will take you more than a couple of minutes or so to read, but if you're the type of person who likes to know why something works the way it does, they can provide some fun additional facts. If you feel those sections might distract you from the practical stuff, ignore them on your first read-through. You can always come back and explore them later when you've mastered the chapter's main material.

1.4 Setting up your lab environment

You're going to be doing a lot of practicing in Windows PowerShell throughout this book, and you'll want to have a lab environment to work in—please don't practice in your company's production environment.

All you'll need to run most of the examples in this book—and to complete all of the labs—is a copy of Windows that has PowerShell v3 installed. The copy can be Windows Vista, Windows 7, Windows Server 2008, Windows Server 2008 R2, Windows 8, or Windows Server 2012. Note that PowerShell might not exist on certain editions of Windows, such as "Starter" editions. If you're going to play with PowerShell, you'll have to invest in a version of Windows that has it. Also note that some of the labs rely on functionality that's new in Windows 8 and Windows Server 2012. At the start of each lab, we'll tell you what operating system you need in order to complete the lab. We do recommend having a Windows 8 or Windows Server 2012 computer to play with—even if it's in a virtual machine.

Keep in mind that, throughout this book, we're assuming you'll be working on a 64-bit operating system, also referred to as an "x64" operating system. As such, it comes with two copies of Windows PowerShell and the graphically oriented Windows PowerShell ISE. In the Start menu (or, in Windows 8, the Start screen), the 64-bit versions of these are listed as "Windows PowerShell" and "Windows PowerShell ISE." The 32-bit versions are identified by an "(x86)" in the shortcut name, and you'll also see "(x86)" in the window's title bar when running those versions. If you're on a 32-bit operating system, you'll have only the 32-bit version of PowerShell, and it won't specifically say "(x86)."

The examples in this book are based on the 64-bit versions of PowerShell and the ISE. If you're not using those, you may sometimes get slightly different results than ours when running examples, and a few of the labs might not work properly. The 32-bit versions are primarily provided for backward compatibility. For example, some shell extensions are available only in 32-bit flavors and can be loaded into only the 32-bit (or "x86") shell. Unless you need to use such an extension, we recommend using the 64-bit shell when you're on a 64-bit operating system. Microsoft's investments going forward are primarily in 64-bit; if you're stuck with a 32-bit operating system, unfortunately that's going to hold you back.

> **TIP** You should be able to accomplish everything in this book with a single computer running PowerShell, although some stuff gets more interesting if

you have two or three computers, all in the same domain, to play with. We've used CloudShare.com as an inexpensive way to spin up several virtual machines in the cloud—if such a scenario interests you, look into that service, or something like it. Note that CloudShare.com isn't currently available in all countries.

1.5 *Installing Windows PowerShell*

Windows PowerShell v3 has been available for most versions of Windows since the release of Windows Server 2008, Windows Server 2008 R2, Windows 7, and later versions. Windows Vista is not supported, but it can still run v2. The shell is preinstalled only on the most recent versions of Windows; it must be manually installed on older versions.

> **TIP** You should check on your version of PowerShell: Open the PowerShell console, type `$PSVersionTable`, and hit Enter. If you get an error, or if the output doesn't say "PSVersion 3.0," then you don't have PowerShell v3.

PowerShell v3 can install "side by side" with v2, which means you won't break anything that depends upon v2 being present. You don't need to have v1, and installing v3 will replace it. No recent, updated Microsoft software depends solely on v1.

If you happen to be using an older version of PowerShell, visit http://download .microsoft.com and enter "powershell 3" into the search box. Locate the correct download for your version of Windows, and install it. You're looking for the Windows Management Framework 3.0 package, with which PowerShell v3 is distributed. Again, be careful to select the right version: "x86" refers to 32-bit packages; "x64" refers to 64-bit packages. You won't see a download for the most recent versions of Windows because PowerShell v3 comes preinstalled on those versions.

> **TIP** PowerShell requires .NET Framework v4 at a minimum, and it prefers to have the latest and greatest version of the framework that you can get. We recommend also installing at least .NET Framework v3.5 SP 1 and .NET Framework v4.0 to get the maximum functionality from the shell.

Installing PowerShell v3 also installs some companion technologies, including the Windows Remote Management (WinRM) service, which you'll learn more about later in this book. PowerShell is installed as a hotfix, which means that once it's installed, it can be a bit tricky to remove. Generally speaking, you won't want to remove it. PowerShell is officially a part of the core Windows operating system, and any bug fixes or updates will come down as additional hotfixes, or even in service packs, as with any other component of Windows.

PowerShell v3 has two components: the standard, text-based console host (PowerShell.exe) and the more visual Integrated Scripting Environment (ISE; PowerShell

_ISE.exe). We use the text-based console most of the time, but you're welcome to use the ISE if you prefer.

> **NOTE** The PowerShell ISE isn't preinstalled on server operating systems. If you want to use it, you'll need to go in to Windows Features (using Server Manager) and manually add the ISE feature (you can also open the PowerShell console and run `Add-WindowsFeature powershell-ise`). The ISE isn't available at all on server installations that don't have the full GUI (for example, Server Core).

Before you go any further, take a few minutes to customize the shell. If you're using the text-based console host, we strongly recommend that you change the font it uses to the Lucida fixed-width font instead of the default console font. The default font makes it difficult to distinguish some of the special punctuation characters that PowerShell uses. Follow these steps to customize the font:

1 Click the control box (that's the PowerShell icon in the upper left of the console window) and select Properties from the menu.
2 In the dialog box that appears, browse through the various tabs to change the font, window colors, window size and position, and so forth.

> **TIP** We strongly recommend you make sure that both the Window Size and Screen Buffer have the same Width values.

Your changes will apply to the default console, meaning they'll stick around when you open new windows.

1.6 *Online resources*

We've mentioned the MoreLunches.com website a couple of times already, and we hope you'll find time to visit. A number of supplementary resources for this book are available there:

- Companion videos for each chapter
- Example answers for each end-of-chapter lab
- Downloadable code listings (so you don't have to type them in from the book)
- Additional articles and bonus chapters
- Links to our Windows PowerShell blogs, which contain even more examples and articles
- Links to Don's Windows PowerShell Frequently Asked Questions (FAQ)
- Links to discussion forums, where you can ask questions or submit feedback about this book

We're passionate about helping folks like you learn Windows PowerShell, and we try to provide as many different resources as we can. We also appreciate your feedback because that helps us come up with ideas for new resources that we can add to the site, and ways to improve future editions of this book. You can contact us through the links on MoreLunches.com. Don can be reached through his company's website, http://ITPro.ConcentratedTech.com, and on Twitter as @concentrateddon. Jeff can be found on his blog, http://jdhitsolutions.com/blog, and on Twitter as @jeffhicks.

1.7   *Being immediately effective with PowerShell*

"Immediately effective" is a phrase we've made our primary goal for this entire book. As much as possible, we'll try to have each chapter focus on something that you could use in a real production environment, right away. That means we'll sometimes gloss over some details in the beginning, but when necessary we promise to circle back and cover those details at the right time. In many cases, we had to choose between hitting you with 20 pages of theory first, or diving right in and accomplishing something without explaining all the nuances, caveats, and details. When those choices came along, we almost always chose to dive right in, with the goal of making you *immediately effective*. But all of those important details and nuances will still be explained at a different time in the book (or, for the subtle details that don't impact the book's content, we may explain them in an online article on MoreLunches.com).

OK, that's enough background. It's time to start being immediately effective. Your first lunch lesson awaits.

Meet PowerShell

This chapter is all about getting you situated and helping you to decide which PowerShell interface you'll use (yes, you have a choice). If you've used PowerShell before, this material might seem redundant, so feel free to *skim* this chapter—you might still find some tidbits here and there that'll help you out down the line.

2.1 *Choose your weapon*

Microsoft provides you with two ways (four, if you're being picky) to work with PowerShell. Figure 2.1 shows the Start screen's All Apps page, with four PowerShell icons. We've highlighted them to help you spot them more easily.

> **TIP** On older versions of Windows, these icons will be on your Start menu. You'll point to All Programs > Accessories > Windows PowerShell to find the icons. You can also select Run from the Start menu, type `PowerShell.exe`, and hit Enter to open the PowerShell console application. On Windows 8 and Windows Server 2012, hold the Windows key on your keyboard and press R to get the Run dialog box. Or, press and release the Windows key, and start typing `powershell` to quickly get to the PowerShell icons.

On a 32-bit operating system, you'll have only two (at most) PowerShell icons; on a 64-bit system, you'll have up to four. These include

- *Windows PowerShell*—64-bit console on a 64-bit system; 32-bit console on a 32-bit system
- *Windows PowerShell (x86)*—32-bit console on a 64-bit system

- *Windows PowerShell ISE*—64-bit graphical console on a 64-bit system; 32-bit graphical console on a 32-bit system
- *Windows PowerShell ISE (x86)*—32-bit graphical console on a 64-bit system

In other words, 32-bit operating systems have only 32-bit PowerShell applications, whereas 64-bit operating systems have both 64-bit and 32-bit versions, and the 32-bit versions include "x86" in their icon names. You'd use the 32-bit versions only when you have a 32-bit shell extension for which a 64-bit version isn't available. Microsoft's fully invested in 64-bit these days, whereas it maintains the 32-bit versions mainly for backward compatibility.

TIP   It's incredibly easy to accidentally launch the wrong application when you're on a 64-bit operating system. Get in the habit of looking at the application window's title bar: if it says "x86," you're running a 32-bit application. The 64-bit extensions (and most new ones are 64-bit) won't be available in a 32-bit application. Our recommendation is to pin a shortcut to your shell of choice to the Start menu.

Figure 2.1   You can use PowerShell in one of four possible ways.

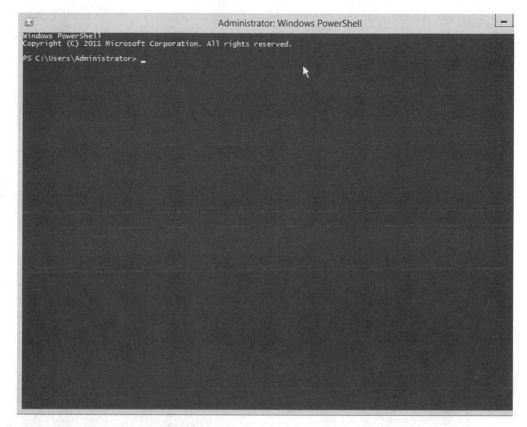

Figure 2.2 The standard PowerShell console window: PowerShell.exe

2.1.1 The console window

Figure 2.2 shows the console window, which is where most folks first meet PowerShell.

We'll start this section by making some arguments against using the PowerShell console application:

- It doesn't support double-byte character sets, which means many non-English languages won't display properly.
- Clipboard operations (copy and paste) use nonstandard keystrokes that are hard to get used to.
- It provides little assistance when it comes to typing (compared to the ISE, which we'll cover next).

That said, the PowerShell console application will be your only option when you're running PowerShell on a server that doesn't have a GUI shell installed (that's any "Server Core" installation, or any Windows Server installation where the Server GUI Shell feature has been removed or not installed). On the plus side,

- The console application is tiny. It loads fast and doesn't use much memory.
- It doesn't require any more .NET Framework stuff than PowerShell itself needs.
- You can set the colors to be green text on a black background and pretend you're working on a 1970s-era mainframe.

If you decide to use the console application, we have a few suggestions for configuring it. You can make all of these configurations by clicking on the window's upper-left-corner control box and selecting Properties; you'll see the dialog box shown in figure 2.3.

On the Options tab, you can increase the size of the Command History Buffer Size. This buffer is how the console remembers what commands you've typed, and how you recall them using the up and down arrows on your keyboard. You can also hit F7 for a pop-up list of commands.

On the Font tab, pick something a bit larger than the default 12 pt font. Please. We don't care if you have 20/10 vision, jack up the font size a bit. PowerShell needs you to be able to quickly distinguish between a lot of similar-looking characters—such as ' (an apostrophe or a single quote) and ` (a backtick or a grave accent)—and a tiny font doesn't help.

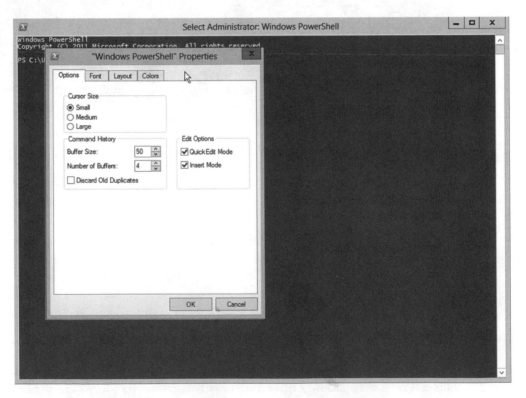

Figure 2.3 **Configuring the console application's properties**

On the Layout tab, set both Width sizes to the same number, and make sure the resulting window fits on your screen. If you fail to do this, it can result in a horizontal scroll bar at the bottom of the window, which can lead to some PowerShell output appearing "wrapped" off the right side of the window, where you'll never see it. We've had students spend half an hour running commands, thinking they were producing no output at all, when in fact the output was scrolled off to the right. Annoying.

Finally, on the Colors tab, don't go nuts. Keep things high contrast and easy to read. Black on medium-gray is quite nice if you don't like the default white on blue.

One thing to keep in mind: This console application isn't PowerShell; it's merely the means by which you interact with PowerShell. The console app itself dates to circa 1985. It's primitive, and you shouldn't expect to have a slick experience with it.

2.1.2 The Integrated Scripting Environment (ISE)

Figure 2.4 shows the PowerShell Integrated Scripting Environment, or ISE.

TIP If you accidentally open the normal console app, you can type `ise` and hit Enter to open the ISE.

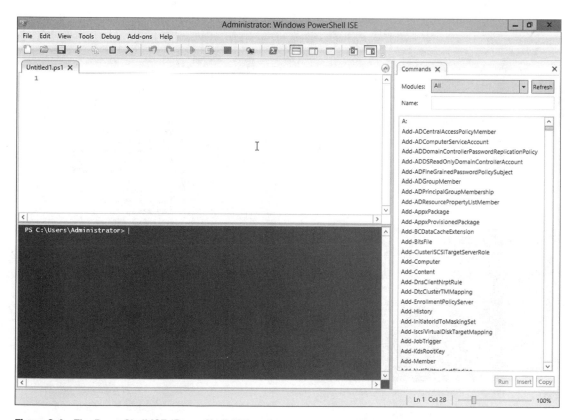

Figure 2.4 The PowerShell ISE (PowerShell_ISE.exe)

Table 2.1 ISE pros and cons

Pros	Cons
ISE is nicer looking and supports double-byte character sets.	It requires Windows Presentation Foundation (WPF), which means it can't run on a server that's had the GUI uninstalled (although it can run in Minimal Server GUI mode, which supports WPF applications).
It does more to help you create PowerShell commands and scripts, as you'll see later in this chapter.	It takes longer to get up and running, but usually only a couple of seconds longer.
It uses normal copy-and-paste keystrokes.	It doesn't support transcription.

We've got a lot of ground to cover with the ISE, and we'll start with table 2.1, which lists its pros and cons.

Let's start with some basic orientation. Figure 2.5 shows ISE's three main areas with labels, and we've highlighted the area of the ISE toolbar that controls these main areas.

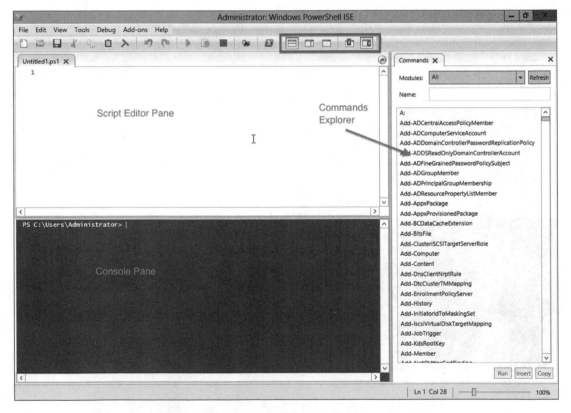

Figure 2.5 The three main areas of the ISE, and the toolbar that controls them

In figure 2.5, the top area is the Script Editor Pane, which we won't be using until the end of this book. In the upper-right corner of that pane, you'll notice a little blue arrow; click it to hide the script editor and maximize the Console Pane, which is the area we'll be using. On the right side is the Commands Explorer, which you can leave open or close by using the little "X" in its upper-right corner. You can also float the Commands Explorer by clicking the next-to-last button in the toolbar. If you close the Commands Explorer and want it back, the last button in the toolbar will bring it back. The first three buttons we've highlighted in the toolbar control the layout of the script editor and the Console Panes. You can set these panes one above the other, side by side, or as a full-screen Script Editor Pane.

In the lower-right corner of the ISE window, you'll find a slider that changes the font size. On the Tools menu, you'll find an Options item that lets you configure custom color schemes and other appearance settings—feel free to play with those.

> **TRY IT NOW** We'll assume you're using the ISE for the remainder of this book and not some other scripting editor. For now, hide the Script Editor Pane and (if you want to) the Commands pane. Set the font size to something you like. If the default color scheme isn't to your liking, change it to something you prefer. If you decide to use the console window instead, you'll be fine—most everything in the book will still work. For the few ISE-specific things we'll show you, we'll be sure to tell you that it works only in the ISE, to give you a chance to switch.

2.2 It's typing class all over again

PowerShell is a command-line interface, and that means you'll do a lot of typing. Typing leaves room for errors—typos. Fortunately, both PowerShell applications provide ways to help minimize typos.

> **TRY IT NOW** The following examples are impossible to illustrate in a book, but they're cool to see in action. Consider following along in your own copy of the shell.

The console application supports tab completion in four areas:

- Type Get-S and press Tab a few times, then try pressing Shift-Tab. PowerShell will cycle back and forth through all of the potential matches—continue to press those keys until you've hit the command you want.
- Type Dir, then a space, then C:\, and then hit Tab. PowerShell will start cycling through available file and folder names from the current folder.
- Type Set-Execu, and hit Tab. Then type a space and a dash (-). Start pressing Tab to see PowerShell cycle through the parameters for the command. You could also type part of a parameter name, like -E, and press Tab to start cycling through matching parameters. Hit Escape to clear the command line.
- Type Set-Execu again, and press Tab. Type a space, then -E, and hit Tab again. Type another space, and hit Tab again. PowerShell will cycle through the legal

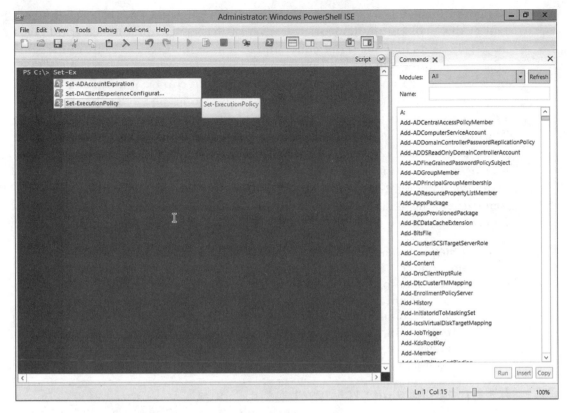

Figure 2.6   IntelliSense works like tab completion in the ISE.

values for that parameter. This works only for parameters that have a pre-defined set of allowable values (the set is called an enumeration). Again, hit Escape to clear the command line—you don't want to run that command yet.

The PowerShell ISE offers something similar to, and better than, tab completion: IntelliSense. This feature operates in all four of the same situations that we showed you for tab completion, except that you get a cool little pop-up menu, like the one shown in figure 2.6. You can use your arrow keys to scroll up or down, find the item you want, hit Tab or Enter to select it, and then keep typing.

IntelliSense works in the ISE's Console Pane and in the Script Editor Pane.

CAUTION   It's *very, very, very, very, very* important to be *very, very, very, very* accurate when you're typing in PowerShell. In some cases, a single misplaced space, quotation mark, or even carriage return can make everything fail. If you're getting errors, double- and triple-check what you've typed.

2.3   *Common points of confusion*

Let's quickly review some of the things that can muck up the works to make sure they don't trip you up as well:

- *Horizontal scroll bars in the console app*—We've learned from years of teaching classes—this trips up people every single time. Configure the console to not have a horizontal scroll bar across the bottom of the window. We explained how to do this earlier in this chapter.
- *The 32-bit versus 64-bit issue*—You should be running a 64-bit version of Windows and using the 64-bit versions of PowerShell's applications (the ones that don't say "(x86)"). We know for some folks it can be a big deal to go buy a 64-bit computer and a 64-bit version of Windows. But that's the investment you'll have to make if you want to use PowerShell effectively. Most of what we cover in this book will work fine on 32-bit, but when you're working in a production environment, 64-bit makes all the difference.
- *Make sure the PowerShell application's window title bar says "Administrator"*—If it doesn't, close the window, right-click the PowerShell icon again, and select Run As Administrator. In a production environment, you might not always do this, and later in the book we'll show you how to specify credentials when you run commands. But for the moment, you need to be sure the shell window says "Administrator" or you'll run into problems later.

2.4 What version is this?

It can be incredibly difficult to figure out which version of PowerShell you're using, in no small part because every released version installs to a directory named "1.0" (which refers to the language engine of the shell, meaning every version has been made backward compatible to v1). With PowerShell v3, there's an easy way to check your version:

```
PS C:\> $PSVersionTable

Name                           Value
----                           -----
PSVersion                      3.0
WSManStackVersion              3.0
SerializationVersion           1.1.0.1
CLRVersion                     4.0.30319.17379
BuildVersion                   6.2.8250.0
PSCompatibleVersions           {1.0, 2.0, 3.0}
PSRemotingProtocolVersion      2.2
```

Type $PSVersionTable and hit Enter. You'll immediately see the version number for every PowerShell-related piece of technology, including PowerShell itself. If this doesn't work, or if it doesn't say "3.0" for "PSVersion," you're not using the right version of PowerShell for this book. Refer to chapter 1 for instructions on getting v3.

> **TRY IT NOW** Don't wait any longer to start using PowerShell. Start by checking your version number to ensure it's 3.0. If it isn't, don't go any further until you've installed v3.

PowerShell v3 can install side by side with v2. In fact, you can run PowerShell.exe -version 2.0 to explicitly run v2. You can set it to run v2 if you have something that isn't v3 compatible (which is rare). PowerShell v3's installer doesn't install v2; you'll be able to run only v2 if it was installed first. The installers for v2 and v3 will both overwrite v1 if it's already installed; they can't exist side by side. All current versions of Microsoft software (including the latest service packs of some older-generation software like Exchange Server 2007) will run with v2 installed.

> **TIP** The newest versions of Windows install PowerShell v3 by default, but include the PowerShell v2 engine. From PowerShell, run `Add-WindowsFeature powershell-v2` to install the v2 engine if you need it.

2.5   *Lab*

Because this is the book's first lab, we'll take a moment and describe how these are supposed to work. For each lab, we'll give you a few tasks that you can try and complete on your own. Sometimes we'll provide a hint or two to get you going in the right direction. From there, you're on your own.

We absolutely guarantee that everything you need to know to complete every lab is either in that same chapter or covered in a previous chapter (and the "previously covered" information is the stuff for which we're most likely to give you a hint). We're not saying the answer will be in plain sight: most often, a chapter will have taught you how to discover something on your own, and you'll have to go through that discovery process to find the answer. It might seem frustrating, but forcing yourself to do it will absolutely make you more successful with PowerShell in the long run. We promise.

Keep in mind that you can find sample answers at MoreLunches.com. Our answers might not exactly match yours, and that will become increasingly true as we move on to more complex material. In fact, you'll often find that PowerShell offers a half dozen or more ways to accomplish almost anything. We'll show you the way we use the most, but if you come up with something different, you're not wrong. Any way that gets the job done is correct.

> **NOTE** For this lab, you'll need any computer running PowerShell v3.

We'll start easy: we just want you to get both the console and the ISE set up to meet your needs. Follow these five steps:

1 Select fonts and colors that work for you.
2 Make sure the console application has no horizontal scroll bar at the bottom. We've already mentioned this about three times in this chapter, so maybe it's important.
3 In the ISE, get the Console Pane maximized; remove or leave the Commands Explorer at your discretion.
4 In both applications, type a single quote, ', and a backtick, `, and make sure you can easily tell the difference. On a U.S. keyboard (at least), a backtick is on one of the upper-left keys, under the Escape key, on the same key as the tilde (~) character.

5 Also type (parentheses), [square brackets], <angle brackets>, and {curly brackets} to make sure the font and size you've selected display well, so that all of these symbols are immediately distinguishable. If there's some visual confusion about which is which, changes fonts or select a bigger font size.

We've already walked you through how to accomplish these steps, so you don't have any answers to check for this lab, other than to be sure you've completed all five of the steps.

2.6 *Further exploration*

What Microsoft gives you isn't the only way to use PowerShell; you'll find other free and commercial editors and shell environments designed specifically for PowerShell, and you should try them out. Even the commercial ones come with a free trial period, so there's no reason not to take them all for a spin.

- *PowerGUI*—You'll find a free edition from http://powergui.org and a professional (commercial) edition from http://quest.com/powershell
- *SAPIEN PrimalScript and PrimalForms*—Two commercial tools from http://primaltools.com
- *PowerSE and PowerWF*—A free editor and a commercial workflow solution from http://powerwf.com
- *Idera PowerShell Plus*—An editor and console environment from http://idera.com

You can likely find others, but these four are the big players and the ones with which we're most familiar. We're not associated with any of these companies (beyond appreciating their work). We're often asked which of these we use the most, at which point we have to admit we use Microsoft's ISE, mainly because we're constantly rebuilding our virtual machines and we're too lazy to keep reinstalling editors (and we haven't gotten around to writing a PowerShell script to do it for us). That said, when we do find ourselves using a third-party tool, it's usually PowerShell Plus, because we like the way it provides an enhanced console as well as a script editor, and we like the integration between the two modes. But you should find an editor that meets your needs and budget.

In January 2012, Don did a write-up of various PowerShell environments. Provided you're reading this book sometime before January 2014 (when the paper expires and will be updated based on available products at that time), you can get the paper at http://library.concentratedtech.com. It was written during the PowerShell v3 era, and applies to specific versions of the products mentioned, but it might give you a good starting point for learning the shell.

Using the help system 3

In the first chapter of this book, we mentioned that discoverability is a key feature that makes graphical user interfaces (GUIs) easier to learn and use, and that command-line interfaces (CLIs) like PowerShell are often more difficult because they lack those discoverability features. In fact, PowerShell has fantastic discoverability features—but they're not that obvious. One of the main discoverability features is its help system.

3.1 *The help system: how you discover commands*

Bear with us for a minute as we climb up on a soapbox and preach to you.

We work in an industry that doesn't place a lot of emphasis on reading, although we do have an acronym, *RTFM*, that we cleverly pass along to users when we wish *they* would "read the friendly manual." Most administrators tend to dive right in, relying on things like tooltips, context menus, and so forth—those GUI discoverability tools—to figure out how to do something. That's how we often work, and we imagine you do the same thing. But let's be clear about one thing:

> *If you aren't willing to read PowerShell's help files, you won't be effective with PowerShell. You won't learn how to use it, you won't learn how to administer products like Windows and Exchange with it, and you might as well stick with the GUI.*

That's about as clear as we can be. It's a blunt statement, but it's absolutely true. Imagine trying to figure out Active Directory Users and Computers, or any other administrative console, without the help of tooltips, menus, and context menus. Trying to learn and use PowerShell without taking the time to read and understand the help files is the same thing. It's like trying to assemble that do-it-yourself

20

furniture from the department store without reading the manual. Your experience will be frustrating, confusing, and ineffective. Why?

- If you need to perform a task and don't know what command to use, the help system is how you'll find that command. Not Google or Bing, but the help system.
- If you run a command and get an error, the help system is what will show you how to properly run the command so you don't get errors.
- If you want to link multiple commands together to perform some complex task, the help system is where you'll find out how each command is able to connect to others. You don't need to search for examples on Google or Bing; you need to learn how to use the commands themselves, so that you can create your own examples and solutions.

We realize our preaching is a little heavy-handed, but 90 percent of the problems we see students struggling with in class, and on the job, could be solved if those folks would find a few minutes to sit back, take some deep breaths, and read the help. And then read this chapter, which is all about helping folks understand the help they're reading.

From here on out, we'll encourage you to read the help for several reasons:

- Although we'll be showing you many commands in our examples, we'll almost never expose the complete functionality, options, and capabilities of each command. You should read the help for each and every command we show you, so that you'll be familiar with the additional things each command can do.
- In the labs, we may give you a hint about which command to use for a task, but we won't give you hints about the syntax. You'll need to use the help system to discover that syntax on your own in order to complete the labs.

We promise you that mastering the help system is the key to becoming a PowerShell expert. No, you won't find every little detail in there, and a lot of super-advanced material isn't documented in the help system, but in terms of being an effective day-to-day administrator, you need to master the help system. This book will make that system understandable, and it will teach you the concepts that the help skips over, but it'll only do this in conjunction with the built-in help.

Stepping off the soapbox now.

Command vs. cmdlet

PowerShell contains many different types of executable commands. Some are called *cmdlets*, some are called *functions*, others are known as *workflows*, and so on. Collectively, they're all *commands*, and the help system works with all of them. A *cmdlet* is something unique to PowerShell, and many of the *commands* you run will be *cmdlets*. But we'll try to consistently use *command* whenever we're talking about the more general class of executable utility.

3.2   *Updatable help*

You may be surprised the first time you fire up help in PowerShell, because, well, there isn't any. But wait, we can explain.

Microsoft included a new feature in PowerShell v3 called "updatable help." PowerShell v3 can download updated, corrected, and expanded help right from the internet. Unfortunately, in order to do that, Microsoft can't ship any help "in the box." When you ask for help on a command, you get an abbreviated, auto-generated version of help, along with a message on how to update the help files, which may look like the following:

```
PS C:\> help Get-Service

NAME
    Get-Service

SYNTAX
    Get-Service [[-Name] <string[]>] [-ComputerName <string[]>]
    [-DependentServices] [-RequiredServices] [-Include <string[]>]
    [-Exclude <string[]>]  [<CommonParameters>]

    Get-Service -DisplayName <string[]> [-ComputerName <string[]>]
    [-DependentServices] [-RequiredServices] [-Include <string[]>]
    [-Exclude <string[]>]  [<CommonParameters>]

    Get-Service [-ComputerName <string[]>] [-DependentServices]
    [-RequiredServices] [-Include <string[]>] [-Exclude <string[]>]
    [-InputObject <ServiceController[]>]  [<CommonParameters>]


ALIASES
    gsv


REMARKS
    Get-Help cannot find the Help files for this cmdlet on this computer.
    It is displaying only partial help.
        -- To download and install Help files for the module that
    includes this cmdlet, use Update-Help.
        -- To view the Help topic for this cmdlet online, type: "Get-Help
    Get-Service -Online" or
            go to http://go.microsoft.com/fwlink/?LinkID=113332.
```

TIP It's impossible to miss the fact that you don't have local help installed–the first time you ask for help, PowerShell will prompt you to update the help content.

Updating PowerShell's help should be your first task. These files are stored in the System32 directory, which means your shell must be running under elevated privileges. If it doesn't say "Administrator" in the PowerShell title bar, you'll likely get an error message:

```
PS C:\> update-help
Update-Help : Failed to update Help for the module(s)
'Microsoft.PowerShell.Management, Microsoft.PowerShell.Utility,
Microsoft.PowerShell.Diagnostics, Microsoft.PowerShell.Core,
```

```
Microsoft.PowerShell.Host, Microsoft.PowerShell.Security,
Microsoft.WSMan.Management' : This command did not update help topics for
the Windows PowerShell core commands or for any modules in the
$pshome\Modules directory. To update these help topics, start Windows
PowerShell with the "Run as Administrator" option and try the command
again.
At line:1 char:1
+ update-help
+ ~~~~~~~~~~~
    + CategoryInfo          : InvalidOperation: (:) [Update-Help], Except
   ion
    + FullyQualifiedErrorId : UpdatableHelpSystemRequiresElevation,Micros
   oft.PowerShell.Commands.UpdateHelpCommand
```

We've boldfaced the important part of the preceding error message—it tells you what the problem is and how to solve it. Run the shell as administrator, run `Update-Help` again, and you'll be good to go in a few minutes.

It's important to get in the habit of updating the help every month or so. Power-Shell can even download updated help for non-Microsoft commands, provided the commands' modules are located in the proper spot and that they've been coded to include the online location for updated help.

Do you have computers that aren't connected to the internet? No problem: Go to one that's connected, and use `Save-Help` to get a local copy of the help. Put it on a file server or somewhere that's accessible to the rest of your network. Then run `Update-Help` with its `-Source` parameter, pointing it to the downloaded copy of the help. That'll let any computer on your network grab the updated help from that central spot, rather than from the internet.

3.3   *Asking for help*

Windows PowerShell provides a cmdlet, `Get-Help`, that accesses the help system. You may see examples (especially on the internet) that show people using the `Help` keyword instead, or even the `Man` keyword (which comes from Unix and means "Manual"). `Man` and `Help` aren't native cmdlets at all—they are *functions*, which are wrappers around the core `Get-Help` cmdlet.

`Help` works much like the base `Get-Help`, but it pipes the help output to `More`, allowing you to have a nice paged view instead of seeing all the help fly by at once. Running `Help Get-Content` and `Get-Help Get-Content` produces the same results, but the former has a page-at-a-time display. You could run `Get-Help Get-Content | More` to produce that paged display, but it's a lot more typing. We'll typically only use `Help`, but we want you to understand that there's some trickery going on under the hood.

> **NOTE**   Technically, `Help` is a function, and `Man` is an alias, or nickname, for `Help`. But you get the same results using either. We'll discuss aliases in the next chapter.

By the way, sometimes that paginated display can be annoying—you have the information you need, but it still wants you to hit the spacebar to display the remaining information. If you encounter this, press Ctrl-C to cancel the command and return to the shell prompt. Within the shell's console window, Ctrl-C always means "break" rather than "copy to the clipboard." But in the more graphically oriented Windows PowerShell ISE, Ctrl-C does copy to the clipboard. A red "stop" button in the toolbar will stop a running command.

> **NOTE**   The `More` command won't work in the ISE. Even if you use `Help` or `Man`, the help content displays all at once rather than a page at a time.

The help system has two main goals: to help you find commands to perform specific tasks, and to help you learn how to use those commands once you've found them.

3.4   *Using help to find commands*

Technically speaking, the help system has no idea what commands are present in the shell. All it knows is what help topics are available, and it's possible for commands to not have a help file, in which case the help system won't know that the commands exist. Fortunately, Microsoft ships a help topic for nearly every cmdlet they produce, which means you usually won't find a difference. In addition, the help system can also access information that isn't related to a specific cmdlet, including background concepts and other general information.

Like most commands, `Get-Help` (and therefore `Help`) has several parameters. One of those—perhaps the most important one—is `-Name`. This parameter specifies the name of the help topic you'd like to access, and it's a positional parameter, so you don't have to type `-Name`—you can just provide the name you're looking for. It also accepts wildcards, which makes the help system useful for discovering commands.

For example, suppose you want to do something with an event log. You don't know what commands might be available, and you decide to search for help topics that cover event logs. You might run either of these two commands:

```
Help *log*
Help *event*
```

The first of these commands returns a list like the following on your computer:

```
Name                          Category  Module
----                          --------  ------
Clear-EventLog                Cmdlet    Microsoft.PowerShell.M...
Get-EventLog                  Cmdlet    Microsoft.PowerShell.M...
Limit-EventLog                Cmdlet    Microsoft.PowerShell.M...
New-EventLog                  Cmdlet    Microsoft.PowerShell.M...
Remove-EventLog               Cmdlet    Microsoft.PowerShell.M...
Show-EventLog                 Cmdlet    Microsoft.PowerShell.M...
Write-EventLog                Cmdlet    Microsoft.PowerShell.M...
Get-AppxLog                   Function  Appx
Get-DtcLog                    Function  MsDtc
Reset-DtcLog                  Function  MsDtc
Set-DtcLog                    Function  MsDtc
Get-LogProperties             Function  PSDiagnostics
```

```
Set-LogProperties              Function  PSDiagnostics
about_Eventlogs                HelpFile
about_Logical_Operators        HelpFile
```

> **NOTE** You'll notice that the preceding list includes commands (and functions) from modules like Appx, MsDtc, and so forth. The help system displays all of these even though you haven't loaded those extensions into memory yet, which helps you discover commands on your computer that you might otherwise have overlooked. It'll discover commands from any extensions that are installed in the proper location, which we'll discuss in chapter 7.

Many of the functions in the previous list seem to have something to do with event logs, and based on a "verb-noun" naming format, all but the last two appear to be help topics related to specific cmdlets. The last two "about" topics provide background information. The last one doesn't seem to have anything to do with event logs, but it came up because it does have "log" in it—part of the word "logical." Whenever possible, we try to search using the broadest term possible—"*event*" or "*log*" as opposed to "*eventlog*"—because we'll get the most results possible.

Once you have a cmdlet that you think will do the job (`Get-EventLog` looks like a good candidate for what you're after in the example), you can ask for help on that specific topic:

```
Help Get-EventLog
```

Don't forget about tab completion! As a reminder, it lets you type a portion of a command name, press Tab, and the shell will complete what you've typed with the closest match. You can continue pressing Tab to cycle through alternative matches.

> **TRY IT NOW** Type `Help Get-Ev` and press Tab. The first match is `Get-Event`, which isn't what you want; pressing Tab again brings up `Get-EventLog`, which is what you're after. You can hit Return to accept the command and display the help for that cmdlet. If you're using the ISE, you don't even have to hit Tab; the list of matching commands pops right up, and you can select one and hit Enter to finish typing it.

You can also use wildcards—mainly the * wildcard, which stands in for zero or more characters—with Help. If PowerShell only finds one match to whatever you've typed, it won't display a list of topics with that one item. Instead, it'll display the contents for that item.

> **TRY IT NOW** Run `Help Get-EventL*` and you should see the help file for `Get-EventLog`, rather than a list of matching help topics.

If you've been following along in the shell, you should now be looking at the help file for `Get-EventLog`. This file is called the summary help, and it's meant to be a short description of the command and a reminder of the syntax. This information is useful when you need to quickly refresh your memory of a command's usage, and it's where we'll begin interpreting the help file itself.

Above and beyond

Sometimes, we'll want to share information that, although nice, isn't essential to your understanding of the shell. We'll put that information into an "Above and beyond" section, like this one. If you skip these, you'll be fine; if you read them, you'll often learn about an alternative way of doing something, or get additional insight into PowerShell.

We mentioned that the Help command doesn't search for cmdlets; it searches for help topics. Because every cmdlet has a help file, we could say that this search retrieves the same results. But you can also directly search for cmdlets using the Get-Command cmdlet (or its alias, Gcm).

Like the Help cmdlet, Get-Command accepts wildcards, meaning you can run something like Gcm *event* to see all of the commands that contain "event" in their name. For better or worse, that list will include not only cmdlets, but also external commands like netevent.dll, which may not be useful.

A better approach is to use the -Noun or -Verb parameters. Because only cmdlet names have nouns and verbs, the results will be limited to cmdlets. Get-Command -noun *event* will return a list of cmdlets dealing with events; Get-Command -verb Get will return all cmdlets capable of retrieving things. You can also use the -CommandType parameter, specifying a type of cmdlet: Get-Command *log* -type cmdlet will show a list of all cmdlets that include "log" in their names, and the list won't include any external applications or commands.

3.5   *Interpreting the help*

PowerShell's cmdlet help files have a particular set of conventions. Learning to understand what you're looking at is the key to extracting the maximum amount of information from these files, and to learning to use the cmdlets themselves more effectively.

3.5.1   *Parameter sets and common parameters*

Most commands can work in a variety of different ways, depending on what you need them to do. For example, here's the syntax section for the Get-EventLog help:

```
SYNTAX
    Get-EventLog [-AsString] [-ComputerName <string[]>] [-List] [<Com
    monParameters>]

    Get-EventLog [-LogName] <string> [[-InstanceId] <Int64[]>] [-Afte
    r <DateTime>] [-AsBaseObject] [-Before <DateTime>] [-ComputerName
     <string[]>] [-EntryType <string[]>] [-Index <Int32[]>] [-Message
     <string>] [-Newest <int>] [-Source <string[]>] [-UserName <strin
    g[]>] [<CommonParameters>]
```

Notice that the command in the previous syntax is listed twice, which indicates that the command supports two *parameter sets*—you can use the command in two distinct ways. Some of the parameters will be shared between the two sets. You'll notice, for example, that both parameter sets include a -ComputerName parameter. But the two parameter sets will always have at least one unique parameter that exists only in that parameter set. In this case, the first set supports -AsString and -List, neither of which is included in the second set; the second set contains numerous parameters that aren't included in the first.

Here's how this works: if you use a parameter that's only included in one set, you're locked into that set and can only use additional parameters that appear within that same set. If you choose to use -List, the only other parameters you can use are -AsString and -ComputerName, because those are the only two other parameters included in the parameter set where -List lives. You couldn't add in the -LogName parameter, because it doesn't live in the first parameter set. That means -List and -LogName are *mutually exclusive*—you'll never use both of them at the same time because they live in different parameter sets.

Sometimes it's possible to run a command with only parameters that are shared between multiple sets. In those cases, the shell will usually select the first-listed parameter set. Because each parameter set implies different behavior, it's important to understand which parameter set you're running.

You'll notice that every parameter set for every PowerShell cmdlet ends with [<CommonParameters>]. This refers to a set of eight parameters that are available on every single cmdlet, no matter how you're using that cmdlet. We're not going to discuss those common parameters now, but we'll discuss some of them later in this book, when we'll use them for a real task. Later in this chapter, though, we'll show you where to learn more about those common parameters, if you're interested.

> **REMEMBER** If you visit http://MoreLunches.com and select this book from the front page, you'll have access to a variety of free companion material. That material includes video demonstrations of key concepts—like parameters and parameter sets—which can help make them easier to see and understand.

3.5.2 *Optional and mandatory parameters*

You don't need every single parameter in order to make a cmdlet run. PowerShell's help lists optional parameters in square brackets. For example, [-ComputerName <string[]>] indicates that the entire -ComputerName parameter is optional. You don't have to use it at all—the cmdlet will probably default to the local computer if you don't specify an alternative name using this parameter. That's also why [<CommonParameters>] is in square brackets—you can run the command without using any of the common parameters.

Almost every cmdlet has at least one optional parameter. You may never need to use some of these parameters, and you may use others on a daily basis. Keep in mind that when you choose to use a parameter, you only have to type enough of the parameter name so that PowerShell can unambiguously figure out which parameter you meant. -L wouldn't be sufficient for -List, for example, because -L could also mean -LogName. But -Li would be a legal abbreviation for -List, because no other parameter starts with -Li.

What if you try to run a command and forget one of the mandatory parameters? Take a look at the help for Get-EventLog, for example, and you'll see that the -LogName parameter is mandatory—the parameter isn't enclosed in square brackets. Try running Get-EventLog without specifying a log name.

TRY IT NOW   Follow along on this example by running Get-EventLog without any parameters.

PowerShell should have prompted you for the mandatory LogName parameter. If you type something like System or Application and hit Return, the command will run correctly. You could also press Ctrl-C to abort the command.

3.5.3   *Positional parameters*

PowerShell's designers knew that some parameters would be used so frequently that you wouldn't want to continually type the parameter names. Those commonly used parameters are often *positional*, meaning that you can provide a value without typing the parameter's name, provided you put that value in the correct position.

There are two ways to identify positional parameters: via the syntax summary or through the full help.

FINDING POSITIONAL PARAMETERS IN THE SYNTAX SUMMARY

You'll find the first way in the syntax summary: the parameter name—only the name—will be surrounded by square brackets. For example, look at the first two parameters in the second parameter set of Get-EventLog:

```
[-LogName] <string> [[-InstanceId] <Int64[]>]
```

The first parameter, -LogName, isn't optional. We can tell because the entire parameter—its name and its value—aren't surrounded by square brackets. But the parameter name is enclosed in square brackets, making it a positional parameter—we could provide the log name without having to type -LogName. And because this parameter appears in the first position within the help file, we know that the log name is the first parameter we have to provide.

The second parameter, -InstanceId, is optional—both it and its value are enclosed in square brackets. Within those, -InstanceId itself is also contained in square brackets, indicating that this is also a positional parameter. It appears in the second position, so we would need to provide a value in the second position if we chose to omit the parameter name.

The -Before parameter (which comes later in the syntax; run Help Get-EventLog and find it for yourself) is optional, because it's entirely enclosed within square brackets. The -Before name isn't in square brackets, which tells us that if we choose to use that parameter, we must type the parameter name (or at least a portion of it).

There are some tricks to using positional parameters:

- It's OK to mix and match positional parameters with those that require their names. Positional parameters must always be in the correct positions. For example, Get-EventLog System -Newest 20 is legal; System will be fed to the -LogName parameter, because that value is in the first position; 20 will go with the -Newest parameter because the parameter name was used.

- It's always legal to specify parameter names, and when you do so, the order in which you type them isn't important. Get-EventLog -newest 20 -Log Application is legal because we've used parameter names (in the case of -LogName, we abbreviated it).
- If you use multiple positional parameters, don't lose track of their positions. Get-EventLog Application 0 will work, with Application being attached to -LogName and 0 being attached to -InstanceId. Get-EventLog 0 Application won't work, because 0 will be attached to -LogName, and no log is named 0.

We'll offer a best practice: use parameter names until you become comfortable with a particular cmdlet and get tired of typing a commonly used parameter name over and over. After that, use positional parameters to save yourself typing. When the time comes to paste a command into a text file for easier reuse, always use the full cmdlet name and type out the complete parameter name—no positional parameters and no abbreviated parameter names. Doing so makes that file easier to read and understand in the future, and because you won't have to type the parameter names repeatedly (that's why you pasted the command into a file, after all), you won't be creating extra typing work for yourself.

FINDING POSITIONAL PARAMETERS IN THE FULL HELP

We said there were two ways to locate positional parameters. The second requires that you open the help file using the -full parameter of the Help command.

> **TRY IT NOW** Run Help Get-EventLog -full. Remember to use the spacebar to view the help file one page at a time, and to press Ctrl-C if you want to stop viewing the file before reaching the end. For now, page through the entire file, which lets you scroll back and review it all.

Page down until you see the help entry for the -LogName parameter. It should look something like the following:

```
-LogName <string>
    Specifies the event log.  Enter the log name (the value of th
    e Log property; not the LogDisplayName) of one event log. Wil
    dcard characters are not permitted. This parameter is require
    d.

    Required?                       true
    Position?                       1
    Default value
    Accept pipeline input?          false
    Accept wildcard characters?     False
```

In the preceding example, you can see that this is a mandatory parameter—it's listed as required. Further, it's a positional parameter, and it occurs in the first position, right after the cmdlet name.

We always encourage students to focus on reading the full help when they're getting started with a cmdlet, rather than only the abbreviated syntax reminder. Reading the help reveals more details, including that description of the parameter's use. You can also see that this parameter doesn't accept wildcards, which means you can't provide a value like App*—you need to type out the full log name, such as Application.

3.5.4   *Parameter values*

The help files also give you clues about what kind of input each parameter accepts. Some parameters, referred to as *switches*, don't require any input value at all. In the abbreviated syntax, they look like the following:

```
[-AsString]
```

And in the full syntax, they look like this:

```
-AsString [<SwitchParameter>]
    Returns the output as strings, instead of objects.

    Required?                   false
    Position?                   named
    Default value
    Accept pipeline input?      false
    Accept wildcard characters? False
```

The [<SwitchParameter>] part confirms that this is a switch, and that it doesn't expect an input value. Switches are never positional; you always have to type the parameter name (or at least an abbreviated version of it). Switches are always optional, which gives you the choice to use them or not.

Other parameters expect some kind of input value, which will always follow the parameter name and be separated from the parameter name by a space (and not by a colon, equal sign, or any other character). In the abbreviated syntax, the type of input expected is shown in angle brackets, like < >:

```
[-LogName] <string>
```

It's shown the same way in the full syntax:

```
-Message <string>
    Gets events that have the specified string in their messages.
     You can use this property to search for messages that contai
    n certain words or phrases. Wildcards are permitted.

    Required?                   false
    Position?                   named
    Default value
    Accept pipeline input?      false
    Accept wildcard characters? True
```

Let's look at some common types of input:

- String—A series of letters and numbers. These can sometimes include spaces, but when they do, the entire string must be contained within quotation marks.

For example, a string value like `C:\Windows` doesn't need to be enclosed in quotes, but `C:\Program Files` does, because it has that space in the middle. For now, you can use single or double quotation marks interchangeably, but it's best to stick with single quotes.

- `Int`, `Int32`, or `Int64`—An integer number (a whole number with no decimal portion).
- `DateTime`—Generally, a string that can be interpreted as a date based on your computer's regional settings. In the United States, that's usually something like `10-10-2010`, with the month, day, and year.

We'll discuss other, more specialized types as we come to them.

You'll also notice some values that have more square brackets:

```
[-ComputerName <string[]>]
```

The side-by-side brackets after `string` don't indicate that something is optional. Instead, `string[]` indicates that the parameter can accept an *array*, a *collection*, or a *list* of strings. In these cases, it's always legal to provide a single value:

```
Get-EventLog Security -computer Server-R2
```

But it's also legal to specify multiple values. A simple way to do so is to provide a comma-separated list. PowerShell treats all comma-separated lists as arrays of values:

```
Get-EventLog Security -computer Server-R2,DC4,Files02
```

Once again, any individual value that contains a space must be enclosed in quotation marks. But the entire list doesn't get enclosed in quotation marks—it's important that only individual values be in quotes. The following is legal:

```
Get-EventLog Security -computer 'Server-R2','Files02'
```

Even though neither of those values needs to be in quotation marks, it's okay to use the quotes if you want to. But the following is wrong:

```
Get-EventLog Security -computer 'Server-R2,Files01'
```

In this case, the cmdlet will be looking for a single computer named `Server-R2,Files01`, which is probably not what you want.

Another way to provide a list of values is to type them into a text file, with one value per line. Here's an example:

```
Server-R2
Files02
Files03
DC04
DC03
```

Next, you can use the `Get-Content` cmdlet to read the contents of that file, and send those contents into the `-computerName` parameter. You do this by forcing the shell to execute the `Get-Content` command first, so that the results get fed to the parameter.

Remember in high school math how parentheses, like ( ), could be used to specify the order of operations in a mathematical expression? The same thing works in PowerShell: by enclosing a command in parentheses, you force that command to execute first:

```
Get-EventLog Application -computer (Get-Content names.txt)
```

The previous example shows a useful trick. We have text files with the names of different classes of computers—web servers, domain controllers, database servers, and so forth—and then we use this trick to run commands against entire sets of computers.

You can also feed a list of values to a parameter in a few other ways, including reading computer names from Active Directory. Those techniques are a bit more complex, though, so we'll get to them in later chapters, after you learn some of the cmdlets you'll need to make the trick work.

Another way you can specify multiple values for a parameter (provided it's a mandatory parameter), is to not specify the parameter at all. As with all mandatory parameters, PowerShell will prompt you for the parameter value. For parameters that accept multiple values, you can type the first value and press Return. PowerShell will then prompt for a second value, which you can type and finish by hitting Return. Keep doing that until you're finished, and press Return on a blank prompt to let PowerShell know you're finished. As always, you can press Ctrl-C to abort the command if you don't want to be prompted for entries.

3.5.5   *Finding command examples*

We tend to learn by example, which is why we'll try to squeeze as many examples into this book as possible. PowerShell's designers know most administrators enjoy having examples, which is why they built a lot of them into the help files. If you've scrolled to the end of the help file for Get-EventLog, you probably noticed almost a dozen examples of how to use the cmdlet.

Let's look at an easier way to get to those examples, if they're all you want to see: use the -example parameter of the Help command, rather than the -full parameter.

```
Help Get-EventLog -example
```

> **TRY IT NOW**   Go ahead and pull up the examples for a cmdlet using this new parameter.

We love having these examples, even though some of them can get complicated. If an example looks too complicated for you, ignore it, and examine the others for now. Or experiment a bit (always on a non-production computer) to see if you can figure out what the example does, and why.

3.6   *Accessing "about" topics*

Earlier in this chapter, we mentioned that PowerShell's help system includes a number of background topics, as well as help for specific cmdlets. These background topics are often called "about" topics, because their filenames all start with "about_". You may also recall from earlier in this chapter that all cmdlets support a set of common parameters. How do you think you could learn more about those common parameters?

TRY IT NOW Before you read ahead, see if you can list the common parameters by using the help system.

We would start by using wildcards. Because the word "common" has been used repeatedly here in the book, that's probably a good keyword to start with:

```
Help *common*
```

It's such a good keyword, in fact, that it'll match only one help topic: About_common_parameters. That topic will display automatically because it's the only match. Paging through the file a bit, you'll find the following list of the eight common parameters:

```
-Verbose
-Debug
-WarningAction
-WarningVariable
-ErrorAction
-ErrorVariable
-OutVariable
-OutBuffer
```

The file says that PowerShell has two additional "risk mitigation" parameters, but those aren't supported by every single cmdlet.

The "about" topics in the help system are tremendously important, but because they're not related to a specific cmdlet, they can be easy to overlook. If you run `help about*` for a list of all of them, you might be surprised at how much extra documentation is hidden away inside the shell.

Table 3.1 lists several third-party scripts and applications that can make PowerShell's help easier to access.

Table 3.1 Third-party scripts and applications for PowerShell help

Resource	URL
A PowerShell script that constructs a graphical browser that lists all of the available help topics	http://mng.bz/5w8E
A dedicated Windows application that lists all of the available help topics	http://www.sapien.com/downloads; log in (free registration required) and look under "Free Tools."
A downloadable Windows Help File that includes the help (and the "about" topics) that come with PowerShell	http://download.microsoft.com (and use search)

3.7   *Accessing online help*

Mere human beings wrote PowerShell's help files, which means they're not error-free. In addition to updating the help files (which you can do by running `Update-Help`), Microsoft also publishes help on its website. The `-online` parameter of PowerShell's help command will attempt to open the web-based help for a given command:

```
Help Get-EventLog -online
```

Microsoft's TechNet website hosts the help, and it's often more up to date than what's installed with PowerShell itself. If you think you've spotted an error in an example or in the syntax, try viewing the online version of the help. Not every single cmdlet in the universe has online help; it's up to each product team (like the Exchange team, the SQL Server team, the SharePoint team, and so forth) to provide that help. But when it's available, it's a nice companion to what's built in.

We like the online help because it lets us read the text in one window (the web browser, where the help is also nicely formatted), as we're typing in PowerShell. Don is fortunate enough to use dual monitors, which makes for a convenient setup.

3.8   *Lab*

NOTE   For this lab, you'll need any computer running PowerShell v3.

We hope this chapter has conveyed the importance of mastering the help system in PowerShell. Now it's time to hone your skills by completing the following tasks. Keep in mind that sample answers can be found on MoreLunches.com. Look for *italicized* words in these tasks, and use them as clues to complete that task.

1   First, run `Update-Help` and ensure it completes without errors. That will get a copy of the help on your local computer. You'll need an internet connection, and the shell needs to run under elevated privileges (which means it must say "Administrator" in the shell window's title bar).

2   Can you find any cmdlets capable of converting other cmdlets' output into *HTML*?

3   Are there any cmdlets that can redirect output into a *file*, or to a *printer*?

4   How many cmdlets are available for working with *processes*? (Hint: remember that cmdlets all use a singular noun.)

5   What cmdlet might you use to *write* to an event *log*?

6   You've learned that aliases are nicknames for cmdlets; what cmdlets are available to create, modify, export, or import *aliases*?

7   Is there a way to keep a *transcript* of everything you type in the shell, and save that transcript to a text file?

8   It can take a long time to retrieve all of the entries from the Security *event* log. How can you get only the 100 most recent entries?

9   Is there a way to retrieve a list of the *services* that are installed on a remote computer?

10   Is there a way to see what *processes* are running on a remote computer?

11   Examine the help file for the Out-File cmdlet. The files created by this cmdlet default to a width of how many characters? Is there a parameter that would enable you to change that width?

12   By default, Out-File will overwrite any existing file that has the same filename as what you specify. Is there a parameter that would prevent the cmdlet from overwriting an existing file?

13   How could you see a list of all *aliases* defined in PowerShell?

14   Using both an alias and abbreviated parameter names, what is the shortest command line you could type to retrieve a list of running processes from a computer named Server1?

15   How many cmdlets are available that can deal with generic objects? (Hint: remember to use a singular noun like "object" rather than a plural one like "objects".)

16   This chapter briefly mentioned *arrays*. What help topic could tell you more about them?

Running commands

When you start looking at PowerShell examples on the internet, it's easy to get the impression that PowerShell is some kind of .NET Framework–based scripting or programming language. Our fellow Microsoft Most Valuable Professional (MVP) award recipients, and hundreds of other PowerShell users, are pretty serious geeks, and we like to dig deep into the shell to see what we can make it do. But almost all of us began right where this chapter starts: running commands. That's what we'll be doing in this chapter: not scripting, not programming, but running commands and command-line utilities.

4.1 Not scripting, but running commands

PowerShell, as its name implies, is a *shell*. It's similar to the Cmd.exe command-line shell that you've probably used previously, and it's even similar to the good old MS-DOS shell that shipped with the first PCs back in the 1980s. It also has a strong resemblance to the Unix shells, like Bash, from the late 1980s, or even the original Unix Bourne shell, introduced in the late 1970s. PowerShell is much more modern, but in the end, PowerShell isn't a scripting language like VBScript or KiXtart.

With those languages, as with most programming languages, you sit down in front of a text editor (even if it's Windows Notepad) and type a series of keywords to form a script. You save that file, and perhaps double-click it to test it. PowerShell *can* work like that, but that's not necessarily the main usage pattern for PowerShell, particularly when you're getting started. With PowerShell, you type a command, add a few parameters to customize the command's behavior, hit Return, and immediately see your results.

Eventually, you'll get tired of typing the same command (and its parameters) over and over again, so you'll copy and paste it all into a text file. Give that file a .PS1 file-name extension, and you suddenly have a "PowerShell script." Now, instead of typing the command over and over, you run that script, and it executes whatever commands are inside. This is the same pattern you may have used with batch files in the Cmd.exe shell, but it's typically far less complex than scripting or programming.

Don't get us wrong: you can get as complex as you need to with PowerShell. In fact, it supports the same kind of usage patterns as VBScript and other scripting or programming languages. PowerShell gives you access to the full underlying power of the .NET Framework, and we've seen PowerShell "scripts" that were practically indistinguishable from a C# program written in Visual Studio. PowerShell supports these different usage patterns because it's intended to be useful to a wide range of audiences. The point is that just because it supports that level of complexity doesn't mean you have to use it at that level, and it doesn't mean you can't be extremely effective with less complexity.

Here's an analogy: You probably drive a car. If you're like us, changing the oil is the most complex mechanical task you'll ever do with your car. We're not car geeks and can't rebuild an engine. We also can't do those cool, high-speed J-turns that you see in the movies. You'll never see us driving a car on a "closed course" in a car commercial, although Jeff dreams about it (he watches too much *Top Gear.*) But the fact that we're not professional stunt drivers doesn't stop us from being extremely effective drivers at a less complex level. Someday we might decide to take up stunt driving for a hobby (our insurance companies will be thrilled), and at that point we'll need to learn a bit more about how our cars work, master some new skills, and so on. The option is always there for us to grow into. But for now, we're happy with what we can accomplish as normal drivers.

For now, we'll stick with being normal "PowerShell drivers," operating the shell at a lower level of complexity. Believe it or not, users at this level are the primary target audience for PowerShell, and you'll find that there's a lot of incredible stuff you can do without going beyond this level. All you need to do is master the ability to run commands within the shell, and you're on your way.

4.2 The anatomy of a command

Figure 4.1 shows the basic anatomy of a complex PowerShell command. We call this the "full-form" syntax of a command, and we've tried to use a somewhat complex command, so that you can see all of the different things that might show up.

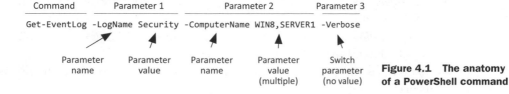

Figure 4.1 The anatomy of a PowerShell command

In order to make sure you're completely familiar with PowerShell's rules, let's cover each of the elements in the previous figure in more detail:

- The cmdlet name is `Get-EventLog`. PowerShell cmdlets always have this verb-noun naming format. We'll explain more about cmdlets in the next section.
- The first parameter name is `-LogName`, and it's being given the value `Security`. Because the value doesn't contain any spaces or punctuation, it doesn't need to be in quotation marks.
- The second parameter name is `-ComputerName`, and it's being given two values: `WIN8` and `SERVER1`. These are in a comma-separated list, and because neither value contains spaces or punctuation, neither value needs to be inside quotation marks.
- The final parameter is `-Verbose`, and it's a switch parameter. That means it doesn't get a value—specifying the parameter is sufficient.
- Note that there's a mandatory space between the command name and the first parameter.
- Parameter names always start with a dash (-).
- There's a mandatory space after the parameter name, and between the parameter's value and the next parameter name.
- There is no space between the dash (-) that precedes a parameter name and the parameter name itself.
- Nothing here is case-sensitive.

Get used to these rules. Start getting really sensitive about accurate, neat typing. Paying attention to spaces and dashes and stuff will minimize the silly errors that PowerShell throws at you.

4.3   *The cmdlet naming convention*

First, let's discuss some terminology. As far as we know, we're the only ones who use this terminology, but we do it consistently, so we may as well explain:

- A *cmdlet* is a native PowerShell command-line utility. These exist only inside of PowerShell and are written in a .NET Framework language like C#. The word "cmdlet" is unique to PowerShell, so if you add it to your search keywords on Google or Bing, the results you get back will be mainly PowerShell-related. The word is pronounced "command-let."
- A *function* can be similar to a cmdlet, but rather than being written in a .NET language, functions are written in PowerShell's own scripting language.
- A *workflow* is a special kind of function that ties into PowerShell's workflow execution system.
- An *application* is any kind of external executable, including command-line utilities like Ping, Ipconfig, and so forth.
- *Command* is the generic term that we use to refer to any or all of the preceding terms.

Microsoft has established a naming convention for cmdlets. That same naming convention *should* be used for functions and workflows, too, although Microsoft can't force anyone but its own developers to follow that rule.

The rule is this: Names start with a standard verb, like Get or Set or New or Pause. You can run `Get-Verb` to see a list of allowable verbs (you'll see about 100, although only about a dozen are common). After the verb is a dash, followed by a singular noun, like Service or Process or EventLog. Developers get to make up their own nouns, so there's no "Get-Noun" cmdlet to display them all.

What's the big deal about this rule? Well, suppose we told you that there were cmdlets named `New-Service`, `Get-Service`, `Get-Process`, `Set-Service`, and so forth. Could you guess what command would create a new Exchange mailbox? Could you guess what command would modify an Active Directory user? If you guessed "Get-Mailbox," you got the first one right. If you guessed "Set-User," you were close: it's `Set-ADUser`, and you'll find the command on domain controllers in the Active-Directory module. The point is that by having this consistent naming convention with a limited set of verbs, it becomes possible for you to guess at command names, and you could then use `Help` or `Get-Command`, along with wildcards, to validate your guess. It becomes easier for you to figure out the names of the commands you need, without having to run to Google or Bing every time.

> **OKAY, OKAY** Not all of the so-called verbs are really verbs. Although Microsoft officially uses the term "verb-noun naming convention," you'll see "verbs" like New, Where, and so forth. You'll get used to it.

4.4 *Aliases: nicknames for commands*

Although PowerShell command names can be nice and consistent, they can also be long. A command name like `Set-WinDefaultInputMethodOverride` is a lot to type, even with Tab completion. Although the command name is clear—looking at it, you can probably guess what it does—it's an *awful* lot to type.

That's where PowerShell aliases come in. An alias is nothing more than a nickname for a command. Tired of typing `Get-Service`? Try this:

```
PS C:\> get-alias -Definition "Get-Service"

Capability      Name
----------      ----
Cmdlet          gsv -> Get-Service
```

Now you know that Gsv is an alias for `Get-Service`.

When using an alias, the command works in exactly the same way. Parameters are the same, everything is the same—the command name is just shorter.

If you're staring at an alias (folks on the internet tend to use them as if we've all memorized all 150 built-in aliases) and can't figure out what it is, ask help:

```
PS C:\> help gsv

NAME
```

```
      Get-Service

SYNOPSIS
      Gets the services on a local or remote computer.

SYNTAX
      Get-Service [[-Name] <String[]>] [-ComputerName <String[]>]
      [-DependentServices [<SwitchParameter>]] [-Exclude <String[]>]
      [-Include <String[]>] [-RequiredServices [<SwitchParameter>]]
      [<CommonParameters>]

      Get-Service [-ComputerName <String[]>] [-DependentServices
      [<SwitchParameter>]] [-Exclude <String[]>] [-Include <String[]>]
      [-RequiredServices [<SwitchParameter>]] -DisplayName <String[]>
      [<CommonParameters>]

      Get-Service [-ComputerName <String[]>] [-DependentServices
      [<SwitchParameter>]] [-Exclude <String[]>] [-Include <String[]>]
      [-InputObject <ServiceController[]>] [-RequiredServices
      [<SwitchParameter>]] [<CommonParameters>]
```

When asked for help about an alias, the help system will always display the help for the full command, which includes the command's complete name.

> **Above and beyond**
>
> You can create your own aliases using `New-Alias`, export a list of aliases with `Export-Alias`, or even import a list of previously created aliases using `Import-Alias`. When you create an alias, it only lasts as long as your current shell session—once you close the window, it's gone. That's why you might want to export them, so that you can more easily reimport them.
>
> We tend to avoid creating and using custom aliases, though, because they're not available to anyone but us. If someone can't look up what "xtd" does, then we're creating confusion and incompatibility.
>
> And "xtd" doesn't do anything. It's a fake alias we made up.

4.5   *Taking shortcuts*

Here's where PowerShell gets tricky. We'd love to tell you that everything we've shown you so far is the only way to do things, but we'd be lying. And, unfortunately, you're going to be out on the internet stealing (er, repurposing) other people's examples, and you'll need to know what you're looking at.

In addition to aliases, which are simply shorter versions of command names, you can also take shortcuts with parameters. You have three ways to do this, each potentially more confusing than the last.

4.5.1   *Truncating parameter names*

PowerShell doesn't force you to type out entire parameter names. Instead of typing -computerName, for example, you could go with -comp. The rule is that you have to type enough of the name for PowerShell to be able to disambiguate. If there's a -computerName parameter, a -common parameter, and a -composite parameter, you'd have to type at least -compu, -commo, and -compo, because that's the minimum number of letters necessary to uniquely identify each.

If you must take shortcuts, this isn't a bad one to take, if you can remember to hit Tab after typing that minimum-length parameter so that PowerShell can finish typing the rest of it for you.

4.5.2 *Parameter name aliases*

Parameters can also have their own aliases, although they can be terribly difficult to find, as they aren't displayed in the help files or anyplace else convenient. For example, the Get-EventLog command has a -computerName parameter. To discover its aliases, you'd run this command:

```
PS C:\> (get-command get-eventlog | select -ExpandProperty parameters).comp
utername.aliases
```

We've boldfaced the command and parameter names; replace these with whatever command and parameter you're curious about. In this case, the output reveals that -Cn is an alias for -ComputerName, so you could run this:

```
PS C:\> Get-EventLog -LogName Security -Cn SERVER2 -Newest 10
```

Tab completion will show you the -Cn alias; if you typed Get-EventLog -C and started pressing Tab, it'd show up. But the help for the command doesn't display -Cn at all, and Tab completion doesn't indicate that -Cn and -ComputerName are the same thing.

4.5.3 *Positional parameters*

When you're looking at a command's syntax in its help file, you can spot positional parameters easily:

```
SYNTAX
    Get-ChildItem [[-Path] <String[]>] [[-Filter] <String>] [-Exclude
    <String[]>] [-Force [<SwitchParameter>]] [-Include <String[]>] [-Name
    [<SwitchParameter>]] [-Recurse [<SwitchParameter>]] [-UseTransaction
    [<SwitchParameter>]] [<CommonParameters>]
```

Here, both -Path and -Filter are positional, and we know that because the parameter name is contained within square brackets. A clearer explanation is available in the full help (help Get-ChildItem -full, in this case), which looks like this:

```
-Path <String[]>
    Specifies a path to one or more locations. Wildcards are
    permitted. The default location is the current directory (.).

    Required?                    false
    Position?                    1
    Default value                Current directory
    Accept pipeline input?       true (ByValue, ByPropertyName)
    Accept wildcard characters?  True
```

That's a clear indication that the -Path parameter is in position 1. For positional parameters, you don't have to type the parameter name—you can provide its value in the correct position. For example,

```
PS C:\> Get-ChildItem c:\users

    Directory: C:\users

Mode                LastWriteTime     Length Name
----                -------------     ------ ----
d----         3/27/2012   11:20 AM           donjones
d-r--         2/18/2012    2:06 AM           Public
```

That's the same as this:

```
PS C:\> Get-ChildItem -path c:\users

    Directory: C:\users

Mode                LastWriteTime     Length Name
----                -------------     ------ ----
d----         3/27/2012   11:20 AM           donjones
d-r--         2/18/2012    2:06 AM           Public
```

The problem with positional parameters is that you're taking on the responsibility of remembering what goes where. You must type all positional parameters first, in the correct order, before you can add any named (non-positional) parameters. If you get the parameter order mixed up, the command fails. For simple commands like Dir, which you've probably used for years, typing -Path feels weird and almost nobody does it. But for more complex commands, which might have three or four positional parameters in a row, it can be tough to remember what goes where.

For example, this is a bit difficult to read and interpret:

```
PS C:\> move file.txt users\donjones\
```

This version, which uses parameter names, is easier to follow:

```
PS C:\> move -Path c:\file.txt -Destination \users\donjones\
```

This version, which puts the parameters in a different order, is allowed when you use the parameter names:
```
PS C:\> move -Destination \users\donjones\ -Path c:\file.txt
```

We tend to recommend against using positional (that is, unnamed) parameters unless you're banging out something quick and dirty at the command line. In anything that will persist, like a batch file or a blog post, include all of the parameter names. We try to do that as much as possible in this book, except in a few instances where we have to shorten the command line to make it fit within the printed pages.

4.6   *Cheating, a bit: Show-Command*

Despite our long experience using PowerShell, the complexity of the commands' syntax can sometimes drive us nuts. One cool new feature of PowerShell v3 is the Show-Command cmdlet. If you're having trouble getting a command's syntax right, with all the spaces, dashes, commas, quotes, and whatnot, Show-Command is your friend. It

Administrator: Windows PowerShell
PS C:\> show-command get-eventlog
Get-EventLog
Parameters for "Get-EventLog":
LogName
List
LogName: *
Security
After:
AsBaseObject
Before:
ComputerName:
localhost
EntryType:
Index:
InstanceId:
Message:
Newest:
100
Source:
UserName:
Common Parameters
Run
Copy
Cancel

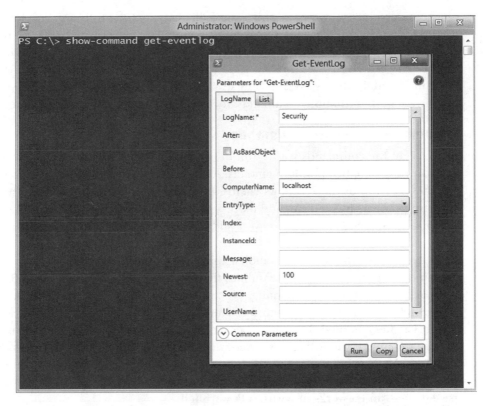

Figure 4.2 `Show-Command` uses a graphical prompt to complete command parameters.

lets you specify the command name you're struggling with and then graphically prompts you for the command's parameters. As shown in figure 4.2, each parameter set (which you learned about in the previous chapter) is on a separate tab, so there's no chance of mixing and matching parameters across sets—pick a tab and stick with it.

When you're done, you can either click Run to run the command or—and we like this option better—click Copy to put the completed command on the clipboard. Back in the shell, paste the command (right-click in the console, or Ctrl-V in the ISE) to look at it. This is a great way to teach yourself the proper syntax, as shown in figure 4.3, and you'll get the proper syntax every time.

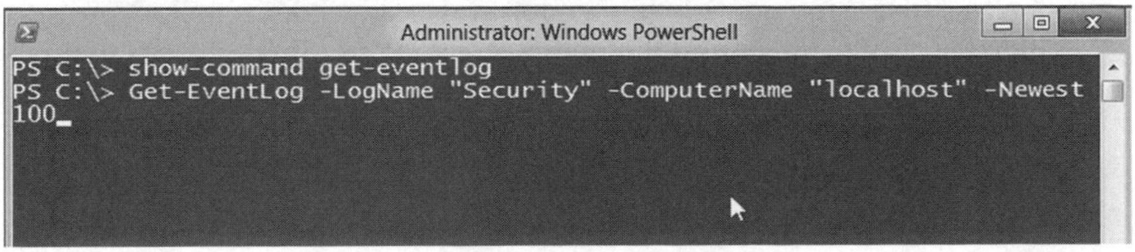

Administrator: Windows PowerShell
PS C:\> show-command get-eventlog
PS C:\> Get-EventLog -LogName "Security" -ComputerName "localhost" -Newest
100

Figure 4.3 `Show-Command` produces the proper command-line syntax based on your entries in its dialog box.

When you produce a command this way, you'll always get the full-form command: full command name, full parameter names, all parameter names typed (that is, nothing entered positionally), and so on. It's a great way to see the perfect, preferred, best-practice way of using PowerShell.

Unfortunately, Show-Command only works with single commands. When you start stringing together multiple commands, it can only help you with one at a time.

4.7   *Support for external commands*

So far, all of the commands you've run in the shell (at least, the ones we've suggested that you run) have been built-in cmdlets. Almost 400 of those cmdlets come built into the latest version of the Windows client operating system, thousands into the server operating system, and you can add more—products like Exchange Server, SharePoint Server, and SQL Server all come with add-ins that each includes hundreds of additional cmdlets.

But you're not limited to the cmdlets that come with PowerShell—you can also use the same external command-line utilities that you have probably been using for years, including Ping, Nslookup, Ipconfig, Net, and so forth. Because these aren't native PowerShell cmdlets, you use them the same way that you always have. PowerShell will launch Cmd.exe behind the scenes, because it knows how to run those external commands, and any results will be displayed within the PowerShell window. Go ahead and try a few old favorites right now. We're often asked how you can use PowerShell to map a regular network drive—one that can be seen from within Explorer. We always use Net Use, and it works fine within PowerShell.

> **TRY IT NOW**   Try running some external command-line utilities that you've used previously. Do they work the same? Do any of them fail?

The Net Use example illustrates an important lesson: with PowerShell, Microsoft (perhaps for the first time ever) isn't saying, "you have to start over and learn everything all over again." Instead, Microsoft is saying, "if you already know how to do something, keep doing it that way. We'll try to provide you with better and more complete tools going forward, but what you already know will still work." One reason there's no "Map-Drive" command within PowerShell is that Net Use already does a good job, so why not keep using it?

> **NOTE**   We've been using that Net Use example for years – ever since Power-Shell v1 first came out. It's still a good story – but PowerShell v3 proves that Microsoft is starting to find the time to create PowerShell-ish ways to do those old tasks. In v3, you'll find that the New-PSDrive command now has a -Persist parameter, which – when used with the FileSystem provider – creates drives that are visible in Explorer.

There are certainly instances where Microsoft has provided better tools than some of the existing, older ones. For example, the native Test-Connection cmdlet provides more options and more flexible output than the old, external Ping command. But if you know how to use Ping, and it's solving whatever need you have, go right on using it. It'll work fine from within PowerShell.

All that said, we do have to deliver a harsh truth: not every single external command will work flawlessly from within PowerShell, at least not without a little tweaking on your part. That's because PowerShell's parser—the bit of the shell that reads what you've typed and tries to figure out what you want the shell to do—doesn't always guess correctly. Sometimes you'll type an external command and PowerShell will mess up, start spitting out errors, and generally not work.

For example, things can get tricky when an external command has a lot of parameters—that's where you'll see PowerShell break the most. We're not going to dive into the details of why it works, but here's a way to run a command that will ensure its parameters work properly:

```
$exe = "C:\Vmware\vcbMounter.exe"
$host = "server"
$user = "joe"
$password = "password"
$machine = "somepc"
$location = "somelocation"
$backupType = "incremental"

& $exe -h $host -u $user -p $password -s "name:$machine" -r $location -t
$backupType
```

This supposes that you have an external command named `vcbMounter.exe` (which is a real-life command-line utility supplied with some of VMWare's virtualization products; if you've never used it or don't have it, that's fine—most old-school command-line utilities work the same way, so this is still a good teaching example). It accepts several parameters:

- `-h` for the host name
- `-u` for the user name
- `-p` for the password
- `-s` for the server name
- `-r` for a location
- `-t` for a backup type

What we've done is put all the various elements—the executable path and name, as well as all of the parameter values—into placeholders, which start with the $ character. That forces PowerShell to treat those values as single units, rather than trying to parse them to see if any of them contain commands or special characters or anything. Then we used the invocation operator (&), passing it the executable name, all of the parameters, and the parameters' values. That pattern will work for almost any command-line utility that's being grumpy about running within PowerShell.

Sound complicated? Well, here's some good news: in PowerShell v3, you don't have to mess around quite so much. Just add two dashes in front of any external command. When you do so, PowerShell won't even try to parse the command, it'll just pass it out to Cmd.exe. That means you can essentially run anything, using the exact syntax you would in Cmd.exe, and not worry about explaining it to PowerShell!

4.8 Dealing with errors

It's inevitable that you'll see some ugly red text as you start working with PowerShell; and probably from time to time even after you're an expert-level shell user. Happens to us all. But don't let the red text stress you out (personally, it takes us back to high school English class and poorly written essays, so "stress" is putting it mildly).

The alarming red text aside, PowerShell's error messages are intended to be helpful. For example, as shown in figure 4.4, they try to show you exactly where PowerShell ran into trouble.

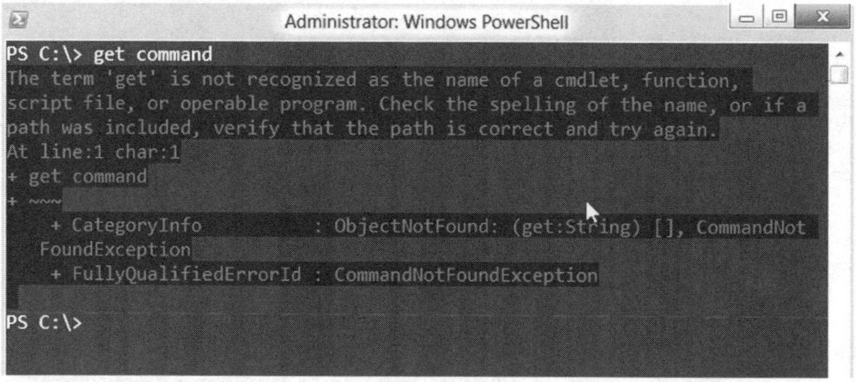

Figure 4.4   Interpreting a PowerShell error message

Error messages almost always include the line and char (character) number where PowerShell got confused. In figure 4.4, it's line 1, char 1—right at the beginning. It's saying, "You typed 'get,' and I have no idea what that means." That's because we typed the command name wrong: it's supposed to be `Get-Command`, not `Get Command`. Oops. What about figure 4.5?

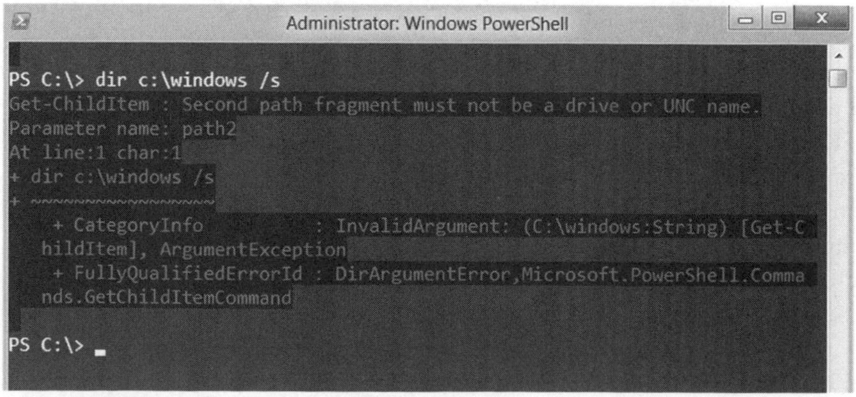

Figure 4.5   What's a "second path fragment?"

The error message in figure 4.5, "Second path fragment must not be a drive or UNC name," is confusing. What second path? We didn't type a second path. We typed one path, `c:\windows`, and a command-line parameter, `/s`. Right?

Well, no. One of the easiest ways to solve this kind of problem is to read the help, and to type the command out completely. If we'd typed `Get-ChildItem -path C:\Windows`, we'd have realized that `/s` isn't the correct syntax. We meant `-recurse`. Sometimes, the error message might not seem helpful—and if it seems like you and PowerShell are speaking different languages, you are. PowerShell obviously isn't going to change its language, so you're probably the one in the wrong, and consulting the help and spelling out the entire command, parameters and all, is often the quickest way to solve the problem. And don't forget to use `Show-Command` to try and figure out the right syntax.

4.9 Common points of confusion

Whenever it seems appropriate, we'll wrap up each chapter with a brief section that covers some of the common mistakes we see when we teach classes. The idea is to help you see what most often confuses other administrators like yourself, and to avoid those problems—or at least to be able to find a solution for them—as you start working with the shell.

4.9.1 Typing cmdlet names

First up is the typing of cmdlet names. It's always verb-noun, like `Get-Content`. All of these are things we'll see newcomers try, but they won't work:

- `Get Content`
- `GetContent`
- `Get=Content`
- `Get_Content`

Part of the problem comes from typos (= instead of -, for example), and part from verbal laziness. We all pronounce the command as "Get Content," verbally omitting the dash. But you've got to type the dash.

4.9.2 Typing parameters

Parameters are also consistently written. A parameter that takes no value, such as `-recurse`, gets a dash before its name. You need to have spaces separating the cmdlet name from its parameters, and the parameters from each other. The following are all correct:

- `Dir -rec` (the shortened parameter name is fine)
- `New-PSDrive -name DEMO -psprovider FileSystem -root \\Server\Share`

But these examples are all incorrect:

- `Dir-rec` (no space between alias and parameter)
- `New-PSDrive -nameDEMO` (no space between parameter name and value)

- `New-PSDrive -name DEMO-psprovider FileSystem` (no space between the first parameter's value and the second parameter's name)

PowerShell isn't normally picky about upper and lowercase, meaning that `dir` and `DIR` are the same, as are `-RECURSE` and `-recurse` and `-Recurse`. But the shell sure is picky about those spaces and dashes.

4.10 Lab

NOTE For this lab, you'll need a Windows 8 or Windows Server 2012 computer running PowerShell v3.

Using what you learned in this chapter, and in the previous chapter on using the help system, complete the following tasks in Windows PowerShell:

1 Display a list of running processes.
2 Display the 100 most recent entries from the Application event log (don't use `Get-WinEvent` for this. We've shown you another command that will do this task).
3 Display a list of all commands that are of the "cmdlet" type (this is tricky—we've shown you `Get-Command`, but you're going to have to read the help to find out how to narrow down the list, as we've asked).
4 Display a list of all aliases.
5 Make a new alias, so you can run `d` to get a directory listing.
6 Display a list of services that begin with the letter *M*. Again, read the help for the necessary command—and don't forget that the asterisk (*) is a near-universal wildcard in PowerShell.
7 Display a list of all Windows Firewall rules. You'll need to use `Help` or `Get-Command` to discover the necessary cmdlet.
8 Display a list only of inbound Windows Firewall rules. You can use the same cmdlet as in the previous task, but you'll need to read its help to discover the necessary parameter and its allowable values.

We hope these tasks seemed straightforward to you. If so—excellent. You were taking advantage of your existing command-line skills to make PowerShell perform a few practical tasks for you. If you're new to the command-line world, these tasks are a good introduction to what you'll be doing in the rest of this book.

Working with providers 5

One of the more potentially confusing aspects of PowerShell is its use of *providers*. We're going to warn you that some of this chapter might seem a bit remedial for you. We expect that you're familiar with Windows' filesystem, for example, and you probably know all the commands you need to manage the filesystem from a command prompt. But bear with us: we're going to point things out in a specific way so that we can use your existing familiarity with the filesystem to help make the concept of providers easier to understand. Also, keep in mind that PowerShell isn't Cmd.exe. You may see some things in this chapter that look familiar, but we assure you that they're doing something quite different than what you're used to.

5.1 What are providers?

A PowerShell provider, or *PSProvider*, is an adapter. It's designed to take some kind of data storage and make it look like a disk drive. You can see a list of installed providers right within the shell:

```
PS C:\> Get-PSProvider

Name            Capabilities                        Drives
----            ------------                        ------
Alias           ShouldProcess                       {Alias}
Environment     ShouldProcess                       {Env}
FileSystem      Filter, ShouldProcess, Credentials  {C, A, D}
Function        ShouldProcess                       {Function}
Registry        ShouldProcess, Transactions         {HKLM, HKCU}
Variable        ShouldProcess                       {Variable}
```

Providers can also be added into the shell, typically along with a module or snap-in, which are the two ways that PowerShell can be extended. (We'll cover those extensions in chapter 7.) Sometimes, enabling certain PowerShell features may create a new PSProvider. For example, when you enable Remoting (which we'll be discussing in chapter 13), you'll get an extra PSProvider, as you can see here:

```
Name                    Capabilities                              Drives
PS C:\> Get-PSProvider

Name                    Capabilities                              Drives
----                    ------------                              ------
Alias                   ShouldProcess                             {Alias}
Environment             ShouldProcess                             {Env}
FileSystem              Filter, ShouldProcess, Credentials        {C, A, D}
Function                ShouldProcess                             {Function}
Registry                ShouldProcess, Transactions               {HKLM, HKCU}
Variable                ShouldProcess                             {Variable}
WSMan                   Credentials                               {WSMan}
```

Notice that each provider has different capabilities. This is important, because it affects the ways in which you can use each provider. These are some of the common capabilities you'll see:

- `ShouldProcess`—Means the provider supports the use of the `-WhatIf` and `-Confirm` parameters, enabling you to "test" certain actions before committing to them.
- `Filter`—Means the provider supports the `-Filter` parameter on the cmdlets that manipulate providers' content.
- `Credentials`—Means the provider permits you to specify alternate credentials when connecting to data stores. There's a `-credential` parameter for this.
- `Transactions`—Means the provider supports the use of transactions, which allows you to use the provider to make several changes, and then either roll back or commit those changes as a single unit.

You use a provider to create a *PSDrive*. A PSDrive uses a single provider to connect to some actual data storage. You're essentially creating a drive mapping, much like you might have in Windows Explorer, but a PSDrive, thanks to the providers, is able to connect to much more than disks. Run the following command to see a list of currently connected drives:

```
PS C:\> Get-PSDrive

Name            Used (GB)       Free (GB)  Provider        Root
----            ---------       ---------  --------        ----
A                                          FileSystem      A:\
Alias                                      Alias
C                    9.88           54.12  FileSystem      C:\
D                    3.34                  FileSystem      D:\
Env                                        Environment
Function                                   Function
HKCU                                       Registry        HKEY_CURRENT_USER
```

```
HKLM                                    Registry        HKEY_LOCAL_MACHINE
Variable                                Variable
```

In the preceding list, you can see that we have three drives using the `FileSystem` provider, two using the `Registry` provider, and so forth. The PSProvider adapts the data store, the PSDrive makes it accessible, and you use a set of cmdlets to see and manipulate the data exposed by each PSDrive. For the most part, the cmdlets you use with a PSDrive have the word "Item" somewhere in their noun:

```
PS C:\> get-command -noun *item*

Capability          Name
----------          ----
Cmdlet              Clear-Item
Cmdlet              Clear-ItemProperty
Cmdlet              Copy-Item
Cmdlet              Copy-ItemProperty
Cmdlet              Get-ChildItem
Cmdlet              Get-Item
Cmdlet              Get-ItemProperty
Cmdlet              Invoke-Item
Cmdlet              Move-Item
Cmdlet              Move-ItemProperty
Cmdlet              New-Item
Cmdlet              New-ItemProperty
Cmdlet              Remove-Item
Cmdlet              Remove-ItemProperty
Cmdlet              Rename-Item
Cmdlet              Rename-ItemProperty
Cmdlet              Set-Item
Cmdlet              Set-ItemProperty
```

We'll be using these cmdlets, and their aliases, to begin working with the providers on our system. Because it's probably the one you're most familiar with, we'll start with the filesystem—that is, the `FileSystem` PSProvider.

5.2　*How the filesystem is organized*

The Windows filesystem is organized around three main types of objects: drives, folders, and files. Drives, the top-level objects, contain both folders and files. Folders are also a kind of container, capable of containing both files and other folders. Files aren't a type of container; they're more of an endpoint object.

You're probably most familiar with viewing the filesystem through Windows Explorer, as shown in figure 5.1, where the hierarchy of drives, folders, and files is visually obvious.

PowerShell's terminology differs somewhat from that of the filesystem. Because a PSDrive might not point to a filesystem—for example, a PSDrive can be mapped to the registry, which is obviously not a filesystem—PowerShell doesn't use the terms "file" and "folder." Instead, it refers to these objects by the more generic term *item*. Both a file and a folder are considered items, although they're obviously different

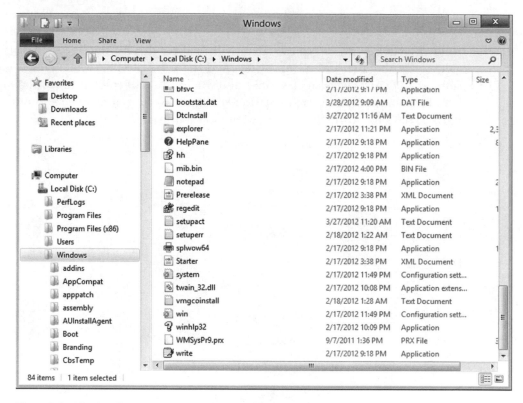

Figure 5.1   Viewing files, folders, and drives in Windows Explorer

types of items. That's why the cmdlet names we showed you previously all use the word "item" in their noun.

Items can, and often do, have properties. For example, a file item might have properties like its last write time, whether or not it's read-only, and so on. Some items, such as folders, can have *child items*, which are the items contained within that item. Knowing those facts should help you make sense of the verbs and nouns in the command list we showed you earlier:

- Verbs like Clear, Copy, Get, Move, New, Remove, Rename, and Set can all apply to items (like files and folders) as well as to item properties (such as the date the item was last written, or whether it's read-only).
- The Item noun refers to individual objects, like files and folders.
- The ItemProperty noun refers to attributes of an item, such as read-only, creation time, length, and so on.
- The ChildItem noun refers to the items (like files and subfolders) contained within an item (like a folder).

Keep in mind that these cmdlets are intentionally generic, because they're meant to work with a variety of different data stores. Some of the cmdlets' capabilities don't make sense in certain situations. As an example, because the FileSystem provider doesn't support the Transactions capability, none of the cmdlets' -UseTransaction parameters will work with items in the filesystem drives. Because the registry doesn't support the Filter capability, the cmdlets' -Filter parameter won't work in the registry drives.

Some PSProviders don't support item properties. For example, the Environment PSProvider is what's used to make the ENV: drive available in PowerShell. This drive provides access to the Windows environment variables, but as the following example shows, they don't have item properties:

```
PS C:\> Get-ItemProperty -Path Env:\PSModulePath
Get-ItemProperty : Cannot use interface. The IPropertyCmdletProvider
interface is not supported by this provider.
At line:1 char:1
+ Get-ItemProperty -Path Env:\PSModulePath
+ ~~~~~~~~~~~~~~~~~~~~~~~~~~~~~~~~~~~~~~~~~~
    + CategoryInfo          : NotImplemented: (:) [Get-ItemProperty], PSN
   otSupportedException
    + FullyQualifiedErrorId : NotSupported,Microsoft.PowerShell.Commands.
   GetItemPropertyCommand
```

The fact that not every PSProvider is the same is perhaps what makes providers so confusing for PowerShell newcomers. You have to think about what each provider is giving you access to, and understand that even when the cmdlet knows how to do something, that doesn't mean the particular provider you're working with will support that operation.

5.3   *How the filesystem is like other data stores*

The filesystem is a model for other forms of storage. For example, figure 5.2 shows the Windows Registry Editor.

The registry is laid out much like the filesystem with folders (registry keys), files (registry values), and so on. It's this broad similarity that makes the filesystem the perfect model, which is why PowerShell connects to data stores as *drives*, exposing *items* and *item properties*. But this similarity only takes you so far: When you dig into the details, the various different forms of storage *are* quite different. That's why the various "item" cmdlets support such a broad range of functionality, and why not every bit of functionality will work with every possible form of storage.

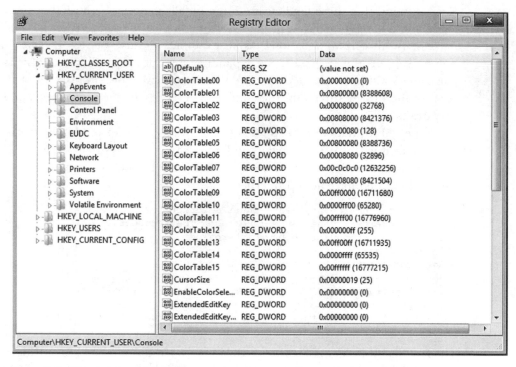

Figure 5.2   The registry and the filesystem have the same kind of hierarchical storage.

5.4   *Navigating the filesystem*

Another cmdlet you'll need to know when working with providers is Set-Location. It's what you use to change the shell's current location to a different container-type item, such as a folder:

```
PS C:\> Set-Location -Path C:\Windows
PS C:\Windows>
```

You're probably more familiar with this command's alias, Cd, which corresponds to the "change directory" command from Cmd.exe:

```
PS C:\Windows> cd 'C:\Program Files'
PS C:\Program Files>
```

Here we've used the alias and passed the desired path as a positional parameter.

One of the trickier tasks in PowerShell is creating new items. For example, how do you create a new directory? Try running New-Item and you'll get an unexpected prompt:

```
PS C:\users\donjones\Documents> new-item testFolder
Type:
```

Remember, the New-Item cmdlet is generic—it doesn't know you want to create a folder. It can create folders, files, registry keys, and much more, but you have to tell it what type of item you want to create:

```
PS C:\users\donjones\Documents> new-item testFolder
Type: directory

    Directory: C:\users\donjones\Documents

Mode                LastWriteTime     Length Name
----                -------------     ------ ----
d----         3/29/2012  10:43 AM            testFolder
```

PowerShell does include a Mkdir command, which most people think is an alias to New-Item. But using Mkdir doesn't require you to enter a type:

```
PS C:\users\donjones\Documents> mkdir test2

    Directory: C:\users\donjones\Documents

Mode                LastWriteTime     Length Name
----                -------------     ------ ----
d----         3/29/2012  10:44 AM            test2
```

What gives? It turns out that Mkdir is a function, not an alias. Internally, it still uses New-Item, but the function adds the -Type Directory parameter for you, making Mkdir behave more like its Cmd.exe predecessor. Keeping this and other little details in mind can help you as you work with providers, because then you know that not every provider is the same, and that the "item" cmdlets are very generic, and they sometimes need a bit more information than you might think at first.

5.5 *Using wildcards and literal paths*

Most of the "item" cmdlets include a -Path property, and by default that property accepts wildcards. Looking at the full help for Get-ChildItem, for example, reveals the following:

```
-Path <String[]>
    Specifies a path to one or more locations. Wildcards are
     permitted. The default location is the current directory (.).

    Required?                    false
    Position?                    1
    Default value                Current directory
    Accept pipeline input?       true (ByValue, ByPropertyName)
    Accept wildcard characters?  True
```

The * wildcard stands in for zero or more characters, whereas the ? wildcard stands in for any single character. You've doubtless used this time and time again, probably with the Dir alias of Get-ChildItem:

```
PS C:\Windows> dir *.exe


    Directory: C:\Windows


Mode                LastWriteTime      Length Name
----                -------------      ------ ----
-a---        2/17/2012    9:17 PM       75264 bfsvc.exe
-a---        2/17/2012   11:21 PM     2355208 explorer.exe
-a---        2/17/2012    9:18 PM      899072 HelpPane.exe
-a---        2/17/2012    9:18 PM       16896 hh.exe
-a---        2/17/2012    9:18 PM      233472 notepad.exe
-a---        2/17/2012    9:18 PM      159744 regedit.exe
-a---        2/17/2012    9:18 PM      125440 splwow64.exe
-a---        2/17/2012   10:09 PM        9728 winhlp32.exe
-a---        2/17/2012    9:18 PM       10240 write.exe
```

The wildcard characters listed in the preceding example are the same ones that Microsoft's filesystems—going all the way back to MS-DOS—have always used. Because those are special wildcard characters, they're not permitted in the names of files and folders. But in PowerShell, the filesystem isn't the only form of storage in use. In most other stores, * and ? are perfectly legal characters for item names. In the registry, for example, you'll find a few values with names that include ?. This presents a problem: When you use * or ? in a path, is PowerShell supposed to treat it as a wildcard character, or as a literal character? If you look for items named "Windows?", do you want the item with "Windows?" as its name, or do you want ? treated as a wildcard, giving you items like "Windows7" and "Windows8" instead?

PowerShell's solution is to provide an alternate -LiteralPath parameter. This parameter doesn't accept wildcards:

```
-LiteralPath <String[]>
    Specifies a path to one or more locations. Unlike the Path
    parameter, the value of the LiteralPath parameter is used exactly
    as it is typed. No characters are interpreted as wildcards. If
    the path includes escape characters, enclose it in single
    quotation marks. Single quotation marks tell Windows PowerShell
    not to interpret any characters as escape sequences.

    Required?                    true
    Position?                    named
    Default value
    Accept pipeline input?       true (ByValue, ByPropertyName)
    Accept wildcard characters?  False
```

When you want * and ? taken literally, you use -LiteralPath instead of the -Path parameter. Note that -LiteralPath isn't positional; if you plan to use it, you have to type -LiteralPath. If you provide a path in the first position, like *.exe in our first example, it'll be interpreted as being for the -Path parameter. Wildcards will also be treated as such.

5.6 *Working with other providers*

One of the best ways to get a feel for these other providers, and how the various "item" cmdlets work, is to play with a PSDrive that isn't the filesystem. Of the providers built into PowerShell, the registry is probably the best example to work with (in part because it's available on every system). Our goal is to turn off the "Aero Peek" feature in Windows.

Start by changing to the HKEY_CURRENT_USER portion of the registry, exposed by the HKCU: drive:

```
PS C:\> set-location -Path hkcu:
```

Next, navigate to the right portion of the registry:

```
PS HKCU:\> set-location -Path software
PS HKCU:\software> get-childitem


    Hive: HKEY_CURRENT_USER\software


Name                            Property
----                            --------
AppDataLow
clients
Microsoft
Mine                            (default) : {}
Parallels
Policies


PS HKCU:\software> set-location microsoft
PS HKCU:\software\microsoft> Get-ChildItem


    Hive: HKEY_CURRENT_USER\software\microsoft


Name                            Property
----                            --------
.NETFramework
Active Setup
Advanced INF Setup
Assistance
AuthCookies
Command Processor               PathCompletionChar : 9
                                EnableExtensions   : 1
                                CompletionChar     : 9
                                DefaultColor       : 0

CTF
EventSystem
Fax
Feeds                           SyncTask : User_Feed_Synchronization-{28B6
                                C75-A5AB-40F7-8BCF-DC87CA308D51
                                          }

FTP                             Use PASV : yes
IdentityCRL                     UpdateDone : 1
Immersive Browser
Internet Connection Wizard      Completed : 1
Internet Explorer
Keyboard
```

```
MediaPlayer
Microsoft Management Console
MSF
PeerNet
RAS AutoDial
Remote Assistance
Speech
SQMClient                       UserId :
                                {73C1117E-B151-4C82-BA8D-BFF6134D1E10}

SystemCertificates
TabletTip
WAB
wfs
Windows
Windows Mail Setup              DelayStartTime   : {186, 248, 138, 82...}
                                DelayInitialized : 2

Windows Media
Windows NT
Windows Script
Windows Script Host
Windows Search
Windows Sidebar
Wisp
```

You're almost finished. You'll notice that we're sticking with full cmdlet names rather than using aliases to emphasize the cmdlets themselves:

```
PS HKCU:\software\microsoft> Set-Location .\Windows
PS HKCU:\software\microsoft\Windows> Get-ChildItem

    Hive: HKEY_CURRENT_USER\software\microsoft\Windows

Name                          Property
----                          --------
CurrentVersion
DWM                           Composition                             : 1
                              EnableAeroPeek                          : 1
                              AlwaysHibernateThumbnails               : 0
                              ColorizationColor                       :
                              3226847725
                              ColorizationColorBalance                : 72
                              ColorizationAfterglow                   :
                              3226847725
                              ColorizationAfterglowBalance            : 0
                              ColorizationBlurBalance                 : 28
                              ColorizationGlassReflectionIntensity    : 50
                              ColorizationOpaqueBlend                 : 0
                              ColorizationGlassAttribute              : 0
Roaming
Shell
TabletPC
Windows Error Reporting       Disabled             : 0
                              MaxQueueCount        : 50
                              DisableQueue         : 0
                              LoggingDisabled      : 0
                              DontSendAdditionalData : 0
```

```
                              ForceQueue             : 0
                              DontShowUI             : 0
                              ConfigureArchive       : 1
                              MaxArchiveCount        : 500
                              DisableArchive         : 0
                              LastQueuePesterTime    : 129773462733828600
```

Note the `EnableAeroPeek` registry value. Let's change it to `0`:

```
PS HKCU:\software\microsoft\Windows> Set-ItemProperty -Path dwm -PSPropert
 EnableAeroPeek -Value 0
```

Let's check it again to make sure the change "took":

```
PS HKCU:\software\microsoft\Windows> Get-ChildItem

    Hive: HKEY_CURRENT_USER\software\microsoft\Windows

Name                            Property
----                            --------
CurrentVersion
DWM                             Composition                              : 1
                                EnableAeroPeek                           : 0
                                AlwaysHibernateThumbnails                : 0
                                ColorizationColor                        :
                                3226847725
                                ColorizationColorBalance                 : 72
                                ColorizationAfterglow                    :
                                3226847725
                                ColorizationAfterglowBalance             : 0
                                ColorizationBlurBalance                  : 28
                                ColorizationGlassReflectionIntensity     : 50
                                ColorizationOpaqueBlend                  : 0
                                ColorizationGlassAttribute               : 0
Roaming
Shell
TabletPC
Windows Error Reporting         Disabled               : 0
                                MaxQueueCount          : 50
                                DisableQueue           : 0
                                LoggingDisabled        : 0
                                DontSendAdditionalData : 0
                                ForceQueue             : 0
                                DontShowUI             : 0
                                ConfigureArchive       : 1
                                MaxArchiveCount        : 500
                                DisableArchive         : 0
                                LastQueuePesterTime    : 129773462733828600
```

Mission accomplished! Using these same techniques, you should be able to work with any provider that comes your way.

5.7   *Lab*

NOTE   For this lab, you'll need any computer running PowerShell v3.

Complete the following tasks:

1   In the registry, go to HKEY_CURRENT_USER\software\microsoft\Windows\ currentversion\explorer. Locate the `Advanced` key, and set its `DontPrettyPath` property to `1`.
2   Create a zero-length file named C:\Test.txt (use `New-Item`).
3   Is it possible to use `Set-Item` to change the contents of C:\Test.txt to `TESTING`? Or do you get an error? If you get an error, why?
4   What are the differences between the `-Filter`, `-Include`, and `-Exclude` parameters of `Get-ChildItem`?

5.8   *Further exploration*

You'll find providers are used for a number of other software packages, including Internet Information Server (IIS), SQL Server, and even Active Directory. In most cases, those products' developers chose to use providers because their software is dynamically extensible. They couldn't know in advance what features would be installed for their products, so they couldn't write a static set of commands. Providers enable developers to expose dynamic structures in a consistent fashion, which lets the IIS and SQL Server teams, in particular, choose to use a combination of cmdlets and providers.

If you have access to these products (for IIS, you'd need v7.5 or later; for SQL Server, we suggest using SQL Server 2012 or later), spend some time exploring their provider model. See how the product teams have arranged the structure of their "drives," and how you can use the cmdlets covered in this chapter to review and change configuration settings and other details.

The pipeline: connecting commands

In chapter 4, you learned that running commands in PowerShell is the same as running commands in any other shell: you type a command name, give it some parameters, and hit Enter. What makes PowerShell special isn't the way it runs commands, but rather the way it allows multiple commands to be connected to each other in powerful, one-line sequences.

6.1 Connect one command to another: less work for you

PowerShell connects commands to each other using something called a *pipeline*. The pipeline provides a way for one command to pass, or *pipe*, its output to another command, allowing that second command to have something to work with.

You've already seen this in action in commands such as Dir | More. You're piping the output of the Dir command into the More command; the More command takes that directory listing and displays it one page at a time. PowerShell takes that same piping concept and extends it to greater effect. In fact, PowerShell's use of a pipeline may seem similar at first to how Unix and Linux shells work. Don't be fooled, though. As you'll come to realize over the next few chapters, PowerShell's pipeline implementation is much richer and more modern.

61

6.2   *Exporting to a CSV or an XML file*

Run a simple command. Here are a few suggestions:

- Get-Process (or Ps)
- Get-Service (or Gsv)
- Get-EventLog Security -newest 100

We picked these commands because they're easy, straightforward commands. We used parentheses to give you the aliases for Get-Process and Get-Service. For Get-EventLog, we specified its mandatory parameter as well as the -newest parameter (which shows you that the command won't take too long to execute).

TRY IT NOW   Go ahead and choose the commands you want to work with. We'll use Get-Process for the following examples; you can stick with one of the three we've listed, or switch between them to see the differences in the results.

What do you see? When we run Get-Process, a table with several columns of information appears on the screen (see figure 6.1).

```
PS C:\> get-process

Handles  NPM(K)    PM(K)      WS(K) VM(M)   CPU(s)     Id ProcessName
-------  ------    -----      ----- -----   ------     -- -----------
     45       5      564       2076    18     0.00   1352 coherence
     29       5      612       1876    38     0.02   1436 coherence
     33       6      756       1028    39     0.02   1444 coherence
    100      10     2660      10848    94     2.61   1220 conhost
    154      10     1620       2948    46     0.13    396 csrss
    196      13     1840       3608    47     0.89    460 csrss
     81       7     1084       3808    53     0.02   2056 dllhost
    105       9     1616       5336    40     0.03   2820 dllhost
    172      18    49016      26712   150     1.44    760 dwm
   1511      95    29212      39916   425     8.20   1288 explorer
      0       0        0         20     0            0 Idle
    631      17     2900       5796    35     0.58    556 lsass
    446      30    56320      15380   181    22.33   1596 MsMpEng
    520      38   104620     111024   699     9.09   1776 powershell
    276      26     3792       8368   105     0.41   3008 prl_cc
    121      11     1612       4332    76     0.08   1476 prl_tools
     90      11     1228       3344    51     0.05   1424 prl_tools_ser...
     83      10     3868       7892    91     0.31    812 regedit
    491      29    14480       8180   615     0.20   2500 SearchIndexer
    195      11     3452       5348    32     0.98    548 services
     36       2      280        788     4     0.05    288 smss
    328      16     3048       5820    47     0.09   1080 spoolsv
    583      37    13512      14056  1386     2.13    404 svchost
    295      12     2116       6240    36     0.13    632 svchost
    313      14     2708       5372    34     0.55    676 svchost
    635      26    14036      12976   118     0.53    736 svchost
    319      23    13244       9668    93     5.05    856 svchost
    574      28     7736       8748   133     0.89    892 svchost
   1071      44    11628      13988   134     3.17    932 svchost
```

Figure 6.1   The output of Get-Process is a table with several columns of information.

It's great to have that information on the screen, but that isn't all you might want to do with the information. For example, if you want to make some charts and graphs of memory and CPU utilization, you might want to export the information into a CSV (comma-separated values) file that could be read into an application like Microsoft Excel.

6.2.1 Exporting to CSV

Exporting to a file is where the pipeline and a second command come in handy:

```
Get-Process | Export-CSV procs.csv
```

Similar to piping `Dir` to `More`, we've piped our processes to `Export-CSV`. That second cmdlet has a mandatory positional parameter that we've used to specify the output filename. Because `Export-CSV` is a native PowerShell cmdlet, it knows how to translate the table normally generated by `Get-Process` into a normal CSV file.

Go ahead and open the file in Windows Notepad to see the results, as shown in figure 6.2:

```
Notepad procs.csv
```

Figure 6.2 Viewing the exported CSV file in Windows Notepad

The first line of the file will be a comment, preceded by a # character, and it identifies the kind of information that's included in the file. In figure 6.2, it's `System .Diagnostics.Process`, which is the under-the-hood name that Windows uses to identify the information related to a running process. The second line will be column headings, and the subsequent lines will list the information for the various processes running on the computer.

You can pipe the output of almost any `Get-` cmdlet to `Export-CSV` and get excellent results. You may also notice that the CSV file contains a great deal more information than what's normally shown on the screen. That's deliberate. The shell knows it couldn't possibly fit all of that information on the screen, so it uses a configuration file, supplied by Microsoft, to select the most important information for on-screen display. In later chapters, we'll show you how to override that configuration to display whatever you want.

Once the information is saved into a CSV file, you can easily email it to a colleague and ask them to view it from within PowerShell. To do this, they'd import the file:

```
Import-CSV procs.csv
```

The shell would read in the CSV file and display the process information. It wouldn't be based on live information, but it would be a snapshot from the exact point in time when you created the CSV file.

6.2.2   *Exporting to XML*

What if CSV files aren't what you need? PowerShell also has an `Export-CliXML` cmdlet, which creates a generic command-line interface (CLI) Extensible Markup Language (XML) file. CliXML is unique to PowerShell, but any program capable of understanding XML can read it. You'll also have a matching `Import-CliXML` cmdlet. Both the import and export cmdlets (such as `Import-CSV` and `Export-CSV`) expect a filename as a mandatory parameter.

> **TRY IT NOW**   Try exporting such things as services, processes, or event log entries to a CliXML file. Make sure you can reimport the file, and try opening the resulting file in Notepad and Internet Explorer to see how each of those applications displays the information.

Does PowerShell include any other import or export commands? You could find out by using the `Get-Command` cmdlet and specifying a `-verb` parameter with either `Import` or `Export`.

> **TRY IT NOW**   See if PowerShell comes with any other import or export cmdlets. You may want to repeat this check after you load new commands into the shell—something you'll do in the next chapter.

6.2.3 Comparing files

Both CSV and CliXML files can be useful for persisting snapshots of information, sharing those snapshots with others, and reviewing those snapshots at a later time. In fact, `Compare-Object` has a great way of using them. It has an alias, `Diff`, which we'll use.

First, run `help diff` and read the help for this cmdlet. We want you to pay attention to three parameters in particular: `-ReferenceObject`, `-DifferenceObject`, and `-Property`.

`Diff` is designed to take two sets of information and compare them to each other. For example, imagine that you ran `Get-Process` on two different computers that were sitting side by side. The computer that's configured exactly the way you want is on the left and is the *reference computer*. The computer on the right might be the same, or it might be somewhat different; it's the *difference computer*. After running the command on each, you'll be staring at two tables of information, and your job is to figure out if any differences exist between the two.

Because these are processes that you're looking at, you're always going to see differences in things like CPU and memory utilization numbers, so we'll ignore those columns. In fact, focus on the Name column, because we want to see if the *difference computer* contains any additional, or any fewer, processes than the *reference computer*. It might take you a while to compare all of the process names from both tables, but you don't have to—that's exactly what `Diff` will do for you.

Let's say you sit down at the reference computer and run this:

```
Get-Process | Export-CliXML reference.xml
```

We prefer using CliXML, rather than CSV, for comparisons like this, because CliXML can hold more information than a flat CSV file. You'd then transport that XML file to the difference computer, and run this command:

```
Diff -reference (Import-CliXML reference.xml)
➥-difference (Get-Process) -property Name
```

Because the previous step is a bit tricky, we'll explain what's happening:

- As in math, parentheses in PowerShell control the order of execution. In the previous example, they force `Import-CliXML` and `Get-Process` to run before `Diff` runs. The output from `Import-CLI` is fed to the `-reference` parameter, and the output from `Get-Process` is fed to the `-difference` parameter.

  The parameter names are `-referenceObject` and `-differenceObject`; keep in mind that you can abbreviate parameter names by typing enough of their names for the shell to be able to figure out which one you want. In this case, `-reference` and `-difference` are more than enough to uniquely identify these parameters. We probably could have shortened them even further to something like `-ref` and `-diff`, and the command would still have worked.

- Rather than comparing the two complete tables, `Diff` focuses on the `Name`, because we gave it the `-property` parameter. If we hadn't, it would think that every process is different because the values of columns like VM, CPU, and PM are always going to be different.

- The result will be a table telling you what's different. Every process that's in the reference set, but not in the difference set, will have a <= indicator (which indicates that the process is present only on the left side). If a process is on the difference computer but not the reference computer, it'll have a => indicator instead. Processes that match across both sets won't be included in the Diff output.

TRY IT NOW Go ahead and try this. If you don't have two computers, start by exporting your current processes to a CliXML file, as we've shown you in the previous example. Then, start some additional processes, such as Notepad, Windows Paint, or Solitaire. Your computer will become the difference computer (on the right), whereas the CliXML file will still be the reference set (on the left).

Here is the output from our test:

```
PS C:\> diff -reference (import-clixml reference.xml) -difference (get
-process) -property name

name                          SideIndicator
----                          -------------
calc                          =>
mspaint                       =>
notepad                       =>
conhost                       <=
powershell_ise                <=
```

This is a useful management trick. If you think of those reference CliXML files as configuration baselines, you can compare any current computer to that baseline and get a difference report. Throughout this book, you'll discover more cmdlets that can retrieve management information, all of which can be piped into a CliXML file to become a baseline. You can quickly build a collection of baseline files for services, processes, operating system configuration, users and groups, and much more, and then use those at any time to compare the current state of a system to that baseline.

TRY IT NOW For fun, try running the Diff command again, but leave off the -property parameter entirely. See the results? Every single process is listed, because values like PM, VM, and so forth have all changed, even though they're the same processes. The output also isn't as useful, because it displays the process's type name and process name.

By the way, you should know that Diff generally doesn't do well at comparing text files. Although other operating systems and shells have a Diff command that's explicitly intended for comparing text files, PowerShell's Diff command works differently. You'll see how differently in this chapter's concluding lab.

NOTE If it seems as though you're using `Get-Process`, `Get-Service`, and `Get-EventLog` often, well, that's on purpose. We guarantee you have access to those cmdlets because they're native to PowerShell and don't require an add-in like Exchange or SharePoint. That said, the skills you're learning will apply to every cmdlet you ever need to run, including those that ship with Exchange, SharePoint, SQL Server, and other server products. Chapter 26 will cover these access details, but for now, focus on *how* to use these cmdlets rather than what the cmdlets are accomplishing. We'll work in some other representative cmdlets at the right time.

6.3 *Piping to a file or a printer*

Whenever you have nicely formatted output—like the tables generated by `Get-Service` or `Get-Process`—you may want to preserve that in a file, or even on paper. Normally, cmdlet output is directed to the screen, which PowerShell refers to as the *host*, but you can change where that output goes. In fact, we've already showed you one way to do so:

```
Dir > DirectoryList.txt
```

The > character is a shortcut added to PowerShell to provide syntactic compatibility with the older Cmd.exe shell. In reality, when you run that command, PowerShell does the following under the hood:

```
Dir | Out-File DirectoryList.txt
```

You can run that same command on your own, instead of using the > syntax. Why would you do so? Because `Out-File` also provides additional parameters that let you specify alternative character encodings (such as UTF8 or Unicode), append content to an existing file, and so forth. By default, the files created by `Out-File` are 80 columns wide, which means sometimes PowerShell might alter command output to fit within 80 characters. That alteration might make the file's contents appear different than when you run the same command on the screen. Read `Out-File`'s help file and see if you can spot a parameter that would let you change the output file width to something other than 80 characters.

> **TRY IT NOW** Don't look here for the answer—open up that help file and see what you can find. We guarantee you'll spot the right parameter in a few moments.

PowerShell has a variety of Out- cmdlets. One is called `Out-Default`, and it's the one the shell uses when you don't specify a different Out- cmdlet. If you run this,

```
Dir
```

you're technically running this,

```
Dir | Out-Default
```

even if you don't realize it. `Out-Default` does nothing more than direct content to `Out-Host`, which means you're running this,

```
Dir | Out-Default | Out-Host
```

without realizing it. `Out-Host` displays information on the screen. What other `Out-` cmdlets can you find?

TRY IT NOW   Time to investigate other `Out-` cmdlets. To get started, try using the `Help` command and wildcards such as `Help Out*`. Another would be to use the `Get-Command` in the same way, such as `Get-Command Out*`. Or, you could specify the `-verb` parameter: `Get-Command -verb Out`. What did you come up with?

`Out-Printer` is probably one of the most useful of the remaining `Out-` cmdlets. `Out-GridView` is also neat; but it requires that you have Microsoft .NET Framework v3.5 and the Windows PowerShell ISE installed, which isn't the case by default on server operating systems. If you do have those installed, try running `Get-Service | Out-GridView` to see what happens. `Out-Null` and `Out-String` have specific uses that we won't get into right now, but you're welcome to read their help files and look at the examples included in those files.

6.4   *Converting to HTML*

Want to produce HTML reports? Easy: pipe your command to `ConvertTo-HTML`. This command produces well-formed, generic HTML that will display in any web browser. It's plain looking, but you can reference a Cascading Style Sheet (CSS) to specify more attractive formatting if desired. Notice that this command doesn't require a filename:

```
Get-Service | ConvertTo-HTML
```

TRY IT NOW   Make sure you run that command yourself—we want you to see what it does before you proceed.

In the PowerShell world, the verb `Export` implies that you're taking data, converting it to some other format, and saving that other format in some kind of storage, such as a file. The verb `ConvertTo` implies only a portion of that process: the conversion to a different format, but not saving it into a file. When you ran the preceding command, you got a screen full of HTML, which probably wasn't what you wanted. Stop for a second: can you think of how you'd get that HTML into a text file on disk?

TRY IT NOW   If you can think of a way, go ahead and try it before you read on.

This command would do the trick:

```
Get-Service | ConvertTo-HTML | Out-File services.html
```

See how connecting more and more commands allows you to have increasingly powerful command lines? Each command handles a single step in the process, and the entire command line as a whole accomplishes a useful task.

PowerShell ships with other `ConvertTo-` cmdlets, including `ConvertTo-CSV` and `ConvertTo-XML`. As with `ConvertTo-HTML`, these don't create a file on disk; they translate command output into CSV or XML, respectively. You could pipe that converted output to `Out-File` to then save it to disk, although it would be shorter to use `Export-CSV` or `Export-CliXML`, because those do both the conversion and the saving.

Above and beyond

Time for a bit more useless background information, although, in this case, it's the answer to a question that many students often ask us: Why would Microsoft provide both `Export-CSV` and `ConvertTo-CSV`, as well as two nearly identical cmdlets for XML?

In certain advanced scenarios, you might not want to save the data to a file on disk. For example, you might want to convert data to XML and then transmit it to a web service, or some other destination. By having distinct `ConvertTo-` cmdlets that don't save to a file, you have the flexibility to do whatever you want.

6.5 Using cmdlets that modify the system: killing processes and stopping services

Exporting and converting aren't the only reasons you might want to connect two commands together. For example, consider—but *please do not run*—this command:

```
Get-Process | Stop-Process
```

Can you imagine what that command would do? We'll tell you: crash your computer. It would retrieve every process and then start trying to end each one of them. It would get to a critical process, like the Local Security Authority, and your computer would probably crash with the famous Blue Screen of Death (BSOD). If you're running PowerShell inside of a virtual machine and want to have a little fun, go ahead and try running that command.

The point is that cmdlets with the same noun (in this case, Process) can often pass information among each other. Typically, you'd specify the name of a specific process rather than trying to stop them all:

```
Get-Process -name Notepad | Stop-Process
```

Services offer something similar: the output from `Get-Service` can be piped to cmdlets like `Stop-Service`, `Start-Service`, `Set-Service`, and so forth.

As you might expect, there are some specific rules about which commands can connect to each other. For example, if you look at a command sequence like `Get-ADUser | New-SQLDatabase`, you would probably not expect it to do anything sensible (although it might well do something nonsensical). In chapter 7, we'll dive into the rules that govern how commands can connect to each other.

We'd like you to know one more thing about cmdlets like `Stop-Service` and `Stop-Process`. These cmdlets modify the system in some fashion, and all cmdlets that modify the system have an internally defined *impact level*. The cmdlet's creator sets this impact level and it can't be changed. The shell has a corresponding `$ConfirmPreference` setting, which is set to `High` by default. Type the following setting name to see your shell's setting:

```
PS C:\> $confirmpreference
High
```

Here's how it works: when a cmdlet's internal impact level is equal to or higher than the shell's `$ConfirmPreference` setting, the shell will automatically ask, "Are you sure?" when the cmdlet does whatever it's trying to do. In fact, if you used a virtual machine to try the crash-your-computer command we mentioned earlier, you probably were asked, "Are you sure?" for each process. When a cmdlet's internal impact level is less than the shell's `$ConfirmPreference` setting, you don't automatically get the "Are you sure?" prompt.

But you can force the shell to ask you whether you're sure:

```
Get-Service | Stop-Service -confirm
```

Next, add the `-confirm` parameter to the cmdlet. This should be supported by any cmdlet that makes some kind of change to the system, and it'll show up in the help file for the cmdlet if it's supported.

A similar parameter is `-whatif`. This is supported by any cmdlet that supports `-confirm`. The `-whatif` parameter isn't triggered by default, but you can specify it whenever you want to:

```
PS C:\> get-process | stop-process -whatif
What if: Performing operation "Stop-Process" on Target "conhost (1920)
".
What if: Performing operation "Stop-Process" on Target "conhost (1960)
".
What if: Performing operation "Stop-Process" on Target "conhost (2460)
".
What if: Performing operation "Stop-Process" on Target "csrss (316)".
```

This tells you what the cmdlet would have done, without letting the cmdlet do it. It's a useful way to preview what a potentially dangerous cmdlet would have done to your computer, to make certain that you want to do that.

6.6   *Common points of confusion*

One common point of confusion in PowerShell revolves around the `Export-CSV` and `Export-CliXML` commands. Both of these commands, technically speaking, create text files. That is, the output of either command can be viewed in Notepad, as shown in figure 6.2. But you have to admit that the text is definitely in a special kind of format—either in comma-separated values or XML.

The confusion tends to set in when someone is asked to read these files back into the shell. Do you use Get-Content (or its aliases, Type or Cat)? For example, suppose you did this:

```
PS C:\> get-eventlog -LogName security -newest 5 | export-csv events.csv
```

Now, try reading that back in by using Get-Content:

```
PS C:\> Get-Content .\events.csv
#TYPE System.Diagnostics.EventLogEntry#security/Microsoft-Windows-Security
-Auditing/4797
"EventID","MachineName","Data","Index","Category","CategoryNumber","EntryT
ype","Message","Source","ReplacementStrings","InstanceId","TimeGenerated",
"TimeWritten","UserName","Site","Container"
"4797","DONJONES1D96","System.Byte[]","263","(13824)","13824","SuccessAudi
t","An attempt was made to query the existence of a blank password for an
account.

Subject:
        Security ID:            S-1-5-21-87969579-3210054174-450162487-100

        Account Name:           donjones
        Account Domain:         DONJONES1D96
        Logon ID:               0x10526

Additional Information:
        Caller Workstation:     DONJONES1D96
        Target Account Name:    Guest
        Target Account Domain:  DONJONES1D96","Microsoft-Windows-Security-
uditing
","System.String[]","4797","3/29/2012 9:43:36 AM","3/29/2012 9:43:36 AM",,
,
"4616","DONJONES1D96","System.Byte[]","262","(12288)","12288","SuccessAudi
t","The system time was changed.
```

We truncated the preceding output, but there's a lot more of the same. Looks like garbage, right? You're looking at the raw CSV data. The command didn't try to interpret, or *parse*, the data at all. Contrast that with the results of Import-CSV:

```
PS C:\> import-csv .\events.csv


EventID            : 4797
MachineName        : DONJONES1D96
Data               : System.Byte[]
Index              : 263
Category           : (13824)
CategoryNumber     : 13824
EntryType          : SuccessAudit
Message            : An attempt was made to query the existence of a
                     blank password for an account.

                     Subject:
                        Security ID:
                     S-1-5-21-87969579-3210054174-450162487-1001
                        Account Name:           donjones
                        Account Domain:         DONJONES1D96
```

```
                        Logon ID:          0x10526

                  Additional Information:
                        Caller Workstation:      DONJONES1D96
                        Target Account Name:     Guest
                        Target Account Domain:   DONJONES1D96
Source               : Microsoft-Windows-Security-Auditing
ReplacementStrings   : System.String[]
InstanceId           : 4797
TimeGenerated        : 3/29/2012 9:43:36 AM
TimeWritten          : 3/29/2012 9:43:36 AM
UserName             :
```

Much nicer, right? The `Import-` cmdlets pay attention to what's in the file, attempt to interpret it, and create a display that looks more like the output of the original command (`Get-EventLog`, in this case). Typically then, if you create a file with `Export-CSV`, you'll read it by using `Import-CSV`. If you create it by using `Export-CliXML`, you'll generally read it by using `Import-CliXML`. By using these commands in pairs, you'll get better results. Use `Get-Content` only when you're reading in a text file and don't want PowerShell attempting to parse the data—that is, when you want to work with the raw text.

6.7   Lab

NOTE   For this lab, you'll need any computer running PowerShell v3.

We've kept this chapter's text slightly shorter because some of the examples we showed you probably took a bit longer to complete, and because we want you to spend more time completing the following hands-on exercises. If you haven't already completed all of the "Try it now" tasks in the chapter, we strongly recommend that you do so before tackling these tasks:

1 What happens if you run `Get-Service | Export-CSV services.csv | Out-File` from the console? Why does that happen?

2 Apart from getting one or more services and piping them to `Stop-Service`, what other means does `Stop-Service` provide for you to specify the service or services you want to stop? Is it possible to stop a service without using `Get-Service` at all?

3 What if you want to create a pipe-delimited file instead of a comma-separated (CSV) file? You would still use the `Export-CSV` command, but what parameters would you specify?

4 Is there a way to eliminate the # comment line from the top of an exported CSV file? That line normally contains type information, but what if you want to omit that from a particular file?

5 `Export-CliXML` and `Export-CSV` both modify the system because they can create and overwrite files. What parameter would prevent them from overwriting

an existing file? What parameter would ask you if you were sure before proceeding to write the output file?

6 Windows maintains several regional settings, which include a default list separator. On U.S. systems, that separator is a comma. How can you tell Export-CSV to use the system's default separator, rather than a comma?

TRY IT NOW   After you've completed this lab, try to complete Review Lab 1, which you'll find in appendix A of this book.

Adding commands

7

One of PowerShell's primary strengths is its extensibility. As Microsoft continues to invest in PowerShell, it develops more and more commands for products like Exchange Server, SharePoint Server, the System Center family, SQL Server, and so on. Typically, when you install these products' management tools, you also get a graphical management console of some kind and one or more extensions for Windows PowerShell.

7.1 How one shell can do everything

We know you're probably familiar with the graphical Microsoft Management Console (MMC), which is why we'll use it as an example of how PowerShell works. The two work similarly when it comes to extensibility, in part because the same Management Frameworks team within Microsoft develops both the MMC and PowerShell.

When you open a new, blank MMC console, it's largely useless. It can't do anything, because the MMC has little built-in functionality. To make it useful, you go to its File menu and select Add/Remove Snapins. In the MMC world, a *snap-in* is a tool, such as Active Directory Users and Computers, DNS Management, DHCP Administration, and so on. You can choose to add as many snap-ins to your MMC as you like, and you can save the resulting console to make it easier to reopen that same set of snap-ins in the future.

Where do snap-ins come from? Once you've installed the management tools associated with a product like Exchange Server, Forefront, or System Center, you'll find those products' snap-ins listed on the Add/Remove Snapins dialog box within the MMC. Most products also install their own preconfigured MMC console files, which do nothing but load up the basic MMC and preload a snap-in or two. You don't have to use those preconfigured consoles if you don't want to, because you can always open a blank MMC console and load the exact snap-ins you want. For example, the preconfigured Exchange Server MMC console doesn't include the Active Directory Sites and Services snap-in, but you can easily create an MMC console that includes Exchange and also Sites and Services.

PowerShell works in almost exactly the same way. Install the management tools for a given product (the option to install management tools is usually included in a product's Setup menu—if you install a product like Exchange Server on Windows 7, the management tools will often be the only thing Setup offers). Doing so will give you any related PowerShell extensions, and it may even create a product-specific management shell.

7.2 About product-specific "management shells"

These product-specific management shells have been a huge source of confusion. We want to clearly state that there is only one Windows PowerShell. There isn't a separate PowerShell for Exchange and Active Directory; it's all a single shell.

Let's take Active Directory as an example. On the Start menu of a Windows Server 2008 R2 domain controller, under Administrative Tools, you'll find an icon for the Active Directory Module for Windows PowerShell. If you right-click that item and select Properties from the context menu, the first thing you should see is the Target field, which will be this:

```
%windir%\system32\WindowsPowerShell\v1.0\powershell.exe
➥-noexit -command import-module ActiveDirectory
```

This command runs the standard PowerShell.exe application and gives it a command-line parameter to run a specific command: `Import-Module ActiveDirectory`. The result is a copy of the shell that has the ActiveDirectory module preloaded. But we can think of no reason why you couldn't open the "normal" PowerShell and run that same command yourself to get the same functionality.

The same holds true for almost every product-specific "management shell" you'll find: Exchange, SharePoint, you name it. Examine the properties of those products' Start menu shortcuts, and you'll find that they open the normal PowerShell.exe and pass a command-line parameter to either import a module, add a snap-in, or load a preconfigured console file (and the console file is simply a list of snap-ins to load automatically).

SQL Server 2008 and SQL Server 2008 R2 are exceptions. Their "product-specific" shell, Sqlps, is a specially compiled version of PowerShell that runs only the SQL Server extensions. Properly called a *mini-shell*, Microsoft tried this approach for the first time in SQL Server. It has been unpopular, and the company won't be using that approach again: SQL Server 2012 uses PowerShell.

You're not constrained to working with the prespecified extensions. Once you open the Exchange management shell, you could run `Import-Module ActiveDirectory`, and provided the ActiveDirectory module was present on your computer, you'd add the Active Directory functionality to that shell. You could also open a normal Power-Shell console and manually add whatever extensions you like.

As we stated earlier in this section, this has been a huge point of confusion for folks, including some who believed there were multiple versions of PowerShell that couldn't cross-utilize each other's functionality. Don even got into an argument on his blog (http://windowsitpro.com/go/DonJonesPowerShell) about it at one point and had to ask members of the PowerShell team to step in and back him up. So trust us: you can have all the functionality you want inside a single shell, and the product-specific shell shortcuts in the Start menu don't in any way limit you or imply that special versions of PowerShell exist for those products.

7.3   *Extensions: finding and adding snap-ins*

PowerShell v3 has two kinds of extensions: modules and snap-ins. We'll look at snap-ins first.

The proper name for a PowerShell snap-in is *PSSnapin*, which distinguishes these from snap-ins for the graphical MMS. PSSnapins were first created for PowerShell v1. A PSSnapin generally consists of one or more DLL files, accompanied by additional XML files that contain configuration settings and help text. PSSnapins have to be installed and registered in order for PowerShell to know they exist.

> **NOTE**   The PSSnapin concept is something Microsoft is moving away from, and you're likely to see fewer and fewer of them in the future. Internally, Microsoft is focusing on delivering extensions as modules.

You can get a list of available snap-ins by running `Get-PSSnapin -registered` from within PowerShell. On our computer, which is a domain controller that happens to have SQL Server 2008 installed, we see this:

```
PS C:\> get-pssnapin -registered

Name        : SqlServerCmdletSnapin100
PSVersion   : 2.0
Description : This is a PowerShell snap-in that includes various SQL
              Server cmdlets.

Name        : SqlServerProviderSnapin100
PSVersion   : 2.0
Description : SQL Server Provider
```

This tells us that we have two snap-ins installed and available, but not loaded. You can view a list of loaded snap-ins by running `Get-PSSnapin`. That list will include all of the core, automatically loaded snap-ins that contain PowerShell's native functionality.

To load a snap-in, run `Add-PSSnapin` and specify the name of the snap-in:

```
PS C:\> add-pssnapin sqlservercmdletsnapin100
```

As is often the case in PowerShell, you don't need to worry about getting uppercase and lowercase letters correct. The shell won't care.

Once a snap-in is loaded, you'll want to figure out what it added to the shell. A PSS-napin can add cmdlets, PSDrive providers, or both to the shell. To find out which cmdlets you've added, use Get-Command (or its alias, Gcm):

```
PS C:\> gcm -pssnapin sqlservercmdletsnapin100

CommandType     Name                     Definition
-----------     ----                     ----------
Cmdlet          Invoke-PolicyEvaluation  Invoke-PolicyEvaluation...
Cmdlet          Invoke-Sqlcmd            Invoke-Sqlcmd [[-Query]...
```

Here we've specified that only the commands from the SqlServerCmdletSnapin100 snap-in be included in the output, and only two were listed. Yes, that's all SQL Server adds in that snap-in, but one of those is capable of executing Transact-SQL (T-SQL) commands. Because you can accomplish almost anything in SQL Server by executing a T-SQL command, the Invoke-Sqlcmd cmdlet makes it possible to do almost anything you might need to do in SQL Server.

To see if the snap-in added any new PSDrive providers, run Get-PSProvider. You can't specify a snap-in with this cmdlet, so you'll have to be familiar with the providers that were already there, and scan through the list manually to spot anything new. Here are our results:

```
PS C:\> get-psprovider

Name            Capabilities             Drives
----            ------------             ------
WSMan           Credentials              {WSMan}
Alias           ShouldProcess            {Alias}
Environment     ShouldProcess            {Env}
FileSystem      Filter, ShouldProcess    {C, A, D}
Function        ShouldProcess            {Function}
Registry        ShouldProcess, Transa... {HKLM, HKCU}
Variable        ShouldProcess            {Variable}
Certificate     ShouldProcess            {cert}
```

Doesn't look like anything new. We're not surprised, because the snap-in we loaded was named SqlServerCmdletSnapin100. If you recall, our list of available snap-ins also included SqlServerProviderSnapin100, suggesting that the SQL Server team, for some reason, packaged its cmdlets and PSDrive provider separately. Let's try adding the second one:

```
PS C:\> add-pssnapin sqlserverprovidersnapin100
PS C:\> get-psprovider

Name            Capabilities             Drives
----            ------------             ------
WSMan           Credentials              {WSMan}
Alias           ShouldProcess            {Alias}
Environment     ShouldProcess            {Env}
FileSystem      Filter, ShouldProcess    {C, A, D}
Function        ShouldProcess            {Function}
Registry        ShouldProcess, Transa... {HKLM, HKCU}
Variable        ShouldProcess            {Variable}
```

```
Certificate          ShouldProcess           {cert}
SqlServer            Credentials             {SQLSERVER}
```

Reviewing the previous output, we see that an SQLSERVER: drive has been added to our shell, powered by the `SqlServer` PSDrive provider. Adding this new drive means we can run `cd sqlserver:` to change to the SQLSERVER: drive, and presumably start exploring databases and stuff.

7.4 *Extensions: finding and adding modules*

PowerShell v3 (and v2) supports a second type of extension called a *module*. Modules are designed to be a little more self-contained, and somewhat easier to distribute, but they work similarly to PSSnapins. But you do need to know a bit more about them in order to find and use them.

Modules don't require advanced registration. Instead, PowerShell automatically looks in a certain set of paths to find modules. The `PSModulePath` environment variable defines the paths where PowerShell expects modules to live:

```
PS C:\> get-content env:psmodulepath
C:\Users\Administrator\Documents\WindowsPowerShell\Modules;C:\Windows
\system32\WindowsPowerShell\v1.0\Modules\
```

As you can see in the previous example, there are two default locations: one in the operating system folder, where system modules live, and one in the Documents folder, where you can add any personal modules. You can also add a module from any other location, provided you know its full path.

> **NOTE** `PSModulePath` isn't something you can modify within PowerShell; it's set as part of your Windows environment. You can change it in the System Control Panel, or you can set it via Group Policy.

The path is important in PowerShell v3. If you have modules located elsewhere, you should add their paths to the `PSModulePath` environment variable. Figure 7.1 shows how you do this from Windows' control panel, not from within PowerShell.

Why is the `PSModulePath` path so important? Because with it, PowerShell can automatically locate all of the modules on your computer. Once it finds your modules, PowerShell *auto-discovers* them. In other words, it will look to you as if all of your modules are loaded all of the time. Ask for help on a module, and you'll get it, without having to load it. Run any command you've found, and PowerShell will automatically load the module containing that command. PowerShell's `Update-Help` command also uses `PSModulePath` to discover what modules you have, and then it seeks out updated help files for each one.

For example, run `Get-Module | Remove-Module` to remove any loaded modules. Then run the following command (your results may differ slightly depending upon which specific version of Windows you're using):

```
PS C:\> help *network*

Name                            Category   Module
----                            --------   ------
Get-BCNetworkConfiguration      Function   BranchCache
Get-DtcNetworkSetting           Function   MsDtc
Set-DtcNetworkSetting           Function   MsDtc
Get-SmbServerNetworkInterface   Function   SmbShare
Get-SmbClientNetworkInterface   Function   SmbShare
```

As you can see, PowerShell discovered several commands (of the "function" variety) that have the word "network" in their name. You could then ask for help on one of these, even though you haven't loaded the module:

```
PS C:\> help Get-SmbServerNetworkInterface
NAME
    Get-SmbServerNetworkInterface

SYNTAX
    Get-SmbServerNetworkInterface [-CimSession <CimSession[]>]
    [-ThrottleLimit <int>] [-AsJob]  [<CommonParameters>]
```

If you want to, you could even run the command, and PowerShell would make sure the module was loaded for you. This auto-discovery and auto-loading functionality is

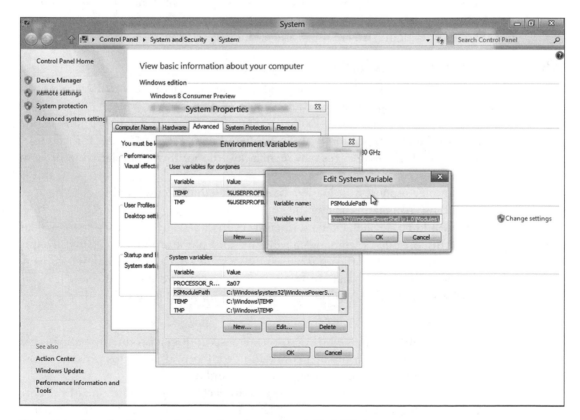

Figure 7.1 Changing the PSModulePath environment variable in Windows

quite useful, helping you to find and use commands that aren't even present in the shell when you start.

> **TIP** You can also use `Get-Module` to retrieve a list of modules available on a remote computer, and use `Import-Module` to load a remote module into your current PowerShell session. You'll learn how to do that in chapter 13 on remote control.

PowerShell's module auto-discovery enables the shell to complete command names (using Tab in the console, or IntelliSense in the ISE), display help, and run commands, even for modules you haven't explicitly loaded into memory. These features make it worth the effort to keep `PSModulePath` complete and up to date.

What if a module isn't located in one of the paths referenced by `PSModulePath`? You would need to run `Import-Module` and specify the complete path to the module, such as C:\MyPrograms\Something\MyModule.

If you have a Start menu shortcut for a product-specific shell—say, SharePoint Server—and you don't know where that product installed its PowerShell module, open the properties for the Start menu shortcut. As we showed you earlier in this chapter, the `Target` property of the shortcut will contain the `Import-Module` command used to load the module, and that will show you the module name and path.

Modules can also add PSDrive providers. You'd use the same technique you used for PSSnapins to identify any new providers: run `Get-PSProvider`.

7.5   *Command conflicts and removing extensions*

Take a close look at the commands we added for both SQL Server and Active Directory. Notice anything special about the commands' names?

Most PowerShell extensions—Exchange Server being a notable exception—add a short prefix to the noun portion of their command names. `Get-ADUser`, for example, or `Invoke-SqlCmd`. These prefixes may seem awkward, but they're designed to prevent command conflicts.

For example, suppose you loaded two modules that each contained a `Get-User` cmdlet. With two commands having the same name and being loaded at the same time, which one would PowerShell execute when you run `Get-User`? The last one loaded, as it turns out. But the other commands having the same name aren't inaccessible. To specifically run either command, you'd have to use a somewhat awkward naming convention that requires both the snap-in name and the command name. If one `Get-User` came from a snap-in called MyCoolPowerShellSnapin, you'd have to run this:

```
MyCoolPowerShellSnapin\Get-User
```

That's a lot of typing, and it's why Microsoft suggests adding a product-specific prefix, like *AD* or *SQL*, to the noun of each command. Adding prefixes helps prevent a conflict and helps make commands easier to identify and use.

If you do wind up with a conflict, you can always choose to remove one of the conflicting extensions. You'd run `Remove-PSSnapin` or `Remove-Module`, along with the snap-in or the module name, to unload an extension.

7.6 *Playing with a new module*

Let's put your newfound knowledge to use. We'll assume that you're using the newest version of Windows, and we'd like you to follow along with the commands we present in this section. More importantly, we want you to follow the process and the thinking that we'll explain, because this is how we teach ourselves to use new commands without rushing out and buying a new book for every single product and feature that we run across. In the concluding lab for this chapter, we'll have you repeat this same process on your own, to learn about an entirely new set of commands.

Our goal is to clear the DNS name resolution cache on our computer. We've no idea if PowerShell can even do this, so we'll start by asking the help system for a clue:

```
PS C:\> help *dns*

Name                              Category   Module

----                              --------   ------
dnsn                              Alias
Resolve-DnsName                   Cmdlet     DnsClient
Clear-DnsClientCache              Function   DnsClient
Get-DnsClient                     Function   DnsClient
Get-DnsClientCache                Function   DnsClient
Get-DnsClientGlobalSetting        Function   DnsClient
Get-DnsClientServerAddress        Function   DnsClient
Register-DnsClient                Function   DnsClient
Set-DnsClient                     Function   DnsClient
Set-DnsClientGlobalSetting        Function   DnsClient
Set-DnsClientServerAddress        Function   DnsClient
Add-DnsClientNrptRule             Function   DnsClient
Get-DnsClientNrptPolicy           Function   DnsClient
Get-DnsClientNrptGlobal           Function   DnsClient
Get-DnsClientNrptRule             Function   DnsClient
Remove-DnsClientNrptRule          Function   DnsClient
Set-DnsClientNrptGlobal           Function   DnsClient
Set-DnsClientNrptRule             Function   DnsClient
```

Ah-ha! As you can see, we have an entire DnsClient module on our computer. The previous list shows the `Clear-DnsClientCache` command, but we're curious about what other commands are available. In order to find out, we'll manually load the module and list its commands:

> **TRY IT NOW** Go ahead and follow along as we run these commands. If you don't have a DnsClient module on your computer, then you're using an older version of Windows. Consider getting a newer version, or even a trial version that you can run inside a virtual machine, so that you can follow along.

```
PS C:\> import-module -Name DnsClient
PS C:\> get-command -Module DnsClient

Capability      Name

----------      ----
CIM             Add-DnsClientNrptRule
CIM             Clear-DnsClientCache
CIM             Get-DnsClient
```

```
CIM              Get-DnsClientCache
CIM              Get-DnsClientGlobalSetting
CIM              Get-DnsClientNrptGlobal
CIM              Get-DnsClientNrptPolicy
CIM              Get-DnsClientNrptRule
CIM              Get-DnsClientServerAddress
CIM              Register-DnsClient
CIM              Remove-DnsClientNrptRule
CIM              Set-DnsClient
CIM              Set-DnsClientGlobalSetting
CIM              Set-DnsClientNrptGlobal
CIM              Set-DnsClientNrptRule
CIM              Set-DnsClientServerAddress
Cmdlet           Resolve-DnsName
```

NOTE   We could have asked for help on Clear-DnsClientCache, or even run the command directly. PowerShell would have loaded the DnsClient module for us in the background. But, because we're exploring, this approach lets us view the module's complete list of commands.

This list of commands looks more or less the same as the earlier list. Fine; let's see what the Clear-DnsClientCache command looks like:

```
PS C:\> help Clear-DnsClientCache

NAME
    Clear-DnsClientCache

SYNTAX
    Clear-DnsClientCache [-CimSession <CimSession[]>] [-ThrottleLimit
    <int>] [-AsJob] [-WhatIf] [-Confirm]  [<CommonParameters>]
```

Seems straightforward, and we don't see any mandatory parameters. Let's try running the command:

```
PS C:\> Clear-DnsClientCache
```

OK, no news is usually good news. Still, it'd be nice to see that the command did something. Let's try this instead:

```
PS C:\> Clear-DnsClientCache -verbose
VERBOSE: The specified name resolution records cached on this machine will
 be removed.
Subsequent name resolutions may return up-to-date information.
```

The -verbose switch is available for all commands, although not all commands do anything with it. In this case, we get a message indicating what's happening, which tells us the command did run.

7.7   *Profile scripts: preloading extensions when the shell starts*

Let's say you've opened PowerShell, and you've loaded several favorite snap-ins and modules. If you took that route, you'd be required to run one command for each snap-in or module you want to load, which can take a few minutes of typing if you have several of them. When you're done using the shell, you close its window. The next time you open a shell window, all of your snap-ins and modules are gone, and you have to run all those commands again to load them back. Horrible. There must be a better way.

We'll show you three better ways. The first involves creating a *console file*. This only memorizes PSSnapins that are loaded—it won't work with any modules you may have loaded. Start by loading in all of the snap-ins you want, and then run this command:

```
Export-Console c:\myshell.psc
```

Running the command creates a small XML file that lists the snap-ins you loaded into the shell.

Next, you'll want to create a new PowerShell shortcut somewhere. The target of that shortcut should be

```
%windir%\system32\WindowsPowerShell\v1.0\powershell.exe
➥-noexit -psconsolefile c:\myshell.psc
```

When you use that shortcut to open a new PowerShell window, your console will load, and the shell will automatically add any snap-ins listed in that console file. Again, modules aren't included. What do you do if you have a mix of snap-ins and modules, or if you have some modules that you always want loaded?

> **TIP** Keep in mind that PowerShell will auto-load modules that are in one of the `PSModulePath` locations. You only need to worry about the following steps if you want to preload modules that aren't in one of the `PSModulePath` locations.

The answer is to use a *profile script*. We've mentioned those before, and we'll cover them in more detail in chapter 25, but for now follow these steps to learn how to use them:

1 In your Documents folder, create a new folder called WindowsPowerShell (no spaces in the folder name).
2 In the newly created folder, use Notepad to create a file named profile.ps1. When you save the file in Notepad, be sure to enclose the filename in quotation marks ("profile.ps1"). Using quotes prevents Notepad from adding a .txt filename extension. If that .txt extension gets added, this trick won't work.
3 In that newly created text file, type your `Add-PSSnapin` and `Import-Module` commands, listing one command per line in order to load your preferred snap-ins and modules.
4 Back in PowerShell, you'll need to enable script execution, which is disabled by default. There are some security consequences to this that we'll discuss in chapter 17 but for now we'll assume you're doing this in a standalone virtual machine, or on a standalone test computer, and that security is less of an issue. In the shell, run `Set-ExecutionPolicy RemoteSigned`. Note that the command

will only work if you've run the shell as *Administrator*. It's also possible for a Group Policy object (GPO) to override this setting; you'll get a warning message if that's the case.

5   Assuming you haven't had any errors or warnings up to this point, close and reopen the shell. It will automatically load profile.ps1, execute your commands, and load your favorite snap-ins and modules for you.

TRY IT NOW   Even if you don't have a favorite snap-in or module yet, creating this simple profile will be good practice. If nothing else, put the command cd \ into the profile script, so that the shell always opens in the root of your system drive. But please don't do this on a computer that's part of your company's production network, because we haven't covered all of the security implications yet.

7.8   *Common points of confusion*

PowerShell newcomers frequently do one thing incorrectly when they start working with modules and snap-ins: they don't read the help. Specifically, they don't use the -example or -full switches when asking for help.

Frankly, looking at built-in examples is the best way to learn how to use a command. Yes, it can be a bit daunting to scroll through a list of hundreds of commands (Exchange Server, for example, adds well over 400 new commands), but using Help and Get-Command with wildcards should make it easier to narrow down the list to whatever noun you think you're after. From there, *read the help*!

7.9   *Lab*

NOTE   For this lab, you'll need a Windows 7, Windows Server 2008 R2, or later computer running PowerShell v3.

As always, we're assuming that you have the latest version of Windows (client or server) on a computer or virtual machine to test with.

For this lab, you only have one task: run the Networking troubleshooting pack. When you successfully do so, you'll be asked for an "Instance ID." Hit Enter, run a Web Connectivity check, and ask for help connecting to a specific web page. Use http://videotraining.interfacett.com as your test URL. We hope you'll get a "No problems were detected" report, meaning you ran the check successfully.

To accomplish this task, you'll need to discover a command capable of getting a troubleshooting pack, and another capable of executing a troubleshooting pack. You'll also need to discover where the packs are located and how they're named. Everything you need to know is in PowerShell, and the help system will find it for you.

That's all the help you get!

Objects: data by another name

We're going to do something a little different in this chapter. We find that Power-Shell's use of objects can be one of its most confusing elements, but at the same time it's also one of the shell's most critical concepts, affecting everything you do in the shell. We've tried different explanations over the years, and we've settled on a couple that each work well for distinctly different audiences. If you have some programming experience and you're comfortable with the concept of objects, we want you to skip to section 8.2. If you don't have a programming background, and haven't programmed or scripted with objects before, start with section 8.1 and read straight through the chapter.

8.1 What are objects?

Take a second to run Get-Process in PowerShell. You should see a table with several columns, but those columns barely scratch the surface of the wealth of information available about processes. Each process object also has a machine name, a main window handle, a maximum working set size, an exit code and time, processor affinity information, and a great deal more. In fact, you'll find more than 60 pieces of information associated with a process. Why does PowerShell show so few of them?

The simple fact is that *most* of the things PowerShell can access offer more information than will comfortably fit on the screen. When you run any command, such as `Get-Process`, `Get-Service`, `Get-EventLog`, or anything, PowerShell constructs—entirely in memory—a table that contains all of the information about those items. In the case of `Get-Process`, that table consists of something like 67 columns, with one row for each process that's running on your computer. Each column contains a bit of information, such as virtual memory, CPU utilization, process name, process ID, and so on. Then, PowerShell looks to see if you've specified which of those columns you want to view. If you haven't (and we haven't shown you how, yet), then the shell looks up a configuration file provided by Microsoft and displays only those table columns that Microsoft thought you'd want to see.

One way to see all of the columns is to use `ConvertTo-HTML`:

```
Get-Process | ConvertTo-HTML | Out-File processes.html
```

That cmdlet doesn't bother filtering down the columns. Instead, it produces an HTML file that contains all of them. That's one way to see the entire table.

In addition to all of those columns of information, each table row also has some actions associated with it. Those actions include what the operating system can do to, or with, the process listed in that table row. For example, the operating system can close a process, kill it, refresh its information, or wait for the process to exit, among other things.

Any time you run a command that produces output, that output takes the form of a table in memory. When you pipe output from one command to another, like this,

```
Get-Process | ConvertTo-HTML
```

the entire table is passed through the pipeline. The table isn't filtered down to a smaller number of columns until every command has run.

Now for some terminology changes. PowerShell doesn't refer to this in-memory table as a "table." Instead, it uses these terms:

- *Object*—This is what we've been calling a "table row." It represents a single thing, like a single process or a single service.
- *Property*—This is what we called a "table column." It represents one piece of information about an object, like a process name, process ID, or service status.
- *Method*—This is what we called an "action." A method is related to a single object and makes that object do something, like killing a process or starting a service.
- *Collection*—This is the entire set of objects, or what we've been calling a "table."

If you ever find the following discussion on objects to be confusing, refer back to this four-point list. Always imagine a *collection* of objects as being a big in-memory table of information, with *properties* as the columns and individual *objects* as the rows.

8.2   *Why PowerShell uses objects*

One of the reasons why PowerShell uses objects to represent data is that, well, you have to represent data *somehow*, right? PowerShell could have stored that data in a format like XML, or perhaps its creators could have decided to use plain-text tables. But they had some specific reasons why they didn't take that route.

The first reason is that Windows itself is an object-oriented operating system—or at least, most of the software that runs on Windows is object oriented. Choosing to structure data as a set of objects is easy, because most of the operating system lends itself to those structures.

Another reason to use objects is because they ultimately make things easier on you and give you more power and flexibility. For the moment, let's pretend that PowerShell doesn't produce objects as the output of its commands. Instead, it produces simple text tables, which is what you probably thought it was doing in the first place. When you run a command like Get-Process, you're getting formatted text as the output:

```
PS C:\> get process

Handles  NPM(K)    PM(K)      WS(K) VM(M)   CPU(s)     Id ProcessName
-------  ------    -----      ----- -----   ------     -- -----------
     39       5     1876       4340    52    11.33   1920 conhost
     31       4      792       2260    22     0.00   2460 conhost
     29       4      828       2284    41     0.25   3192 conhost
    574      12     1864       3896    43     1.30    316 csrss
    181      13     5892       6348    59     9.14    356 csrss
    306      29    13936      18312   139     4.36   1300 dfsrs
    125      15     2528       6048    37     0.17   1756 dfssvc
   5159    7329    85052      86436   118     1.80   1356 dns
```

What if you wanted to do something else with this information? Perhaps you want to make a change to all of the processes running Conhost. To do this, you'd have to filter the list down a bit. In a Unix or Linux shell, you'd use a command like Grep, telling it, "Look at this text list for me. Keep only those rows where columns 58–64 contain the characters 'conhost.' Delete all of the other rows." The resulting list would contain only those processes you specified:

```
Handles  NPM(K)    PM(K)      WS(K) VM(M)   CPU(s)     Id ProcessName
-------  ------    -----      ----- -----   ------     -- -----------
     39       5     1876       4340    52    11.33   1920 conhost
     31       4      792       2260    22     0.00   2460 conhost
     29       4      828       2284    41     0.25   3192 conhost
```

You'd then pipe that text to another command, perhaps telling it to extract the process ID from the list. "Go through this and get the characters from columns 52–56, but drop the first two (header) rows." The result might be this:

```
1920
2460
3192
```

Finally, you'd pipe *that* text to yet *another* command, asking it to kill the processes (or whatever else you were trying to do) represented by those ID numbers.

This is, in fact, exactly how Unix and Linux administrators work. They spend a lot of time learning how to get better at parsing text, using tools like Grep, Awk, and Sed, and becoming proficient in the use of regular expressions. Going through this learning process makes it easier for them to define the text patterns they want their computer to look for. Unix and Linux folks like programming languages like Perl because those languages contain rich text-parsing and text-manipulation functions.

But this text-based approach does present some problems:

- You can spend more time messing around with text than doing your real job.
- If the output of a command changes—say, moving the ProcessName column to the start of the table—then you have to rewrite all of your commands, because they're all dependent on things like column positions.
- You have to become proficient in languages and tools that parse text. Not because your job involves parsing text, but because parsing text is a means to an end.

PowerShell's use of objects helps to remove all of that text-manipulation overhead. Because objects work like tables in memory, you don't have to tell PowerShell which text column a piece of information is located at. Instead, you tell it the column name, and PowerShell knows exactly where to go to get that data. Regardless of how you arrange the final output on the screen or in a file, the in-memory table is always the same, so you never have to rewrite your commands because a column moved. You spend a lot less time on overhead tasks, and more time focusing on what you want to accomplish.

True, you do have to learn a few syntax elements that let you instruct PowerShell properly, but you'll have to learn a *lot* less than if you were working in a purely text-based shell.

8.3   *Discovering objects: Get-Member*

If objects are like a giant table in memory, and PowerShell only shows you a portion of that table on the screen, how can you see what else you have to work with? If you're thinking that you should use the `Help` command, we're glad, because we've certainly been pushing that down your throat in the previous few chapters. Unfortunately, you'd be wrong.

The help system only documents background concepts (in the form of the "about" help topics) and command syntax. To learn more about an object, you use a different command: `Get-Member`. You should become comfortable using this command—so much so, in fact, that you start looking for a shorter way to type it. We'll give you that right now: the alias `Gm`.

You can use `Gm` after any cmdlet that normally produces some output. For example, you already know that running `Get-Process` produces some output on the screen. You can pipe it to `Gm`:

```
Get-Process | Gm
```

Whenever a cmdlet produces a collection of objects, as `Get-Process` does, the entire collection remains accessible until the end of the pipeline. It's not until every command has run that PowerShell filters down the columns of information to be displayed and creates the final text output you see. Therefore, in the preceding example, Gm has complete access to all of the process objects' properties and methods, because they haven't been filtered down for display yet. Gm looks at each object and constructs a list of the objects' properties and methods. It looks a bit like this:

```
PS C:\> get-process | gm

    TypeName: System.Diagnostics.Process

Name                    MemberType      Definition
----                    ----------      ----------
Handles                 AliasProperty   Handles = Handlecount
Name                    AliasProperty   Name = ProcessName
NPM                     AliasProperty   NPM = NonpagedSystemMemo...
PM                      AliasProperty   PM = PagedMemorySize
VM                      AliasProperty   VM = VirtualMemorySize
WS                      AliasProperty   WS = WorkingSet
Disposed                Event           System.EventHandler Disp...
ErrorDataReceived       Event           System.Diagnostics.DataR...
Exited                  Event           System.EventHandler Exit...
OutputDataReceived      Event           System.Diagnostics.DataR...
BeginErrorReadLine      Method          System.Void BeginErrorRe...
BeginOutputReadLine     Method          System.Void BeginOutputR...
CancelErrorRead         Method          System.Void CancelErrorR...
CancelOutputRead        Method          System.Void CancelOutput...
```

We've trimmed the preceding list a bit because it's long, but hopefully you get the idea.

> **TRY IT NOW** Don't take our word for it. This is the perfect time to follow along and run the same commands we do, in order to see their complete output.

By the way, it may interest you to know that all of the properties, methods, and other things attached to an object are collectively called its *members,* as if the object itself were a country club and all of these properties and methods belonged to the club. That's where Get-Member takes its name from: it's getting a list of the objects' members. But remember, because the PowerShell convention is to use singular nouns, the cmdlet name is Get-Member, not "Get-Members."

> **IMPORTANT** It's easy to overlook, but pay attention to the first line of output from Get-Member. It's the TypeName, which is the unique name assigned to that particular type of object. It may seem unimportant now—after all, who cares what it's named? But it's going to become crucial in the next chapter.

8.4   Object attributes, or "properties"

When you examine the output of Gm, you'll notice several different kinds of properties:

- ScriptProperty
- Property
- NoteProperty
- AliasProperty

> **Above and beyond**
>
> Normally, objects in the .NET Framework—which is where all of PowerShell's objects come from—have only "properties." PowerShell dynamically adds the other stuff: `ScriptProperty`, `NoteProperty`, `AliasProperty`, and so on. If you happen to look up an object type in Microsoft's MSDN documentation (you can plug the object's `TypeName` into your favorite search engine to find the MSDN page), you won't see these extra properties.
>
> PowerShell has an Extensible Type System (ETS) that's responsible for adding these last-minute properties. Why does it do this? In some cases, it's to make objects more consistent, such as adding a `Name` property to objects that natively only have something like `ProcessName` (that's what an `AliasProperty` is for). Sometimes it's to expose information that's deeply buried in the object (process objects have a few `ScriptProperties` that do this).
>
> Once you're in PowerShell, these properties all behave the same way. But don't be surprised when they don't show up on the official documentation page: the shell adds these extras, often to make your life easier.

For your purposes, these properties are all the same. The only difference is in how the properties were originally created, but that's not something you need to worry about. To you, they're all "properties," and you'll use them the same way.

A property always contains a value. For example, the value of a process object's ID property might be 1234, and the Name property of that object might have a value of Notepad. Properties describe something about the object: its status, its ID, its name, and so on. In PowerShell, properties are often read-only, meaning you can't change the name of a service by assigning a new value to its Name property. But you can retrieve the name of a service by reading its Name property. We'd estimate that 90 percent of what you'll do in PowerShell will involve properties.

8.5   Object actions, or "methods"

Many objects support one or more methods, which, as we mentioned earlier, are actions that you can direct the object to take. A process object has a Kill method, which terminates the process. Some methods require one or more input arguments that provide additional details for that particular action, but this early in your PowerShell education you won't be running into any of those. In fact, you may spend months or even years working with PowerShell and never need to execute a single object method. That's because many of those actions are also provided by cmdlets.

For example, if you need to terminate a process, you have three ways to do so. One way would be to retrieve the object and then somehow execute its Kill method. Another way would be to use a couple of cmdlets:

```
Get-Process -Name Notepad | Stop-Process
```

You could also accomplish that by using a single cmdlet:

```
Stop-Process -name Notepad
```

Our focus with this book is entirely on using PowerShell cmdlets to accomplish tasks. They provide the easiest, most administrator-centric, most task-focused way of accomplishing things. Using methods starts to edge into .NET Framework programming, which can be more complicated and can require a lot more background information. For that reason, you'll rarely—if ever—see us execute an object method in this book. In fact, our general philosophy at this point is, "if you can't do it with a cmdlet, go back and use the GUI." You won't feel that way for your entire career, we promise, but for now it's a good way to stay focused on the "PowerShell way" of doing things.

> **Above and beyond**
>
> You don't need to know about them at this stage in your PowerShell education, but in addition to properties and methods, objects can also have *events*. An event is an object's way of notifying you that something happened to it. A process object, for example, can trigger its Exited event when the process ends. You can attach your own commands to those events, so that, for example, an email gets sent when a process exits. Working with events in this fashion is an advanced topic, and beyond the scope of this book.

8.6 Sorting objects

Most PowerShell cmdlets produce objects in a deterministic fashion, which means that they tend to produce objects in the same order every time you run the command. Both services and processes, for example, are listed in alphabetical order by name. Event log entries tend to come out in chronological order. What if we want to change that?

For example, suppose we want to display a list of processes, with the biggest consumers of virtual memory (VM) at the top of the list, and the smallest consumers at the bottom. We would need to somehow reorder that list of objects based on the VM property. PowerShell provides a simple cmdlet, Sort-Object, which does exactly that:

```
Get-Process | Sort-Object -property VM
```

> **TRY IT NOW** We're hoping that you'll follow along and run these same commands. We won't be pasting the output into the book because these tables are somewhat long, but you'll get substantially the same thing on your screen if you're following along.

That command isn't exactly what we wanted. It did sort on VM, but it did so in ascending order, with the largest values at the bottom of the list. Reading the help for Sort-Object, we see that it has a -descending parameter that should reverse the sort order. We also notice that the -property parameter is positional, so we don't need to type the parameter name. We'll also tell you that Sort-Object has an alias, Sort, so you can save yourself a bit of typing for the next try:

```
Get-Process | Sort VM -desc
```

We also abbreviated -descending to -desc, and we have the result we wanted. The -property parameter accepts multiple values (which we're sure you saw in the help file, if you looked).

In the event that two processes are using the same amount of virtual memory, we'd like them sorted by process ID, and the following command will accomplish that:

```
Get-Process | Sort VM,ID -desc
```

As always, a comma-separated list is the way to pass multiple values to any parameter that supports them.

8.7 *Selecting the properties you want*

Another useful cmdlet is Select-Object. It accepts objects from the pipeline, and you can specify the properties that you'd like displayed. This enables you to access properties that are normally filtered out by PowerShell's configuration rules, or to trim down the list to a few properties that interest you. This can be useful when piping objects to ConvertTo-HTML, because that cmdlet usually builds a table containing every property.

Compare the results of these two commands:

```
Get-Process | ConvertTo-HTML | Out-File test1.html
```

```
Get-Process | Select-Object -property Name,ID,VM,PM |
➥Convert-ToHTML | Out-File test2.html
```

> **TRY IT NOW**   Go ahead and run each of these commands separately, and then examine the resulting HTML files in Internet Explorer to see the differences.

Take a look at the help for Select-Object (or you can use its alias, Select). The -property parameter appears to be positional, which means we could shorten that last command to:

```
Get-Process | Select Name,ID,VM,PM | ConvertTo-HTML | Out-File test3.html
```

Spend some time experimenting with Select-Object. In fact, try variations of the following command, which allows the output to appear on the screen:

```
Get-Process | Select Name,ID,VM,PM
```

Try adding and removing different process object properties from that list and reviewing the results. How many properties can you specify and still get a table as the output? How many properties force PowerShell to format the output as a list rather than as a table?

Above and beyond

Select-Object also has -First and -Last parameters, which let you keep a subset of the objects in the pipeline. For example, Get-Process | Select -First 10 would keep the first ten objects. There's no criteria involved, like keeping certain processes; it's merely grabbing the first (or last) ten.

CAUTION People often get mixed up about two PowerShell commands: `Select-Object` and `Where-Object`, which you haven't seen yet. `Select-Object` is used to choose the properties (or columns) you want to see, and it can also select an arbitrary subset of output rows (using `-First` and `-Last`). `Where-Object` removes, or filters, objects out of the pipeline based on some criteria you specify.

8.8 Objects until the end

The PowerShell pipeline always contains objects until the last command has been executed. At that time, PowerShell looks to see what objects are in the pipeline, and then looks at its various configuration files to see which properties to use to construct the onscreen display. It also decides whether that display will be a table or a list, based on some internal rules and on its configuration files. (We'll explain more about those rules and configurations, and how you can modify them, in an upcoming chapter.)

An important fact is that the pipeline can contain many different kinds of objects over the course of a single command line. For the next few examples, we're going to take a single command line and physically type it so that only one command appears on a single line of text. That'll make it a bit easier to explain what we're talking about.

Here's the first one:

```
Get-Process |
Sort-Object VM -descending |
Out-File c:\procs.txt
```

In this example, you start by running `Get-Process`, which puts process objects into the pipeline. The next command is `Sort-Object`. That doesn't change what's in the pipeline; it changes only the order of the objects, so at the end of `Sort-Object`, the pipeline still contains processes. The last command is `Out-File`. Here, PowerShell has to produce output, so it takes whatever's in the pipeline—processes—and formats them according to its internal rule set. The results go into the specified file.

Next up is a more complicated example:

```
Get-Process |
Sort-Object VM -descending |
Select-Object Name,ID,VM
```

This starts off in the same way. `Get-Process` puts process objects into the pipeline. Those go to `Sort-Object`, which sorts them and puts the same process objects into the pipeline. But `Select-Object` works a bit differently. A process object always has the exact same members. In order to trim down the list of properties, `Select-Object` can't remove the properties you don't want, because the result wouldn't be a process object anymore. Instead, `Select-Object` creates a new kind of custom object called a `PSObject`. It copies over the properties you do want from the process, resulting in a custom object being placed into the pipeline.

TRY IT NOW Try running this three-cmdlet command line, keeping in mind that you should type the whole thing on a single line. Notice how the output is different from the normal output of `Get-Process`?

When PowerShell sees that it's reached the end of the command line, it has to decide how to lay out the text output. Because there are no longer any process objects in the pipeline, PowerShell won't use the default rules and configurations that apply to process objects. Instead, it looks for rules and configurations for a PSObject, which is what the pipeline now contains. Microsoft didn't provide any rules or configurations for PSObjects, because they're meant to be used for custom output. Instead, PowerShell takes its best guess and produces a table, on the theory that those three pieces of information probably will still fit in a table. The table isn't as nicely laid out as the normal output of Get-Process, though, because the shell lacks the additional configuration information needed to make a nicer-looking table.

You can use Gm to see the different objects that wind up in the pipeline. Remember, you can add Gm after any cmdlet that produces output:

```
Get-Process | Sort VM -descending | gm
Get-Process | Sort VM -descending | Select Name,ID,VM | gm
```

> **TRY IT NOW**   Try running those two command lines separately, and notice the difference in the output.

Notice that, as part of the Gm output, PowerShell shows you the type name for the object it saw in the pipeline. In the first case, that was a System.Diagnostics.Process object, but in the second case the pipeline contains a different kind of object. Those new "selected" objects only contained the three properties specified—Name, ID, and VM—plus a couple of system-generated members.

Even Gm produces objects and places them into the pipeline. After running Gm, the pipeline no longer contains either process or the "selected" objects; it contains the type of object produced by Gm: a Microsoft.PowerShell.Commands.MemberDefinition. You can prove that by piping the output of Gm to Gm itself:

```
Get-Process | Gm | Gm
```

> **TRY IT NOW**   You'll definitely want to try this, and think hard about it to make sure it makes sense to you. You start with Get-Process, which puts process objects into the pipeline. Those go to Gm, which analyzes them and produces its own MemberDefinition objects. Those are then piped to Gm, which analyzes them and produces output that lists the members of a MemberDefinition object.

A key to mastering PowerShell is learning to keep track of what kind of object is in the pipeline at any given point. Gm can help you do that, but sitting back and verbally walking yourself through the command line is also a good exercise that can help clear up confusion.

8.9   *Common points of confusion*

Our classroom students tend to make a few common mistakes as they get started with PowerShell. Most of these go away with a little experience, but we'll direct your attention to them with the following list, to give you a chance to catch yourself if you start heading down the wrong path.

- Remember that the PowerShell help files don't contain information on objects' properties. You'll need to pipe the objects to Gm (Get-Member) to see a list of properties.
- Remember that you can add Gm to the end of any pipeline that normally produces results. A command line like Get-Process -name Notepad | Stop-Process doesn't normally produce results, so tacking | Gm onto the end won't produce anything either.
- Pay attention to neat typing. Put a space on either side of every pipeline character, because your command lines should read like Get-Process | Gm and not like Get-Process|Gm. That spacebar key is extra-large for a reason—use it.
- Remember that the pipeline can contain different types of objects at each step. Think about what type of object is in the pipeline, and focus on what the next command will do to that *type* of object.

8.10 *Lab*

NOTE For this lab, you'll need any computer running PowerShell v3.

This chapter has probably covered more, and more difficult, new concepts than any chapter to this point. We hope we were able to make sense of it all, but these exercises will help you cement what you've learned. See if you can complete all of the exercises, and remember to supplement your learning with the companion videos and sample solutions at MoreLunches.com. Some of these tasks will draw on skills you've learned in previous chapters, to refresh your memory and keep you sharp.

1 Identify a cmdlet that will produce a random number.
2 Identify a cmdlet that will display the current date and time.
3 What type of object does the cmdlet from task #2 produce? (What is the *type name* of the object produced by the cmdlet?)
4 Using the cmdlet from task #2 and Select-Object, display only the current day of the week in a table like the following (caution: the output will right-align, so make sure your PowerShell window doesn't have a horizontal scroll bar):

```
DayOfWeek
---------
   Monday
```

5 Identify a cmdlet that will display information about installed hotfixes.
6 Using the cmdlet from task #5, display a list of installed hotfixes. Sort the list by the installation date, and display only the installation date, the user who installed the hotfix, and the hotfix ID. Remember that the column headers shown in a command's default output aren't necessarily the real property names—you'll need to look up the real property names to be sure.

7 Repeat task #6, but this time sort the results by the hotfix description, and include the description, the hotfix ID, and the installation date. Put the results into an HTML file.

8 Display a list of the 50 newest entries from the Security event log (you can use a different log, such as System or Application, if your Security log is empty). Sort the list with the oldest entries appearing first, and with entries made at the same time sorted by their index. Display the index, time, and source for each entry. Put this information into a text file (not an HTML file, but a plain text file). You may be tempted to use `Select-Object` and its `-first` or `-last` parameters to achieve this; don't. There's a better way. Also, avoid using `Get-WinEvent` for now; a better cmdlet is available for this particular task.

The pipeline, deeper

9

At this point, you've learned to be pretty effective with PowerShell's pipeline. Running commands (like `Get-Process | Sort VM -desc | ConvertTo-HTML | Out-File procs.html`) is powerful, accomplishing in one line what used to take several lines of script. But you can do even better. In this chapter, we'll dig deeper into the pipeline and uncover some of its most powerful capabilities.

9.1 The pipeline: enabling power with less typing

One of the reasons we like PowerShell so much is that it enables us to be more effective administrators without having to write complex scripts, like we used to have to do in VBScript. But the key to powerful one-line commands lies in the way the PowerShell pipeline works.

Let us be clear: You could skip this chapter and still be effective with PowerShell, but you would in most cases have to resort to VBScript-style scripts and programs. Although PowerShell's pipeline capabilities can be complicated, they're probably easier to learn than more-complicated programming skills. By learning to manipulate the pipeline, you can be much more effective without needing to write scripts.

The whole idea here is to get the shell to do more of your work for you, with as little typing as possible. We think you'll be surprised at how well the shell can do that!

9.2 How PowerShell passes data down the pipeline

Whenever you string two commands together, PowerShell has to figure out how to get the output of the first command to the input of the second command. In the upcoming examples, we're going to refer to the first command as *Command A*.

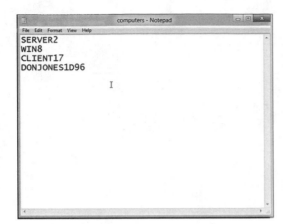

Figure 9.1   Creating a text file containing computer names, with one name per line

That's the command that produces something. The second command will be *Command B*, which needs to accept Command A's output and then do its own thing.

```
PS C:\> CommandA | CommandB
```

For example, suppose you have a text file that contains one computer name on each line, as shown in figure 9.1.

You might want to use those computer names as the input to some command, telling that command which computers you want it to run against. Consider this example:

```
PS C:\> Get-Content .\computers.txt | Get-Service
```

When Get-Content runs, it places the computer names into the pipeline. PowerShell then has to decide how to get those to the Get-Service command. The trick with PowerShell is that commands can only accept input on a parameter. That means PowerShell has to figure out which parameter of Get-Service will accept the output of Get-Content. This figuring-out process is called *pipeline parameter binding*, and it's what we'll be covering in this chapter. PowerShell has two methods it can use to get the output of Get-Content onto a parameter of Get-Service. The first method the shell will try is called ByValue; if that doesn't work, it'll try ByPropertyName.

9.3   *Plan A: pipeline input ByValue*

With this pipeline parameter binding method, PowerShell looks at the type of object produced by Command A and tries to see if any parameter of Command B can accept that type of object from the pipeline. You can determine this for yourself: first, pipe the output of Command A to Get-Member, to see what type of object Command A is producing. Then, examine the full help of Command B (for example, Help Get-Service -full) to see if any parameter accepts that type of data from the pipeline ByValue. Figure 9.2 shows what you might discover.

What you'll find is that Get-Content produces objects of the type System.String (or String for short). You'll also find that Get-Service does have a parameter that

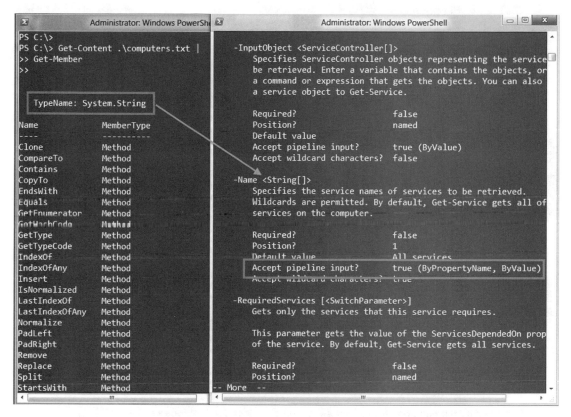

Figure 9.2   Comparing the output of `Get-Content` to the input parameters of `Get-Service`

accepts `String` from the pipeline `ByValue`. The problem is that it's the `-Name` parameter, which according to the help "specifies the service names of services to be retrieved." That isn't what we wanted—our text file, and therefore our `String` objects, are computer names, not service names. If we ran the following,

```
PS C:\> Get-Content .\computers.txt | Get-Service
```

we'd be attempting to retrieve services named SERVER2, WIN8, and so forth, which is probably not going to work.

PowerShell only permits one parameter to accept a given type of object from the pipeline `ByValue`. This means that because the `-Name` parameter accepts `String` from the pipeline `ByValue`, no other parameter can do so. That dashes our hopes for trying to pipe computer names from our text file to `Get-Service`.

In this case, pipeline input is working, but it isn't achieving the results we'd hoped for. Let's consider a different example, where we do get the results we want. Here's the command line:

```
PS C:\> get-process -name note* | Stop-Process
```

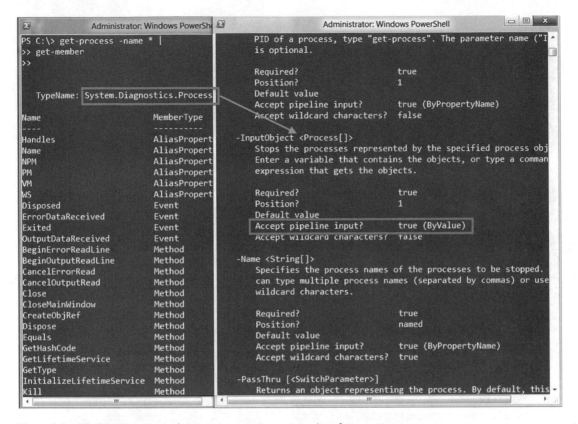

Figure 9.3   Binding the output of `Get-Process` to a parameter of `Stop-Process`

Let's pipe the output of Command A to `Get-Member` and examine the full help for Command B. Figure 9.3 shows what you'll find.

`Get-Process` produces objects of the type `System.Diagnostics.Process` (note that we limited the command to processes whose names start with note*; we made sure a copy of Notepad was running so that the command would produce some output). `Stop-Process` can accept those `Process` objects from the pipeline `ByValue`; it does so on its `-InputObject` parameter. According to the help, that parameter "stops the processes represented by the specified process objects." In other words, Command A will get one or more `Process` objects, and Command B will stop (or *kill*) them.

This is a good example of pipeline parameter binding in action, and it also illustrates an important point in PowerShell: For the most part, commands sharing the same noun (as `Get-Process` and `Stop-Process` do) can usually pipe to each other `ByValue`.

Let's cover one more example:

```
PS C:\> get-service -name s* | stop-process
```

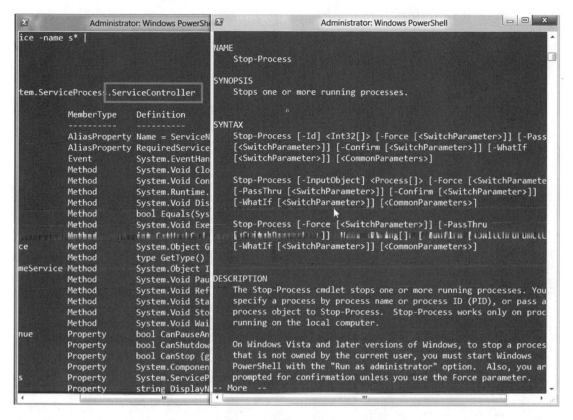

Figure 9.4 Examining the output of `Get-Service` and the input parameters of `Stop-Process`

On the face of it, this might not seem to make any sense. But let's see this through by piping Command A's output to `Get-Member`, and re-examining the help for Command B. Figure 9.4 shows what you should find.

`Get-Service` produces objects of the type `ServiceController` (technically, `System .ServiceProcess.ServiceController`, but you can usually take the last bit of the `TypeName` as a shortcut). Unfortunately, there isn't a single parameter of `Stop-Process` that can accept a `ServiceController` object. That means the `ByValue` approach has failed, and PowerShell will try its backup plan: `ByPropertyName`.

9.4   *Plan B: pipeline input ByPropertyName*

With this approach, you're still looking to attach the output of Command A to parameters of Command B. But ByPropertyName is slightly different than ByValue. With this backup method, it's possible for multiple parameters of Command B to become involved. Once again, pipe the output of Command A to Get-Member, and then look at the syntax for Command B. Figure 9.5 shows what you should find: The output of Command A has one property whose name corresponds to a parameter on Command B.

A lot of folks will overthink what's happening here, so let's be clear on how simple the shell is being: it's literally looking for property names that match parameter names. That's it. Because the property "Name" is spelled the same as the parameter "-Name," the shell will try to connect the two.

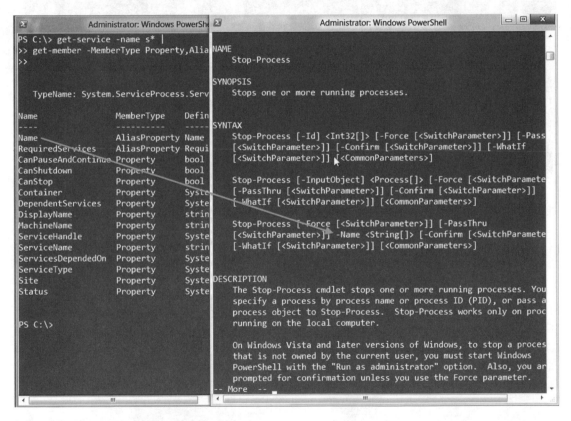

Figure 9.5   Mapping properties to parameters

But it can't do so right away: first it needs to see if the -Name parameter will accept input from the pipeline ByPropertyName. A glance at the full help, shown in figure 9.6, is required to make this determination.

In this case, -Name does accept pipeline input ByPropertyName, so this connection will work. Now, here's the trick: unlike ByValue, where only one parameter would be involved, ByPropertyName will connect every matching property and parameter (provided each parameter has been designed to accept pipeline input ByPropertyName).

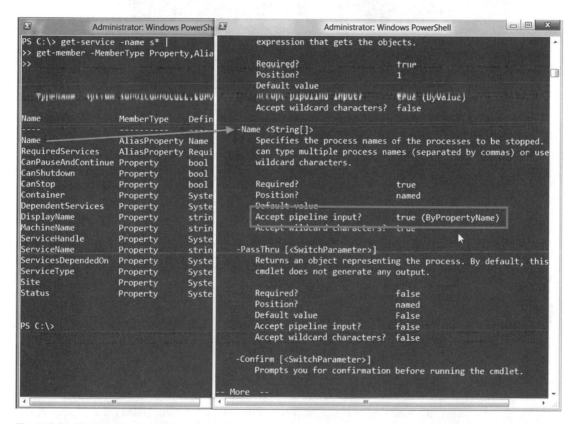

Figure 9.6   Checking to see if `Stop-Process`'s `-Name` parameter accepts pipeline input `ByPropertyName`

Figure 9.7   Attempting to pipe Get-Service to Stop-Process

In the case of our current example, only Name and -Name match. The results? Examine figure 9.7.

A bunch of error messages. The problem is that services' names are usually things like ShellHWDetection and SessionEnv, whereas the services' executables might be things like svchost.exe. Stop-Process only deals with those executable names. But even though the Name property connects to the -Name parameter via the pipeline, the values inside the Name property don't make sense to the -Name parameter, which leads to the errors.

Let's look at a more successful example. Create a simple comma-separated values (CSV) file in Notepad, using the example in figure 9.8.

Save the file as Aliases.csv. Now, back in the shell, try importing it, as shown in figure 9.9. You should also pipe the output of Import-CSV to Get-Member, so that you can examine the output's members.

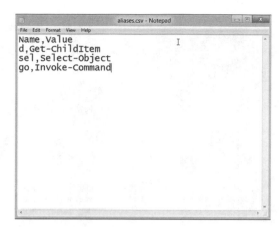

Figure 9.8 Create this CSV file in Windows Notepad.

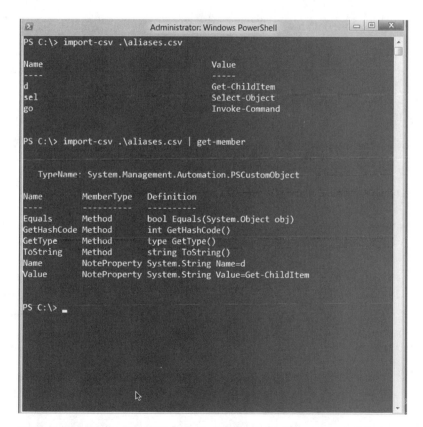

Figure 9.9 Importing the CSV file and checking its members

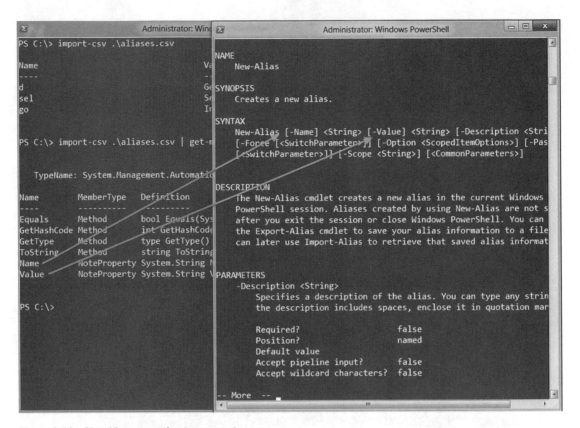

Figure 9.10 Matching properties to parameter names

You can clearly see that the columns from the CSV file become properties, and each data row in the CSV file becomes an object. Now, examine the help for New-Alias, as shown in figure 9.10.

Both of the properties—Name and Value—correspond to parameter names of New-Alias. Obviously, this was done on purpose—when you create the CSV file, you can name those columns anything you want. Now, check to see if -Name and -Value accept pipeline input ByPropertyName, as shown in figure 9.11.

Both parameters do, meaning this trick will work. Try running the command:

```
PS C:\> import-csv .\aliases.csv | new-alias
```

The result will be three new aliases, named d, sel, and go, which point to the commands Get-ChildItem, Select-Object, and Invoke-Command, respectively. This is a powerful technique for passing data from one command to another, and for accomplishing complex tasks in a minimum number of commands.

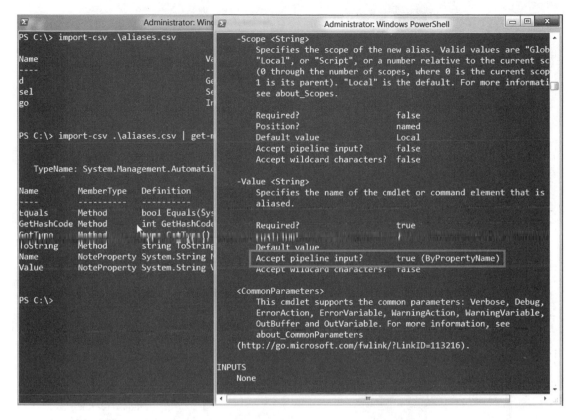

Figure 9.11 Looking for parameters that accept pipeline input `ByPropertyName`

9.5 *When things don't line up: custom properties*

The CSV example was cool, but it's pretty easy to make property and parameter names line up when you're creating the input from scratch. Things get tougher when you're forced to deal with objects that are created for you, or data that's being produced by someone else.

For this example, we're going to introduce a new command that you might not have access to: `New-ADUser`. It's part of the ActiveDirectory module, which you'll find on any Windows Server 2008 R2 (or later) domain controller. You can also get that module on a client computer by installing Microsoft's Remote Server Administration Tools (RSAT). But for now, don't worry about running the command; follow along with the example.

`New-ADUser` has a number of parameters, each designed to accept information about a new Active Directory user. Here are some examples:

- `-Name` (this is mandatory)
- `-samAccountName` (technically not mandatory, but you have to provide it to make the account usable)

- -Department
- -City
- -Title

We could cover the others, but let's work with these. All of them accept pipeline input ByPropertyName.

For this example, we'll again assume you're getting a CSV file, but it's coming from your company's Human Resources or Personnel department. You've given them your desired file format a dozen times, but they persist in giving you something that's close, but not quite right, as shown in figure 9.12.

Figure 9.12 Working with the CSV file provided by Human Resources

As you can see in figure 9.12, the shell can import the CSV file fine, resulting in three objects with four properties apiece. The problem is that the dept property won't line up with the -Department parameter of New-ADUser, the login property is meaningless, and you don't have samAccountName or Name properties—both of which are required if you want to be able to run this command to create new users:

```
PS C:\> import-csv .\newusers.csv | new-aduser
```

How can you fix this? Obviously, you could open the CSV file and fix it, but that's a lot of manual work over time, and the whole point of PowerShell is to reduce manual labor. Why not set up the shell to fix it instead? Look at the following example:

```
PS C:\> import-csv .\newusers.csv |
>> select-object -property *,
>>  @{name='samAccountName';expression={$_.login}},
>>  @{label='Name';expression={$_.login}},
>>  @{n='Department';e={$_.Dept}}
>>
```

```
login           : DonJ
dept            : IT
city            : Las Vegas
title           : CTO
samAccountName  : DonJ
Name            : DonJ
Department      : IT

login           : GregS
dept            : Custodial
city            : Denver
title           : Janitor
samAccountName  : GregS
Name            : GregS
Department      : Custodial

login           : JeffH
dept            : IT
city            : Syracuse
title           : Network Engineer
samAccountName  : JeffH
Name            : JeffH
Department      : IT
```

That's some pretty funky syntax, so let's break it down:

- We used `Select-Object` and its `-Property` parameter. We started by specifying the property `*`, which means "all of the existing properties." Notice that the `*` is followed by a comma, which means we're continuing the list of properties.

- We then created a hash table, which is the construct starting with `@{` and ending with `}`. Hash tables consist of one or more key=value pairs, and `Select-Object` has been programmed to look for some specific keys, which we'll provide to it.

- The first key `Select-Object` wants can be `Name`, `N`, `Label`, or `L`, and the value for that key is the name of the property we want to create. In the first hash table, we specified `samAccountName`, in the second, `Name`, and in the third, `Department`. These correspond to the parameter names of `New-ADUser`.

- The second key that `Select-Object` needs can be either `Expression` or `E`. The value for this key is a script block, contained within {curly brackets}. Within that script block, you use the special `$_` placeholder to refer to the existing piped-in object (the original row of data from the CSV file) followed by a period. `$_` lets you access one property of the piped-in object, or one column of the CSV file. This specifies the contents for the new properties.

TRY IT NOW Go ahead and create the CSV file that's shown in figure 9.12. Then try running the exact command we did above—you can type it exactly as shown.

What we've done is taken the contents of the CSV file—the output of `Import-CSV`—and modified it, dynamically, in the pipeline. Our new output matches what `New-ADUser` wants to see, so we can now create new users by running this command:

```
PS C:\> import-csv .\newusers.csv |
>> select-object -property *,
>>  @{name='samAccountName';expression={$_.login}},
>>  @{label='Name';expression={$_.login}},
>>  @{n='Department';e={$_.Dept}} |
>> new-aduser
>>
```

The syntax might be a bit ugly, but this is an incredibly powerful technique. It's also usable in many other places in PowerShell, and you'll see it again in upcoming chapters. You'll even see it in the examples contained in PowerShell's help files: Run `Help Select -Example` and look for yourself.

9.6   *Parenthetical commands*

Sometimes, no matter how hard you try, you can't make pipeline input work. For example, consider the `Get-WmiObject` command. You'll learn more about it in an upcoming chapter, but for right now, look at the help for its `-ComputerName` property, as shown in figure 9.13.

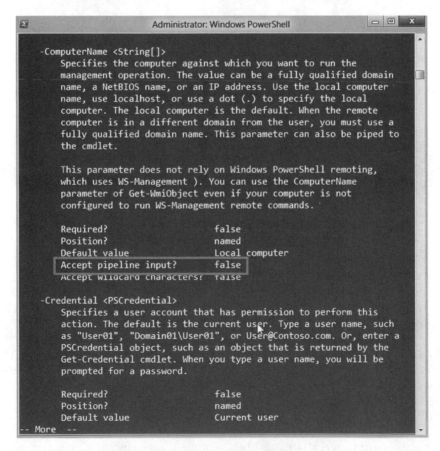

Figure 9.13   Reading the full help for `Get-WmiObject`

This parameter doesn't accept computer names from the pipeline. How can we retrieve names from someplace—like our text file, which contains one computer name per line—and feed them to the command? The following won't work:

```
PS C:\> get-content .\computers.txt | get-wmiobject -class win32_bios
```

The `String` objects produced by `Get-Content` won't match the `-computerName` parameter of `Get-WmiObject`. What can we do? Use parentheses:

```
PS C:\> Get-WmiObject -class Win32_BIOS -ComputerName (Get-Content .\comput
ers.txt)
```

Think back to high school algebra class, and you'll recall that parentheses mean "do this first." That's what PowerShell does: it runs the parenthetical command first. The results of that command—in this case, a bunch of `String` objects—are fed to the parameter. Because `-ComputerName` happens to want a bunch of `String` objects, the command works.

> **TRY IT NOW** If you have a couple of computers with which you can test this, go ahead and try that command. Put the correct computer names or IP addresses into your own Computers.txt file. This will work best for computers all in the same domain, because permissions will be taken care of more easily in that environment.

The parenthetical command trick is powerful because it doesn't rely on pipeline parameter binding at all—it takes objects and sticks them right into the parameter. But the technique doesn't work if your parenthetical command isn't generating the exact type of object that the parameter expects, which means sometimes you'll have to manipulate things a bit. Let's look at how.

9.7 *Extracting the value from a single property*

Earlier in this chapter, we showed you an example of using parentheses to execute `Get-Content`, feeding its output to the parameter of another cmdlet:

```
Get-Service -computerName (Get-Content names.txt)
```

Rather than getting your computer names from a static text file, you might want to query them from Active Directory. With the ActiveDirectory module (available on a Windows Server 2008 R2 or later domain controller, and installable with the Remote Server Administration Tools, or RSAT), you could query all of your domain controllers:

```
get-adcomputer -filter * -searchbase "ou=domain controllers,
➥dc=company,dc=pri"
```

Could you use the same parentheses trick to feed computer names to `Get-Service`? For example, would this work?

```
Get-Service -computerName (Get-ADComputer -filter *
➥-searchBase "ou=domain controllers,dc=company,dc=pri")
```

Above and beyond

If you don't have a domain controller handy, that's okay—we'll quickly tell you what you need to know about the `Get-ADComputer` command.

First, it's contained in a module named ActiveDirectory. As we already mentioned, that module installs on any Windows Server 2008 R2 or later domain controller, and it's available in the RSAT to install on a client computer that belongs to a domain.

Second, the command—as you might expect—retrieves computer objects from the domain.

Third, it has two useful parameters. `-Filter *` will retrieve all computers, and you could specify other filter criteria to limit the results, such as specifying a single computer name. The `-SearchBase` parameter tells the command where to start looking for computers; in this example, we're having it start in the Domain Controllers organizational unit (OU) of the Company.com domain:

```
get-adcomputer -filter * -searchbase "ou=domain controllers,
   dc=company,dc=pri"
```

Fourth, computer objects have a `Name` property, which contains the computers' host name.

We realize that throwing this kind of command at you—which, depending on your lab environment, you might not have access to—might be a bit unfair. But it's an incredibly useful command for the scenarios we're looking at, and it's one you'd definitely want to use in a production environment. Provided you can keep the preceding four facts in mind, you should be fine for this chapter.

Sadly, it won't. Look at the help for `Get-Service`, and you'll see that the `-computerName` parameter expects `String` values.

Run this instead:

```
get-adcomputer -filter * -searchbase "ou=domain controllers,
   dc=company,dc=pri" | gm
```

`Get-Member` reveals that `Get-ADComputer` is producing objects of the type `ADComputer`. Those aren't `String` objects, so `-computerName` won't know what to do with them. But the `ADComputer` objects do have a `Name` property. What you need to do is extract the values of the objects' `Name` properties, and feed those values, which are computer names, to the `-ComputerName` parameter.

> **TIP** This is an important fact about PowerShell, and if you're a bit lost right now, STOP and reread the preceding paragraphs. `Get-ADComputer` produces objects of the type `ADComputer`; `Get-Member` proves it. The `-ComputerName` parameter of `Get-Service` can't accept an `ADComputer` object; it accepts only `String` objects, as shown in its help file. Therefore, that parenthetical command won't work as written.

Once again, the `Select-Object` cmdlet can rescue you, because it includes an `-expandProperty` parameter, which accepts a property name. It will take that property, extract its values, and return those values as the output of `Select-Object`. Consider this example:

```
get-adcomputer -filter * -searchbase "ou=domain controllers,
➥dc=company,dc=pri" | Select-Object -expand name
```

You should get a simple list of computer names. Those can be fed to the `-computerName` parameter of `Get-Service` (or any other cmdlet that has a `-computerName` parameter):

```
Get-Service -computerName (get-adcomputer -filter *
➥-searchbase "ou=domain controllers,dc=company,dc=pri" |
➥Select-Object -expand name)
```

> **TIP** Once again, this is an important concept. Normally, a command like `Select-Object -Property Name` produces objects that happen to only have a `Name` property, because that's all we specified. The `-computerName` parameter doesn't want some random object that has a `Name` property; it wants a `String`, which is a much simpler value. `-Expand Name` goes into the `Name` property and extracts its values, resulting in simple strings being returned from the command.

Again, this is a cool trick that makes it possible to combine an even wider variety of commands with each other, saving you typing and making PowerShell do more of the work.

Now that you've seen all that coolness with `Get-ADComputer`, let's look at a similar example using commands you should have access to. We're assuming you're running the latest version of Windows, but for this example you don't need to be in a domain, or have access to a domain controller or even to a server OS. We're going to stick with the general theme of "getting computer names" because that's such a common production need.

Start by creating a CSV file in Notepad that looks like the one in figure 9.14. If you provide computer names that are valid on your network, you'll be able to run the example commands. If you only have one computer, use "localhost" as the host name, and enter it three or four times. It'll still work.

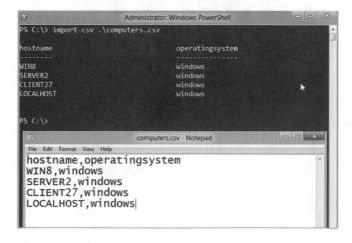

Figure 9.14 Make sure you can import your CSV file using `Import-CSV` and get results similar to those shown here.

Now let's say that you want to get a list of running processes from each of these computers. If you examine the help for Get-Process, as shown in figure 9.15, you'll see that its -computerName parameter does accept pipeline input ByPropertyName. It expects its input to be objects of the type String. We're not going to fuss around with pipeline input, though; we're going to focus on property extraction. The relevant information in the help file is the fact that -ComputerName needs one or more String objects.

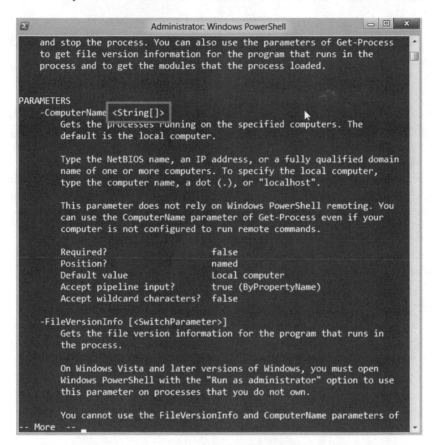

Figure 9.15   Verifying the data type needed by the -ComputerName parameter

Back to basics: start by seeing what Command A produces by piping it to Get-Member. Figure 9.16 shows the results.

Import-CSV's PSCustomObject output isn't a String, so the following won't work:

```
PS C:\> Get-Process -computerName (import-csv .\computers.csv)
```

Let's try selecting the HostName field from the CSV, and see what that produces. You should see what's shown in figure 9.17.

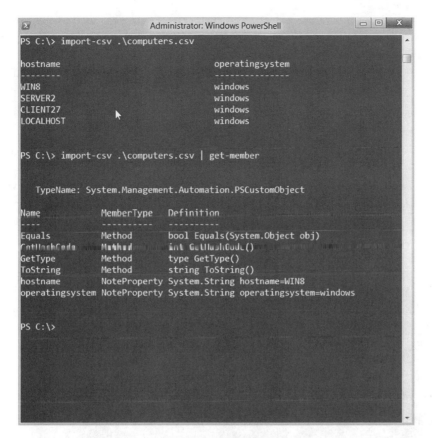

Figure 9.16 `Import-CSV` produces objects of the type `PSCustomObject`.

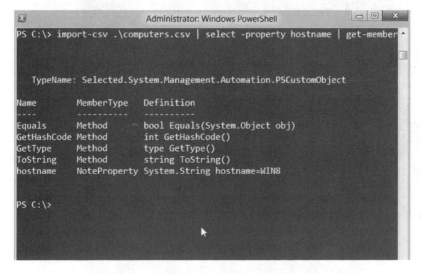

Figure 9.17 Selecting a single property still gives you a `PSCustomObject`.

You've still got a PSCustomObject, but it has fewer properties than before. That's the point about Select-Object and its -Property parameter: it doesn't change the fact that you're outputting an entire object.

The -ComputerName parameter can't accept a PSCustomObject, so this still won't work:

```
PS C:\> Get-Process -computerName (import-csv .\computers.csv |
select -property hostname)
```

This is where the -ExpandProperty parameter works. Again, let's try it on its own and see what it produces, as shown in figure 9.18.

Because the Hostname property contained text strings, -ExpandProperty was able to expand those values into plain String objects, which is what -ComputerName wants. This means the following will work:

```
PS C:\> Get-Process -computerName (import-csv .\computers.csv |
select -expand hostname)
```

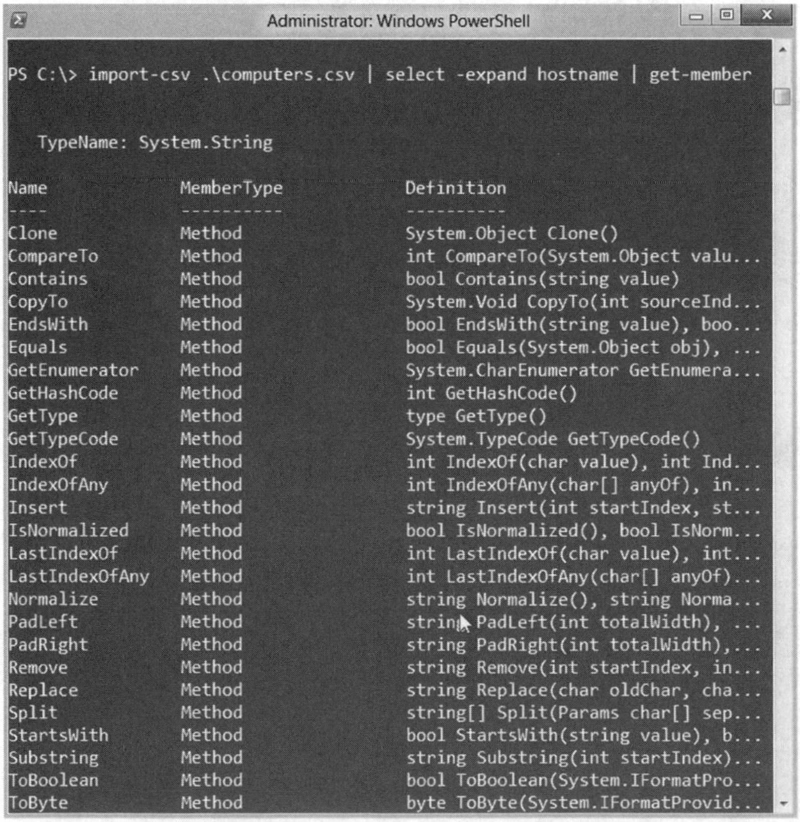

Figure 9.18   You finally have a String object as output!

This is a powerful technique. It can be a little hard to grasp at first, but understanding that a property is kind of like a box can help. With `Select -Property`, you're deciding what boxes you want, but you've still got boxes. With `Select -ExpandProperty`, you're extracting the contents of the box, and getting rid of the box entirely. You're left with the contents.

9.8 Lab

NOTE For this lab, you'll need any computer running PowerShell v3.

Once again, we've covered a lot of important concepts in a short amount of time. The best way to cement your new knowledge is to put it to immediate use. We recommend doing the following tasks in order, because they build on each other to help remind you what you've learned and to help you find practical ways to use that knowledge.

To make this a bit trickier, we're going to force you to consider the `Get-ADComputer` command. Any Windows Server 2008 R2 or later domain controller has this command installed, but you don't need one. You only need to know three things:

- The `Get-ADComputer` command has a `-filter` parameter; running `Get-ADComputer -filter *` will retrieve all computer objects in the domain.
- Domain computer objects have a `Name` property that contains the computer's host name.
- Domain computer objects have the `TypeName` `ADComputer`, which means `Get-ADComputer` produces objects of the type `ADComputer`.

That's all you should need to know. With that in mind, complete these tasks:

NOTE You're not being asked to run these commands. Instead, you're being asked if these commands will function or not, and why. You've been told how `Get-ADComputer` works, and what it produces; you can read the help to discover what other commands expect and accept.

1 Would the following command work to retrieve a list of installed hotfixes from all computers in the specified domain? Why or why not? Write out an explanation, similar to the ones we provided earlier in this chapter.
```
Get-Hotfix -computerName (get-adcomputer -filter * |
Select-Object -expand name)
```

2 Would this alternative command work to retrieve the list of hotfixes from the same computers? Why or why not? Write out an explanation, similar to the ones we provided earlier in this chapter.
```
get-adcomputer -filter * |
Get-HotFix
```

3 Would this third version of the command work to retrieve the list of hotfixes from the domain computers? Why or why not? Write out an explanation, similar to the ones we provided earlier in this chapter.

```
get-adcomputer -filter * |
Select-Object @{l='computername';e={$_.name}} |
Get-Hotfix
```

4 Write a command that uses pipeline parameter binding to retrieve a list of running processes from every computer in an Active Directory (AD) domain. Don't use parentheses.

5 Write a command that retrieves a list of installed services from every computer in an AD domain. Don't use pipeline input; instead use a parenthetical command (a command in parentheses).

6 Sometimes Microsoft forgets to add a pipeline parameter binding to a cmdlet. For example, would the following command work to retrieve information from every computer in the domain? Write out an explanation, similar to the ones we provided earlier in this chapter.

```
get-adcomputer -filter * |
    Select-Object @{l='computername';e={$_.name}} |
Get-WmiObject -class Win32_BIOS
```

9.9 *Further exploration*

We find that many students have difficulty embracing this pipeline input concept, mainly because it's so abstract. If you find yourself in that situation, head to More-Lunches.com. Find this book's cover image or name, and click on it. Scroll to the Downloads section, and download the Pipeline Input Workbook. Print as many copies as you like, grab a pencil, and start using it to walk through examples like `Get-Service | Stop-Service`. The workbook provides step-by-step instructions for working through the entire pipeline input process.

Formatting—and why it's done on the right

Let's quickly review: you know that PowerShell cmdlets produce objects, and that those objects often contain more properties than PowerShell shows by default. You know how to use Gm to get a list of all of an object's properties, and you know how to use Select-Object to specify the properties you want to see. Up to this point in the book, you've relied on PowerShell's default configuration and rules to determine how the final output will appear on the screen (or in a file, or in hardcopy form). In this chapter, you'll learn to override those defaults and create your own formatting for your commands' output.

10.1 Formatting: making what you see prettier

We don't want to give you the impression that PowerShell is a full-fledged management-reporting tool, because it isn't. But PowerShell has good capabilities for collecting information about computers, and, with the right output, you can certainly produce reports using that information. The trick is getting the right output, and that's what formatting is all about.

On the surface, PowerShell's formatting system can seem easy to use—and for the most part that's true. But the formatting system also contains some of the trickiest "gotchas" in the entire shell, so we want to make sure you understand how it works and why it does what it does. We're not just going to show you a few new commands here; rather, we'll explain how the entire system works, how you can interact with it, and what limitations you might run into.

10.2   *About the default formatting*

Run our old friend Get-Process again, and pay special attention to the column headers. Notice that they don't exactly match the property names. Instead, they each have a specific width, alignment, and so forth. All that configuration stuff has to come from someplace, right? You'll find it in one of the .format.ps1xml files that install with PowerShell. Specifically, formatting directions for process objects are in DotNetTypes.format.ps1xml.

> **TRY IT NOW**   You'll definitely want to have PowerShell open so that you can follow along with what we're about to show you. This will help you understand what the formatting system is up to under the hood.

We'll begin by changing to the PowerShell installation folder and opening DotNetTypes.format.ps1xml. Be careful not to save any changes to this file. It's digitally signed, and any changes that you save—even a single carriage return or space added to the file—will break the signature and prevent PowerShell from using the file.

```
PS C:\>cd $pshome
PS C:\>notepad dotnettypes.format.ps1xml
```

Next, find out the exact type of object returned by Get-Process:

```
PS C:\>get-process | gm
```

Now follow these steps:

1   Copy and paste the complete type name, System.Diagnostics.Process, to the clipboard. To do so, use your cursor to highlight the type name, and press Return to copy it to the clipboard.
2   Switch over to Notepad and press Ctrl-F to open the Find window.
3   In the Find window, paste in the type name you copied to the clipboard. Click Find Next.
4   The first thing you find will probably be a ProcessModule object, not a Process object, so click Find Next again and again until you locate System.Diagnostics.Process in the file. Figure 10.1 shows what you should have found.

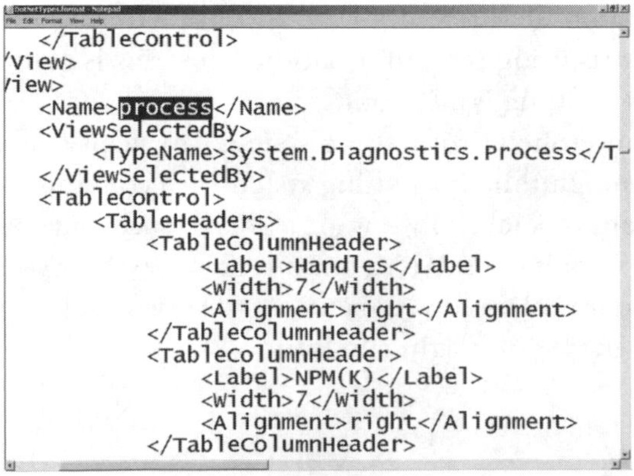

Figure 10.1   Locating the process view in Windows Notepad

What you're now looking at in Notepad is the set of directions that govern how a process is displayed by default. Scroll down a bit, and you'll see the definition for a *table view*, which you should expect because you already know that processes display in a multicolumn table. You'll see the familiar column names, and if you scroll down a bit more you'll see where the file specifies which property will display in each column. You'll see definitions for column widths and alignments too. When you're done browsing, close Notepad, being careful not to save any changes that you may have accidentally made to the file, and go back to PowerShell.

When you run `Get-Process`, here's what happens in the shell:

1. The cmdlet places objects of the type `System.Diagnostics.Process` into the pipeline.
2. At the end of the pipeline is an invisible cmdlet called `Out-Default`. It's always there, and its job is to pick up whatever objects are in the pipeline after all of your commands have run.
3. `Out-Default` passes the objects to `Out-Host`, because the PowerShell console is designed to use the screen (called the *host*) as its default form of output. In theory, someone could write a shell that uses files or printers as the default output instead, but nobody has that we know of.
4. Most of the `Out-` cmdlets are incapable of working with normal objects. Instead, they're designed to work with special formatting instructions. So when `Out-Host` sees that it has been handed normal objects, it passes them to the formatting system.
5. The formatting system looks at the type of the object and follows an internal set of formatting rules (we'll cover those in a moment). It uses those rules to produce formatting instructions, which are passed back to `Out-Host`.
6. Once `Out-Host` sees that it has formatting instructions, it follows those instructions to construct the onscreen display.

All of this happens whenever you manually specify an `Out-` cmdlet, too. For example, run `Get-Process | Out-File procs.txt`, and `Out-File` will see that you've sent it some normal objects. It will pass those to the formatting system, which creates formatting instructions and passes them back to `Out-File`. `Out-File` then constructs the text file based on those instructions. So the formatting system becomes involved any time objects need to be converted into human-readable textual output.

What rules does the formatting system follow in step 5, above? For the first formatting rule, the system looks to see if the type of object it's dealing with has a predefined view. That's what you saw in DotNetTypes.format.ps1xml: a predefined view for a `Process` object. There are a few other .format.ps1xml files installed with PowerShell, and they're all loaded by default when the shell starts. You can create your own predefined views as well, although doing so is beyond the scope of this book.

The formatting system looks for predefined views that specifically target the object type it's dealing with—meaning that in this case it's looking for the view that handles `System.Diagnostics.Process` objects.

What if there is no predefined view? For example, try running this:

```
Get-WmiObject Win32_OperatingSystem | Gm
```

Grab that object's type name (or at least the "Win32_OperatingSystem" part), and try to find it in one of the .format.ps1xml files. We'll save you some time by telling you that you won't find it.

This is where the formatting system takes its next step, or what we call the second formatting rule: it looks to see if anyone has declared a `default display property set` for that type of object. You'll find those in a different configuration file, Types.ps1xml. Go ahead and open it in Notepad now (again, be careful not to save any changes to this file) and use the Find function to locate Win32_OperatingSystem. Once you do, scroll down a bit and you'll see `DefaultDisplayPropertySet`. It's shown in figure 10.2. Make a note of the six properties listed there.

Now, go back to PowerShell and run this:

```
Get-WmiObject Win32_OperatingSystem
```

Do the results look familiar? They should: the properties you see are there solely because they're listed as defaults in Types.ps1xml. If the formatting system finds a `default display property set`, it will use that set of properties for its next decision. If it doesn't find one, the next decision will consider all of the object's properties.

That next decision—the third formatting rule—is about what kind of output to create. If the formatting system will display four or fewer properties, it will use a table. If there are five or more properties, it will use a list. That's why the `Win32 _OperatingSystem` object wasn't displayed as a table: there were six properties, triggering a list. The theory is that more than four properties might not fit well into an ad hoc table without truncating information.

Now you know how the default formatting works. You also know that most `Out-` cmdlets will automatically trigger the formatting system, so that they can get the formatting instructions they need. Next let's look at how we can control that formatting system ourselves, and override the defaults.

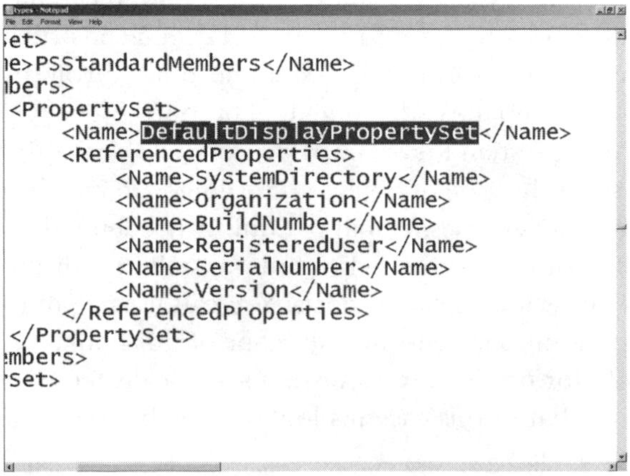

Figure 10.2   Locating a `DefaultDisplayPropertySet` in Notepad

10.3 Formatting tables

There are four formatting cmdlets in PowerShell, and we'll work with the three that provide the most day-to-day formatting capability (the fourth is briefly discussed in an "Above and beyond" section near the end of this chapter). First up is Format-Table, which has an alias, Ft.

If you read the help file for Format-Table, you'll notice that it has a number of parameters. These are some of the most useful ones, along with examples of how to use them:

- -autoSize—Normally PowerShell tries to make a table fill the width of your window (the exception is when a predefined view, like the one for processes, defines column widths). That means a table with relatively few columns will have a lot of space in between those columns, which isn't always attractive. By adding the -autosize parameter, you force the shell to try to size each column to hold its contents, and no more. This makes the table a bit "tighter" in appearance, and it will take a bit of extra time for the shell to start producing output. That's because it has to examine every object that will be formatted to find the longest values for each column. Try the following example both with and without the -autosize parameter.

  ```
  Get-WmiObject Win32_BIOS | Format-Table -autoSize
  ```

- -property—This parameter accepts a comma-separated list of properties that should be included in the table. These properties aren't case-sensitive, but the shell will use whatever you type as the column headers, so you can get nicer-looking output by properly casing the property names ("CPU" instead of "cpu," for example). This parameter accepts wildcards, meaning you can specify * to include all properties in the table, or something like c* to include all properties starting with *c*. Notice that the shell will still only display the properties it can fit in the table, so not every property you specify may display. This parameter is positional, so you don't have to type the parameter name, provided the property list is in the first position. Try these examples (the last one is shown in figure 10.3):

  ```
  Get-Process | Format-Table -property *
  Get-Process | Format-Table -property ID,Name,Responding -autoSize
  Get-Process | Format-Table * -autoSize
  ```

- -groupBy—This parameter generates a new set of column headers each time the specified property value changes. This only works well when you have first sorted the objects on that same property. An example is the best way to see how this works:

  ```
  Get-Service | Sort-Object Status | Format-Table -groupBy Status
  ```

- -wrap—If the shell has to truncate information in a column, it will end that column with ellipses (...) to visually indicate that information was suppressed. This parameter enables the shell to wrap information, which will make the table longer, but will preserve all of the information you wanted to display. Here's an example:

  ```
  Get-Service | Format-Table Name,Status,DisplayName -autoSize -wrap
  ```

```
Administrator: Windows PowerShell                                        _ □ x
PS C:\> ps | ft -auto

Handles NPM(K)   PM(K)   WS(K) VM(M)   CPU(s)     Id ProcessName
------- ------   -----   ----- -----   ------     -- -----------
     38      6    1984    4552    57    43.88   2196 conhost
     31      4     796    2272    22     0.14   2508 conhost
     29      4     832    2300    41     2.27   2888 conhost
     32      5     976    2904    46     0.11   3236 conhost
    506     13    1900    4064    48     3.78    320 csrss
    213     12    7928    5892    53    54.17    372 csrss
    296     30   14576   19516   143    20.83   1300 dfsrs
    122     15    2584    6188    41     0.63   1760 dfssvc
   5157   7329   85720   87088   122     4.48   1356 dns
     65      7    1824    4684    53     0.25    324 dwm
    669     40   27176   41668   174     8.28   2100 explorer
    129      9    3032    5056    38     8.95   2500 fdhost
     48      6    1020    3244    25     0.02   2432 fdlauncher
      0      0       0      24     0             0 Idle
    134     14    5760   11684    68     0.08   1420 inetinfo
    100     14    2988    4876    39     0.13   1464 ismserv
   1332    111   34368   30308   164    67.03    484 lsass
    194     11    2820    5676    30     7.55    492 lsm
    308     42   52244   52348   559    11.03   1236 Microsoft.ActiveDirecto...
    146     18    3228    7180    60     0.09   2576 msdtc
   1793     44  473460  492088  1010    53.44   3028 powershell
    545     54  128788  133564   766   224.25   3760 powershell_ise
```

Figure 10.3   Creating an auto-size table of processes

TRY IT NOW   You should run through all of these examples in the shell, and feel free to mix and match these techniques. Experiment a bit to see what works, and what sort of output you can create.

10.4   *Formatting lists*

Sometimes you need to display more information than will fit horizontally in a table, which can make a list useful. `Format-List` is the cmdlet you'll turn to, or you can use its alias, `Fl`.

   This cmdlet supports some of the same parameters as `Format-Table`, including `-property`. In fact, `Fl` is another way of displaying the properties of an object. Unlike `Gm`, `Fl` will also display the values for those properties, so that you can see what kind of information each property contains:

```
Get-Service | Fl *
```

Figure 10.4 shows an example of the output. We often use `Fl` as an alternative way of discovering the properties of an object.

TRY IT NOW   Read the help for `Format-List` and try experimenting with its different parameters.

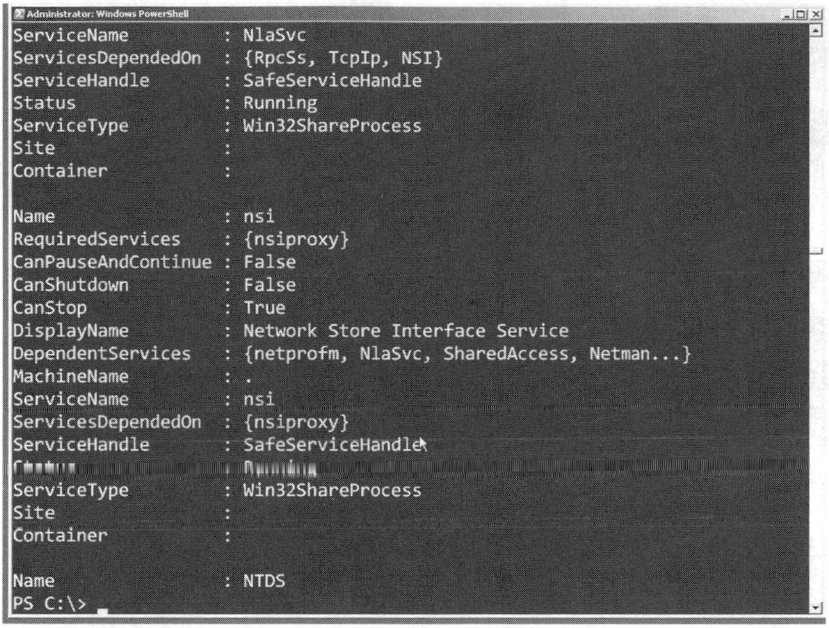

Figure 10.4 Reviewing services displayed in list form

10.5 *Formatting wide*

The last cmdlet, Format-Wide (or its alias, Fw), displays a wide list. It's able to display only the values of a single property, so its -property parameter accepts only one property name, not a list, and it can't accept wildcards.

By default, Format-Wide will look for an object's Name property, because Name is a commonly used property and usually contains useful information. The display will generally default to two columns, but a -columns parameter can be used to specify more columns:

```
Get-Process | Format-Wide name -col 4
```

Figure 10.5 shows an example of what you should see.

TRY IT NOW Read the help for Format-Wide, and try experimenting with its different parameters.

```
Administrator: Windows PowerShell                                              _|□|x|
PS C:\> get-process | format-wide name -col 4


conhost            conhost            conhost            conhost
csrss              csrss              dfsrs              dfssvc
dns                dwm                explorer           fdhost
fdlauncher         Idle               inetinfo           ismserv
lsass              lsm                Microsoft.Activ... msdtc
powershell         powershell_ise     PresentationFon... services
smss               spoolsv            sqlservr           sqlwriter
svchost            svchost            svchost            svchost
svchost            svchost            svchost            svchost
svchost            svchost            svchost            svchost
svchost            System             taskhost           TPAutoConnect
TPAutoConnSvc      vds                vmtoolsd           VMUpgradeHelper
VMwareTray         VMwareUser         wininit            winlogon
WmiPrvSE



PS C:\>
```

Figure 10.5   **Displaying process names in a wide list**

10.6   *Custom columns and list entries*

Flip back to the previous chapter, and review section 9.5, "When things don't line up: custom properties." In that section, we showed you how to use a hash table construct to add custom properties to an object. Both Format-Table and Format-List can use those same constructs to create custom table columns or custom list entries.

You might do this to provide a column header that's different from the property name being displayed:

```
Get-Service |
Format-Table @{n='ServiceName';e={$_.Name}},Status,DisplayName
```

Or, you might put a more complex mathematical expression in place:

```
Get-Process |
Format-Table Name,
@{n='VM(MB)';e={$_.VM / 1MB -as [int]}} -autosize
```

Figure 10.6 shows the output of the preceding command. We admit, we're cheating there a little bit by throwing in a bunch of stuff that we haven't talked about yet.

We might as well talk about it now:

- Obviously, we're starting with Get-Process, a cmdlet you're more than familiar with by now. If you run Get-Process | Fl *, you'll see that the VM property is in bytes, although that's not how the default table view displays it.
- We're telling Format-Table to start with the process's Name property.

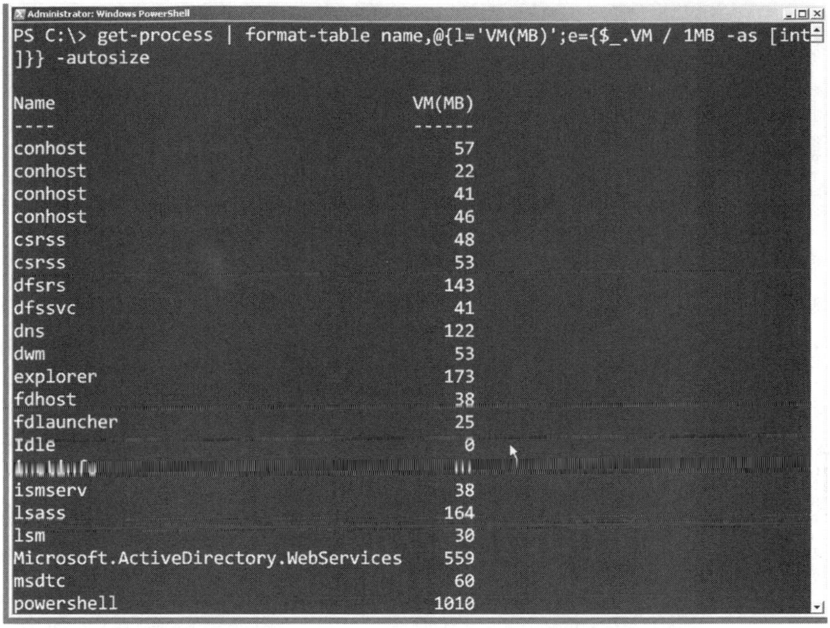

Figure 10.6   Creating a custom, calculated table column

- Next, we're creating a custom column that will be labeled VM(MB). The value, or expression, for that column takes the object's normal VM property and divides it by 1MB. The slash is PowerShell's division operator, and PowerShell recognizes the shortcuts KB, MB, GB, TB, and PB as denoting kilobyte, megabyte, gigabyte, terabyte, and petabyte respectively.

- The result of that division operation will have a decimal component that we don't want to see. The -as operator enables us to change the data type of that result from a floating-point value to, in this case, an integer value (specified by [int]). The shell will round up or down, as appropriate, when making that conversion. The result is a whole number with no fractional component.

Above and beyond

We'd like you to try repeating this example:

```
Get-Process |
Format-Table Name,
@{n='VM(MB)';e={$_.VM / 1MB -as [int]}} -autosize
```

But this time don't type it all on one line. Type it exactly as it's shown here in the book, on three lines total. You'll notice after typing the first line, which ends with a pipe character, that PowerShell changes its prompt. That's because you ended the shell in a pipe, and the shell knows that there are more commands coming. It will enter this same "waiting for you to finish" mode if you hit Return without properly closing all curly braces, quotation marks, and parentheses.

(continued)

If you didn't mean to enter that extended-typing mode, hit Ctrl-C to abort, and start over. In this case, you could type the second line of text and hit Return, and then type the third line and hit Return. In this mode, you'll have to hit Return one last time, on a blank line, to tell the shell you're done. When you do so, it will execute the command as if it had been typed on a single, continuous line.

We wanted to show you this little division-and-changing trick because it can be useful in creating nicer-looking output. We won't spend much more time in this book on these operations (although we will tell you that * is used for multiplication, and as you might expect + and - are for addition and subtraction).

Unlike `Select-Object`, whose hash tables can only accept a `Name` and `Expression` key (although it'll also accept `N`, `L`, and `Label` for `Name`, and will accept `E` for `Expression`), the `Format-` commands can handle additional keys that are intended to control the visual display. These additional keys are most useful with `Format-Table`:

- `FormatString` specifies a formatting code, causing the data to be displayed according to the specified format. This is mainly useful with numeric and date data. Go to MSDN's "Formatting Types" page (http://msdn.microsoft.com/en-us/library/26etazsy.aspx) to review the available codes for standard numeric and date formatting, and for custom numeric and date formatting.
- `Width` specifies the desired column width.
- `Alignment` specifies the desired column alignment, either `Left` or `Right`.

Using those additional keys makes it a bit easier to achieve the previous example's results, and even to improve upon them:

```
Get-Process |
Format-Table Name,
@{n='VM(MB)';e={$_.VM};formatstring='F2';align='right'} -autosize
```

Now we don't have to do the division, because PowerShell will format the number as a fixed-point value having two decimal places, and it will right-align the result.

10.7 *Going out: to a file, a printer, or the host*

Once something is formatted, you have to decide where it will go.

If a command line ends in a `Format-` cmdlet, the formatting instructions created by the `Format-` cmdlet will go to `Out-Default`, which forwards them to `Out-Host`, which displays them on the screen:

```
Get-Service | Format-Wide
```

You could also manually pipe the formatting instructions to `Out-Host`, which would accomplish exactly the same thing:

```
Get-Service | Format-Wide | Out-Host
```

Alternatively, you can pipe formatting instructions to either `Out-File` or `Out-Printer` to direct formatted output to a file or to hardcopy. As you'll read later, in "Common points of confusion," only one of those three `Out-` cmdlets should ever follow a `Format-` cmdlet on the command line.

Keep in mind that both `Out-Printer` and `Out-File` default to a specific character width for their output, which means a hardcopy or a text file might look different from what would display on the screen. The cmdlets have a `-width` parameter that enables you to change the output width, if desired, to accommodate wider tables.

10.8   *Another out: GridViews*

`Out-GridView` provides another useful form of output. Note that this isn't technically formatting; in fact, `Out-GridView` entirely bypasses the formatting subsystem. No `Format-` cmdlets are called, no formatting instructions are produced, and no text output is displayed in the console window. `Out-GridView` can't receive the output of a `Format-` cmdlet—it can only receive the regular objects output by other cmdlets.

Figure 10.7 shows what the grid view looks like.

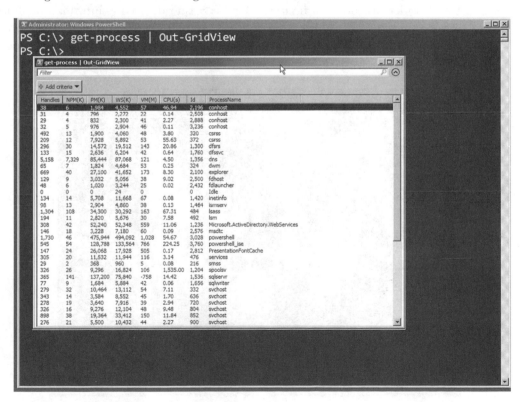

Figure 10.7   The results of the `Out-GridView` cmdlet

10.9   Common points of confusion

As we mentioned at the start of this chapter, the formatting system has most of the "gotchas" that trip up PowerShell newcomers. There are two main things that our classroom students tend to run across, so we'll try to help you avoid them.

10.9.1   Always format right

It's incredibly important that you remember one rule from this chapter: *format right*. Your `Format-` cmdlet should be the last thing on the command line, with `Out-File` or `Out-Printer` as the only exceptions. The reason for this rule is that the `Format-` cmdlets produce formatting instructions, and only an `Out-` cmdlet can properly consume those instructions. If a `Format-` cmdlet is last on the command line, the instructions will go to `Out-Default` (which is always at the end of the pipeline), which will forward them to `Out-Host`, which is happy to work with formatting instructions.

Try running this command to illustrate the need for this rule:

```
Get-Service | Format-Table | Gm
```

You'll notice, as shown in figure 10.8, that `Gm` isn't displaying information about your service objects because the `Format-Table` cmdlet doesn't output service objects. It consumes the service objects you pipe in, and it outputs formatting instructions—which is what `Gm` sees and reports on.

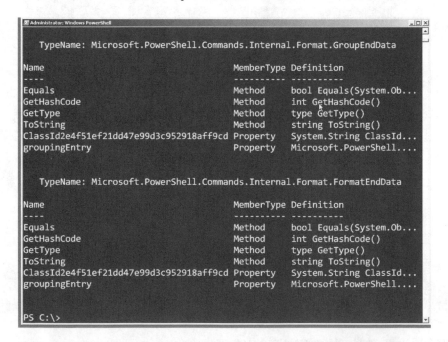

Figure 10.8   Formatting cmdlets produce special formatting instructions, which aren't meaningful to humans.

Now try this:

```
Get-Service | Select Name,DisplayName,Status | Format-Table |
ConvertTo-HTML | Out-File services.html
```

Go ahead and open Services.html in Internet Explorer, and you'll see some crazy results. You didn't pipe service objects to `ConvertTo-HTML`; you piped formatting instructions, so that's what got converted to HTML. This illustrates why a `Format-` cmdlet, if you use one, either has to be the last thing on the command line or has to be second-to-last with the last cmdlet being `Out-File` or `Out-Printer`.

Also know that `Out-GridView` is unusual (for an `Out-` cmdlet, at least) in that it *won't* accept formatting instructions and *will* only accept normal objects. Try these two commands to see the difference:

```
PS C:\>Get-Process | Out-GridView
PS C:\>Get-Process | Format-Table | Out-GridView
```

That's why we explicitly mentioned `Out-File` and `Out-Printer` as the only cmdlets that should follow a `Format-` cmdlet (technically, `Out-Host` can also follow a `Format-` cmdlet, but there's no need because ending the command line with the `Format-` cmdlet will get the output to `Out-Host` anyway).

10.9.2 *One type of object at a time, please*

The next thing to avoid is putting multiple kinds of objects into the pipeline. The formatting system looks at the first object in the pipeline and uses the type of that object to determine what formatting to produce. If the pipeline contains two or more kinds of objects, the output won't always be complete or useful.

For example, run this:

```
Get-Process; Get-Service
```

That semicolon allows us to put two commands onto a single command line, without piping the output of the first cmdlet into the second one. This means both cmdlets will run independently, but they will put their output into the same pipeline. As you'll see if you try this or look at figure 10.9, the output starts out fine, displaying process objects. But the output breaks down when it's time to display the service objects. Rather than producing the table you're used to, PowerShell reverts to a list. The formatting system isn't designed to take multiple kinds of objects and make the results look as attractive as possible.

What if you want to combine information drawn from two (or more) different places into a single form of output? You absolutely can, and you can do so in a way that the formatting system can deal with nicely. But that's an advanced topic that we won't get to in this book.

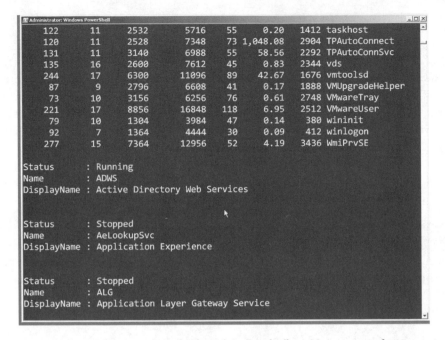

Figure 10.9   Putting two types of objects into the pipeline at once can confuse PowerShell's formatting system.

Above and beyond

Technically, the formatting system *can* handle multiple types of objects—if you tell it how. Run `Dir | Gm` and you'll notice that the pipeline contains both `DirectoryInfo` and `FileInfo` objects (`Gm` has no problem working with pipelines that contain multiple kinds of objects and will display member information for all of them). When you run `Dir` by itself, the output is perfectly legible. That's because Microsoft provides a predefined custom formatting view for `DirectoryInfo` and `FileInfo` objects, and that view is handled by the `Format-Custom` cmdlet.

`Format-Custom` is mainly used to display different predefined custom views. You could technically create your own predefined custom views, but the necessary XML syntax is complicated and isn't publicly documented at this time, so custom views are limited to what Microsoft provides.

Microsoft's custom views do get a lot of usage, though. PowerShell's help information is stored as objects, for example, and the formatted help files you see on the screen are the result of feeding those objects into a custom view.

10.10 Lab

NOTE For this lab, you'll need any computer running PowerShell v3.

See if you can complete the following tasks:

1 Display a table of processes that includes only the process names, IDs, and whether or not they're responding to Windows (the `Responding` property has that information). Have the table take up as little horizontal room as possible, but don't allow any information to be truncated.

2 Display a table of processes that includes the process names and IDs. Also include columns for virtual and physical memory usage, expressing those values in megabytes (MB).

3 Use `Get-EventLog` to display a list of available event logs. (Hint: you'll need to read the help to learn the correct parameter to accomplish that.) Format the output as a table that includes, in this order, the log display name and the retention period. The column headers must be "LogName" and "RetDays."

4 Display a list of services so that a separate table is displayed for services that are started and services that are stopped. Services that are started should be displayed first. (Hint: you'll use a `-groupBy` parameter).

10.11 Further exploration

This is the perfect time to experiment with the formatting system. Try using the three main `Format-` cmdlets to create different forms of output. The labs in upcoming chapters will often ask you to use specific formatting, so you might as well hone your skills with these cmdlets and start memorizing the more often-used parameters that we've covered in this chapter.

Filtering and comparisons

Up to this point, you've been working with whatever output the shell gave you: all the processes, all the services, all the event log entries, all the hotfixes. But this type of output isn't always going to be what you want. Often you'll want to narrow down the results to a few items that specifically interest you. That's what you'll learn to do in this chapter.

11.1 Making the shell give you just what you need

The shell offers two broad models for narrowing down results, and they're both referred to as *filtering*. In the first model, you try to instruct the cmdlet that's retrieving information for you to retrieve only what you've specified. In the second model, which takes an iterative approach, you take everything the cmdlet gives you and use a second cmdlet to filter out the things you don't want.

Ideally, you'll use the first model, which we call *early filtering*, as much as possible. It may be as simple as telling the cmdlet what you're after. For example, with `Get-Service`, you can tell it which service names you want:

```
Get-Service -name e*,*s*
```

But if you want `Get-Service` to return only the running services, regardless of their names, you can't tell the cmdlet to do that for you, because it doesn't offer any parameters to specify that information.

Similarly, if you're using Microsoft's ActiveDirectory module, all of its `Get-` cmdlets support a `-filter` parameter. Although you can tell it `-filter *` to get all objects, we don't recommend it because of the load it can impose on a domain controller in large domains. Instead, you can specify criteria like the following, which explain precisely what you want:

```
Get-ADComputer -filter "Name -like '*DC'"
```

Once again, this technique is ideal because the cmdlet only has to retrieve matching objects. We call this the *filter left* technique.

11.2 Filter left

"Filter left" means putting your filtering criteria as far to the left, or toward the beginning, of the command line as possible. The earlier you can filter out unwanted objects, the less work the remaining cmdlets on the command line will have to do, and the less unnecessary information will have to be transmitted across the network to your computer.

The downside of the filter left technique is that every single cmdlet can implement its own means of specifying filtering, and every cmdlet will have varying abilities to perform filtering. With `Get-Service`, for example, you can only filter on the `Name` property of the services. But with `Get-ADComputer` you can filter on any Active Directory attribute that a `Computer` object might have. Being effective with the filter left technique requires you to learn a lot about how various cmdlets operate, which can mean a somewhat steeper learning curve. But you'll benefit from better performance.

When you're not able to get a cmdlet to do all of the filtering you need, you can turn to a core PowerShell cmdlet called `Where-Object` (which has an alias of `Where`). This uses a generic syntax, and you can use it to filter any kind of object once you've retrieved it and put it into the pipeline.

To use `Where-Object`, you'll need to learn how to tell the shell what you want to filter, and that involves using the shell's comparison operators. Interestingly, some filter left techniques—such as the `-filter` parameter of the `Get-` cmdlets in the Active-Directory module—use the same comparison operators, so you'll be killing two birds with one stone. But some cmdlets (we're thinking about `Get-WmiObject`, which we'll discuss later in the chapter) use an entirely different filtering and comparison language, which we'll cover when we discuss those cmdlets.

11.3 Comparison operators

In computers, a *comparison* always involves taking two objects or values and testing their relationship to one another. You might be testing to see if they're equal, or to see if one is greater than another, or if one of them matches a text pattern of some kind. You indicate the kind of relationship you want to test by using a *comparison operator*. The result of the test is always a Boolean value: `True` or `False`. Put another way, either the tested relationship is as you specified, or it isn't.

PowerShell uses the following comparison operators. Note that when comparing text strings, these aren't case-sensitive. That means an uppercase letter is seen as equal to a lowercase letter.

- -eq—Equality, as in 5 -eq 5 (which is True) or "hello" -eq "help" (which is False)
- -ne—Not equal to, as in 10 -ne 5 (which is True) or "help" -ne "help" (which is False, because they're, in fact, equal, and we were testing to see if they were unequal)
- -ge and -le—Greater than or equal to, and less than or equal to, as in 10 -ge 5 (True) or Get-Date -le '2012-12-02' (which will depend on when you run this, and shows how dates can be compared)
- -gt and -lt—Greater than and less than, as in 10 -lt 10 (False) or 100 -gt 10 (True)

For string comparisons, you can also use a separate set of case-sensitive operators if needed: -ceq, -cne, -cgt, -clt, -cge, -cle.

If you want to compare more than one thing at once, you can use the Boolean operators -and and -or. Each of those takes a subexpression on either side, and we usually enclose them in parentheses to make the line easier to read:

- (5 -gt 10) -and (10 -gt 100) is False, because one or both subexpressions were False
- (5 -gt 10) -or (10 -lt 100) is True, because at least one subexpression was True

In addition, the Boolean -not operator reverses True and False. This can be useful when you're dealing with a variable or a property that already contains True or False, and you want to test for the opposite condition. For example, if we wanted to test whether a process wasn't responding, we could do the following (we're going to use $__ as a placeholder for a process object):

```
$_.Responding -eq $False
```

Windows PowerShell defines $False and $True to represent the False and True Boolean values. Another way to write that comparison would be as follows:

```
-not $_.Responding
```

Because Responding normally contains True or False, the -not will reverse False to True. If the process isn't responding (meaning Responding is False), then our comparison will return True, indicating that the process is "not responding." We prefer the second technique because it reads, in English, more like what we're testing for: "I want to see if the process isn't responding." You'll sometimes see the -not operator abbreviated as an exclamation mark (!).

A couple of other comparison operators are useful when you need to compare strings of text:

- -like accepts * as a wildcard, so you can compare to see if "Hello" -like "*ll*" (that would be True). The reverse is -notlike, and both are case-insensitive; use -clike and -cnotlike for case-sensitive comparisons.

- -match makes a comparison between a string of text and a regular expression pattern. -notmatch is its logical opposite, and as you might expect, -cmatch and -cnotmatch provide case-sensitive versions. Regular expressions are beyond the scope of what we'll cover in this book.

The neat thing about the shell is that you can run almost all of these tests right at the command line (the exception is the one where we used the $_ placeholder—it won't work by itself, but you'll see where it will work in the next section).

TRY IT NOW   Go ahead and try any—or all—of these comparisons. Type them on a line, like 5 -eq 5, hit Return, and see what you get.

You can find the other available comparison operators in the about_comparison _operators help file, and you'll learn about a few of the other ones in chapter 25.

Above and beyond

If a cmdlet doesn't use the PowerShell-style comparison operators discussed in section 11.3, it probably uses the more traditional, programming language-style comparison operators that you might remember from high school or college (or even your daily work):

- = equality
- <> inequality
- <= less than or equal to
- >= greater than or equal to
- > greater than
- < less than

If Boolean operators are supported, they're usually the words AND and OR; some cmdlets may support operators such as LIKE as well. For example, you'll find support for all of these operators in the -filter parameter of Get-WmiObject; we'll repeat this list when we discuss that cmdlet in chapter 14.

Every cmdlet's designers get to pick how (and if) they'll handle filtering; you can often get examples of what they decided to do by reviewing the cmdlet's full help, including the usage examples near the end of the help file.

11.4   *Filtering objects out of the pipeline*

Once you've written a comparison, where do you use it? Well, using the comparison language we just outlined, you can use it with the -filter parameter of some cmdlets, perhaps most notably the ActiveDirectory module's Get- cmdlets. You can also use it with the shell's generic filtering cmdlet, Where-Object.

For example, do you want to get rid of all but the running services?

```
Get-Service | Where-Object -filter { $_.Status -eq 'Running' }
```

The `-filter` parameter is positional, which means you'll often see this typed without it, and with the alias `Where`:

```
Get-Service | Where { $_.Status -eq 'Running' }
```

If you get used to reading that aloud, it sounds sensible: "where status equals running." Here's how it works: when you pipe objects to `Where-Object`, it examines each one of them using its filter. It places one object at a time into the `$_` placeholder and then runs the comparison to see if it's `True` or `False`. If it's `False`, the object is dropped from the pipeline. If the comparison is `True`, the object is piped out of `Where-Object` to the next cmdlet in the pipeline. In this case, the next cmdlet is `Out-Default`, which is always at the end of the pipeline (as we discussed in chapter 8) and which kicks off the formatting process to display your output.

That `$_` placeholder is a special creature: you've seen it used before (in chapter 10), and you'll see it in one or two more contexts. You can only use this placeholder in the specific places where PowerShell looks for it, and this happens to be one of those places. As you learned in chapter 10, the period tells the shell that you're not comparing the entire object, but rather just one of its properties, `Status`.

We hope you're starting to see where `Gm` comes in handy. It gives you a quick and easy way to discover what properties an object has, which lets you turn around and use those properties in a comparison like this one. Always keep in mind that the column headers in PowerShell's final output don't always reflect the property names. For example, run `Get-Process` and you'll see a column like PM(MB); run `Get-Process | Gm` and you'll see that the actual property name is `PM`. That's an important distinction: always verify property names using `Gm`, not with a `Format-` cmdlet.

Above and beyond

PowerShell v3 introduced a new "simplified" syntax for `Where-Object`. You can use it only when you're doing a single comparison; if you need to compare multiple items, you still have to use the original syntax, which is what you've seen in this section.

Folks debate whether or not this simplified syntax is helpful. It looks something like this:

```
Get-Service | Where Status -eq 'Running'
```

Obviously, that's a bit easier to read: it dispenses with the {curly brackets} and doesn't require the use of the awkward-looking `$_` placeholder. But this new syntax doesn't mean you can forget about the old syntax, which you still need for more complex comparisons:

```
Get-WmiObject -Class Win32_Service |
   Where { $_.State -ne 'Running' -and $_.StartMode -eq 'Auto' }
```

What's more, there are six years' worth of examples out on the internet that all use the old syntax, which means you have to know it to use them. You also have to know the new syntax, because it will now start cropping up in developer's examples. Having to know two sets of syntax isn't exactly "simplified," but at least you know what's what.

And by the way, we acknowledge that the previous command isn't an ideal example. We could have used the `-Filter` parameter of `Get-WmiObject`, which would be more efficient. But we wanted to use this illustration to point out that the "old" `Where-Object` syntax still has some uses.

11.5 *The iterative command-line model*

We want to go on a brief tangent with you now to talk about what we call the Power-Shell Iterative Command-Line Model, or PSICLM. (There's no reason for it to have an acronym, but it's fun to try to pronounce.) The idea behind PSICLM is that you don't need to construct these large, complex command lines all at once and entirely from scratch. Start small.

Let's say you want to measure the amount of virtual memory being used by the ten most virtual, memory-hungry processes. But if PowerShell itself is one of those processes, you don't want it included in the calculation. Let's take a quick inventory of what you need to do:

1 Get processes
2 Get rid of everything that's PowerShell
3 Sort them by virtual memory
4 Only keep the top ten or bottom ten, depending on how we sort them
5 Add up the virtual memory for whatever is left

We believe you know how to do the first three of these steps. The fourth is accomplished using your old friend, `Select-Object`.

TRY IT NOW Take a moment and read the help for `Select-Object`. Can you find any parameters that would enable you to keep the first or last number of objects in a collection?

We hope you found the answer.

Finally, you need to add up the virtual memory. This is where you'll need to find a new cmdlet, probably by doing a wildcard search with `Get-Command` or `Help`. You might try the `Add` keyword, or the `Sum` keyword, or even the `Measure` keyword.

TRY IT NOW See if you can find a command that would measure the total of a numeric property like virtual memory. Use `Help` or `Get-Command` with the `*` wildcard.

As you're trying these little tasks (and not reading ahead for the answer), you're making yourself into a PowerShell expert. Once you think you have the answer, you might start in on the iterative approach.

To start with, you need to get processes. That's easy enough:

```
Get-Process
```

TRY IT NOW   Follow along in the shell, and run these commands. After each, examine the output, and see if you can predict what you need to change for the next iteration of the command.

Next, you need to filter out what you don't want. Remember, "filter left" means you want to get the filter as close to the beginning of the command line as possible. In this case, we'll use `Where-Object` to do the filtering, because we want it to be the next cmdlet. That's not as good as having the filtering occur on the first cmdlet, but it's better than filtering later on down the pipeline.

In the shell, hit the up arrow on the keyboard to recall your last command, and then add the next command:

```
Get-Process | Where-Object -filter { $_.Name -notlike 'powershell*' }
```

We're not sure if it's "powershell" or "powershell.exe," so we're using a wildcard comparison to cover all our bases. Any process that isn't like those names will remain in the pipeline.

Run that to test it, and then hit the up arrow again to add the next bit:

```
Get-Process | Where-Object -filter { $_.Name -notlike 'powershell*' } |
Sort VM -descending
```

Hitting Return lets you check your work, and the up arrow will let you add the next piece of the puzzle:

```
Get-Process | Where-Object -filter { $_.Name -notlike 'powershell*' } |
Sort VM -descending | Select -first 10
```

Had you sorted in the default ascending order, you would have wanted to keep the `-last 10` before adding this last bit:

```
Get-Process | Where-Object -filter { $_.Name -notlike 'powershell*' } |
Sort VM -descending | Select -first 10 |
Measure-Object -property VM -sum
```

We hope you were able to figure out at least the name of that last cmdlet, if not the exact syntax used here.

This model—running a command, examining the results, recalling it, and modifying it for another try—is what differentiates PowerShell from more traditional scripting languages. Because PowerShell is a command-line shell, you get those immediate results, and also the ability to quickly and easily modify your command if the results weren't what you expected. You should also be seeing the power you have when you combine even the handful of cmdlets you've learned to this point in the book.

11.6   *Common points of confusion*

Any time we introduce `Where-Object` in a class, we usually come across two main sticking points. We tried to hit those concepts hard in the preceding discussion, but if you have any doubts, we'll clear them up now.

11.6.1 *Filter left, please*

You want your filtering criteria to go *as close to the beginning of the command line as possible*. If you can accomplish the filtering you need on the first cmdlet, do so; if not, try to filter in the second cmdlet so that the subsequent cmdlets have as little work to do as possible.

Also, try to accomplish filtering as close to the source of the data as possible. For example, if you're querying services from a remote computer and need to use Where-Object—as we did in one of this chapter's examples—consider using Power-Shell remoting to have the filtering occur on the remote computer, rather than bringing all of the objects to your computer and filtering them there. You'll tackle remoting in chapter 13, and we'll mention this idea of filtering at the source again there.

11.6.2 *When $_ is allowed*

The special $_ placeholder is only valid in the places where PowerShell knows to look for it. When it's valid, it contains one object at a time from the ones that were piped into that cmdlet. Keep in mind that what's in the pipeline can and will change throughout the pipeline, as various cmdlets execute and produce output.

Also be careful of nested pipelines—the ones that occur inside a parenthetical command. For example, the following can be tricky to figure out:

```
Get-Service -computername (Get-Content c:\names.txt |
Where-Object -filter { $_ -notlike '*dc' }) |
Where-Object -filter { $_.Status -eq 'Running' }
```

Let's walk through that:

1 You start with Get-Service, but that isn't the first command that will execute. Because of the parentheses, Get-Content will execute first.
2 Get-Content is piping its output—which consists of simple String objects—to Where-Object. That Where-Object is inside the parentheses, and within its filter, $_ represents the String objects piped in from Get-Content. Only those strings that don't end in "dc" will be retained and output by Where-Object.
3 The output of Where-Object becomes the result of the parenthetical command, because Where-Object was the last cmdlet inside the parentheses. Therefore, all of the computer names that don't end in "dc" will be sent to the -computername parameter of Get-Service.
4 *Now* Get-Service executes, and the ServiceController objects it produces will be piped to Where-Object. *That* instance of Where-Object will put one service at a time into its $_ placeholder, and it will keep only those services whose status property is Running.

Sometimes we feel like our eyes are crossing with all the curly braces, periods, and parentheses, but that's how PowerShell works, and if you can train yourself to walk through the command carefully, you'll be able to figure out what it's doing.

11.7   Lab

NOTE   For this lab, you'll need a Windows 8 or Windows Server 2012 computer running PowerShell v3.

Remember that `Where-Object` isn't the only way to filter, and it isn't even the one you should turn to first. We've kept this chapter brief to allow you more time to work on the hands-on examples, so keeping in mind the principle of *filter left*, try to accomplish the following:

1   Import the NetAdapter module (available in the latest version of Windows, both client and server). Using the `Get-NetAdapter` cmdlet, display a list of non-virtual network adapters (that is, adapters whose `Virtual` property is `False`, which PowerShell represents with the special `$False` constant).

2   Import the DnsClient module (available in the latest version of Windows, both client and server). Using the `Get-DnsClientCache` cmdlet, display a list of A and AAAA records from the cache. Hint: if your cache comes up empty, try visiting a few web pages first to force some items into the cache.

3   Display a list of hotfixes that are security updates.

4   Using `Get-Service`, is it possible to display a list of services that have a start type of `Automatic`, but that aren't currently started? Answer "Yes" or "No" to this question. You don't need to write a command to accomplish this.

5   Display a list of hotfixes that were installed by the Administrator, and which are updates. Note that some hotfixes won't have an "installed by" value—that's OK.

6   Display a list of all processes running with either the name "Conhost" or the name "Svchost".

11.8   *Further exploration*

Practice makes perfect, so try filtering some of the output from the cmdlets you've already learned about, such as `Get-Hotfix`, `Get-EventLog`, `Get-Process`, `Get-Service`, and even `Get-Command`. For example, you might try to filter the output of `Get-Command` to show only cmdlets. Or use `Test-Connection` to ping several computers, and only show the results from computers that didn't respond. We're not suggesting that you need to use `Where-Object` in every case, but you should practice using it when it's appropriate.

A practical interlude

12

It's time to put some of your new knowledge to work. In this chapter, we're not even going to try and teach you anything new—instead, we're going to walk you through a detailed example using what you've learned. This is meant to be an absolutely real-world example: we're going to set ourselves a task, and then let you follow our thought processes as we figure out how to complete it. This chapter is really the epitome of what this book is all about, because instead of just handing you the answer on how to do something, we're helping you realize that *you can teach yourself*.

12.1 Defining the task

First of all, we're going to assume that you're working on Windows 8 or on Windows Server 2012, and that you obviously have PowerShell v3 installed (it comes with those operating systems). If you don't have one of those versions of Windows, we strongly recommend downloading a trial version, if possible, or spinning up a virtual machine using a service like CloudShare.com. While PowerShell v3 will run on older versions of Windows, those versions don't supply the same deep administrative integration as the newest versions of Windows.

Our goal is to use PowerShell to create a new scheduled task. We want this to be a real scheduled task, one we could see in Windows' Task Scheduler when we're done. Every day at 3 a.m., we want the task to remove all print jobs from a local printer named "Accounting." Let's say that jobs sometimes get hung, because it's an old and recalcitrant piece of hardware, and we want a fresh start every morning.

12.2   *Finding the commands*

The first step in solving any task is to figure out which commands will do it for you. We're going to start a bit backwards, and figure out the printer side of the task first. That way, we can run the commands interactively to make sure they're doing what we think they are. Then, when we go to put them in a scheduled task, we're only going to be fighting one problem at a time.

We start by looking for print commands. Notice that we chose to use *print* as our keyword, rather than *printer*. Whenever possible, use a shorter form of a word to get a broader set of results.

```
PS C:\> help *print*

Name                          Category  Module

----                          --------  ------
Add-Printer                   Function  printmanagement
Add-PrinterDriver             Function  printmanagement
Add-PrinterPort               Function  printmanagement
Get-PrintConfiguration        Function  printmanagement
Get-Printer                   Function  printmanagement
Get-PrinterDriver             Function  printmanagement
Get-PrinterPort               Function  printmanagement
Get-PrinterProperty           Function  printmanagement
Get-PrintJob                  Function  printmanagement
Remove-Printer                Function  printmanagement
Remove-PrinterDriver          Function  printmanagement
Remove-PrinterPort            Function  printmanagement
Remove-PrintJob               Function  printmanagement
Rename-Printer                Function  printmanagement
Restart-PrintJob              Function  printmanagement
Resume-PrintJob               Function  printmanagement
Set-PrintConfiguration        Function  printmanagement
Set-Printer                   Function  printmanagement
Set-PrinterProperty           Function  printmanagement
Suspend-PrintJob              Function  printmanagement
Out-Printer                   Cmdlet    Microsoft.PowerShell.U
```

TRY IT NOW   You should definitely be following along with the commands we run in this chapter. Make sure you're seeing what we see, and make sure it's giving you the same information that we're claiming. What's important here isn't accomplishing the task—what's important is *how* we figure it out.

That's promising! There's Get-PrintJob and Remove-PrintJob. If you look at the help for Remove-PrintJob, you'll see that it has an -InputObject parameter, which accepts pipeline input ByValue. That means we should be able to get a job, and then pipe it to Remove-PrintJob to remove that job:

```
-InputObject <CimInstance#MSFT_PrintJob>

    Required?                  true
    Position?                  0
    Accept pipeline input?     true (ByValue)
```

```
Parameter set name          jobObject
Aliases                     None
Dynamic?                    False
```

A quick test on a non-production printer shows that `Get-PrintJob -printer "Accounting"` | `Remove-PrintJob` will remove all outstanding print jobs. So that's one part of our job. Now for the scheduled task part.

```
PS C:\> help *task*

Name                                   Category   Module

----                                   --------   ------

Disable-NetAdapterEncapsulated...      Function   NetAdapter
Enable-NetAdapterEncapsulatedP...      Function   NetAdapter
Get-NetAdapterEncapsulatedPack...      Function   NetAdapter
Set-NetAdapterEncapsulatedPack...      Function   NetAdapter
Get-CertificateNotificationTask        Cmdlet     PKI
New-CertificateNotificationTask        Cmdlet     PKI
Remove-CertificateNotification...      Cmdlet     PKI
Get-ClusteredScheduledTask             Function   ScheduledTasks
Get-ScheduledTask                      Function   ScheduledTasks
Get-ScheduledTaskInfo                  Function   ScheduledTasks
New-ScheduledTask                      Function   ScheduledTasks
New-ScheduledTaskAction                Function   ScheduledTasks
New-ScheduledTaskPrincipal             Function   ScheduledTasks
New-ScheduledTaskSettingsSet           Function   ScheduledTasks
New-ScheduledTaskTrigger               Function   ScheduledTasks
```

Great—there are several commands (well, functions, but same thing) in a module called ScheduledTasks. Let's narrow our search down to just that module:

```
PS C:\> get-command -module scheduledtasks

Capability      Name

----------      ----

CIM             Get-ClusteredScheduledTask
CIM             Get-ScheduledTask
CIM             Get-ScheduledTaskInfo
CIM             New-ScheduledTask
CIM             New-ScheduledTaskAction
CIM             New-ScheduledTaskPrincipal
CIM             New-ScheduledTaskSettingsSet
Cmdlet, Script  New-ScheduledTaskTrigger
CIM             Register-ClusteredScheduledTask
CIM             Register-ScheduledTask
CIM             Set-ClusteredScheduledTask
CIM             Set-ScheduledTask
CIM             Start-ScheduledTask
CIM             Stop-ScheduledTask
CIM             Unregister-ClusteredScheduledTask
CIM             Unregister-ScheduledTask
```

Excellent. Now we know what commands we're after. We just have to figure out how to use them.

12.3   *Learning to use the commands*

We want to create a new scheduled task, so New-ScheduledTask seems like a grand place to start.

```
PS C:\> help new-scheduledtask -full

NAME
    New-ScheduledTask

SYNTAX
    New-ScheduledTask [[-Action] <CimInstance#MSFT_TaskAction[]>]
    [[-Trigger] <CimInstance#MSFT_TaskTrigger[]>] [[-Settings]
    <CimInstance#MSFT_TaskSettings>] [[-Principal]
    <CimInstance#MSFT_TaskPrincipal>] [[-Description] <string>]
    [-CimSession <CimSession[]>] [-ThrottleLimit <int>] [-AsJob]
    [<CommonParameters>]
```

There don't appear to be any mandatory parameters here, but the help suggests that -Trigger will be how we specify when the task should run, -Action will be what the task does, and we can probably ignore everything else. The help file indicates that those parameters each take an object as input—a TaskTrigger and TaskAction object, respectively. So we need to figure out how to make those objects. We could just read the examples at the end of the help, but let's make this challenging and not do so for now.

Fortunately, we still have that list of commands from the ScheduledTasks module, and the list includes a New-ScheduledTaskTrigger and a New-ScheduledTaskAction command. Hopefully you can see where this is going:

```
PS C:\> help New-ScheduledTaskTrigger

NAME
    New-ScheduledTaskTrigger

SYNOPSIS

SYNTAX
    New-ScheduledTaskTrigger [-RandomDelay <TimeSpan>] [-At] <DateTime>
    -Once [<CommonParameters>]

    New-ScheduledTaskTrigger [-DaysInterval <Int32>] [-RandomDelay
    <TimeSpan>] [-At] <DateTime> -Daily [<CommonParameters>]

    New-ScheduledTaskTrigger [-WeeksInterval <Int32>] [-RandomDelay
    <TimeSpan>] [-At] <DateTime> -DaysOfWeek <DayOfWeek[]> -Weekly
    [<CommonParameters>]

    New-ScheduledTaskTrigger [-RandomDelay <TimeSpan>] [[-User] <String>]
    -AtLogOn [<CommonParameters>]

    New-ScheduledTaskTrigger [[-RandomDelay] <TimeSpan>] -AtStartup
    [<CommonParameters>]
```

Well, we don't want any random stuff. The second parameter set has mandatory -Daily and -At parameters, and that seems promising. Let's see if we can quickly create a trigger using those:

```
PS C:\> New-ScheduledTaskTrigger -daily -at 0300

WARNING: column "Enabled" does not fit into the display and was removed

Id         Frequency     Time                  DaysOfWeek
--         ---------     ----                  ----------
0          Daily         1/1/0001 12:00:00 AM
```

No, not quite right. It didn't like our time format because it created it for midnight. Let's try again:

```
PS C:\> New-ScheduledTaskTrigger -daily -at '3:00 am'

WARNING: column "Enabled" does not fit into the display and was removed.

Id         Frequency     Time                  DaysOfWeek
--         ---------     ----                  ----------
0          Daily         4/18/2012 3:00:00 AM
```

There we go. So that's the command to create the trigger we want. Excellent. Notice that both attempts produced a trigger with ID 0, and that there's no command in the module to "Get-ScheduledTaskTrigger," so that suggests that PowerShell isn't tracking these things in memory. The command produces a trigger, and doesn't store it. Good to know—and it shows the importance of looking at each piece of data (even a lowly ID number) and thinking about what it might mean.

Now for the action:

```
PS C:\> help New-ScheduledTaskAction

NAME
    New-ScheduledTaskAction

SYNTAX
    New-ScheduledTaskAction [-Execute] <string> [[-Argument] <string>]
    [[-WorkingDirectory] <string>] [-Id <string>] [-CimSession
    <CimSession[]>] [-ThrottleLimit <int>] [-AsJob]  [<CommonParameters>]
```

We have played with scheduled tasks in the GUI before, so we know that -WorkingDirectory sets the folder in which the task runs. -Argument probably passes command-line arguments to whatever we're running, so we're going to guess that -Execute specifies whatever it is we want to run. Let's give it a shot:

```
PS C:\> New-ScheduledTaskAction -Execute 'dir'


Id               :
Arguments        :
Execute          : dir
WorkingDirectory :
PSComputerName   :
```

Yeah, okay, seems plausible. Let's try the entire thing:

```
PS C:\> New-ScheduledTask -Action (New-ScheduledTaskAction -Execute 'Get-Pr
intJob -printer "Accounting"') -Trigger (New-ScheduledTaskTrigger -daily
-at '3:00 am') -Description "Reset accounting printer daily at 3am"
```

But having run that, we're not seeing anything in the Task Scheduler GUI (once we eventually found it in the new "Metro" Start screen, of course). Rats. Back to the command list for the module:

```
PS C:\> gcm -Module scheduledtasks

Capability      Name

----------      ----
CIM             Get-ClusteredScheduledTask
CIM             Get-ScheduledTask
CIM             Get-ScheduledTaskInfo
CIM             New-ScheduledTask
CIM             New-ScheduledTaskAction
CIM             New-ScheduledTaskPrincipal
CIM             New-ScheduledTaskSettingsSet
Cmdlet, Script  New-ScheduledTaskTrigger
CIM             Register-ClusteredScheduledTask
CIM             Register-ScheduledTask
CIM             Set-ClusteredScheduledTask
CIM             Set-ScheduledTask
CIM             Start-ScheduledTask
CIM             Stop-ScheduledTask
CIM             Unregister-ClusteredScheduledTask
CIM             Unregister-ScheduledTask
```

Hmm. There's that `Register-ScheduledTask`, which is starting to look interesting. "New" usually means "make something," but maybe we have to also "register" the new task in order for Windows to realize it exists.

```
NAME
    Register-ScheduledTask

SYNTAX
    Register-ScheduledTask [-TaskName] <string> [[-TaskPath] <string>]
    [-Action] <CimInstance#MSFT_TaskAction[]> [[-Trigger]
    <CimInstance#MSFT_TaskTrigger[]>] [[-Settings]
    <CimInstance#MSFT_TaskSettings>] [[-User] <string>] [[-Password]
    <string>] [[-RunLevel] <RunLevelEnum> {Limited | Highest}]
    [[-Description] <string>] [-Force] [-CimSession <CimSession[]>]
    [-ThrottleLimit <int>] [-AsJob]  [<CommonParameters>]
```

Looks really similar to `New-ScheduledTask`, only with more. This, for example, has a -TaskName parameter, where we could presumably give our task a name—that makes sense. We're also seeing -User and -Password, which we'd expected to see on a scheduled task. Okay, let's try this instead:

```
PS C:\> Register-ScheduledTask -TaskName "ResetAccountingPrinter" -Descript
ion "Resets the Accounting print queue at 3am daily" -Action (New-Scheduled
TaskAction -Execute 'Get-PrintJob -printer "Accounting"') -Trigger (New-Sch
eduledTaskTrigger -daily -at '3:00 am')

WARNING: column "State" does not fit into the display and was removed.

TaskPath                                TaskName
--------                                --------
\                                       ResetAccountingPrinter
```

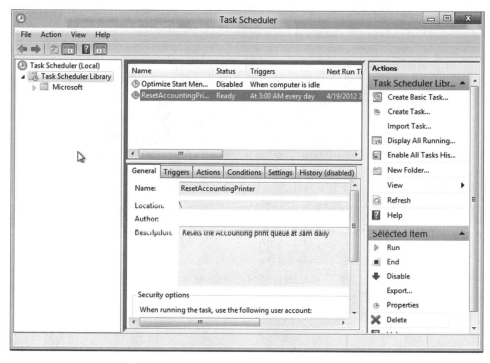

Figure 12.1   Verifying the scheduled task in the Task Scheduler GUI

Well, that looks like it did something. Back to the GUI where—as shown in figure 12.1—our task exists. SWEET! Sorry... we get excited when these things finally work.

Awesome. We feel like superheroes right now. But the point isn't that we got it done—the point is that we *figured out how* to get it done. And we really, truly did, too. When we sat down to write this chapter we deliberately picked a task we'd been told was possible but had never done before. You've seen every bit of exploration and error that went along with our learning and discovery process.

12.4   *Tips for teaching yourself*

Again, the real point of this book is to teach you to teach yourself—and that's what this chapter has tried to illustrate. Here are a few tips:

- Don't be afraid of the help, and be sure to read the examples. We say that over and over and over, and it's like nobody believes us. We still see students, right in front of us in classes, secretly going to Google to find examples. What's so scary about the help files? If you're willing to read someone's blog, why not give the examples in the help files a shot first?
- Pay attention. Every bit of information on the screen is potentially important—don't mentally skip over the stuff that you're not immediately looking for. That's easy to do, but don't. Instead, look at each thing, and try to figure out

what it's for, and what information you can derive from it. For example, when triggers were being created with an ID of 0, rather than each trigger getting a new, sequential ID number, we felt safe assuming that PowerShell wasn't storing those triggers in some list somewhere. That meant we'd need to pass the trigger from a parenthetical command, rather than creating it in one step and then retrieving it later.

- Don't be afraid to fail. Hopefully you've got a virtual machine you can play in—so use it. Students are constantly asking us questions like, "hey, if I do such-and-such, what will happen?" to which we've started replying, "no idea—try it." Experimentation is good. In a virtual machine, the worst that can happen is you have to roll back to a snapshot, right? So give it a whirl, whatever you're working on.

- If one thing doesn't work, don't bang your head against a wall with it—try something else. We got the time format wrong when we specified `0300`, and we were too lazy to read the examples to see what was correct. Rather than trying endless permutations—03:00, 03:00:00, and so on—we tried a different tack, putting in `'3:00 am'` as a string. It worked. Or do the smart thing and read the examples!

- We used our familiarity with the GUI Task Scheduler to intuit some things about the commands we ran, such as the `-Execute` switch. Don't let the fact that you're in a command-line shell erase your past experiences with Windows—try to think about how what you're doing now might relate to what you've done in the past.

Obviously, everything gets easier with time, patience, and practice—but be sure that you're *thinking* along the way.

12.5　Lab

> **NOTE**　For this lab, you'll need a Windows 8 or Windows Server 2012 computer running PowerShell v3.

Okay, now it's your turn. We're assuming that you're working in a virtual machine or other machine that it's okay to mess up a little in the name of learning. Please don't do this in a production environment on a mission-critical computer!

Windows 8 and Windows Server 2012 include a module for working with file shares. Your task is to create a directory called "LABS" on your computer and share it. For the sake of this exercise, you can assume the folder and share don't already exist. Don't worry about NTFS permissions, but make sure that the share permissions are set so that Everyone has read/write access, and local Administrators have full control. Because the share will be primarily for files, you want to set the share's caching mode for documents. Your script should output an object showing the new share and its permissions.

Remote control: one to one, and one to many

When we first started to use PowerShell (in version 1), we were playing around with the `Get-Service` command and noticed that it had a `-computerName` parameter. Hmmm... does that mean it can get services from other computers, too? After a bit of experimenting, we discovered that's exactly what it did. We were excited and started to look for `-computerName` parameters on other cmdlets. But we were disappointed to find there were only a few. With v2 a few more were added, but the number of commands that have this parameter are vastly outnumbered by the commands that don't.

What we've realized since that time is that PowerShell's creators are a bit lazy—and that's a good thing. Because they didn't want to have to code a `-computerName` parameter for every single cmdlet, they created a shell-wide system called *remoting*. This system enables you to run any cmdlet on a remote computer. In fact, you can even run commands that exist on the remote computer but that don't exist on your own computer—meaning you don't always have to install every single administrative cmdlet on your workstation. This remoting system is powerful, and it offers a number of interesting administrative capabilities.

> **NOTE** Remoting is a huge, complex technology. We'll introduce you to it in this chapter and cover usage scenarios that you'll deal with 80 to 90 percent of the time. But we can't cover it all, so in the "Further exploration" section at the end of this chapter, we'll point you to a must-have resource that covers remoting's configuration options.

13.1   *The idea behind remote PowerShell*

Remote PowerShell works somewhat similarly to Telnet and other age-old remote control technologies. When you run a command, it's running *on* the remote computer. Only the results of that command come back to your computer. But rather than using Telnet or SSH, PowerShell uses a new communications protocol called Web Services for Management (WS-MAN).

WS-MAN operates entirely over HTTP or HTTPS, making it easy to route through firewalls if necessary (because each of those protocols uses a single port to communicate). Microsoft's implementation of WS-MAN comes in the form of a background service, Windows Remote Management (WinRM). WinRM is installed along with PowerShell v2 and is started by default on server operating systems like Windows Server 2008 R2. It's installed on Windows 7 by default, but the service is disabled. It's also included with PowerShell v3, and it's enabled by default on Windows Server 2012.

You've already learned that Windows PowerShell cmdlets all produce objects as their output. When you run a remote command, its output objects need to be put into a form that can be easily transmitted over a network using the HTTP (or HTTPS) protocol. XML, it turns out, is an excellent way to do that, so PowerShell automatically *serializes* those output objects into XML. The XML is transmitted across the network and is then *deserialized* on your computer back into objects that you can work with inside PowerShell. Serialization and deserialization are really just a form of format conversion: one from objects to XML (serialization), and from XML to objects (deserialization).

Why should you care how this output is returned? Because those serialized-then-deserialized objects are only snapshots, of sorts; they don't update themselves continually. For example, if you were to get the objects that represent the processes running on a remote computer, what you'd get back would only be accurate for the exact point in time at which those objects were generated. Values like memory usage and CPU utilization won't be updated to reflect subsequent conditions. In addition, you can't tell the deserialized objects to do anything—you can't instruct one to stop itself, for example.

Those are basic limitations of remoting, but they don't stop you from doing some amazing stuff. In fact, you can tell a remote process to stop itself, but you have to be a bit clever about it. We'll show you how later in this chapter.

To make remoting work, you have two basic requirements:

- Both your computer and the one you want to send commands to must be running Windows PowerShell v2 or v3. Windows XP is the oldest version of Windows on which you can install PowerShell v2, so it's the oldest version of Windows that can participate in remoting.
- Ideally, both computers need to be members of the same domain, or of trusted/trusting domains. It's possible to get remoting to work outside of a domain, but it's tricky, and we won't be covering it in this chapter. To learn more about that scenario, open PowerShell and run `help about_remote _troubleshooting`.

TRY IT NOW We hope you'll be able to follow along with some of the examples in this chapter. To participate, you'll ideally have a second test computer (or a virtual machine) that's in the same Active Directory domain as the test computer you've been using up to this point. You can run any version of Windows on that second computer, provided you have PowerShell v2 or v3 installed. If you can't set up an additional computer or virtual machine, use "localhost" to create remoting connections to your current computer. You're still using remoting, but it isn't as exciting to be "remote controlling" the computer at which you're sitting.

13.2 *WinRM overview*

Let's talk a bit about WinRM, because you're going to have to configure it in order to use remoting. Once again, you only need to configure WinRM—and PowerShell remoting—on those computers that will *receive* incoming commands. In most of the environments we've worked in, the administrators have enabled remoting on every Windows-based computer (keep in mind that PowerShell and remoting are supported all the way back to Windows XP). Doing so gives you the ability to remote into client desktop and laptop computers in the background (meaning the users of those computers won't know you're doing so), which can be tremendously useful.

WinRM isn't unique to PowerShell. In fact, Microsoft is starting to use it for more and more administrative communications—even things that use other protocols today. With that in mind, Microsoft made WinRM able to route traffic to multiple administrative applications—not only PowerShell. WinRM acts as a dispatcher: when traffic comes in, WinRM decides which application needs to deal with that traffic. All WinRM traffic is tagged with the name of a recipient application, and those applications must register as *endpoints* with WinRM so that WinRM will listen for incoming traffic on their behalf. This means you'll not only need to enable WinRM, but you'll also need to tell PowerShell to register as an *endpoint* with WinRM. Figure 13.1 illustrates how the pieces fit together.

As shown, you can have dozens or even hundreds of WinRM endpoints on your system (PowerShell calls them *session configurations*). Each endpoint can point to a different application, and you can even have endpoints that point to the same application but provide different permissions and functionality. For example, you could create a PowerShell endpoint that only allowed one or two commands, and make it available to specific users in your environment. We won't be diving that deep into remoting in this chapter, but chapter 23 will.

Figure 13.1 also illustrates the WinRM *listener,* which in the figure is of the HTTP variety. A listener sits and waits for incoming network traffic on behalf of WinRM— kind of like a web server listening for incoming requests. A listener "listens" on a specific port, and on a specific IP address, although the default listener created by Enable-PSRemoting listens on *all* local IP addresses.

The listener connects to the defined endpoint. One way to create an endpoint is to open a copy of PowerShell—making sure that you're running it as an Administrator—

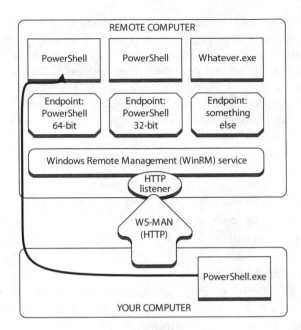

Figure 13.1 The relationship between WinRM, WS-MAN, endpoints, and PowerShell

and run the `Enable-PSRemoting` cmdlet. You might sometimes see references to a different cmdlet, called `Set-WSManQuickConfig`. You don't need to run that one; `Enable-PSRemoting` will call it for you, and `Enable-PSRemoting` performs a few extra steps that are necessary to get remoting up and running. All told, the cmdlet will start the WinRM service, configure it to start automatically, register PowerShell as an endpoint, and even set up a Windows Firewall exception to permit incoming WinRM traffic.

> **TRY IT NOW** Go ahead and enable remoting on your second computer (or on the first one, if that's the only one you have to work with). Make sure you're running PowerShell as an administrator (it should say "Administrator" in the window's title bar). If you're not, close the shell, right-click the PowerShell icon in the Start menu, and select Run as Administrator from the context menu. If you receive an error message when you enable remoting, stop and figure it out. You won't be able to proceed until `Enable-PSRemoting` runs without error.

Figure 13.2 shows one of the most common errors you can get when you run `Enable-PSRemoting`.

The error in figure 13.2 typically only occurs on client computers, and the error message—once you dig into it—tells you exactly what the problem is. We've got at least one network adapter set to "Public." Remember that Windows Vista and later versions assign a network type—Work, Home, or Public—to each network adapter. Anything set to "Public" can't have Windows Firewall exceptions, so when `Enable-PSRemoting` tries to create one, it fails. The only solution is to go into Windows and modify the network adapter setting so that whatever network you're on is either "Work" or "Home." But

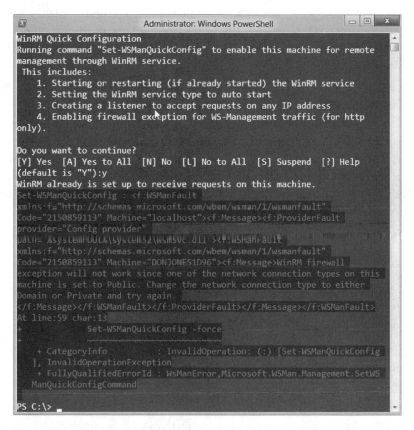

Figure 13.2 The most common error you'll get when you enable remoting on a client computer

don't do this if you're connected to a public network (like a public wireless hotspot), because you'll be turning off some valuable security protections.

NOTE You don't have to worry about this much on server operating systems, because they don't have the same restrictions in the OS.

If you're not excited about having to run around to every computer to enable remoting, don't worry: you can also do it with a Group Policy object (GPO), too. The necessary GPO settings are built into Windows Server 2008 R2 (and later) domain controllers (and you can download an ADM template from http://download.Microsoft.com to add these GPO settings to an older domain's domain controllers). Open a GPO and look under Computer Configuration > Administrative Templates > Windows Components. Near the bottom of the list, you'll find both Remote Shell and Windows Remote Management. For now, we'll assume you'll run `Enable-PSRemoting` on those computers that you want to configure, because at this point you're probably only playing around with a virtual machine or two.

NOTE   PowerShell's about_remote_troubleshooting help topic provides more coverage on using GPOs. Look for the "How to enable remoting in an enterprise" and "How to enable listeners by using a Group Policy" sections within that help topic.

WinRM v2 (which is what PowerShell v2 and v3 use) defaults to using TCP port 5985 for HTTP and 5986 for HTTPS. Those ports help to ensure it won't conflict with any locally installed web servers, which tend to listen to 80 and 443 instead. The default remoting setup created by Enable-PSRemoting only sets up the non-encrypted HTTP listener for port 5985. You can configure WinRM to use alternative ports, but we don't recommend doing so. If you leave those ports alone, all of PowerShell's remoting commands will run normally. If you change the ports, you'll have to always specify an alternative port when you run a remoting command, which means more typing for you.

  If you absolutely must change the port, you can do so by running this command:

```
Winrm set winrm/config/listener?Address=*+Transport=HTTP
➥@{Port="1234"}
```

In this example, "1234" is the port you want to use. Modify the command to use HTTPS instead of HTTP to set the new HTTPS port.

DON'T TRY IT NOW   Although you may want to change the port in your production environment, don't change it on your test computer. Leave WinRM using the default configuration so that the remainder of this book's examples will work for you without modification.

We should admit that there is a way to configure WinRM on client computers to use alternative default ports, which means you don't have to constantly specify an alternative port when you run commands. But for now let's stick with the defaults Microsoft came up with. We'll also note that you can create multiple listeners for WinRM—say, one for HTTP and one for encrypted HTTPS traffic, or others for different IP addresses. All of them will deliver traffic to whatever endpoints you've configured on the computer.

NOTE   If you do happen to browse around in the Group Policy object settings for Remote Shell, you'll notice you can specify how long a remoting session can sit idle before the server kills it, how many concurrent users can remote into a server at once, how much memory and how many processes each remote shell can use, how many remote shells a given user can open at once, and so on. These are all great ways to help ensure your servers don't get overly burdened by forgetful administrators. By default, however, you *do* have to be an Administrator to use remoting, so you don't need to worry about ordinary users clogging up your servers.

13.3 *Using Enter-PSSession and Exit-PSSession for one-to-one remoting*

PowerShell uses remoting in two distinct ways. The first is called *one-to-one*, or 1:1, remoting (the second is one-to-many, or 1:n, remoting, and you'll see it in the next section). With one-to-one remoting, you're accessing a shell prompt on a single remote computer. Any commands you run will run directly on that computer, and you'll see results in the shell window. This is vaguely similar to using Remote Desktop Connection, except that you're limited to the command-line environment of Windows PowerShell. This kind of remoting also uses a *fraction* of the resources that Remote Desktop requires, so it imposes much less overhead on your servers.

To establish a one-to-one connection with a remote computer, run the following command:

```
Enter-PSSession -computerName Server-R2
```

(You'll need to provide the correct computer name instead of `Server-R2`.)

Assuming you enabled remoting on your remote computer, and you're all in the same domain, and your network is functioning correctly, you should get a connection going. PowerShell lets you know that you've succeeded by changing the shell prompt:

```
[server-r2] PS C:\>
```

The shell prompt tells you that everything you're doing is taking place on Server-R2 (or whichever server you connected to). You can run whatever commands you like. You can even import any modules or add any PSSnapins that happen to reside on that remote computer.

> **TRY IT NOW** Go ahead and try to create a remoting connection to your second computer or virtual machine. If you haven't done so, you'll also need to enable remoting on that computer before you try to connect to it. Note that you're going to need to know the real computer name of the remote computer; WinRM won't, by default, permit you to connect by using its IP address or a DNS alias.

Your permissions and privileges carry over across the remote connection. Your copy of PowerShell will pass along whatever security token it's running under (it does this with Kerberos, so it doesn't pass your username or password across the network). Any command you run on the remote computer will run under your credentials, so you'll be able to do anything you'd normally have permission to do. It's as if you logged into that computer's console and used its copy of PowerShell directly.

Well, almost. Let's look at a couple of differences:

- Even if you have a PowerShell profile script on the remote computer, it won't run when you connect using remoting. We haven't fully covered profile scripts yet (they're in chapter 25), but suffice it to say, they're a batch of commands that run automatically each time you open the shell. Folks use them to automatically load shell extensions and modules and so forth. That doesn't happen when you remote into a computer, so be aware of that.

- You're still restricted by the remote computer's execution policy. Let's say your local computer's policy is set to RemoteSigned, which means you can run local, unsigned scripts. That's great, but if the remote computer's policy is set to the default, Restricted, it won't be running any scripts for you when you're remoting into it.

Aside from those two fairly minor caveats, you should be good to go. But wait—what do you do when you're finished running commands on the remote computer? Many PowerShell cmdlets come in pairs, with one cmdlet doing something and the other doing the opposite. In this case, if Enter-PSSession gets you *into* the remote computer, can you guess what would get you *out* of the remote computer? If you guessed Exit-PSSession, give yourself a prize. The command doesn't need any parameters; run it and your shell prompt will change back to normal, and the remote connection will close automatically.

> **TRY IT NOW** Go ahead and exit the remoting session, if you created one. We're done with it for now.

What if you forget to run Exit-PSSession and instead close the PowerShell window? Don't worry. PowerShell and WinRM are smart enough to figure out what you did, and the remote connection will close all by itself.

We do have one caution to offer. When you're remoting into a computer, don't run Enter-PSSession *from that computer* unless you fully understand what you're doing. Let's say you work on Computer A, which runs Windows 7, and you remote into Server-R2. Then, at the PowerShell prompt, you run this:

```
[server-r2] PS C:\>enter-pssession server-dc4
```

This causes Server-R2 to maintain an open connection to Server-DC4, which can start to create a "remoting chain" that's hard to keep track of, and which imposes unnecessary overhead on your servers. There may be times when you *have* to do this—we're thinking mainly of instances where a computer like Server-DC4 sits behind a firewall and you can't access it directly, so you use Server-R2 as a middleman to hop over to Server-DC4. But, as a general rule, try to avoid remote chaining.

> **CAUTION** Some people refer to "remote chaining" as "the second hop," and it's a major PowerShell "gotcha." We offer a hint: If the PowerShell prompt is displaying a computer name, then you're done. You can't issue any more remote control commands until you exit that session and "come back" to your computer. Enabling multi-hop remoting is something we'll discuss in chapter 23.

When you're using this one-to-one remoting, you don't need to worry about objects being serialized and deserialized. As far as you're concerned, you're typing directly on the remote computer's console. If you retrieve a process and pipe it to `Stop-Process`, it'll stop running, as you'd expect it to.

13.4 *Using Invoke-Command for one-to-many remoting*

The next trick—and honestly, this is one of the coolest things in Windows Power-Shell—is to send a command to *multiple remote computers at the same time*. That's right, full-scale distributed computing. Each computer will independently execute the command and send the results back to you. It's all done with the `Invoke-Command` cmdlet, and it's called *one-to-many*, or 1:n, remoting.

The command looks something like this:

```
Invoke-Command -computerName Server-R2,Server-DC4,Server12
-command { Get-EventLog Security -newest 200 |
Where { $_.EventID  eq 1212 }}
```

TRY IT NOW Go ahead and run this command. Substitute the name of your remote computer (or computers) where we put our three server names.

Everything in those outermost curly braces, the {}, will get transmitted to the remote computers—all three of them. By default, PowerShell will talk to up to 32 computers at once; if you specified more than that, it will queue them up, and as one computer completes, the next one in line will begin. If you have an awesome network and powerful computers, you could raise that number by specifying the `-throttleLimit` parameter of `Invoke-Command`—read the command's help for more information.

Be careful about the punctuation

We need to further consider the syntax for a one-to-many remoting example, because this is a case where PowerShell's punctuation can get confusing, and that confusion can make you do the wrong thing when you start constructing these command lines on your own.

Here's the example to consider:

```
Invoke-Command  -computerName Server-R2,Server-DC4,Server12
-command { Get-EventLog Security -newest 200 |
Where { $_.EventID -eq 1212 }}
```

There are two commands in this example that use curly braces: `Invoke-Command` and `Where` (which is an alias for `Where-Object`). `Where` is entirely nested within the outer set of braces. The outermost set of braces encloses everything that's being sent to the remote computers for execution:

```
Get-EventLog Security -newest 200 | Where { $_.EventID -eq 1212 }
```

It can be tough to follow that nesting of commands, particularly in a book like this one, where the physical width of the page makes it necessary to display the command across several lines of text.

Be sure you can identify the exact command that's being sent to the remote computer, and that you understand the use for each matched set of curly braces.

We should tell you that you won't see the -command parameter in the help for Invoke-Command, but the command we just showed you will work fine. The -command parameter is an *alias,* or nickname, for the -scriptblock parameter that you *will* see listed in the help. We have an easier time remembering -command, so we tend to use it instead of -scriptblock, but they both work the same way.

If you read the help for Invoke-Command carefully (see how we're continuing to push those help files?), you'll also notice a parameter that lets you specify a script file, rather than a command. That parameter lets you send an entire script from your local computer to the remote computers—meaning you can automate some complex tasks and have each computer do its own share of the work.

> **TRY IT NOW** Make sure you can identify the -scriptblock parameter in the help for Invoke-Command, and that you can spot the parameter that would enable you to specify a file path and name instead of a script block.

We want to circle back to the -computerName parameter we mentioned at the beginning of the chapter for a bit. When we first used Invoke-Command, we typed a comma-separated list of computer names, as we did in the previous example. But we work with a lot of computers, and we don't want to have to type them all in every time. We keep text files for some of our common computer categories, like web servers and domain controllers. Each text file contains one computer name per line, and that's it—no commas, no quotes, no nothing. PowerShell makes it easy for us to use those files:

```
Invoke-Command -command { dir }
➥-computerName (Get-Content webservers.txt)
```

The parentheses here force PowerShell to execute Get-Content first—the same way parentheses work in math. The results of Get-Command are then stuck into the -computerName parameter, which works against each of the computers listed in the file.

We also sometimes want to query computer names from Active Directory, which is a bit trickier. We can use the Get-ADComputer command (from the ActiveDirectory module; it's available in the Windows 7 Remote Server Administration Tools and on Windows Server 2008 R2 and later domain controllers) to retrieve computers, but we can't stick that command in parentheses as we did with Get-Content. Why not? Because Get-Content produces simple strings of text, which -computerName is expecting. Get-ADComputer, on the other hand, produces entire computer objects, and the -computerName parameter won't know what to do with them.

If we want to use Get-ADComputer, we need to find a way to get only the *values* from those computer objects' Name properties. We'll show you how in the following example:

```
Invoke-Command -command { dir } -computerName (
➥Get-ADComputer -filter * -searchBase "ou=Sales,dc=company,dc=pri" |
➥Select-Object -expand Name )
```

> **TRY IT NOW** If you're running PowerShell on a Windows Server 2008 R2 domain controller, or on a Windows 7 computer that has the Remote Server Administration Tools installed, you can run Import-Module ActiveDirectory

and try the preceding command. If your test domain doesn't have a Sales OU that contains a computer account, then change `ou=Sales` to `ou=Domain Controllers`, and be sure to change `company` and `pri` to the appropriate values for your domain (for example, if your domain is mycompany.org, you'd substitute `mycompany` for `company` and `org` for `pri`).

Within the parentheses, we've piped the computer objects to `Select-Object`, and we've used its `-expand` parameter. We're telling it to expand the `Name` property of whatever came in—in this case, those computer objects. The result of that entire parenthetical expression will be a bunch of computer names, not computer objects—and computer names are exactly what the `-computerName` parameter wants to see.

> **NOTE**   We hope the previous discussion of the `-Expand` parameter triggered some déjà vu: You first saw that parameter in chapter 9. If you need to, flip back to that chapter for a refresher.

To be thorough, we should mention that the `-filter` parameter of `Get-ADComputer` specifies that all computers should be included in the command's output. The `-searchBase` parameter tells the command to start looking for computers in the specified location—in this case, the Sales OU of the company.pri domain. Again, the `Get-ADComputer` command is available only on Windows Server 2008 R2 (and later) domain controllers, and on Windows 7 (and later) client computers where you've installed the Remote Server Administration Tools (RSAT).

13.5   *Differences between remote and local commands*

We want to explain a bit about the differences between running commands using `Invoke-Command` and running those same commands locally, as well as the differences between remoting and other forms of remote connectivity. For this discussion, we'll use this command as our example:

```
Invoke-Command -computerName Server-R2,Server-DC4,Server12
➥-command { Get-EventLog Security -newest 200 |
➥Where { $_.EventID -eq 1212 }}
```

Let's look at some alternatives and see why they're different.

13.5.1 *Invoke-Command versus -ComputerName*

Here's an alternative way to perform that same basic task:

```
Get-EventLog Security -newest 200
➥-computerName Server-R2,Server-DC4,Server12
➥| Where { $_.EventID -eq 1212 }
```

In the previous example, we used the `-computerName` parameter of `Get-EventLog`, rather than invoking the entire command remotely. We'll get more or less the same results, but there are some important differences in how this version of the command executes:

- The computers will be contacted sequentially rather than in parallel, which means the command may take longer to execute.
- The output won't include a PSComputerName property, which may make it harder for us to tell which result came from which computer.
- The connection won't be made using WinRM, but will instead use whatever underlying protocol the .NET Framework decides to use. We don't know what that is, and it might be harder to get the connection through any firewalls between us and the remote computer.
- We're querying 200 records from each of the three computers, and only then are we filtering through them to find the ones with EventID 1212. That means we're probably bringing over a lot of records we don't want.
- We're getting back event log objects that are fully functional.

These differences apply to any cmdlet that has a -computerName parameter. Generally speaking, it can be more efficient and effective to use Invoke-Command rather than a cmdlet's -computerName parameter.

Here's what would have happened if we'd used the original Invoke-Command instead:

- The computers would have been contacted in parallel, meaning the command could complete somewhat more quickly.
- Thc output would have included a PSComputerName property, enabling us to more easily distinguish the output from each computer.
- The connection would have been made through WinRM, which uses a single predefined port that can make it easier to get through any intervening firewalls.
- Each computer would have queried the 200 records and filtered them *locally*. The only data transmitted across the network would have been the result of that filtering, meaning that only the records we cared about would have been transmitted.
- Before transmitting, each computer would have serialized its output into XML. Our computer would have received that XML and deserialized it back into something that looks like objects. But they wouldn't have been real event log objects, and that might limit what we could do with them once they were on our computer.

That last point is a big distinction between using a -computerName parameter and using Invoke-Command. Let's discuss that distinction.

13.5.2 *Local versus remote processing*

We'll cite our original example again:

```
Invoke-Command -computerName Server-R2,Server-DC4,Server12
➥-command { Get-EventLog Security -newest 200 |
➥Where { $_.EventID -eq 1212 }}
```

Now, compare it to this alternative:

```
Invoke-Command -computerName Server-R2,Server-DC4,Server12
➥-command { Get-EventLog Security -newest 200 } |
➥Where { $_.EventID -eq 1212 }
```

The differences are subtle. Well, we see only one difference: we moved one of those curly braces.

In the second version, only `Get-EventLog` is being invoked remotely. All of the results generated by `Get-EventLog` will be serialized and sent to our computer, where they'll be deserialized into objects and then piped to `Where` and filtered. The second version of the command is less efficient, because a lot of unnecessary data is being transmitted across the network, and our one computer has to filter the results from three computers, rather than those three computers filtering their own results for us. The second version, then, is a bad idea.

Let's look at two versions of another command, starting with the following:

```
Invoke-Command -computerName Server-R2
➥-command { Get-Process -name Notepad } |
➥Stop-Process
```

Now let's look at the second version:

```
Invoke-Command -computerName Server-R2
➥-command { Get-Process -name Notepad |
➥Stop-Process }
```

Once again, the only difference between these two is the placement of a curly brace. But in this example, the first version of the command won't work.

Look carefully: we're sending `Get-Process -name Notepad` to the remote computer. The remote computer retrieves the specified process, serializes it into XML, and sends it to us across the network. Our computer receives that XML, deserializes it back into an object, and pipes it to `Stop-Process`. The problem is that the deserialized XML doesn't contain enough information for our computer to realize that the process came from a *remote machine.* Instead, our computer will try to stop the Notepad process *running locally,* which isn't what we want at all.

The moral of the story is to always complete as much of your processing on the remote computer as possible. The only thing you should expect to do with the results of `Invoke-Command` is to display them or store them as a report, or a data file, or so forth. The second version of our command follows that advice: what's being sent to the remote computer is `Get-Process -name Notepad | Stop-Process`, so the entire command—both getting the process and stopping it—happens on the remote computer. Because `Stop-Process` doesn't normally produce any output, there won't be any objects to serialize and send to us, so we won't see anything on our local console. But the command will do what we want: stop the Notepad process *on the remote computer,* not on our local machine.

Whenever we use `Invoke-Command`, we always look at the commands after it. If we see commands for formatting, or for exporting data, we're fine, because it's OK to do those things with the results of Invoke-Command. But if Invoke-Command is followed by action cmdlets—ones that start, stop, set, change, or do something else—then we sit back and try to think about what we're doing. Ideally, we want all of those actions to happen on the remote computer, not on our local computer.

13.5.3 *Deserialized objects*

Another caveat to keep in mind about remoting is that the objects that come back to your computer aren't fully functional. In most cases, they lack methods, because they're no longer "attached" to "live" software.

 For example, run this on your local computer and you'll notice that a Service-Controller object has numerous methods associated with it:

```
PS C:\> get-service | get-member

    TypeName: System.ServiceProcess.ServiceController

Name                       MemberType    Definition
----                       ----------    ----------
Name                       AliasProperty Name = ServiceName
RequiredServices           AliasProperty RequiredServices = ServicesDep
Disposed                   Event         System.EventHandler Disposed(S
Close                      Method        System.Void Close()
Continue                   Method        System.Void Continue()
CreateObjRef               Method        System.Runtime.Remoting.ObjRef
Dispose                    Method        System.Void Dispose()
Equals                     Method        bool Equals(System.Object obj)
ExecuteCommand             Method        System.Void ExecuteCommand(int
GetHashCode                Method        int GetHashCode()
GetLifetimeService         Method        System.Object GetLifetimeServi
GetType                    Method        type GetType()
InitializeLifetimeService  Method        System.Object InitializeLifeti
Pause                      Method        System.Void Pause()
Refresh                    Method        System.Void Refresh()
Start                      Method        System.Void Start(), System.Vo
Stop                       Method        System.Void Stop()
WaitForStatus              Method        System.Void WaitForStatus(Syst
CanPauseAndContinue        Property      bool CanPauseAndContinue {get;
CanShutdown                Property      bool CanShutdown {get;}
CanStop                    Property      bool CanStop {get;}
Container                  Property      System.ComponentModel.IContain
DependentServices          Property      System.ServiceProcess.ServiceC
```

Now get some of those same objects via remoting:

```
PS C:\> Invoke-Command -ScriptBlock { Get-Service } -ComputerName
    DONJONESE408 | Get-Member

    TypeName: Deserialized.System.ServiceProcess.ServiceController

Name        MemberType    Definition
----        ----------    ----------
ToString    Method        string ToString(), string ToString(string
    format, System.I
Name        NoteProperty  System.String Name=AeLookupSvc
```

```
PSComputerName          NoteProperty System.String PSComputerName=DONJONESE408
PSShowComputerName      NoteProperty System.Boolean PSShowComputerName=True
RequiredServices        NoteProperty
     Deserialized.System.ServiceProcess.ServiceController[] Req
RunspaceId              NoteProperty System.Guid RunspaceId=6dc9e130-f7b2-4db4-
     8b0d-3863033d7df
CanPauseAndContinue Property      System.Boolean {get;set;}
CanShutdown         Property      System.Boolean {get;set;}
CanStop             Property      System.Boolean {get;set;}
Container           Property       {get;set;}
DependentServices   Property
     Deserialized.System.ServiceProcess.ServiceController[] {ge
DisplayName         Property      System.String {get;set;}
MachineName         Property      System.String {get;set;}
ServiceHandle       Property      System.String {get;set;}
ServiceName         Property      System.String {get;set;}
ServicesDependedOn  Property
     Deserialized.System.ServiceProcess.ServiceController[] {ge
ServiceType         Property      System.String {get;set;}
Site                Property       {get;set;}
Status              Property      System.String {get;set;}
```

The methods—except the universal `ToString()` method common to all objects—are gone. This is a read-only copy of the object; you can't tell it to do things like stop, pause, resume, and so forth. So any actions you want taken as the result of your command should be included in the script block that's sent to the remote computer; that way, the objects are still live and contain all of their methods.

13.6 But wait, there's more

The previous examples have all used ad hoc remoting connections, meaning that we specified computer names. If you're going to be reconnecting to the same computer (or computers) several times within a short period of time, you can create reusable, persistent connections to use instead. We'll cover that technique in chapter 20.

   We should also acknowledge that not every company is going to allow PowerShell remoting to be enabled—at least, not right away. Companies with extremely restrictive security policies may, for example, have firewalls on all client and server computers, which would block the remoting connection. If your company is one of those, see if an exception is in place for Remote Desktop Protocol (RDP). We find that's a common exception, because administrators obviously need some remote connectivity to servers. If RDP is allowed, try to make a case for PowerShell remoting. Because remoting connections can be audited (they look like network logins, much like accessing a file share would appear in the audit log), they're locked down by default to only permit Administrators to connect. It's not that different from RDP in terms of security risks, and it imposes much less overhead on the remote machines than RDP does.

13.7   *Remote options*

Read their help files, and you'll notice that both `Invoke-Command` and `Enter-PSSession` have a `-SessionOption` parameter, which accepts a `<PSSessionOption>` object. What's that all about?

As we just explained, both of those commands initiate a new PowerShell connection, or *session*, when they run. They do their thing, and then close that session automatically for you. A *session option* is a set of options that you can specify to change the way the session is created. The `New-PSSessionOption` command does the magic. Among other things, you can use it to specify the following:

- Open, cancellation, and idle timeouts
- Elimination of the normal data stream compression or encryption
- Various proxy-related options, for when the traffic is passing through a proxy server
- Skips of the remote machine's SSL certificate, name, and other security features

For example, here's how you could open a session and skip the machine name check:

```
PS C:\> Enter-PSSession -ComputerName DONJONESE408
➥-SessionOption (New-PSSessionOption -SkipCNCheck)
[DONJONESE408]: PS C:\Users\donjones\Documents>
```

Review the help for `New-PSSessionOption` to see what it can do for you; in chapter 20 we'll be using a few of those options to accomplish some advanced remoting tasks.

13.8   *Common points of confusion*

Whenever we start using remoting in a class we're teaching, we've found some common problems that will crop up over the course of the day:

- Remoting only works, by default, with the remote computer's real computer name. You can't use DNS aliases or IP addresses. In chapter 23, we'll discuss some of the background behind this limitation and show you how to work around it.
- Remoting is designed to be more or less automatically configuring within a domain. If every computer involved, and your user account, all belong to the same domain (or trusting domains), things will typically work great. If not, you'll need to run `help about_remote_troubleshooting` and dig into the details. One area where you might have to do this is if you're remoting across domains. You may have to do a tiny bit of configuration in order for that to work, and the help file describes it in detail.
- When you invoke a command, you're asking the remote computer to launch PowerShell, run your command, and then close PowerShell. The next command you invoke on that same remote computer will be starting from scratch—anything that was run in the first invocation will no longer be in effect. If you

need to run a whole series of related commands, put them all into the same invocation.

- Make absolutely certain that you're running PowerShell as an administrator, particularly if your computer has User Account Control (UAC) enabled. If the account you're using doesn't have Administrator permissions on the remote computer, use the -credential parameter of Enter-PSSession or Invoke-Command to specify an alternative account that does have Administrator permissions.

- If you're using a local firewall product other than the Windows Firewall, Enable-PSRemoting won't set up the necessary firewall exceptions. You'll need to do it manually. If your remoting connection will need to traverse a regular firewall, such as one implemented on a router or proxy, it'll also need a manually entered exception for the remoting traffic.

- Don't forget that any settings in a Group Policy object (GPO) override anything you configure locally. We've seen administrators struggle for hours to get remoting to work, only to finally discover that a GPO was overriding everything they did. In some cases, a well-meaning colleague may have put GPO into place a long time ago and forgotten it was there. Don't assume that there's no GPO affecting you; check and see for sure.

13.9 Lab

NOTE For this lab, you'll need any computer running PowerShell v3. Ideally, you'll want to have two computers that are each members of the same Active Directory domain, but if you have only one computer to test with, that's fine.

It's time to combine some of what you've learned about remoting with what you've learned in previous chapters. See if you can accomplish the following tasks:

1 Make a one-to-one connection with a remote computer (or with "localhost" if you only have one computer). Launch Notepad.exe. What happens?

2 Using Invoke-Command, retrieve a list of services that aren't started from one or two remote computers (it's OK to use "localhost" twice if you only have one computer). Format the results as a wide list. (Hint: it's OK to retrieve results and have the formatting occur on your computer—don't include the Format- cmdlets in the commands that are invoked remotely.)

3 Use Invoke-Command to get a list of the top ten processes for virtual memory (VM) usage. Target one or two remote computers, if you can; if you only have one computer, target "localhost" twice.

4 Create a text file that contains three computer names, with one name per line. It's OK to use the same computer name, or "localhost," three times if you only have access to one remote computer. Then use Invoke-Command to retrieve the 100 newest Application event log entries from the computer names listed in that file.

13.10 *Further exploration*

We could cover a lot more about remoting in PowerShell—enough that you'd be reading about it for *another* month of lunches. Unfortunately, some of its trickier bits aren't well documented. We suggest heading up to http://PowerShellBooks.com, where Don and fellow MVP Dr. Tobias Weltner have put together a comprehensive (and free!) *Secrets of PowerShell Remoting* mini ebook for you. The guide rehashes some of the basics you learned in this chapter, but it primarily focuses on detailed, step-by-step directions (with color screenshots) that show how to configure a variety of remoting scenarios. The guide is updated periodically, so you'll want to check back every few months to make sure you've got the latest edition. Don't forget that you can also reach Don with your questions at http://bit.ly/AskDon.

Using Windows Management Instrumentation

We've been looking forward to writing this chapter, and dreading it at the same time. Windows Management Instrumentation (WMI) is probably one of the best things Microsoft has ever offered to administrators. At the same time, it's also one of the worst things the company has ever inflicted on us. WMI offers a way to gather an amazing amount of system information from a computer. But it can sometimes feel arcane, and the documentation is far from user friendly. In this chapter, we'll introduce you to WMI the PowerShell way, showing you how it works and explaining some of its less-beautiful aspects, to provide you with full disclosure on what you're up against.

We want to emphasize that WMI is an external technology; PowerShell merely interfaces with it. The focus in this chapter will be on how PowerShell does that, and not on the underlying guts of WMI itself. If you'd like to explore WMI further, we'll offer some suggestions at the end of this chapter. Keep in mind that Power-Shell v3 has made some amazing strides in minimizing how much you have to touch WMI yourself, which greatly improves the situation.

14.1 *WMI essentials*

A typical Windows computer will contain tens of thousands of pieces of management information, and WMI seeks to organize that into something that's approachable and more or less sensible.

At the top level, WMI is organized into *namespaces*. Think of a namespace as a sort of folder that ties to a specific product or technology. For example, the root\CIMv2 namespace contains all of the Windows operating system and computer hardware information; the root\MicrosoftDNS namespace includes all of the information about DNS Server (assuming you've installed that role on your computer). On client computers, root\SecurityCenter contains information about firewall, antivirus, and antispyware utilities.

> **NOTE** The contents of root\SecurityCenter will differ depending on what's installed on your computer, and newer versions of Windows use root\SecurityCenter2 instead, which is one example of how confusing WMI can be.

Figure 14.1 shows some of the namespaces on our computer—we generated this by using the WMI Control snap-in for the Microsoft Management Console (MMC).

Within a namespace, WMI is divided into a series of *classes*. A class represents a management component that WMI knows how to query. For example, the Antivirus-Product class in root\SecurityCenter is designed to hold information about antispyware products; the Win32_LogicalDisk class in root\CIMv2 is designed to hold information about logical disks. But even though a class exists on a computer doesn't mean that the computer has any of those components: the Win32_TapeDrive class is present on all versions of Windows, whether or not a tape drive is installed.

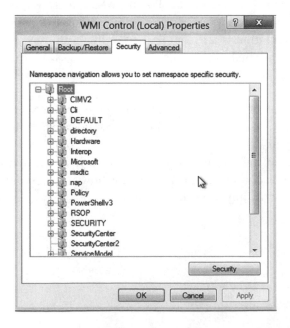

Figure 14.1 Browsing the WMI namespaces

NOTE Once again, not every computer contains the same WMI namespaces or classes. For example, newer Windows computers have a `Root\SecurityCenter2` namespace in addition to the `Root\SecurityCenter` namespace; the former, on newer computers, contains all the good stuff.

Let's look at a quick example of querying the `AntiSpywareProduct` from `root\SecurityCenter2` so you can see the instance that's returned:

```
PS C:\> Get-CimInstance -Namespace root\securitycenter2 -ClassName antispyw
areproduct
```

NOTE This example requires PowerShell v3, and we'll explain the `Get-CimInstance` command in just a bit.

When you have one or more manageable components, you'll have an equal number of *instances* for that class. An instance is a real-world occurrence of something represented by a class. If your computer has a single BIOS (and they all do), you'll have 1 instance of `Win32_BIOS` in `root\CIMv2`; if your computer has 100 background services installed, you'll have 100 instances of `Win32_Service`. Note that the class names in `root\CIMv2` tend to start with either `Win32_` (even on 64-bit machines) or `CIM_` (which stands for Common Information Model, the standard upon which WMI is built). In other namespaces, those class name prefixes aren't usually used. Also, it's possible for class names to be duplicated across namespaces. It's rare, but WMI allows for it, because each namespace acts as a kind of container and boundary. When you're referring to a class, you'll also have to refer to its namespace, so that WMI knows where to look for the class and so that it doesn't get confused between two classes that have the same name but live in different namespaces.

All of these instances and classes and whatnot live in something called the *WMI repository*. In older versions of Windows, the repository could sometimes become corrupted and unusable and you would have to rebuild it; that's less common since Windows 7.

On the surface, using WMI seems fairly simple: you figure out which class contains the information you want, query that class's instances from WMI, and then examine the instances' properties to see the management information. In some cases, you may ask an instance to execute a method in order to initiate an action or start a configuration change.

14.2 *The bad news about WMI*

Unfortunately, for most of its life (the situation has recently changed), Microsoft didn't exercise a lot of internal control over WMI. The company established a set of programming standards, but the product groups were more or less left to their own devices for how to implement classes and whether or not to document them. The result is that WMI can be a confusing mishmash.

Within the `root\CIMv2` namespace, for example, few classes have any methods that allow you to change configuration settings. Properties are read-only, meaning that you must have a method to make changes; if a method doesn't exist, you can't use WMI to make changes for that class. When the IIS team adopted WMI (for IIS version 6), they implemented parallel classes for a lot of elements. A website, for example, could be represented by one class that had the typical read-only properties, but also by a second class that had writable properties you could change. Confusing—and this confusion was made worse by the lack of good documentation on how to use those classes, because the IIS team originally intended them to be used mainly by their own tools, not directly by administrators. The IIS team has since backed away from WMI as a management interface, and since v7.5 has focused on PowerShell cmdlets and a PSProvider instead.

Microsoft doesn't have a rule that says a product *has* to use WMI, or that if it does use WMI it must expose every possible component through WMI. Microsoft's DHCP server is inaccessible to WMI, as is its old WINS server. Although you can query the configuration of a network adapter, you can't retrieve its link speed, because that information isn't supplied. Although most of the `Win32_` classes are well documented, few of the classes in other namespaces are documented at all. WMI isn't searchable, so the process of finding the class you need can be time-consuming and frustrating (although we'll try to help with that in the next section).

The good news is that Microsoft is making an effort to provide PowerShell cmdlets for as many administration tasks as possible. For example, WMI used to be the only practical way to programmatically restart a remote computer, using a method of the `Win32_OperatingSystem` class. Now, PowerShell provides a `Restart-Computer` cmdlet. In some cases, cmdlets will use WMI internally, but you won't have to deal with WMI directly in those cases. Cmdlets can provide a more consistent interface for you, and they're almost always better documented. WMI isn't going away, but over time you'll probably have to deal with it—and its eccentricities—a lot less.

In fact, in PowerShell v3 (particularly on the newest versions of Windows) you'll notice a lot of "CIM" commands, as shown in figure 14.2 (which is the partial output of `Get-Command`). In most cases, these are "wrappers" around some piece of WMI, giving you a more PowerShell-centric way of interacting with WMI. You use these as you would any command, including asking for help, which makes them more consistent with the rest of PowerShell and helps to hide some of the underlying WMI eccentricities.

14.3 *Exploring WMI*

Perhaps the easiest way to get started with WMI is to put PowerShell aside for a second and explore WMI on its own. We use a free WMI Explorer tool available from SAPIEN Technologies (http://www.sapien.com/downloads; free registration required). We locate most of what we need in WMI with this tool. It does require a lot of browsing and patience—we're not pretending this is a perfect process—but it eventually gets us there.

You don't need to install the tool, which means you can easily copy it to a USB flash drive and carry it to whatever computer you're using. Because each computer can have different WMI namespaces and classes, you'll want to run the tool directly on whatever computer you're planning to query, so that you can see that computer's WMI repository.

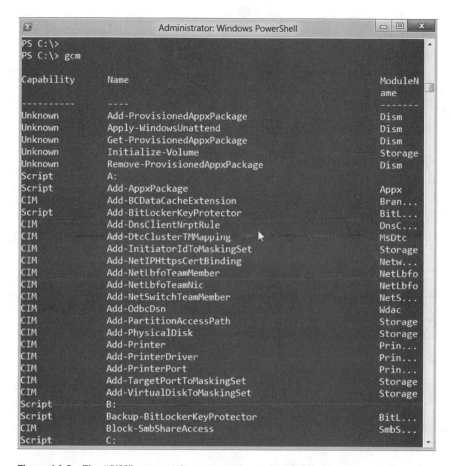

Figure 14.2 The "CIM" commands are wrappers around WMI classes.

Let's say we needed to query a bunch of client computers to see what their icon spacing is set to. That's a task related to the Windows desktop, and it's a core part of the operating system, so we started in the root\CIMV2 class, shown in the tree view on the left side of the WMI Explorer (see figure 14.3). Clicking the namespace brings up a list of its classes in the right side, and we took a guess on "Desktop" as a keyword. Scrolling to the right, we eventually found Win32_Desktop and clicked on that. Doing so enables the details pane at the bottom, and we clicked on the Properties tab to see what was available. About a third of the way down, we found IconSpacing, which is listed as an integer.

Obviously, search engines are another good way to find the class you want. We tend to prefix queries with "wmi," as in "wmi icon spacing," and that will often pull up an example or two that can point us in the right direction. The example might be VBScript-related, or might even be in a .NET language like C# or Visual Basic, but that's OK because we're only after the WMI class name. For example, we searched for

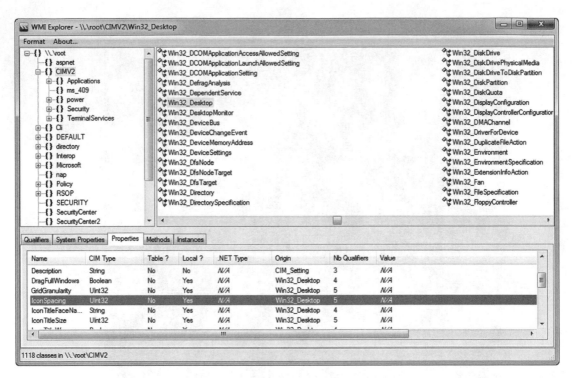

Figure 14.3   WMI Explorer

"wmi icon spacing" and turned up http://stackoverflow.com/questions/202971/formula-or-api-for-calulating-desktop-icon-spacing-on-windows-xp as the first result. On that page we found some C# code:

```
ManagementObjectSearcher searcher = new
    ManagementObjectSearcher("root\\CIMV2","SELECT * FROM Win32_Desktop");
```

We've no idea what any of that means, but `Win32_Desktop` looks like a WMI class name. Our next search will be for that class name, because such a search will often turn up whatever documentation exists. We'll cover the documentation a bit later in this chapter.

Another approach is to use PowerShell itself. For example, suppose we wanted to do something with disks. We'll start by guessing at the right namespace, but we happen to know that `root\CIMv2` contains all of the core OS and hardware stuff, so we'll run this command:

```
PS C:\> Get-WmiObject -Namespace root\CIMv2 -list | where name -like '*dis
*'

   NameSpace: ROOT\CIMv2

Name                              Methods                Properties
----                              -------                ----------
CIM_LogicalDisk                   {SetPowerState, R...   {Access, Avail...
Win32_LogicalDisk                 {SetPowerState, R...   {Access, Avail...
Win32_MappedLogicalDisk           {SetPowerState, R...   {Access, Avail...
CIM_DiskPartition                 {SetPowerState, R...   {Access, Avail...
```

```
Win32_DiskPartition                 {SetPowerState, R...  {Access, Avail...
CIM_DiskDrive                       {SetPowerState, R...  {Availability,...
Win32_DiskDrive                     {SetPowerState, R...  {Availability,...
CIM_DisketteDrive                   {SetPowerState, R...  {Availability,...
CIM_DiskSpaceCheck                  {Invoke}              {AvailableDisk...
Win32_LogicalDiskRootDirectory      {}                    {GroupComponen...
Win32_DiskQuota                     {}                    {DiskSpaceUsed...
Win32_LogonSessionMappedDisk        {}                    {Antecedent, D...
CIM_LogicalDiskBasedOnPartition     {}                    {Antecedent, D...
Win32_LogicalDiskToPartition        {}                    {Antecedent, D...
CIM_LogicalDiskBasedOnVolumeSet     {}                    {Antecedent, D...
Win32_DiskDrivePhysicalMedia        {}                    {Antecedent, D...
CIM_RealizesDiskPartition           {}                    {Antecedent, D...
Win32_DiskDriveToDiskPartition      {}                    {Antecedent, D...
Win32_OfflineFilesDiskSpaceLimit    {}                    {AutoCacheSize...
Win32_PerfFormattedData_Counters... {}                    {Caption, Desc...
Win32_PerfRawData_Counters_FileS... {}                    {Caption, Desc...
Win32_PerfFormattedData_PerfDisk... {}                    {AvgDiskBytesP...
```

Eventually, we find Win32_LogicalDisk.

> **NOTE** The classes whose names start with CIM_ are often "base" classes, and you don't use them directly. The Win32_ versions of the classes are Windows-specific. Also note that the Win32_ prefix is used only in this particular namespace—other namespaces don't prefix class names that way.

14.4 *Choose your weapon: WMI or CIM*

In PowerShell v3, you have two ways to interact with WMI:

- *The so-called "WMI cmdlets,"* such as Get-WmiObject *and* Invoke-WmiMethod— These are legacy cmdlets, meaning they still work, but Microsoft isn't investing in further development of them. They communicate over remote procedure calls (RPCs), which can only pass through a firewall if that firewall supports stateful inspection (in other words, it's hard).
- *The new "CIM cmdlets,"* such as Get-CimInstance *and* Invoke-CimMethod—These are more or less equivalent to the old "WMI cmdlets," although they communicate over WS-MAN (implemented by the Windows Remote Management service) instead of using RPCs. This is Microsoft's way forward, and running Get-Command -noun CIM* reveals that Microsoft offers a lot more functionality through these commands.

Make no mistake: all of these commands use the same WMI back end. The main difference is in how they communicate, and in how you use them. On older systems that don't have PowerShell installed, or that don't have Windows Remote Management enabled, the WMI cmdlets will often still work (the technology was introduced for Windows NT 4.0 SP3 and later). For newer systems where PowerShell is installed and Windows Remote Management is enabled, the CIM cmdlets provide the best experience—and are where Microsoft will continue building functionality and making performance improvements.

14.5 *Using Get-WmiObject*

With the `Get-WmiObject` cmdlet, you can specify a namespace, a class name, and even the name of a remote computer—and alternative credentials, if needed—to retrieve all instances of that class from the computer specified.

You can even provide filter criteria if you want fewer than all of the instances of the class. You can get a list of classes from a namespace. Here's the syntax:

```
Get-WmiObject -namespace root\cimv2 -list
```

Note that namespace names use a backslash, not a forward slash.

To retrieve a class, specify the namespace and class name:

```
Get-WmiObject -namespace root\cimv2 -class win32_desktop
```

The `root\CIMv2` namespace is the system default namespace on Windows XP Service Pack 2 and later, so if your class is in that namespace, you don't need to specify it. Also, the `-class` parameter is positional, so if you provide the class name in the first position, the cmdlet works the same.

Here are two examples, including one that uses the `Gwmi` alias instead of the full cmdlet name:

```
PS C:\> Get-WmiObject win32_desktop
PS C:\> gwmi antispywareproduct -namespace root\securitycenter2
```

> **TRY IT NOW** You should start following along at this point, running each of the commands we show you. For commands that include a remote computer name, you can substitute `localhost` if you don't have another remote computer that you can test against.

For many WMI classes, PowerShell has configuration defaults that specify which properties are shown. `Win32_OperatingSystem` is a good example because it only displays six of its properties, in a list, by default. Keep in mind that you can always pipe the WMI objects to `Gm` or to `Format-List *` to see all of the available properties; `Gm` will also list available methods. Here's an example:

```
PS C:\> Get-WmiObject win32_operatingsystem | gm


   TypeName: System.Management.ManagementObject#root\cimv2\Win32_Operating
System

Name                            MemberType   Definition
----                            ----------   ----------
Reboot                          Method       System.Managemen...
SetDateTime                     Method       System.Managemen...
Shutdown                        Method       System.Managemen...
Win32Shutdown                   Method       System.Managemen...
Win32ShutdownTracker            Method       System.Managemen...
BootDevice                      Property     System.String Bo...
BuildNumber                     Property     System.String Bu...
BuildType                       Property     System.String Bu...
Caption                         Property     System.String Ca...
CodeSet                         Property     System.String Co...
```

```
CountryCode                                 Property    System.String Co...
CreationClassName                           Property    System.String Cr...
```

We've truncated this output to save space, but you'll see the whole thing if you run the same command.

The `-filter` parameter lets you specify criteria for retrieving specific instances. This can be a bit tricky to use, so here's an example of its worst-case use:

```
PS C:\> gwmi -class win32_desktop -filter "name='COMPANY\\Administrator'"

__GENUS                 : 2
__CLASS                 : Win32_Desktop
__SUPERCLASS            : CIM_Setting
__DYNASTY               : CIM_Setting
__RELPATH               : Win32_Desktop.Name="COMPANY\\Administrator"
__PROPERTY_COUNT        : 21
__DERIVATION            : {CIM_Setting}
__SERVER                : SERVER-R2
__NAMESPACE             : root\cimv2
__PATH                  : \\SERVER-R2\root\cimv2:Win32_Desktop.Name="COMPANY
                          \\Administrator"
BorderWidth             : 1
Caption                 :
CoolSwitch              :
CursorBlinkRate         : 530
Description             :
DragFullWindows         : False
GridGranularity         :
IconSpacing             : 43
IconTitleFaceName       : Tahoma
IconTitleSize           : 8
IconTitleWrap           : True
Name                    : COMPANY\Administrator
Pattern                 : 0
ScreenSaverActive       : False
ScreenSaverExecutable   :
ScreenSaverSecure       :
ScreenSaverTimeout      :
SettingID               :
Wallpaper               :
WallpaperStretched      : True
WallpaperTiled          : False
```

There are some things you should notice about this command and its output:

- The filter criteria are usually enclosed in double quotation marks.
- The filter comparison operators aren't the normal PowerShell `-eq` or `-like` operators. Instead, WMI uses more traditional, programming-like operators, such as =, >, <, <=, >=, and <>. You can use the keyword LIKE as an operator, and when you do your comparison value you have to use % as a character wildcard, as in `"NAME LIKE '%administrator%'"`. Note that you can't use * as a wildcard, as you can elsewhere in PowerShell.

- String comparison values are enclosed in single quotation marks, which is why the outermost quotes that contain the entire filter expression must be double quotes.
- Backslashes are escape characters for WMI, so when you need to use a literal backslash, as in this example, you have to use two backslashes instead.
- The output of Gwmi always includes a number of system properties. PowerShell's default display configuration often suppresses these, but they'll be displayed if you're deliberately listing all properties, or if the class doesn't have a default. System property names start with a double underscore. Here are two particularly useful ones:
  - __SERVER contains the name of the computer from which the instance was retrieved. This can be useful when retrieving WMI information from multiple computers at once. This property is duplicated in the easier-to-remember PSComputerName property.
  - __PATH is an absolute reference to the instance itself, and it can be used to requery the instance if necessary.

The cmdlet can retrieve not only from remote computers but from multiple computers, using any technique that can produce a collection of strings that contains either computer names or IP addresses. Here's an example:

```
PS C:\> Gwmi Win32_BIOS -comp server-r2,server3,dc4
```

Computers are contacted sequentially, and if one computer isn't available, the cmdlet will produce an error, skip that computer, and move on to the next. Unavailable computers generally must time out, which means the cmdlet will pause for about 30–45 seconds until it gives up, produces the error, and moves on.

Once you retrieve a set of WMI instances, you can pipe them to any -Object cmdlet, to any Format- cmdlet, or to any of the Out-, Export-, or ConvertTo- cmdlets. For example, here's how you could produce a custom table from the Win32_BIOS class:

```
PS C:\> Gwmi Win32_BIOS | Format-Table SerialNumber,Version -auto
```

In chapter 10, we showed you a technique you can use to produce custom columns using the Format-Table cmdlet. That technique can come in handy when you wish to query a couple of WMI classes from a given computer and aggregate the results into a single table. To do so, you create a custom column for the table and have that column's expression execute a whole new WMI query. The syntax for the command can be confusing, but the results are impressive:

```
PS C:\> gwmi -class win32_bios -computer server-r2,localhost | format-table
 @{l='ComputerName';e={$_.__SERVER}},@{l='BIOSSerial';e={$_.SerialNumber}},
@{l='OSBuild';e={gwmi -class win32_operatingsystem -comp $_.__SERVER | sele
ct-object -expand BuildNumber}} -autosize

ComputerName BIOSSerial                                          OSBuild
------------ ----------                                          ------
SERVER-R2    VMware-56 4d 45 fc 13 92 de c3-93 5c 40 6b 47 bb 5b 86 7600
```

The preceding syntax can be a bit easier to parse if you copy it into the PowerShell ISE and format it a bit:

```
gwmi -class win32_bios -computer server-r2,localhost |
 format-table
  @{l='ComputerName';e={$_.__SERVER}},
  @{l='BIOSSerial';e={$_.SerialNumber}},
  @{l='OSBuild';e={
    gwmi -class win32_operatingsystem -comp $_.__SERVER |
    select-object -expand BuildNumber}
  } -autosize
```

Here's what's happening:

- Get-WmiObject is querying Win32_BIOS from two computers.
- The results are being piped to Format-Table. Format-Table is being told to create three custom columns:
  - The first column is named ComputerName, and it's using the __SERVER system property from the Win32_BIOS instance.
  - The second column is named BIOSSerial, and it's using the SerialNumber property of the Win32_BIOS instance.
  - The third column is named OSBuild. This column is executing a whole new Get-WmiObject query, retrieving the Win32_OperatingSystem class from the __SERVER system property of the Win32_BIOS instance (of the same computer). That result is being piped to Select-Object, which is selecting the contents of the BuildNumber property of the Win32_OperatingSystem instance and using that as the value for the OSBuild column.

That syntax is complex, but it offers powerful results. It's also a great example of how much you can achieve by stringing together a few carefully selected PowerShell cmdlets.

As we've mentioned, some WMI classes include methods. You'll see how to use those in chapter 16; doing so can be a bit complicated, and the topic deserves its own chapter.

14.6 Using Get-CimInstance

Get-CimInstance is new in PowerShell v3, and it works a lot like Get-WmiObject with a few major syntactical differences:

- You use -ClassName instead of -Class (although you only have to type -Class, so if that's all you remember, it's fine).
- There's no -List parameter to list all the classes in a namespace. Instead, run Get-CimClass and use the -Namespace parameter to list classes.
- There's no -Credential parameter; if you intend to query from a remote computer and need to provide alternative credentials, send Get-CimInstance via Invoke-Command (which you learned in the previous chapter).

For example,

```
PS C:\> Get-CimInstance -ClassName Win32_LogicalDisk

DeviceID   DriveType ProviderName   VolumeName        Size       FreeSpace
--------   --------- ------------   ----------        ----       ---------
A:         2
C:         3                                          687173... 580806...
D:         5                        HB1_CCPA_X64F... 358370... 0
```

If you want to query a remote computer using alternate credentials, you can use a command like this:

```
PS C:\> invoke-command -ScriptBlock { Get-CimInstance -ClassName win32_proc
ess } -ComputerName WIN8 -Credential DOMAIN\Administrator
```

14.7   *WMI documentation*

We mentioned earlier that a search engine is often the best way to find whatever WMI documentation exists. The `Win32_` classes are well documented in Microsoft's MSDN Library site, but a search engine remains the easiest way to land on the right page. Enter the name of the class in Google or Bing, and the first hit will usually be a page on http://msdn.microsoft.com.

14.8   *Common points of confusion*

Because we've spent the last ten chapters telling you to use the built-in PowerShell help, you might be inclined to run something like `help win32_service` right inside PowerShell. Sadly, that won't work. The operating system itself doesn't contain any WMI documentation, so PowerShell's help function wouldn't have any place to go look for it. You're stuck with whatever help you can find online—and much of that will be from other administrators and programmers, not from Microsoft. Search for "root\SecurityCenter", for example, and you won't find a single Microsoft documentation page in the results, which is unfortunate.

The different filter criteria that WMI uses are also common points of confusion. You should always provide a filter whenever you need anything other than all of the available instances, but you'll have to memorize that different filter syntax. The filter syntax is passed along to WMI and not processed by PowerShell, which is why you have to use the syntax that WMI prefers, instead of the native PowerShell operators.

Part of what makes WMI confusing for some of our classroom students is that, although PowerShell provides an easy way to query information from WMI, WMI isn't integrated into PowerShell. WMI is an external technology, and it has its own rules and its own way of working. Although you can get to it from within PowerShell, it won't behave exactly like other cmdlets and techniques that are integrated completely within PowerShell. Keep that in mind, and watch for little points of confusion that result from WMI's individuality.

14.9   Lab

NOTE   For this lab, you'll need any computer running PowerShell v3.

Take some time to complete the following hands-on tasks. Much of the difficulty in using WMI is in finding the class that will give you the information you need, so much of the time you'll spend in this lab will be tracking down the right class. Try to think in keywords (we'll provide some hints), and use a WMI explorer to quickly search through classes (the WMI Explorer we use lists classes alphabetically, making it easier for us to validate our guesses). Keep in mind that PowerShell's help system can't help you find WMI classes.

1   What class can you use to view the current IP address of a network adapter? Does the class have any methods that you could use to release a DHCP lease? (Hint: *network* is a good keyword here.)

2   Create a table that shows a computer name, operating system build number, operating system description (caption), and BIOS serial number. (Hint: you've seen this technique, but you'll need to reverse it a bit and query the OS class first, then query the BIOS second.)

3   Query a list of hotfixes using WMI. (Hint: Microsoft formally refers to these as *quick fix engineering*.) Is the list different from that returned by the `Get-Hotfix` cmdlet?

4   Display a list of services, including their current statuses, their start modes, and the accounts they use to log on.

5   Can you find a class that will display a list of installed software *products*? Do you consider the resulting list to be complete?

TRY IT NOW   After you've completed this lab, try completing review lab 2, which you will find in appendix A of this book.

14.10   Further exploration

WMI is a vast, complex technology, and someone could easily write an entire book about it. In fact, someone did: *PowerShell and WMI* by fellow MVP Richard Siddaway (Manning, 2012). The book provides tons of examples and discusses some of the new capabilities of the CIM cmdlets introduced in PowerShell v3. We heartily recommend this book to anyone interested in learning more about WMI.

If you've found WMI to be thoroughly confusing or frustrating, don't worry. That's a common reaction. But we have some good news: in PowerShell v3, you can often use WMI without seeming to "touch" WMI. That's because Microsoft has written literally hundreds of cmdlets that "wrap around" WMI. These cmdlets provide help, discoverability, examples, and all the good things cmdlets give you, but they use WMI internally. This makes it easier to take advantage of the power of WMI without having to deal with its frustrating elements.

Multitasking with
background jobs

Everyone's always telling you to "multitask," right? Why shouldn't PowerShell help you out with that by doing more than one thing at a time? It turns out that Power-Shell can do exactly that, particularly for longer-running tasks that might involve multiple target computers. Make sure you've read chapters 13 and 14 before you dive into this chapter, because we'll be taking those remoting and WMI concepts a step farther.

15.1 Making PowerShell do multiple things at the same time

You should think of PowerShell as a single-threaded application, meaning that it can do only one thing at once. You type a command, you hit Return, and the shell waits for that command to execute. You can't run a second command until the first command finishes.

But with its background jobs functionality, PowerShell has the ability to move a command onto a separate background thread (a separate, background PowerShell process). That enables the command to run in the background, as you continue to use the shell for some other task. But you have to make that decision before running the command; after you press Return, you can't decide to move a long-running command into the background.

After commands are in the background, PowerShell provides mechanisms to check on their status, retrieve any results, and so forth.

15.2 *Synchronous versus asynchronous*

Let's get a few bits of terminology out of the way first. PowerShell runs normal commands *synchronously*, meaning you hit Return and then wait for the command to complete. Moving a job into the background allows it to run *asynchronously*, meaning you can continue to use the shell for other tasks as the command completes.

Let's look at some important differences between running commands in these two ways:

- When you run a command synchronously, you can respond to input requests. When you run commands in the background, there's no opportunity to see input requests—in fact, they'll stop the command from running.
- Synchronous commands produce error messages when something goes wrong. Background commands produce errors, but you won't see them immediately. You'll have to make arrangements to capture them, if necessary. (Chapter 22 discusses how you do that.)
- If you omit a required parameter on a synchronous command, PowerShell can prompt you for the missing information. On a background command, it can't, so the command will fail.
- The results of a synchronous command start displaying as soon as they become available. With a background command, you wait until the command finishes running and then retrieve the cached results.

We typically run commands synchronously to test them out and get them working properly, and only run them in the background after we know they're fully debugged and working as we expect. We follow these measures to ensure the command will run without problems, and that it will have the best chance of completing in the background.

PowerShell refers to background commands as *jobs*, and you can create jobs in several ways, and there are several commands you can use to manage them.

Above and beyond

Technically, the jobs we'll discuss in this chapter are just one kind of job you'll encounter. Jobs are an extension point for PowerShell, meaning it's possible for someone (either in Microsoft or as a third party) to create other things called jobs that look and work a bit differently than what we'll describe in this chapter. In fact, scheduled jobs, which we'll cover later in this chapter, work a bit differently than the "normal" jobs that we'll cover first, and you may run into other kinds of jobs as you extend the shell for different purposes. We want you to know that little detail, and to know that what you're learning applies only to the native, regular jobs that come with PowerShell.

15.3   *Creating a local job*

The first type of job we'll cover is perhaps the easiest: a local job. This is a command that runs more or less entirely on your local computer (with exceptions that we'll cover in a second) and that runs in the background.

To launch one of these jobs, you use the `Start-Job` command. A `-scriptblock` parameter lets you specify the command (or commands) to run. PowerShell will make up a default job name (Job1, Job2, and so on), or you can specify a custom job name by using the `-Name` parameter. If you need the job to run under alternative credentials, a `-credential` parameter will accept a DOMAIN\Username credential and prompt you for the password. Rather than specifying a script block, you can specify the `-FilePath` parameter to have the job execute an entire script file full of commands.

Here's a simple example:

```
PS C:\> start-job -scriptblock { dir }

Id             Name          State      HasMoreData    Location
--             ----          -----      -----------    --------
1              Job1          Running    True           localhost
```

The result of the command is the job object that was created, and as the previous example shows, the job begins running immediately. The job is also assigned a sequential job ID number, which is shown in the table.

We said these jobs run entirely on your local computer, and that's true. But the commands in the job are allowed to access remote computers, which would be the case if you ran a command that supported a `-computerName` parameter. Here's an example:

```
PS C:\> start-job -scriptblock {
➥get-eventlog security -computer server-r2
}

Id             Name          State      HasMoreData    Location
--             ----          -----      -----------    --------
3              Job3          Running    True           localhost
```

> **TRY IT NOW**   We hope you'll follow along and run all of these commands. If you only have a single computer to work with, refer to its computer name and use localhost as an alternative, so that PowerShell will act like it's dealing with two computers.

The processing for this job will happen on your local computer. It will contact the specified remote computer (SERVER-R2 in this example), so the job is, in a way, a "remote job." But because the command itself is running locally, we still refer to this as a local job.

Sharp-eyed readers will note that the first job we created was named Job1 and given the ID 1, but the second job was Job3 with ID 3. It turns out that every job has at least one *child job*, and the first child job (a child of Job1) was given the name Job2 and the ID 2. We'll get to child jobs a bit later in this chapter.

Here's something to keep in mind: although local jobs run locally, they do require the infrastructure of PowerShell's remoting system, which we covered in chapter 13. If you haven't enabled remoting, you won't be able to start local jobs.

15.4 WMI, as a job

Another way to start a job is to use `Get-WmiObject`. As we explained in the previous chapter, the `Get-WmiObject` command can contact one or more remote computers, but it does so sequentially. That means a long list of computer names can cause the command to take a long time to process, so that command is a natural choice for moving to a background job. To do so, you use `Get-WmiObject` as usual but add the `-AsJob` parameter. You don't get to specify a custom job name at this point; you're stuck with the default job name that PowerShell applies.

> **TRY IT NOW** If you're running the same commands on your test system, you'll need to create a text file called allservers.txt. We put it in the root of our C: drive (because that's where we have PowerShell focused for these examples), and we put several computer names in the file, listing one name per line. You can list your computer name and localhost to duplicate the results we're showing you.

```
PS C:\> get-wmiobject win32_operatingsystem -computername
➥ (get-content allservers.txt) -asjob

WARNING: column "Command" does not fit into the display and was removed.

Id            Name            State       HasMoreData       Location
--            ----            -----       -----------       --------
5             Job5            Running     False             server-r2,lo...
```

This time, the shell will create one top-level parent job (Job5, which is shown in the output of the command), and it will create one child job for each computer that you specified. You can see that the Location column in the output table lists as many of the computer names as will fit, indicating that the job will be running against those computers.

It's important to understand that `Get-WmiObject` executes only on your computer; the cmdlet is using normal WMI communications to contact the remote computers you specified. It'll still do this one at a time and follow the usual defaults of skipping computers that aren't available, and so forth. In fact, it works identically to using `Get-WmiObject` synchronously, except that the cmdlet runs in the background.

> **TRY IT NOW** You have commands other than `Get-WmiObject` that can start a job. Try running `Help * -parameter asjob` to see if you can find all of them.

Note that the newer `Get-CimInstance` command, which you learned about in chapter 14, doesn't have an `-AsJob` parameter. If you want to use it in a job, run either `Start-Job` or `Invoke-Command` (which you'll learn about next), and include `Get-CimInstance` (or for that matter, any of the new CIM commands) in the script block.

15.5 *Remoting, as a job*

Let's review the final technique you can use to create a new job: PowerShell's remoting capabilities, which you learned about in chapter 13. As with `Get-WmiObject`, you start this kind of job by adding an `-AsJob` parameter, but this time you'll add it to the `Invoke-Command` cmdlet.

There's an important difference here: whatever command you specify in the `-scriptblock` (or `-command`, which is an alias for the same parameter) will be transmitted in parallel to each computer you specify. Up to 32 computers can be contacted at once (unless you modify the `-throttleLimit` parameter to allow more or fewer), so if you specify more than 32 computer names, only the first 32 will start. The rest will start after the first set begins to finish, and the top-level job will show a completed status after all of the computers finish.

Unlike the other two ways to start a job, this technique requires you to have PowerShell v2 or v3 installed on each target computer, and remoting to be enabled in PowerShell on each target computer. Because the command physically executes on each remote computer, you're distributing the computing workload, which can help improve performance for complex or long-running commands. The results come back to your computer and are stored with the job until you're ready to review them.

In the following example, you'll also see the `-JobName` parameter that lets you specify a job name other than the boring default:

```
PS C:\> invoke-command -command { get-process }
➥-computername (get-content .\allservers.txt )
➥-asjob -jobname MyRemoteJob

WARNING: column "Command" does not fit into the display and was removed.

Id          Name          State     HasMoreData    Location
--          ----          -----     -----------    --------
8           MyRemoteJob   Running   True           server-r2,lo...
```

15.6 *Getting job results*

The first thing you'll probably want to do after starting a job is check to see if your jobs have finished. The `Get-Job` cmdlet will retrieve every job currently defined by the system, and show you each one's status:

```
PS C:\> get-job

Id          Name          State       HasMoreData    Location
--          ----          -----       -----------    --------
1           Job1          Completed   True           localhost
3           Job3          Completed   True           localhost
5           Job5          Completed   True           server-r2,lo...
8           MyRemoteJob   Completed   True           server-r2,lo...
```

You can also retrieve a specific job by using its ID or its name. We suggest that you do that and pipe the results to `Format-List *`, because you've gathered some valuable information:

```
PS C:\> get-job -id 1 | format-list *

State          : Completed
HasMoreData    : True
StatusMessage  :
Location       : localhost
Command        :   dir
JobStateInfo   : Completed
Finished       : System.Threading.ManualResetEvent
InstanceId     : e1ddde9e-81e7-4b18-93c4-4c1d2a5c372c
Id             : 1
Name           : Job1
ChildJobs      : {Job2}
Output         : {}
Error          : {}
Progress       : {}
Verbose        : {}
Debug          : {}
Warning        : {}
```

TRY IT NOW   If you're following along, keep in mind that your job IDs and names might be a bit different than ours. Focus on the output of Get-Job to retrieve your job IDs and names, and substitute yours in the examples.

The ChildJobs property is one of the most important pieces of information there is, and we'll cover it in a moment.

To retrieve the results from a job, use Receive-Job. But before you run this, you need to know a few things:

- You have to specify the job from which you want to receive results. You can do this by job ID or job name, or by getting jobs with Get-Job and piping them to Receive-Job.
- If you receive the results of the parent job, those results will include all output from all child jobs. Alternatively, you can choose to get the results from one or more child jobs.
- Normally, receiving the results from a job clears them out of the job output cache, so you can't get them a second time. Specify -keep to keep a copy of the results in memory. Or you can output the results to CliXML, if you want to retain a copy to work with.
- The job results may be deserialized objects, which you learned about in chapter 13. That means they're a snapshot from the point in time when they were generated, and they may not have any methods that you can execute. But you can pipe the job results directly to cmdlets such as Sort-Object, Format-List, Export-CSV, ConvertTo-HTML, Out-File, and so on, if desired.

Here's an example:

```
PS C:\> receive-job -id 1

    Directory: C:\Users\Administrator\Documents
```

```
Mode              LastWriteTime       Length Name
----              -------------       ------ ----
d----        11/21/2009  11:53 AM            Integration Services Script C
                                             omponent
d----        11/21/2009  11:53 AM            Integration Services Script T
                                             ask
d----         4/23/2010   7:54 AM            SQL Server Management Studio
d----         4/23/2010   7:55 AM            Visual Studio 2005
d----        11/21/2009  11:50 AM            Visual Studio 2008
```

The preceding output shows an interesting set of results. Here's a quick reminder of the command that launched this job in the first place:

```
PS C:\> start-job -scriptblock { dir }
```

Although our shell was in the C:\ drive when we ran this, the directory in the results is C:\Users\Administrator\Documents. As you can see, even local jobs take on a slightly different context when they run, which may result in a change of location. Don't ever make assumptions about file paths from within a background job: use absolute paths to make sure you can refer to whatever files your job command may require. If we wanted the background job to get a directory of C:\, we should have run the following command:

```
PS C:\> start-job -scriptblock { dir c:\ }
```

When we received the results from job 1, we didn't specify -keep. If we try to get those same results again, we'll get nothing, because the results are no longer cached with the job:

```
PS C:\> receive-job -id 1
PS C:\>
```

Here's how you would force the results to stay cached in memory:

```
PS C:\> receive-job -id 3 -keep

   Index Time            EntryType    Source                 InstanceID Messa
                                                                        ge

   ----- ----            ---------    ------                 ---------- -----
    6542 Oct 04 11:55    SuccessA...  Microsoft-Windows...         4634 An...
    6541 Oct 04 11:55    SuccessA...  Microsoft-Windows...         4624 An...
    6540 Oct 04 11:55    SuccessA...  Microsoft-Windows...         4672 Sp...
    6539 Oct 04 11:54    SuccessA...  Microsoft-Windows...         4634 An...
```

You'll eventually want to free up the memory that's being used to cache the job results, and we'll cover that in a bit. But first, let's look at a quick example of piping the job results directly to another cmdlet:

```
PS C:\> receive-job -name myremotejob | sort-object PSComputerName |
➥Format-Table -groupby PSComputerName

   PSComputerName: localhost
```

Handles	NPM(K)	PM(K)	WS(K)	VM(M)	CPU(s)	Id	ProcessName	PSComputerName
195	10	2780	5692	30	0.70	484	lsm	loca...
237	38	40704	36920	547	3.17	1244	Micro...	loca...
146	17	3260	7192	60	0.20	3492	msdtc	loca...
1318	100	42004	28896	154	15.31	476	lsass	loca...

This was the job we started by using `Invoke-Command`. As always, the cmdlet has added the `PSComputerName` property so we can keep track of which object came from which computer. Because we retrieved the results from the top-level job, this included all of the computers we specified, which allows this command to sort them on the computer name and then create an individual table group for each computer.

`Get-Job` can also keep you informed about which jobs have results remaining:

```
PS C:\> gct job

WARNING: column "Command" does not fit into the display and was removed.

Id          Name          State       HasMoreData   Location
--          ----          -----       -----------   --------
1           Job1          Completed   False         localhost
3           Job3          Completed   True          localhost
5           Job5          Completed   True          server-r2,lo...
8           MyRemoteJob   Completed   False         server-r2,lo...
```

The HasMoreData column will be `False` when no output is cached with that job. In the case of Job1 and MyRemoteJob, we have already received those results and didn't specify `-keep` at that time.

15.7 Working with child jobs

We mentioned earlier that all jobs consist of one top-level parent job and at least one child job. Let's look at a job again:

```
PS C:\> get-job -id 1 | format-list *

State           : Completed
HasMoreData     : True
StatusMessage   :
Location        : localhost
Command         :  dir
JobStateInfo    : Completed
Finished        : System.Threading.ManualResetEvent
InstanceId      : e1ddde9e-81e7-4b18-93c4-4c1d2a5c372c
Id              : 1
Name            : Job1
ChildJobs       : {Job2}
Output          : {}
Error           : {}
Progress        : {}
Verbose         : {}
Debug           : {}
Warning         : {}
```

TRY IT NOW   Don't follow along for this part, because if you've been following along up to now, you've already received the results of Job1. If you'd like to try this, start a new job by running `Start-Job -script { Get-Service }`, and use that new job's ID instead of the ID number 1 we used in our example.

You can see that Job1 has a child job, Job2. You can get it directly now that you know its name:

```
PS C:\> get-job -name job2 | format-list *

State         : Completed
StatusMessage :
HasMoreData   : True
Location      : localhost
Runspace      : System.Management.Automation.RemoteRunspace
Command       :  dir
JobStateInfo  : Completed
Finished      : System.Threading.ManualResetEvent
InstanceId    : a21a91e7-549b-4be6-979d-2a896683313c
Id            : 2
Name          : Job2
ChildJobs     : {}
Output        : {Integration Services Script Component, Integration Servic
                es Script Task, SQL Server Management Studio, Visual Studi
                o 2005...}
Error         : {}
Progress      : {}
Verbose       : {}
Debug         : {}
Warning       : {}
```

Sometimes, a job will have too many child jobs to list in that form, so you may want to list them a bit differently, as follows:

```
PS C:\> get-job -id 1 | select-object -expand childjobs

WARNING: column "Command" does not fit into the display and was removed.

Id          Name          State        HasMoreData     Location
--          ----          -----        -----------     --------
2           Job2          Completed    True            localhost
```

This technique will create a table of the child jobs for job ID 1, and the table can be whatever length it needs to be to list them all.

   You can receive the results from any individual child job by specifying its name or ID with `Receive-Job`.

15.8   *Commands for managing jobs*

Jobs also use three more commands. For each of these, you can specify a job either by giving its ID, giving its name, or by getting the job and piping it to one of these cmdlets:

- `Remove-Job`—This deletes a job, and any output still cached with it, from memory.

- `Stop-Job`—If a job seems to be stuck, this command will terminate it. You'll still be able to receive whatever results were generated to that point.
- `Wait-Job`—This is useful if a script is going to start a job and you want the script to continue only when the job is done. This command forces the shell to stop and wait until the job is completed, and then allows the shell to continue.

For example, to remove the jobs that we've already received output from, we'd use the following command:

```
PS C:\> get-job | where { -not $_.HasMoreData } | remove-job
PS C:\> get-job
```

```
WARNING: column "Command" does not fit into the display and was removed.

Id          Name         State        HasMoreData    Location
--          ----         -----        -----------    --------
3           Job3         Completed    True           localhost
5           Job5         Completed    True           server-r2,lo...
```

Jobs can also fail, meaning that something went wrong with their execution. Consider this example:

```
PS C:\> invoke-command -command { nothing } -computer notonline -asjob -job
name ThisWilLFail
```

```
WARNING: column "Command" does not fit into the display and was removed.

Id          Name           State        HasMoreData    Location
--          ----           -----        -----------    --------
11          ThisWilLFail   Failed       False          notonline
```

Here, we started a job with a bogus command and targeted a non-existent computer. The job immediately failed, as shown in its status. We don't need to use `Stop-Job` at this point; the job isn't running. But we can get a list of its child jobs:

```
PS C:\> get-job -id 11 | format-list *
```

```
State        : Failed
HasMoreData  : False
StatusMessage :
Location     : notonline
Command      :  nothing
JobStateInfo : Failed
Finished     : System.Threading.ManualResetEvent
InstanceId   : d5f47bf7-53db-458d-8a08-07969305820e
Id           : 11
Name         : ThisWilLFail
ChildJobs    : {Job12}
Output       : {}
Error        : {}
Progress     : {}
Verbose      : {}
Debug        : {}
Warning      : {}
```

And we can then get that child job:

```
PS C:\> get-job -name job12
```

```
WARNING: column "Command" does not fit into the display and was removed.
```

```
Id            Name           State        HasMoreData      Location
--            ----           -----        -----------      --------
12            Job12          Failed       False            notonline
```

As you can see, no output was created for this job, so you won't have any results to retrieve. But the job's errors are stored in the results, and you can get them by using Receive-Job:

```
PS C:\> receive-job -name job12
Receive-Job : [notonline] Connecting to remote server failed with the foll
owing error message : WinRM cannot process the request. The following erro
r occured while using Kerberos authentication: The network path was not fo
und.
```

The full error is much longer; we've truncated it here to save some space. You'll notice that the error includes the computer name that the error came from, [notonline]. What happens if only one of the computers can't be reached? Let's try:

```
PS C:\> invoke-command -command { nothing }
➥-computer notonline,server-r2 -asjob -jobname ThisWilLFail
```

```
WARNING: column "Command" does not fit into the display and was removed.
```

```
Id            Name           State        HasMoreData      Location
--            ----           -----        -----------      --------
13            ThisWilLFail   Running      True             notonline,se...
```

After waiting for a bit, we'll run the following:

```
PS C:\> get-job
```

```
WARNING: column "Command" does not fit into the display and was removed.
```

```
Id            Name           State        HasMoreData      Location
--            ----           -----        -----------      --------
13            ThisWilLFail   Failed       False            notonline,se...
```

The job still failed, but let's look at the individual child jobs:

```
PS C:\> get-job -id 13 | select -expand childjobs
```

```
WARNING: column "Command" does not fit into the display and was removed.
```

```
Id            Name           State        HasMoreData      Location
--            ----           -----        -----------      --------
14            Job14          Failed       False            notonline
15            Job15          Failed       False            server-r2
```

OK, they both failed. We have a feeling we know why Job14 didn't work, but what's wrong with Job15?

```
PS C:\> receive-job -name job15
Receive-Job : The term 'nothing' is not recognized as the name of a cmdlet
, function, script file, or operable program. Check the spelling of the na
me, or if a path was included, verify that the path is correct and try aga
in.
```

Ah, that's right, we told it to run a bogus command. As you can see, each child job can fail for different reasons, and PowerShell will track each one individually.

15.9 Scheduled jobs

PowerShell v3 introduces support for scheduled jobs—a PowerShell-friendly way of creating tasks in Windows' Task Scheduler. These jobs work differently from the jobs we've discussed up to this point; as we wrote earlier, jobs are an extension point in PowerShell, meaning there can be many kinds of job that work slightly differently. The scheduled jobs feature is one of those different kinds of job.

You start a scheduled job by creating a trigger (New-JobTrigger) that defines when the task will run. You can also set options for the job (New-ScheduledTaskOption). Then you register the job (Register-ScheduledJob) with Task Scheduler. This creates the job definition in Task Scheduler's XML format, on disk, and creates a folder hierarchy to contain the results of the job each time it runs.

Let's look at an example:

```
PS C:\> Register-ScheduledJob -Name DailyProcList -ScriptBlock { Get-Proces
s } -Trigger (New-JobTrigger -Daily -At 2am) -ScheduledJobOption (New-Sched
uledJobOption -WakeToRun -RunElevated)

WARNING: column "Enabled" does not fit into the display and was removed.

Id         Name            JobTriggers      Command
--         ----            -----------      -------
1          DailyProcList   {1}              Get-Process
```

This creates a new job that will run Get-Process every day at 2 a.m., waking the computer if necessary, and running under elevated privileges. After the job runs, you can come back into PowerShell and run Get-Job to see a standard job for each time the scheduled task completed:

```
PS C:\> get-job

WARNING: column "Command" does not fit into the display and was removed.

Id   Name            State       HasMoreData    Location
--   ----            -----       -----------    --------
6    DailyProcList   Completed   True           localhost
9    DailyProcList   Completed   True           localhost
```

Unlike normal jobs, receiving the results from scheduled jobs won't delete the results, because they're cached on disk and not in memory. You can continue to receive the results over and over. When you remove the job, the results will be removed from disk, too. As shown in figure 15.1, this output resides in a specific folder on disk, and Receive-Job is capable of reading those files.

You can control the number of stored result sets by using the -MaxResultCount parameter of Register-ScheduledJob.

Figure 15.1   Scheduled job output is stored on disk

15.10 *Common points of confusion*

Jobs are usually straightforward, but we've seen folks do one thing that does cause confusion. Don't do this:

```
PS C:\> invoke-command -command { Start-Job -scriptblock { dir } }
-computername Server-R2
```

Doing so starts up a temporary connection to SERVER-R2 and starts a local job. Unfortunately, that connection immediately terminates, so you have no way to reconnect and retrieve that job. In general, then, don't mix and match the three ways of starting jobs.

The following is also a bad idea:

```
PS C:\> start-job -scriptblock { invoke-command -command { dir }
-computername SERVER-R2 }
```

That's completely redundant; keep the Invoke-Command section and use the -AsJob parameter to have it run in the background.

Less confusing, but equally interesting, are the questions our classroom students often ask about jobs. Probably the most important of these is, "Can we see jobs started by someone else?" The answer is no, except for scheduled jobs. Normal jobs are contained entirely within the PowerShell process, and although you could see that another user was running PowerShell, you wouldn't be able to see inside that process. It's like any other application: you could see that another user was running Microsoft Office Word, for example, but you couldn't see what documents they were editing, because those documents exist entirely inside of Word's process.

Jobs only last as long as your PowerShell session is open. After you close it, any jobs defined within it disappear. Jobs aren't defined anywhere outside of PowerShell, so they depend upon its process continuing to run in order to maintain themselves.

Scheduled jobs are the exception to the previous statement: anyone with permission can see them, modify them, delete them, and retrieve their results, because they're stored on disk. Note that they're stored under your user profile, so it would normally require an administrator to get the files (and results) out of your profile.

15.11 Lab

> **NOTE** For this lab, you'll need a Windows 8 or Windows Server 2012 computer running PowerShell v3.

The following exercises should help you understand how to work with the different types of jobs and tasks in PowerShell. As you work through these exercises, don't feel you have to write a one-line solution. Sometimes it's easier to break things down into separate steps.

1 Create a one-time background job to find all the PowerShell scripts on the C: drive. Any task that might take a long time to complete is a great candidate for a job.

2 You realize it would be helpful to identify all PowerShell scripts on some of your servers. How would you run the same command from task 1 on a group of remote computers?

3 Create a background job that will get the latest 25 errors from the system event log on your computer and export them to a CliXML file. You want this job to run every day, Monday through Friday at 6:00 a.m., in order for it to be ready for you to look at when you come in to work.

4 What cmdlet would you use to get the results of a job, and how would you save the results in the job queue?

16

Working with many objects, one at a time

The whole point of PowerShell is to automate administration, and that often means you'll want to perform some tasks with multiple targets. You might want to reboot several computers, reconfigure several services, modify several mailboxes, and so on. In this chapter, you'll learn three distinct techniques for accomplishing these and other multiple-target tasks: batch cmdlets, WMI methods, and object enumeration.

16.1 Automation for mass management

We know this isn't a book about VBScript, but we want to use a VBScript example to briefly illustrate the way that multiple-target administration—what Don likes to call *mass management*—has been approached in the past. Consider this example (you don't need to type this in and run it—we're going to discuss the approach, not the results):

```
For Each varService in colServices
  varService.ChangeStartMode("Automatic")
Next
```

This kind of approach isn't only common in VBScript but is common throughout the world of programming. The following steps illustrate what it does:

1 Assume that the variable `colServices` contains multiple services. It doesn't matter how they got in there, because you could retrieve the services in many

different ways. What matters is that you've already retrieved the services and put them into this variable.

　2　The For Each construct will go through, or *enumerate*, the services one at a time. As it does this, it'll place each service into the variable varService. Within the construct then, varService will contain only a single service. If colServices contained 50 services, then the construct's contents would execute 50 times, and each time varService would contain a different one of the 50 services.

　3　Within the construct, a method is executed each time—in this example, ChangeStartMode()—to perform some task.

If you think about it carefully, you'll realize that this code isn't doing something to a bunch of services at once. Instead, it's doing something to one service at a time, exactly as you would if you were manually reconfiguring the services by using the graphical user interface. The only difference is that this code makes the computer go through the services one at a time.

Computers are good at repeating things over and over, so this isn't a horrible approach. The problem is that this approach requires us to give the computer a longer and fairly complicated set of instructions. Learning the language necessary to give that set of instructions can take time, which is why a lot of administrators try to avoid VBScript and other scripting languages.

PowerShell can duplicate this approach, and we'll show you how later in this chapter, because sometimes you have to resort to this method. But the approach of having the computer enumerate objects isn't the most efficient way to use PowerShell. In fact, PowerShell offers two other techniques that are easier to learn and easier to type, and they're often more powerful.

16.2　*The preferred way: "batch" cmdlets*

As you've learned in several previous chapters, many PowerShell cmdlets can accept batches, or *collections*, of objects to work with.

In chapter 6, for example, you learned how objects can be piped from one cmdlet to another, like this (please don't run this—it could crash your computer):

```
Get-Service | Stop-Service
```

This is an example of batch administration using a cmdlet. In this case, Stop-Service is specifically designed to accept one service object, or many service objects, from the pipeline, and then stop them. Set-Service, Stop-Process, Move-ADObject, and Move-Mailbox are all examples of cmdlets that accept one or more input objects and then perform some task or action with each of them. You don't need to manually enumerate the objects using a construct, as we did in the VBScript example in the previous section. PowerShell knows how to work with batches of objects and can handle them for you with a less complex syntax.

These so-called *batch cmdlets* (that's our name for them—it's not an official term) are our preferred way of performing mass management. For example, let's suppose we need to change the start mode of three services. Rather than using an approach like the VBScript one, we could do this:

```
Get-Service -name BITS,Spooler,W32Time | Set-Service -startuptype Automatic
```

In a way, Get-Service is also a kind of batch cmdlet, because it's capable of retrieving services from multiple computers. Suppose you need to change those same three services across a set of three computers:

```
Get-Service -name BITS,Spooler,W32Time -computer Server1,Server2,Server3 |
Set-Service -startuptype Automatic
```

One potential downside of this approach is that cmdlets that perform an action often don't produce any output indicating that they've done their job. That means you won't have any visual output from either of the preceding commands, which can be disconcerting. But those cmdlets often have a -passThru parameter, which tells them to output whatever objects they accepted as input. You could have Set-Service output the same services it modified, and have Get-Service re-retrieve those services to see if the change took effect.

Here's an example of using -passThru with a different cmdlet:

```
Get-Service -name BITS -computer Server1,Server2,Server3 |
Start-Service -passthru |
Out-File NewServiceStatus.txt
```

This command would retrieve the specified service from the three computers listed. The services would be piped to Start-Service, which would not only start them, but also output the updated service objects. Those service objects would be piped to Out-File, telling it to store the updated service status in a text file.

Once more: this is our recommended way to work in PowerShell. If a cmdlet exists to do whatever you want, you should use it. Ideally, authors write cmdlets to work with batches of objects, but that isn't always the case (cmdlet authors are still learning the best ways to write cmdlets for us administrators), but it's the ideal.

16.3   *The WMI way: invoking WMI methods*

Unfortunately, we don't always have cmdlets that can take whatever action we need, and that's true when it comes to the items we can manipulate through Windows Management Instrumentation (WMI, which we tackled in chapter 14).

> **NOTE**   We'll walk you through a brief storyline meant to help you experience how folks use PowerShell. Some things may seem redundant, but bear with us—the experience itself is valuable.

For example, consider the Win32_NetworkAdapterConfiguration class in WMI. This class represents the configuration bound to a network adapter (adapters can have multiple configurations, but for now let's assume they have only one configuration apiece, which is common on client computers). Let's say that our goal is to enable DHCP on all of our computer's Intel network adapters—we don't want to enable any of the RAS or other virtual adapters.

We might start by trying to query the desired adapter configurations, which would allow us to get something like the following as output:

```
DHCPEnabled        : False
IPAddress          : {192.168.10.10, fe80::ec31:bd61:d42b:66f}
DefaultIPGateway   :
DNSDomain          :
ServiceName        : E1G60
Description        : Intel(R) PRO/1000 MT Network Connection
Index              : 7

DHCPEnabled        : True
IPAddress          :
DefaultIPGateway   :
DNSDomain          :
ServiceName        : E1G60
Description        : Intel(R) PRO/1000 MT Network Connection
Index              : 12
```

To achieve this output, we'd need to query the appropriate WMI class and filter it to allow only configurations with "Intel" in their descriptions to be included. The following command will do it (notice that the % acts as a wildcard within the WMI filter syntax):

```
PS C:\> gwmi win32_networkadapterconfiguration
➥-filter "description like '%intel%'"
```

TRY IT NOW You're welcome to follow along with the commands we're running in this section of the chapter. You may need to tweak the commands slightly to make them work. For example, if your computer doesn't have any Intel-made network adapters, you'd need to change the filter criteria appropriately.

Once we have those configuration objects in the pipeline, we want to enable DHCP on them (you can see that one of our adapters doesn't have DHCP enabled). We might start by looking for a cmdlet named something like "Enable-DHCP." Unfortunately, we won't find it, because there's no such thing. There aren't any cmdlets that are capable of dealing directly with WMI objects in batches.

Our next step would be to see if the object itself has a method that's capable of enabling DHCP. To find out, we'll pipe those configuration objects to `Get-Member` (or its alias, `Gm`):

```
PS C:\> gwmi win32_networkadapterconfiguration
➥-filter "description like '%intel%'" | gm
```

Right near the top of the resulting list, we should see the method we're after, `EnableDHCP()`:

```
TypeName: System.Management.ManagementObject#root\cimv2\Win32_NetworkAd
apterConfiguration

Name                      MemberType   Definition
----                      ----------   ----------
DisableIPSec              Method       System.Management.ManagementB...
EnableDHCP                Method       System.Management.ManagementB...
```

```
EnableIPSec                    Method        System.Management.ManagementB...
EnableStatic                   Method        System.Management.ManagementB...
```

The next step, which a lot of PowerShell newcomers try, is to pipe the configuration objects to the method:

```
PS C:\> gwmi win32_networkadapterconfiguration
➥-filter "description like '%intel%'" | EnableDHCP()
```

Sadly, that won't work. You can't pipe objects to a method; you can only pipe to a cmdlet. `EnableDHCP` isn't a PowerShell cmdlet. Rather, it's an action that's directly attached to the configuration object itself. The old, VBScript-style approach would look a lot like the VBScript example we showed you at the start of this chapter, but with PowerShell you can do something simpler.

Although there's no "batch" cmdlet called Enable-DHCP, you can use a generic cmdlet called `Invoke-WmiMethod`. This cmdlet is specially designed to accept a batch of WMI objects, such as our `Win32_NetworkAdapterConfiguration` objects, and to invoke one of the methods attached to those objects. Here's the command we'd run:

```
PS C:\> gwmi win32_networkadapterconfiguration
➥-filter "description like '%intel%'" |
➥Invoke-WmiMethod -name EnableDHCP
```

You have a few things to keep in mind:

- The method name isn't followed by parentheses.
- The method name isn't case-sensitive.
- `Invoke-WmiMethod` can accept only one kind of WMI object at a time. In this case, we're sending it only `Win32_NetworkAdapterConfiguration` objects, which means it'll work as expected. It's OK to send it more than one object (that's the whole point, in fact), but all of the objects have to be of the same type.
- You can use `-WhatIf` and `-Confirm` with `Invoke-WmiMethod`. But you can't use those when calling a method directly from an object.

The output of `Invoke-WmiMethod` can be a little confusing. WMI always produces a result object, and it has a lot of system properties (whose names start with two underscore characters). In our case, the command produced the following:

```
__GENUS          : 2
__CLASS          : __PARAMETERS
__SUPERCLASS     :
__DYNASTY        : __PARAMETERS
__RELPATH        :
__PROPERTY_COUNT : 1
__DERIVATION     : {}
__SERVER         :
__NAMESPACE      :
__PATH           :
ReturnValue      : 0

__GENUS          : 2
__CLASS          : __PARAMETERS
__SUPERCLASS     :
```

```
__DYNASTY          : __PARAMETERS
__RELPATH          :
__PROPERTY_COUNT   : 1
__DERIVATION       : {}
__SERVER           :
__NAMESPACE        :
__PATH             :
ReturnValue        : 84
```

The only useful information in the preceding output is the one property that doesn't start with two underscores: ReturnValue. That number tells us the result of the operation. A Google search for "Win32_NetworkAdapterConfiguration" turns up the documentation page, and we can then click through to the EnableDHCP method to see the possible return values and what they mean. Figure 16.1 shows what we discovered:

Zero means success, whereas 84 means that the IP isn't enabled on that adapter configuration and DHCP can't be enabled. But which bit of the output went with which of our two network adapter configurations? It's difficult to tell, because the output doesn't tell you which specific configuration object produced it. That's unfortunate, but it's the way WMI works.

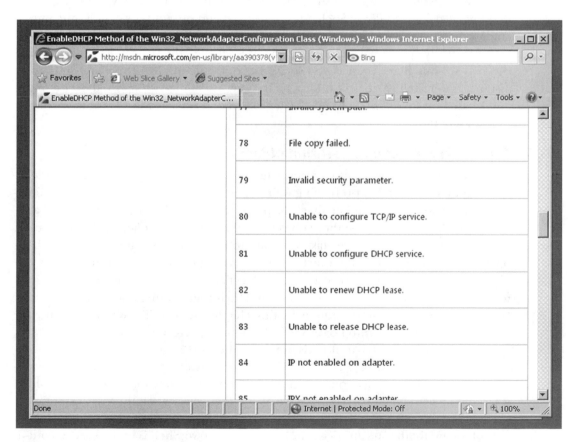

Figure 16.1 Looking up return values for a WMI method's results

Invoke-WmiMethod will work for most situations where you have a WMI object that has a method that you want to execute. It works well when querying WMI objects from remote computers too. Our basic rule is, "if you can get to something by using Get-WmiObject, then Invoke-WmiObject can execute its methods."

If you recall what you learned in chapter 14, you'll know that Get-WmiObject and Invoke-WmiMethod are the "legacy" cmdlets for working with WMI; their successors are Get-CimInstance and Invoke-CimMethod. They work more or less the same way:

```
PS C:\> Get-CimInstance -classname win32_networkadapterconfiguration
➥-filter "description like '%intel%'" |
➥Invoke-CimMethod -methodname EnableDHCP
```

In chapter 14, we offered suggestions for when to use WMI or CIM, and those apply here: WMI works with the broadest range of computers (currently), although it requires difficult-to-firewall RPC network traffic; CIM requires the newer and easier WS-MAN traffic, but that isn't installed by default on older versions of Windows.

But wait—there's one more thing. We're discussing WMI in this section, and back in chapter 14 we mentioned that Microsoft had done a lot to inadvertently hide WMI from you, wrapping key WMI functionality into cmdlets. Try running help Set-NetIPAddress in PowerShell. On a newer version of Windows, you'll find a great cmdlet that wraps around much of the underlying WMI complexity. Instead of all this WMI fussing, we could have used that cmdlet to change the IP address. That's one of the real lessons here: Even if you've read about something on the internet, don't assume PowerShell v3 doesn't offer a better way. Much of what's posted on the internet is based on PowerShell v1 and v2, and the cmdlet coverage in v3 is at least four or five times better.

16.4 *The backup plan: enumerating objects*

Unfortunately, we've run across a few situations where Invoke-WmiObject couldn't execute a method—it kept returning weird error messages. We've also run into situations where we have a cmdlet that can produce objects, but we know of no batch cmdlet to which we can pipe those objects to take some kind of action. In either case, you can still perform whatever task you want to perform, but you'll have to fall back on the old VBScript-style approach of instructing the computer to enumerate the objects and perform your task against one object at a time. PowerShell offers two ways to accomplish this: one is using a cmdlet, and the other is using a scripting construct. We'll focus on the first technique in this chapter, and we'll save the second for chapter 21, which dives into PowerShell's built-in scripting language.

As an example of how to do this, we'll use the Win32_Service WMI class. Specifically, we'll use the Change() method. This is a complex method that can change several elements of a service at once. Figure 16.2 shows its online documentation (which we found by searching for "Win32_Service" and then clicking on the Change method).

Reading this page, you'll discover that you don't have to specify every single parameter of the method. You can specify Null (which in PowerShell is in the special built-in $null variable) for any parameters that you want to omit.

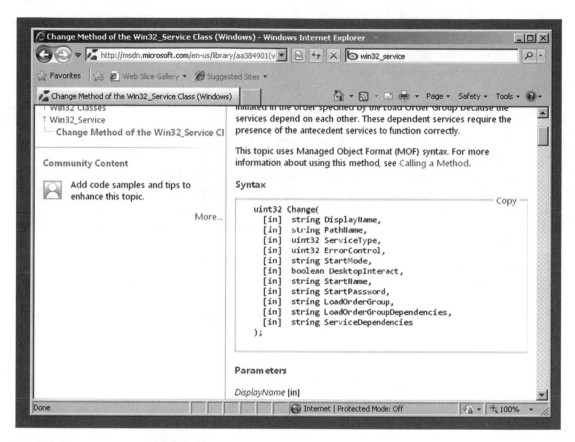

Figure 16.2 Documentation page for the Change() method of Win32_Service

For this example, we want to change the service's startup password, which is the eighth parameter. To do this, we'll need to specify $null for the first seven parameters. That means our method execution might look something like the following:

```
Change($null, $null, $null, $null, $null, $null, $null, "P@ssw0rd")
```

By the way, neither Get-Service nor Set-Service are capable of displaying or setting a service's logon password. But WMI can do it, so we're using WMI.

Because we can't use the Set-Service batch cmdlet, which would normally be our preferred approach, we'll try our second approach, which is to use Invoke-WmiMethod. The cmdlet has a parameter, -ArgumentList, where we can specify the arguments for the method. The following is an example of what we tried, along with the results we received:

```
PS C:\> gwmi win32_service -filter "name = 'BITS'" | invoke-wmimethod -name
 change -arg $null,$null,$null,$null,$null,$null,$null,"P@ssw0rd"
Invoke-WmiMethod : Input string was not in a correct format.
At line:1 char:62
+ gwmi win32_service -filter "name = 'BITS'" | invoke-wmimethod <<<<  -nam
```

```
e change -arg $null,$null,$null,$null,$null,$null,$null,"P@ssw0rd"
   + CategoryInfo          : NotSpecified: (:) [Invoke-WmiMethod], Forma
  tException
   + FullyQualifiedErrorId : System.FormatException,Microsoft.PowerShell
  .Commands.InvokeWmiMethod
```

NOTE We're using `Get-WmiObject`, but `Get-CimInstance` has virtually the same syntax.

At this point, we have to make a decision. It's possible that we're running the command incorrectly, so we have to decide if we want to spend a lot of time figuring it out. It's also possible that `Invoke-WmiMethod` doesn't work well with the `Change()` method, in which case we could be spending a lot of time trying to fix something over which we have no control.

Our usual choice in these situations is to try a different approach: we're going to ask the computer (well, the shell) to enumerate the service objects, one at a time, and execute the `Change()` method on each of them, one at a time. To do this, we'll use the `ForEach-Object` cmdlet:

```
PS C:\> gwmi win32_service -filter "name = 'BITS'" | foreach-object {$_.cha
nge($null,$null,$null,$null,$null,$null,$null,"P@ssw0rd") }


__GENUS           : 2
__CLASS           : __PARAMETERS
__SUPERCLASS      :
__DYNASTY         : __PARAMETERS
__RELPATH         :
__PROPERTY_COUNT  : 1
__DERIVATION      : {}
__SERVER          :
__NAMESPACE       :
__PATH            :
ReturnValue       : 0
```

In the documentation, we found that a `ReturnValue` of 0 meant success, which means we've achieved our goal. But let's look at that command in more detail, with some nicer formatting:

```
Get-WmiObject Win32_Service -filter "name = 'BITS'" |
➥ForEach-Object -process {
➥  $_.change($null,$null,$null,$null,$null,$null,$null,"P@ssw0rd")
➥}
```

This command has lots going on. The first line should make sense: we're using `Get-WmiObject` to retrieve all instances of `Win32_Service` that match our filter criteria, which is looking for services that have the name "BITS." (As usual, we're picking on the BITS service because it's less essential than some others we could have picked, and breaking it won't crash our computer.) We're piping those `Win32_Service` objects to the `ForEach-Object` cmdlet.

Let's break down the previous example into its component elements:

- First, you'll see the cmdlet name: ForEach-Object.
- Next, we're using the -Process parameter to specify a script block. We didn't originally type the -Process parameter name, because it's a positional parameter. But that script block—everything contained within the curly braces—is the value for the -Process parameter. We went ahead and included the parameter name when we reformatted the command for easier reading.
- ForEach-Object will execute its script block once for each object that was piped into ForEach-Object. Each time the script block executes, the next piped-in object will be placed into the special $_ placeholder.
- By following $_ with a period, we're telling the shell we want to access a property or method of the current object.
- In the example, we're accessing the Change() method. Note that the method's parameters are passed as a comma-separated list, contained within parentheses. We've used $null for the parameters we don't want to change and provided our new password as the eighth parameter. The method accepts more parameters, but because we don't want to change the ninth, tenth, or eleventh ones, we can omit them entirely. (We could also have specified $null for the last three parameters.)

We've definitely covered a complicated syntax. Figure 16.3 breaks it down for you:

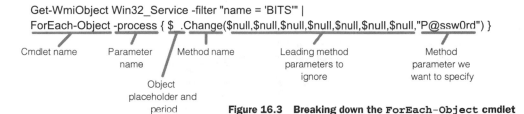

Figure 16.3 Breaking down the ForEach-Object cmdlet

You can use this exact same pattern for any WMI method. Why would you ever use Invoke-WmiMethod instead? Well, it usually does work, and it's a bit easier to type and read. But if you'd prefer to only have to memorize one way of doing things, this ForEach-Object way works well.

We have to caution you that the examples you see on the internet might be a lot less easy to read. PowerShell gurus often tend to use aliases, positional parameters, and shortened parameter names, which reduces readability (but saves on typing). Here's the same command again, in super-short form:

```
PS C:\> gwmi win32_service -fi "name = 'BITS'" |
% {$_.change($null,$null,$null,$null,$null,$null,$null,"P@ssw0rd") }
```

Let's review what we changed:

- We used the alias Gwmi instead of Get-WmiObject.
- We abbreviated -filter to -fi.

- We used the % alias instead of ForEach-Object. Yes, the percent sign is an alias to that cmdlet. We find that to be tough to read, but lots of folks use it.
- We removed the -process parameter name again, because it's a positional parameter.

We don't like using aliases and abbreviated parameter names when we're sharing scripts, posting them in our blogs, and so forth, because it makes them too difficult for someone else to read. If you're going to save something in a script file, it's worth your time to type everything out (or use Tab completion to let the shell type it out for you).

If you ever want to use this example, there are a few things you might change (as illustrated in figure 16.4):

- You would change the WMI class name, and your filter criteria, to retrieve whatever WMI objects you want.
- You would modify the method name from Change to whatever method you want to execute.
- You would modify the method's parameter (also called *argument*) list to whatever your method needs. This is always a comma-separated list contained within parentheses. It's OK for the parentheses to be completely empty for methods that have no parameters, such as the EnableDHCP() method we introduced earlier in this chapter.

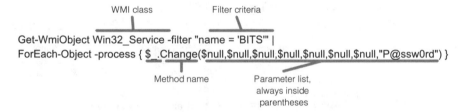

Figure 16.4   The changes you would make to the previous example to execute a different WMI method

Was this approach the best way to achieve our goal? Looking at the help for Set-Service, we see that it doesn't offer a way to change passwords, which Get-Wmi-Object and Get-CimInstance both do. This leads us to conclude that, even in PowerShell v3, WMI is the way to go for this particular task.

16.5   *Common points of confusion*

The techniques we've covered in this chapter are among the most difficult in Power-Shell, and they often cause the most confusion in our classes. Let's look at some of the problems students tend to run into, and provide some alternative explanations that we hope will help you avoid the same issues.

16.5.1 *Which way is the right way?*

We use the term *batch cmdlet* or *action cmdlet* to refer to any cmdlet that performs some action against a group, or collection, of objects all at once. Rather than having to instruct the computer to "go through this list of things, and perform this one action with each of those things," you can send the whole group to a cmdlet, and the cmdlet handles it.

Microsoft is getting better about providing these kinds of cmdlets with its products, but its coverage isn't 100% yet (and probably won't be for many years, because of the many complex Microsoft products that exist). But when a cmdlet does exist, we prefer to use it. That said, other PowerShell developers prefer alternate ways, depending on what they learned first and what they remember most easily. All of the following are exactly the same:

```
Get-Service -name *B* | Stop-Service                              ◄—❶ Batch cmdlet

Get-Service -name *B* | ForEach-Object { $_.Stop() }             ◄—❷ ForEach-Object

Get-WmiObject Win32_Service -filter "name LIKE '%B%' |           ◄—❸ WMI
➥Invoke-WmiMethod -name StopService

Get-WmiObject Win32_Service -filter "name LIKE '%B%' |           ◄—  WMI and
➥ForEach-Object { $_.StopService() }                              ❹ ForEach-Object

Stop-Service -name *B*                                       ◄—❺ Stop-Service
```

Let's look at how each approach works:

- The first approach is to use a batch cmdlet ❶. Here, we're using `Get-Service` to retrieve all services with a "B" in their name, and then stop them.
- The second approach is similar. But rather than using a batch cmdlet, we're piping the services to `ForEach-Object`, and asking it to execute each service's `Stop()` method ❷.
- The third technique is to use WMI, rather than the shell's native service-management cmdlets ❸. We're retrieving the desired services (again, any with "B" in their name), and piping them to `Invoke-WmiMethod`. We're telling it to invoke the `StopService` method, which is the method name that the WMI service objects use.
- The fourth way uses `ForEach-Object` instead of `Invoke-WmiMethod` but accomplishes exactly the same thing ❹. This is a combination of ❷ and ❸, not a whole new way of doing things.
- The fifth technique uses `Stop-Service` ❺ directly, because its `-Name` parameter (in PowerShell v3) accepts wildcards.

Heck, there's even a sixth approach—using PowerShell's scripting language to do the same thing. You'll find lots of ways to accomplish almost anything in PowerShell, and none of them are wrong. Some are easier than others to learn, remember, and repeat, which is why we've focused on the techniques we have, in the order that we did.

Our examples also illustrate some important differences between using native cmdlets and WMI:

- Native cmdlets' filtering criteria usually use * as a wildcard character, where WMI filtering uses the percent sign (%)—don't confuse that percent sign for the ForEach-Object alias. This percent sign is enclosed within the value of Get-WmiObject's -filter parameter, and it isn't an alias.
- Native objects often have similar capabilities to WMI ones, but the syntax may differ. In our example, the ServiceController objects produced by Get-Service have a Stop() method; when we access those same services through the WMI Win32_Service class, the method name becomes StopService().
- Native filtering often uses native comparison operators, such as -eq; WMI uses programming-style operators such as = or LIKE.

Which should you use? It doesn't matter, because there's no right way. You may even end up using a mix of these, depending on the circumstances and the capabilities that the shell is able to offer you for the task at hand.

16.5.2 *WMI methods versus cmdlets*

When should you use a WMI method or a cmdlet to accomplish a task? It's a simple choice:

- If you retrieved something by using Get-WmiObject, you'll take action on that something by using a WMI method. You can execute the method by using Invoke-WmiMethod or the ForEach-Object approach.
- If you retrieved something by using an approach other than Get-WmiObject, you'll use a native cmdlet to take action against that something. Or, if whatever you retrieved has a method but no supporting cmdlet, you might use the ForEach-Object approach to execute that method.

Notice that the lowest common denominator here is ForEach-Object: its syntax is perhaps the most difficult, but you can always use it to accomplish whatever task you need to do.

You can never pipe anything to a method. You can only pipe from one cmdlet to another. If a cmdlet doesn't exist to do what you need, but a method does, then you pipe to ForEach-Object and have it execute the method.

For example, suppose you retrieve something using a Get-Something cmdlet. You want to delete that something, but there's no Delete-Something or Remove-Something cmdlet. But the something objects do have a Delete method. You can do this:

```
Get-Something | ForEach-Object { $_.Delete() }
```

16.5.3 *Method documentation*

Always remember that piping objects to Get-Member reveals methods. Again, let's use the fictional Get-Something cmdlet as an example:

```
Get-Something | Get-Member
```

PowerShell's built-in help system doesn't document WMI methods; you'll need to use a search engine (usually searching on the WMI class name) to locate WMI method instructions and examples. You also won't find methods of non-WMI objects documented in PowerShell's built-in help system. For example, if you get a member list for a service object, you can see that methods named `Stop` and `Start` exist:

```
TypeName: System.ServiceProcess.ServiceController

Name                       MemberType    Definition
----                       ----------    ----------
Name                       AliasProperty Name = ServiceName
RequiredServices           AliasProperty RequiredServices = ServicesDepe...
Disposed                   Event         System.EventHandler Disposed(Sy...
Close                      Method        System.Void Close()
Continue                   Method        System.Void Continue()
CreateObjRef               Method        System.Runtime.Remoting.ObjRef ...
Dispose                    Method        System.Void Dispose()
Equals                     Method        bool Equals(System.Object obj)
ExecuteCommand             Method        System.Void ExecuteCommand(int ...
GetHashCode                Method        int GetHashCode()
GetLifetimeService         Method        System.Object GetLifetimeService()
GetType                    Method        type GetType()
InitializeLifetimeService  Method        System.Object InitializeLifetim...
Pause                      Method        System.Void Pause()
Refresh                    Method        System.Void Refresh()
Start                      Method        System.Void Start(), System.Voi...
Stop                       Method        System.Void Stop()
ToString                   Method        string ToString()
WaitForStatus              Method        System.Void WaitForStatus(Syste...
```

To find the documentation for these, focus on the `TypeName`, which in this case is `System.ServiceProcess.ServiceController`. Search for that complete type name in a search engine, and you'll usually come across the official developer documentation for that type, which will lead to the documentation for the specific method you're after.

16.5.4 *ForEach-Object confusion*

The `ForEach-Object` cmdlet has a punctuation-heavy syntax, and adding in a method's own syntax can create an ugly command line. We've compiled some tips for breaking any mental logjams:

- Try to use the full cmdlet name instead of its `%` or `ForEach` alias. The full name can be easier to read. If you're using someone else's example, replace aliases with the full cmdlet names.
- The script block enclosed in curly braces executes once for each object that's piped into the cmdlet.
- Within the script block, the `$_` represents one of the piped-in objects.
- Use `$_` by itself to work with the entire object you piped in; follow `$_` with a period to work with individual methods or properties.

- Method names are always followed by parentheses, even if the method doesn't require any parameters. When parameters are required, they're delimited by commas and included within the parentheses.

16.6 Lab

NOTE   For this lab, you'll need any computer running PowerShell v3.

Try to answer the following questions and complete the specified tasks. This is an important lab, because it draws on skills you've learned in many previous chapters, and you should be continuing to use and reinforce these skills as you progress through the remainder of this book.

1   What method of a `ServiceController` object (produced by `Get-Service`) will pause the service without stopping it completely?
2   What method of a `Process` object (produced by `Get-Process`) would terminate a given process?
3   What method of a WMI `Win32_Process` object would terminate a given process?
4   Write four different commands that could be used to terminate all processes named "Notepad", assuming that multiple processes might be running under that same name.

Security alert!

By now, you're probably starting to get a feel for how powerful PowerShell can be—and you're wondering if maybe all of that power might be a security problem. It *might* be. Our goal in this chapter is to help you understand exactly how PowerShell can impact security in your environment, and to show you how to configure PowerShell to provide exactly the balance of security and power you require.

17.1 Keeping the shell secure

When PowerShell was introduced in late 2006, Microsoft didn't exactly have a spotless record on security and scripting. After all, VBScript and Windows Script Host (WSH) were probably two of the most popular virus and malware vectors of the time, serving as entry points for such infamous viruses as "I Love You," "Melissa," and many others. When the PowerShell team announced that they were creating a new command-line shell that would offer unprecedented power and functionality, as well as scripting capabilities, we're sure alarms went off, people were evacuated from buildings, and everyone gnashed their teeth in dismay.

But it's OK. PowerShell was created after the famous "Trustworthy Computing Initiative" that Bill Gates started within Microsoft. That initiative had a real effect within the company: each product team is required to have a skilled software security expert sit in on their design meetings, code reviews, and so forth. That expert is referred to as—and we're not making this up—the product's "Security Buddy." PowerShell's Security Buddy was one of the authors of *Writing Secure Code*, Microsoft's own bible for writing software that's less easily exploited by attackers. You can be assured that PowerShell is as secure as any such product can possibly be—at least, it's that secure by default. Obviously, you can change the defaults, but when you do that, you should consider the security ramifications, and not only the functional ones. That's what this chapter will help you accomplish.

17.2   *Windows PowerShell security goals*

We need to be clear about what PowerShell does and doesn't do when it comes to security, and the best way to do that is to outline some of PowerShell's security goals.

First and foremost, PowerShell doesn't apply any additional layers of permissions on anything it touches. That means PowerShell will only enable you to do what you already have permission to do. If you can't create new users in Active Directory by using the graphical console, you won't be able to do so in PowerShell either. Power-Shell is another means of exercising whatever permissions you already have.

PowerShell is also not a way to bypass any existing permissions. Let's say you want to deploy a script to your users, and you want that script to do something that your users don't normally have permission to do. That script isn't going to work for them. If you want your users to do something, you need to give them permission to do it; PowerShell can only accomplish things that the person running a command or script already has permission to do.

PowerShell's security system isn't designed to prevent anyone from typing in, and running, whatever commands they have permission to execute. The idea is that it's somewhat difficult to trick a user into typing a long, complicated command, so Power-Shell doesn't apply any security beyond the user's existing permissions. But we know from past experience that it's easy to trick users into running a script, which might well contain malicious commands. This is why most of PowerShell's security is

Above and beyond

It's beyond the scope of this book, but we do want you to be aware of *other* ways to let your users execute a script that runs under credentials other than their own. You can typically accomplish this through a technique called *script packaging*, and it's a feature of some commercial script development environments, such as SAPIEN PrimalScript (www.primaltools.com).

After creating a script, you use the packager to bundle the script into an executable (.EXE) file. This isn't compilation in the programming sense of the term: the executable isn't standalone, and it requires that PowerShell be installed in order to run. You can configure the packager to encrypt alternative credentials into the executable. That way, when someone runs the executable, it launches the packaged script under whatever credentials you specify, rather than under the user's own credentials.

The packaged credentials aren't 100 percent safe. The package does include the username and password, although most packagers adequately encrypt them. It's safe to say that most users won't be able to discover the username and password, but it's completely possible for a skilled encryption expert to decrypt the username and password.

designed with the goal of preventing users from *unintentionally* running scripts. The "unintentionally" part is important: nothing in PowerShell's security is intended to prevent a determined user from running a script. The idea is only to prevent users from being *tricked* into running scripts from untrusted sources.

PowerShell's security is also not a defense against malware. Once you have malware on your system, that malware can do anything you have permission to do. It might use PowerShell to execute malicious commands, but it might as easily use any of a dozen other techniques to damage your computer. Once you have malware on your system, you're "owned," and PowerShell isn't a second line of defense. You'll continue to need antimalware software to prevent malware from getting onto your system in the first place. This is a hugely important concept that a lot of people miss: even though a piece of malware might use PowerShell to do harm doesn't make that malware Power-Shell's problem. Your antimalware software must stop the malware. Nothing in Power-Shell is designed or intended to protect an already compromised system.

17.3 *Execution policy and code signing*

The first security measure PowerShell includes is an *execution policy.* This is a machine-wide setting that governs the scripts that PowerShell will execute. As we stated earlier in this chapter, the intent of this setting is to help prevent users from being tricked into running a script.

17.3.1 *Execution policy settings*

The default setting is `Restricted`, which prevents scripts from being executed at all. That's right: by default, you can use PowerShell to interactively run commands, but you can't use it to run scripts. If you try, you'll get the following error message:

```
File C:\test.ps1 cannot be loaded because the execution of scripts is disa
bled on this system. Please see "get-help about_signing" for more details.
At line:1 char:7
+ ./test <<<<
    + CategoryInfo        : NotSpecified: (:) [], PSSecurityException
    + FullyQualifiedErrorId : RuntimeException
```

You can view the current execution policy by running `Get-ExecutionPolicy`. You can change the execution policy in one of three ways:

- *By running the* `Set-ExecutionPolicy` *command.* This changes the setting in the HKEY_LOCAL_MACHINE portion of the Windows registry and usually must be run by an administrator, because regular users don't have permission to write to that portion of the registry.
- *By using a Group Policy object (GPO).* Windows Server 2008 R2 comes with the Windows PowerShell-related settings built right in; for older domain controllers you can download an ADM template to extend Group Policy. You'll find it at http://mng.bz/U6tJ. You can also visit http://download.microsoft.com and punch in "PowerShell ADM" as a search term.

As shown in figure 17.1, the PowerShell settings are located under Computer Configuration > Policies > Administrative Templates > Windows Components > Windows PowerShell. Figure 17.2 displays the policy setting as enabled. When configured via a Group Policy object, the setting in the Group Policy will override any local setting. In fact, if you try to run `Set-ExecutionPolicy`, it'll work, but a warning message will tell you that your new setting had no effect due to a Group Policy override.

- *By manually running PowerShell.exe and using its* `-ExecutionPolicy` *command-line switch.* When you run it in this fashion, the specified execution policy will override any local setting as well as any Group Policy–defined setting.

You can set the execution policy to one of five settings (note that the Group Policy object only provides access to the middle three of the following list):

- `Restricted`—This is the default, and scripts aren't executed. The only exceptions are a few Microsoft-supplied scripts that set up PowerShell's default configuration settings. Those scripts carry a Microsoft digital signature and won't execute if modified.
- `AllSigned`—PowerShell will execute any script that has been digitally signed by using a code-signing certificate issued by a trusted Certification Authority (CA).

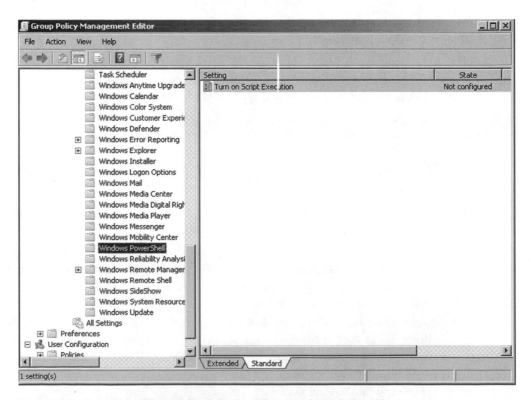

Figure 17.1   Finding the Windows PowerShell settings in a Group Policy object

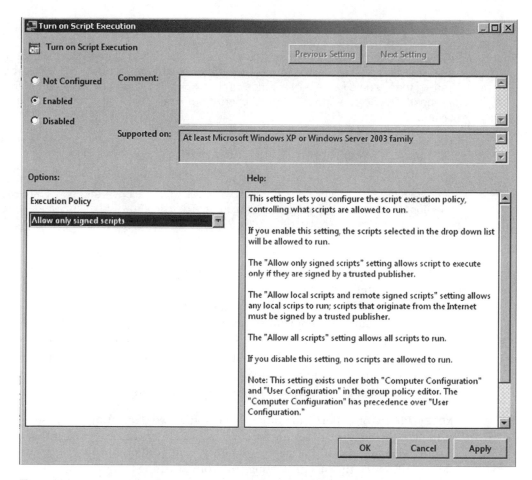

Figure 17.2 Changing the Windows PowerShell execution policy in a Group Policy object

- `RemoteSigned`—PowerShell will execute any local script, and will execute remote scripts if they've been digitally signed by using a code-signing certificate issued by a trusted CA. "Remote scripts" are those that exist on a remote computer, usually accessed by a Universal Naming Convention (UNC) path. Scripts marked as having come from the internet are also considered "remote"; Internet Explorer, Firefox, and Outlook all mark downloads as having come from the internet. Some versions of Windows can distinguish between internet paths and UNC paths; in those cases, UNC paths on the local network aren't considered "remote."

- `Unrestricted`—All scripts will run. We don't like nor recommend this setting, because it provides too little protection.

- `Bypass`—This special setting is intended for use by application developers who are embedding PowerShell within their application. This setting bypasses the configured execution policy and should be used only when the hosting application is providing its own layer of script security.

Wait, what?

Did you notice that you could set the execution policy in a Group Policy object, but also override it using a parameter of PowerShell.exe? What good is a GPO-controlled setting that people can easily override? This emphasizes that the execution policy is intended only to protect *uninformed* users from *unintentionally* running *anonymous* scripts.

The execution policy isn't intended to stop an informed user from doing anything intentional. It's not that kind of security setting.

In fact, the odds of someone using a PowerShell script to propagate malware aren't necessarily all that high. A smart malware coder would access the .NET Framework functionality directly, without going to the trouble of using PowerShell as a middleman.

Microsoft recommends that you use `RemoteSigned` when you want to run scripts, and that you use it only on computers where scripts must be executed. According to Microsoft, all other computers should be left at `Restricted`. The company says that `RemoteSigned` provides a good balance between security and convenience; `AllSigned` is stricter but it requires all of your scripts to be digitally signed. The PowerShell community as a whole is more divided, with a range of opinions on what a good execution policy is. For now, we'll go with Microsoft's recommendation and let you explore the topic more on your own, if you wish.

This would be a good time for us to discuss digital signing in depth.

NOTE   Plenty of experts, including Microsoft's own "Scripting Guy," suggest using the `Unrestricted` setting for `ExecutionPolicy`. Their feeling is that the feature doesn't provide a layer of security, and you shouldn't give yourself false confidence that it's protecting you from anything.

17.3.2 *Digital code signing*

Digital code signing, *code signing* for short, is the process of applying a cryptographic signature to a text file. Signatures appear at the end of the file and look something like the following:

```
<!-- SIG # Begin signature block -->
<!-- MIIXXAYJKoZIhvcNAQcCoIIXTTCCF0kCAQExCzAJBgUrDgMCGgUAMGkGCisGAQQB -->
<!-- gjcCAQSgWzBZMDQGCisGAQQBgjcCAR4wJgIDAQAABBAfzDtgWUsITrck0sYpfvNR -->
<!-- AgEAAgEAAgEAAgEAMCEwCQYFKw4DAhoFAAQUJ7qroHx47PI1dIt4lBg6Y5Jo -->
<!-- UVigghIxMIIEYDCCA0ygAwIBAgIKLqsR3FD/XJ3LwDAJBgUrDgMCHQUAMHAxKzAp -->
<!-- YjcCn4FqI4n2XGOPsFq7OddgjFWEGjP1O5igggyiX4uzLLehpcur2iC2vzAZhSAU -->
<!-- DSq8UvRB4F4w45IoaYfBcOLzp6vOgEJydg4wggR6MIIDYqADAgECAgphBieBAAAA -->
<!-- ZngnZui2t++Fuc3uqv0SpAtZIikvz0DZVgQbdrVtZG1KVNvd8d6/n4PHgN9/TAI3 -->
<!-- an/xvmG4PNGSdjy8Dcbb5otiSjgByprAttPPf2EKUQrFPzREgZabAatwMKJbeRS4 -->
<!-- kd6Qy+RwkCn1UWIeaChbs0LJhix0jm38/pLCCOo1nL79E1sxJumCe6GtqjdWOIBn -->
<!-- KKe66D/GX7eGrfCVg2Vzgp4gG7fHADFEh3OcIvoILWc= -->
<!-- SIG # End signature block -->
```

The signature contains two important pieces of information: First, it lists the identity of the company or organization that signed the script. Second, it includes an encrypted copy of the script, which PowerShell can decrypt. Understanding how this works requires a bit of background information, which will also help you make some important decisions about security in your environment.

In order to create a digital signature, you need to have a code-signing certificate. Also referred to as Class 3 certificates, these are available from commercial CAs like Cybertrust, GoDaddy, Thawte, VeriSign, and others. You might also obtain one from your company's internal public-key infrastructure (PKI), if you have one. Class 3 certificates are normally issued only to organizations and companies, not to individuals, although your company may issue them internally to specific users. Before issuing a certificate, the CA is responsible for verifying the identity of the recipient—the certificate is a kind of digital identification card, listing the holder's name and other details. Before issuing a certificate to XYZ Corporation, for example, a CA needs to verify that an authorized representative of XYZ Corporation is making the request. This verification process is the single most important step in the entire security framework, and you should only trust a CA that you know does a good job of verifying the identities of the companies to which it issues certificates. If you're not familiar with a CA's verification procedures, you *should not trust* that CA.

Trust is configured in Windows' Internet Properties control panel (and can also be configured by Group Policy). In that control panel, select the Content tab, and then click Publishers. In the resulting dialog box, select the Trusted Root Certification Authorities tab. As shown in figure 17.3, you'll see a list of the CAs that your computer trusts.

When you trust a CA, you also trust all certificates issued by it. If someone uses a certificate to sign a malicious script, you can use the signature itself to track down the

Figure 17.3 Configuring your computer's Trusted Root Certification Authorities

author—that's why signed scripts are considered more "trusted" than unsigned scripts. But if you place your trust in a CA that does a bad job of verifying identities, a malicious script author might be able to obtain a fraudulent certificate, and you wouldn't be able to use their signature to track them down. That's why choosing which CAs to trust is such a big responsibility.

Once you've obtained a Class 3 certificate (specifically, you need one packaged as an Authenticode certificate—CAs usually offer different varieties for different operating systems and programming languages), you install it on your computer. Once installed, you can then use PowerShell's `Set-AuthenticodeSignature` cmdlet to apply a digital signature to a script. Run `help about_signing` in the shell to learn more. Many commercial script development environments (PrimalScript, PowerShell Plus, PowerGUI, and others) can also apply signatures, and can even do that automatically when you save a script, making the signing process more transparent for you.

Signatures not only provide information about the script author's identity, they also ensure that the script hasn't been modified since the author signed it. It works as follows:

1. The script author holds a digital certificate, which consists of two cryptographic keys: a public key and a private key.
2. When signing a script, the signature is encrypted using the private key. Only the script author has access to that key, and only the public key can decrypt the signature. The signature contains a copy of the script.
3. When PowerShell runs the script, it uses the author's public key (which is included along with the signature) to decrypt the signature. If the decryption fails, the signature was tampered with, and the script won't run. If the copy of the script within the signature doesn't match the clear-text copy, the signature is considered broken, and the script won't run.

Figure 17.4 illustrates the entire process that PowerShell goes through when trying to run a script. You can see how the `AllSigned` execution policy is somewhat more secure: under that setting, only scripts containing a signature will execute, meaning that you'll always be able to identify a script's author. You'll also have to sign every script you want to run, and resign them any time you change them, which can be inconvenient.

17.4 *Other security measures*

PowerShell has two other key security measures that are in effect at all times, and they shouldn't be modified.

First, Windows doesn't consider the .PS1 filename extension (which is what the shell uses to identify PowerShell scripts) an executable file type. Double-clicking a .PS1 file will normally open it in Notepad for editing, rather than execute it. This configuration is intended to help prevent users from unknowingly executing a script, even if the execution policy would allow it.

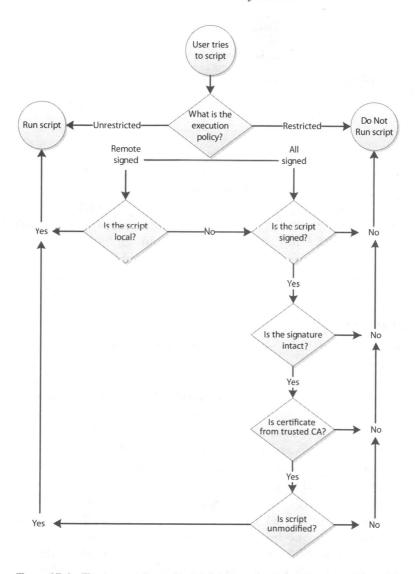

Figure 17.4 The process PowerShell follows when attempting to execute a script

Second, you can't run a script within the shell by typing its name. The shell never searches the current directory for scripts, which means if you have a script named test.ps1, changing to its folder and typing test or test.ps1 won't run the script.

Here's an example:

```
PS C:\> test
The term 'test' is not recognized as the name of a cmdlet, function, scrip
t file, or operable program. Check the spelling of the name, or if a path
was included, verify that the path is correct and try again.
At line:1 char:5
+ test <<<<
```

```
    + CategoryInfo          : ObjectNotFound: (test:String) [], CommandNo
  tFoundException
    + FullyQualifiedErrorId : CommandNotFoundException

Suggestion [3,General]: The command test was not found, but does exist in t
he current location. Windows PowerShell doesn't load commands from the curr
ent location by default. If you trust this command, instead type ".\test".
See "get-help about_Command_Precedence" for more details.
PS C:\>
```

As you can see in the previous example, PowerShell does detect the script but warns you that you have to type either an absolute or relative path in order to run the script. Because the script is located in C:, you could run either `C:\test`, which is an absolute path, or run `.\test`, which is a relative path that points to the current folder.

The purpose of this security feature is to guard against a type of attack called command hijacking. The attack involves putting a script into a folder, and giving it the same name as a built-in command, such as `Dir`. With PowerShell, you never put a path in front of a command name—if you run `Dir`, you know you're running the command; if you run `.\Dir`, you know you're running a script named Dir.ps1.

17.5   *Other security holes?*

As we discussed earlier in this chapter, PowerShell's security focuses primarily on preventing users from unknowingly running untrusted scripts. No security measures can stop a user from manually typing commands into the shell, or from copying the entire contents of a script and pasting them into the shell (although the commands might not have the same effect when run in that fashion). It's a little more difficult to convince a user to do that, and to explain to them how to do it, which is why Microsoft didn't focus on that scenario as a potential attack vector. But remember, PowerShell doesn't grant your users any additional permissions—they'll only be able to do those things that you've permitted them to do.

Someone could call a user on the phone, or send an email, and walk them through the process of opening PowerShell, typing a few commands, and damaging their computer. But that same someone could also talk a user through an attack using something other than PowerShell. It'd be as easy (or difficult, depending on your viewpoint) to convince a user to open Explorer, select the Program Files folder, and hit Delete on the keyboard. In some ways, that would be easier than walking a user through the equivalent PowerShell command.

We point this out only because people tend to get nervous about the command line and its seemingly infinite reach and power, but the fact is that you and your users can't do anything with the shell that you couldn't do in a half dozen other ways.

17.6   *Security recommendations*

As we mentioned earlier, Microsoft recommends the use of the `RemoteSigned` execution policy for computers where you need to run scripts. You can also consider using `AllSigned` or even `Unrestricted`.

`AllSigned` is a bit less convenient, but you can make it more convenient by following these two recommendations:

- Commercial CAs charge up to $900 per year for a code-signing certificate. If you don't have an internal PKI that can provide a free one, you can make your own. Run `help about_signing` for information on obtaining and using Makecert .exe, a tool that will make a certificate that will be trusted only by your local computer. If that's the only place where you need to run scripts, it's a quick and free way to obtain a certificate.
- Edit scripts in one of the editors we mentioned, each of which can sign the script for you each time you save the file. That makes the signing process transparent and automatic, making it more convenient.

As we've already stated, we don't think you should change the .PS1 filename association. We've seen some folks modify Windows to recognize .PS1 as an executable, meaning that you can double-click a script to run it. That takes us right back to the bad old days of VBScript, and you probably want to avoid that.

We want to point out that none of the scripts we supply on MoreLunches.com are digitally signed. That means it's possible for those to be modified without our (or your) knowledge. Before you run any of those scripts, you should take the time to review them, understand what they're supposed to do, and make sure they match what's in this book (if appropriate). We didn't sign the scripts specifically because we *want you to take that time*: you should be in the habit of carefully reviewing anything you download from the internet, no matter how "trusted" the author may seem.

17.7 Lab

NOTE For this lab, you'll need any computer running PowerShell v3.

Your task in this lab is simple—so simple, in fact, that we won't even post a sample solution on MoreLunches.com. We want you to configure your shell to allow script execution. Use the `Set-ExecutionPolicy` cmdlet, and we suggest using the `RemoteSigned` policy setting. You're welcome to use `AllSigned`, but it'll be impractical for the purposes of this book's remaining labs. You could also choose `Unrestricted`.

That said, if you're using PowerShell in a production environment, please make sure that the execution policy setting you choose is compatible with your organization's security rules and procedures. We don't want you getting in trouble for the sake of this book and its labs.

Variables: a place to store your stuff

18

We've already mentioned that PowerShell contains a scripting language, and in a few more chapters we'll start to play with it. But once you start scripting, you tend to start needing *variables*, so we'll get those out of the way in this chapter. You can use variables in a lot of places other than long, complex scripts, so we'll also use this chapter to show you some practical ways to use them.

18.1 Introduction to variables

A simple way to think of a variable is as a box in the computer's memory that has a name. You can put whatever you want into the box: a single computer name, a collection of services, an XML document, and so on. You access the box by using its name, and when accessing it, you can put things in it, add things to it, or retrieve things from it. Those things stay in the box, allowing you to retrieve them over and over.

PowerShell doesn't place a lot of formality around variables. For example, you don't have to explicitly announce or declare your intention to use a variable before you do so. You can also change the types of the contents of a variable: one moment, you might have a single process in it, and the next moment you can store a bunch of computer names in it. A variable can even contain multiple different things, such as a collection of services *and* a collection of processes (although we admit that, in those cases, using the variable's contents can be tricky).

18.2　*Storing values in variables*

Everything in PowerShell—and we do mean *everything*—is treated as an object. Even a simple string of characters, such as a computer name, is considered an object. For example, piping a string to `Get-Member` (or its alias, `Gm`) reveals that the object is of the type `System.String` and that it has a great many methods you can work with (we're truncating the following list to save space):

```
PS C:\> "SERVER-R2" | gm

    TypeName: System.String

Name            MemberType      Definition
----            ----------      ----------
Clone           Method          System.Object Clone()
CompareTo       Method          int CompareTo(System.Object valu...
Contains        Method          bool Contains(string value)
CopyTo          Method          System.Void CopyTo(int sourceInd...
EndsWith        Method          bool EndsWith(string value), boo...
Equals          Method          bool Equals(System.Object obj), ...
GetEnumerator   Method          System.CharEnumerator GetEnumera...
GetHashCode     Method          int GetHashCode()
GetType         Method          type GetType()
GetTypeCode     Method          System.TypeCode GetTypeCode()
IndexOf         Method          int IndexOf(char value), int Ind...
IndexOfAny      Method          int IndexOfAny(char[] anyOf), in...
```

> **TRY IT NOW**　Run this same command in PowerShell to see if you get the complete list of methods—and even a property—that comes with a `System.String` object.

Although that string is technically an object, like everything else in the shell, you'll find that folks tend to refer to it as a simple *value*. That's because, in most cases, what you're concerned about is the string itself—`"SERVER-R2"` in the previous example—and you're less concerned about retrieving information from properties. That's different from, say, a process, where the entire process object is a big, abstract data construct, and you're usually dealing with individual properties such as VM, PM, Name, CPU, ID, and so forth. A `String` is an object, but it's a much less complicated object than something like a `Process`.

　　PowerShell allows you to store these simple values in a variable. To do this, specify the variable, and use the equal sign operator—the *assignment* operator—followed by whatever you want to put within the variable. Here's an example:

```
PS C:\> $var = "SERVER-R2"
```

> **TRY IT NOW**　You'll want to follow along with these examples, because then you'll be able to replicate the results we demonstrate. You should use your test server's name rather than SERVER-R2.

It's important to note that the dollar sign ($) isn't part of the variable's name. In our example, the variable name is var. The dollar sign is a cue to the shell that what follows is going to be a variable name, and that we want to access the contents of that variable. In this case, we're setting the contents of the variable.

- Let's look at some key points to keep in mind about variables and their names:
- Variable names usually contain letters, numbers, and underscores, and it's most common for them to begin with a letter or an underscore.
- Variable names can contain spaces, but the name must be enclosed in curly braces. For example, `${My Variable}` is how you represent a variable named "My Variable". Personally, we dislike variable names that contain spaces because they require more typing and they're harder to read.
- Variables don't persist between shell sessions. When you close the shell, any variables you created go away.
- Variable names can be quite long—long enough that you don't need to worry about how long. Try to make variable names sensible. For example, if you'll be putting a computer name into a variable, use `computername` as the variable name. If a variable will contain a bunch of processes, then `processes` is a good variable name.
- Except for folks who have a VBScript background, PowerShell users don't typically use variable name prefixes to indicate what's stored in the variable. For example, in VBScript, `strComputerName` was a common type of variable name, indicating that the variable stored a string (the "str" part). PowerShell doesn't care if you do that, but it's no longer considered a desirable practice by the community at large.

To retrieve the contents of a variable, use the dollar sign followed by the variable name, as shown in the following example. Again, the dollar sign tells the shell you want to access the *contents* of a variable; following it with the variable name tells the shell which variable you're accessing.

```
PS C:\> $var
SERVER-R2
```

You can use a variable in place of a value in almost any situation. For example, when using WMI, you have the option to specify a computer name. The command might normally look like this:

```
PS C:\> get-wmiobject win32_computersystem -comp SERVER-R2

Domain             : company.pri
Manufacturer       : VMware, Inc.
Model              : VMware Virtual Platform
Name               : SERVER-R2
PrimaryOwnerName   : Windows User
TotalPhysicalMemory : 3220758528
```

You can substitute a variable for any of the values:

```
PS C:\> get-wmiobject win32_computersystem -comp $var

Domain              : company.pri
Manufacturer        : VMware, Inc.
Model               : VMware Virtual Platform
Name                : SERVER-R2
PrimaryOwnerName    : Windows User
TotalPhysicalMemory : 3220758528
```

By the way, we realize that var is a pretty generic variable name. We'd normally use computername, but in this specific instance we plan to reuse $var in several situations, so we decided to keep it generic. Don't let this example stop you from using more sensible variable names in real life.

We may have put a string into $var to begin with, but we can change that anytime we want:

```
PS C:\> $var = 5
PS C:\> $var | gm

   TypeName: System.Int32

Name        MemberType Definition
----        ---------- ----------
CompareTo   Method     int CompareTo(System.Object value), int CompareT...
Equals      Method     bool Equals(System.Object obj), bool Equals(int ...
GetHashCode Method     int GetHashCode()
GetType     Method     type GetType()
GetTypeCode Method     System.TypeCode GetTypeCode()
ToString    Method     string ToString(), string ToString(string format...
```

In the preceding example, we placed an integer into $var, and then we piped $var to Gm. You can see that the shell recognizes the contents of $var as a System.Int32, or a 32-bit integer.

18.3 Using variables: fun tricks with quotes

Because we're talking about variables, this is a good time to cover a neat PowerShell feature. To this point in the book, we've advised you to generally enclose strings within single quotation marks. The reason for that is PowerShell treats everything enclosed in single quotation marks as a literal string.

Consider the following example:

```
PS C:\> $var = 'What does $var contain?'
PS C:\> $var
What does $var contain?
```

In the preceding example, you can see that the $var within single quotes is treated as a literal.

But in double quotation marks that's not the case. Check out the following trick:

```
PS C:\> $computername = 'SERVER-R2'
PS C:\> $phrase = "The computer name is $computername"
PS C:\> $phrase
The computer name is SERVER-R2
```

We started our example by storing SERVER-R2 in the variable $computername. Next, we stored "The computer name is $computername" in the variable $phrase. When we did this, we used double quotes. PowerShell automatically seeks out dollar signs within double quotes, and replaces any variables it finds *with their contents*. Because we displayed the contents of $phrase, $computername was replaced with SERVER-R2, the contents of the variable.

This replacement action only happens when the shell initially parses the string. At this point, $phrase contains "The computer name is SERVER-R2"—it doesn't contain the "$computername" string. We can test that by trying to change the contents of $computername to see if $phrase updates itself:

```
PS C:\> $computername = 'SERVER1'
PS C:\> $phrase
The computer name is SERVER-R2
```

As you can see, the $phrase variable stayed the same.

Another facet of this double-quotes trick is the PowerShell escape character. This character is the backtick (`` ` ``), and on a U.S. keyboard it's located on one of the upper-left keys, usually below the Escape key and often on the same key as the tilde (~) character. The problem is that, in some fonts, it's practically indistinguishable from a single quote. In fact, we usually configure our shell to use the Consolas font, because that makes distinguishing the backtick easier than when using the Lucida Console or Raster fonts.

> **TRY IT NOW**   Click the control box in the upper-left corner of your PowerShell window, and select Properties. On the Font tab, select the Consolas font as shown in figure 18.1. Click OK, and type a single quote and a backtick so you can see the difference between these characters. Figure 18.1 shows what it looks like on our system. Can't see the difference? We barely can, either, even when using a large font size. It's a tough distinction, but make sure you're comfortable distinguishing between these characters in whatever font face and size you select.

Let's look at what this escape character does. It removes whatever special meaning might be associated with the character after it, or in some cases, it adds special meaning to the following character. We have an example of this first use:

```
PS C:\> $computername = 'SERVER-R2'
PS C:\> $phrase = "`$computername contains $computername"
PS C:\> $phrase
$computername contains SERVER-R2
```

When we assigned the string to $phrase, we used $computername twice. The first time, we preceded the dollar sign with a backtick. Doing this took away the dollar sign's special meaning as a variable indicator and made it a literal dollar sign. You can see in the preceding output, on the last line, that $computername was stored in the variable. We didn't use the backtick the second time, so $computername was replaced with the contents of that variable.

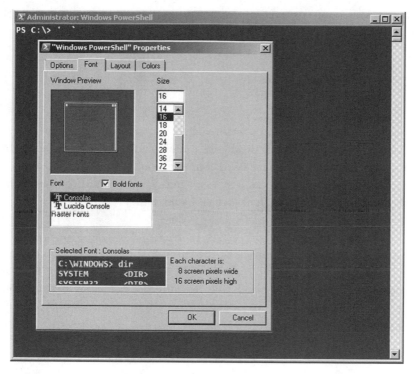

Figure 18.1 Setting a font that makes it easier to distinguish the backtick character from the single quote

Now, let's look at an example of the second way a backtick can work:

```
PS C:\> $phrase = "`$computername`ncontains`n$computername"
PS C:\> $phrase
$computername
contains
SERVER-R2
```

Look carefully, and you'll notice we used `n twice in the phrase—once after the first $computername and once after contains. In the example, the backtick is adding a special meaning. Normally, "n" is a letter, but with the backtick in front of it, it becomes a carriage return and line feed (think "n" for "new line").

Run help about_escape for more information, including a list of other special escape characters. You can, for example, use an escaped "t" to insert a tab, or an escaped "a" to make your computer beep (think "a" for "alert").

18.4 Storing many objects in a variable

To this point, we've been working with variables that contain a single object, and those objects have all been simple values. We've worked directly with the objects themselves, rather than with their properties or methods. Let's now try putting a bunch of objects into a single variable.

One way to do this is to use a comma-separated list, because PowerShell recognizes those lists as collections of objects:

```
PS C:\> $computers = 'SERVER-R2','SERVER1','localhost'
PS C:\> $computers
SERVER-R2
SERVER1
Localhost
```

Notice that we were careful in the previous example to put the commas outside the quotation marks. If we'd put them inside, we'd have had a single object that included commas and three computer names. With our method, we get three distinct objects, all of which are String types. As you can see, when we examined the contents of the variable, PowerShell displayed each object on its own line.

18.4.1 *Working with single objects in a variable*

You can also access individual elements in the variable, one at a time. To do this, specify an index number for the object you want, in square brackets. The first object is always at index number 0, the second is at index number 1, and so forth. You can also use an index of -1 to access the last object, -2 for the next-to-last object, and so on. Here's an example:

```
PS C:\> $computers[0]
SERVER-R2
PS C:\> $computers[1]
SERVER1
PS C:\> $computers[-1]
localhost
PS C:\> $computers[-2]
SERVER1
```

The variable itself has a property that lets you see how many objects are in it:

```
PS C:\> $computers.count
3
```

You can also access the properties and methods of the objects inside the variable as if they were properties and methods of the variable itself. This is a bit easier to see, at first, with a variable that contains a single object:

```
PS C:\> $computername.length
9
PS C:\> $computername.toupper()
SERVER-R2
PS C:\> $computername.tolower()
server-r2
PS C:\> $computername.replace('R2','2008')
SERVER-2008
PS C:\> $computername
SERVER-R2
```

In the previous example, we're using the $computername variable we created earlier in the chapter. If you remember, that variable contained an object of the type System .String, and you should have seen the complete list of properties and methods of that type when you piped a string to Gm in section 18.2. We've used the Length property, as well as the ToUpper(), ToLower(), and Replace() methods. In each case, we had to follow the method name with parentheses, even though neither ToUpper() nor ToLower() require any parameters inside those parentheses. Also, none of these methods changed what was in the variable—you can see that on the last line. Instead, each method created a new String based on the original one, as modified by the method.

18.4.2 *Working with multiple objects in a variable*

When a variable contains multiple objects, the steps can get a bit trickier. Even if every object inside the variable is of the same type, as is the case with our $computers variable, PowerShell v2 didn't let you *call a method, or access a property, on multiple objects at the same time.* If you tried to do so, you got an error:

```
PS C:\> $computers.toupper()
Method invocation failed because [System.Object[]] doesn't contain a metho
d named 'toupper'.
At line:1 char:19
+ $computers.toupper <<<< ()
    + CategoryInfo          : InvalidOperation: (toupper:String) [], Runt
    imeException
    + FullyQualifiedErrorId : MethodNotFound
```

Instead, you would have to specify which object within the variable you want, and then access a property or execute a method on that specific object:

```
PS C:\> $computers[0].tolower()
server-r2
PS C:\> $computers[1].replace('SERVER','CLIENT')
CLIENT1
```

Again, these methods are producing new strings, not changing the ones inside the variable. You can test that by examining the contents of the variable:

```
PS C:\> $computers
SERVER-R2
SERVER1
Localhost
```

What if you want to change the contents of the variable? You'd assign a new value to one of the existing objects:

```
PS C:\> $computers[1] = $computers[1].replace('SERVER','CLIENT')
PS C:\> $computers
SERVER-R2
CLIENT1
Localhost
```

You can see in this example that we changed the second object in the variable, rather than producing a new string. We point this out in case you're dealing with computers that only have PowerShell v2 installed; the behavior has changed a bit for v3, as we'll see in a bit.

18.4.3 *Other ways to work with multiple objects*

We want to show you two other options for working with the properties and methods of a bunch of objects contained in a variable. The previous examples only executed methods on a single object within the variable. If you wanted to run the `ToLower()` method on every object within the variable, and store the results back into the variable, you'd do something like this:

```
PS C:\> $computers = $computers | ForEach-Object { $_.ToLower() }
PS C:\> $computers
server-r2
client1
localhost
```

This example is a bit complicated, so let's break it down in figure 18.2. We started the pipeline with `$computers =`, which means the results of the pipeline will be stored in that variable. Those results will overwrite whatever was in the variable previously.

The pipeline begins with `$computers` being piped to `ForEach-Object`. The cmdlet will enumerate each object in the pipeline (we have three computer names, which are `String` objects), and execute its script block for each. Within the script block, the `$_` placeholder will contain one piped-in object at a time, and we're executing the `ToLower()` method of each object. The new `String` objects produced by `ToLower()` will be placed into the pipeline—and into the `$computers` variable.

You can do something similar with properties by using `Select-Object`. This example will select the `Length` property of each object you pipe to the cmdlet:

```
PS C:\> $computers | select-object length

                                                          Length
                                                          ------
                                                               9
                                                               7
                                                               9
```

Because the property is numeric, PowerShell right-aligns the output.

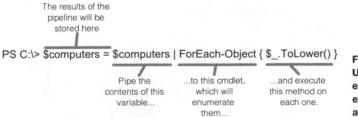

The results of the pipeline will be stored here

```
PS C:\> $computers = $computers | ForEach-Object { $_.ToLower() }
```

Pipe the contents of this variable...

...to this cmdlet, which will enumerate them...

...and execute this method on each one.

Figure 18.2 Using `ForEach-Object` to execute a method against each object contained within a variable

18.4.4 *Unrolling Properties and Methods in PowerShell v3*

All this business of "you can't access properties and methods when a variable contains multiple objects" proved to be extremely confusing for users of PowerShell v1 and v2. So confusing that, for v3, Microsoft made an important change, called *automatic unrolling*. Essentially, it means you now *can* access properties and methods using a variable that contains multiple objects:

```
$services = Get-Service
$services.Name
```

Under the hood, PowerShell "sees" that you're trying to access a property, in that example. It also sees that the collection in $services doesn't have a Name property – but that the individual objects within the collection do. So it implicitly enumerates, or unrolls, the objects, and grabs the Name property of each. This is equivalent to:

```
Get-Service | ForEach-Object { Write-Output $_.Name }
```

And also equivalent to:

```
Get-Service | Select-Object -ExpandProperty Name
```

Which are the two ways you'd have had to do this in v1 and v2. The same thing works for methods:

```
$objects = Get-WmiObject –class Win32_Service -filter "name='BITS'"
$objects.ChangeStartMode('Disabled')
```

Just bear in mind that this is a PowerShell v3 feature – don't expect it to work this way on older versions of PowerShell.

18.5 *More tricks with double quotes*

We have another cool technique you can use with double quotes, which is a somewhat conceptual extension of the variable-replacement trick. Suppose, for example, that you've put a bunch of services into the $service variable. Now, you want to put only the name of the first one into a string:

```
PS C:\> $services = get-service
PS C:\> $firstname = "$services[0].name"
PS C:\> $firstname
AeLookupSvc ALG AllUserInstallAgent AppIDSvc Appinfo AppMgmt AudioEndpoint
Builder Audiosrv AxInstSV BDESVC BFE BITS BrokerInfrastructure Browser bth
serv CertPropSvc COMSysApp CryptSvc CscService DcomLaunch defragsvc Device
AssociationService DeviceInstall Dhcp Dnscache dot3svc DPS DsmSvc Eaphost
EFS ehRecvr ehSched EventLog EventSystem Fax fdPHost FDResPub fhsvc FontCa
che gpsvc hidserv hkmsvc HomeGroupListener HomeGroupProvider IKEEXT iphlps
vc KeyIso KtmRm LanmanServer LanmanWorkstation lltdsvc lmhosts LSM Mcx2Svc
 MMCSS MpsSvc MSDTC MSiSCSI msiserver napagent NcaSvc NcdAutoSetup Netlogo
n Netman netprofm NetTcpPortSharing NlaSvc nsi p2pimsvc p2psvc Parallels C
oherence Service Parallels Tools Service PcaSvc PeerDistSvc PerfHost pla P
lugPlay PNRPAutoReg PNRPsvc PolicyAgent Power PrintNotify ProfSvc QWAVE Ra
sAuto RasMan RemoteAccess RemoteRegistry RpcEptMapper RpcLocator RpcSs Sam
Ss SCardSvr Schedule SCPolicySvc SDRSVC seclogon SENS SensrSvc SessionEnv
```

```
SharedAccess ShellHWDetection SNMPTRAP Spooler sppsvc SSDPSRV SstpSvc stis
vc StorSvc svsvc swprv SysMain SystemEventsBroker TabletInputService TapiS
rv TermService Themes THREADORDER TimeBroker TrkWks TrustedInstaller UI0De
tect UmRdpService upnphost VaultSvc vds vmicheartbeat vmickvpexchange vmic
rdv vmicshutdown vmictimesync vmicvss VSS W32Time wbengine WbioSrvc Wcmsvc
 wcncsvc WcsPlugInService WdiServiceHost WdiSystemHost WdNisSvc WebClient
Wecsvc wercplsupport WerSvc WiaRpc WinDefend WinHttpAutoProxySvc Winmgmt W
inRM WlanSvc wlidsvc wmiApSrv WMPNetworkSvc WPCSvc WPDBusEnum wscsvc WSear
ch WSService wuauserv wudfsvc WwanSvc[0].name
```

Err, oops. The `[` immediately after `$services` in the example isn't normally a legal character in a variable name, which caused PowerShell to try and replace `$services`. Doing this jammed the name of every service into your string. The `[0].name` part wasn't replaced at all.

The solution is to put all of that into an expression:

```
PS C:\> $services = get-service
PS C:\> $firstname = "The first name is $($services[0].name)"
PS C:\> $firstname
The first name is AeLookupSvc
```

Everything within `$()` is evaluated as a normal PowerShell command, and the result is placed into the string, replacing anything that was already there. Again, this only works in double quotes. This `$()` construct is called a *subexpression.*

We have another cool trick you can do in PowerShell v3. Sometimes, you'll want to put something more complicated into a variable, and then display that variable's contents within quotation marks. In PowerShell v3, the shell is smart enough to enumerate all of the objects in a collection even when you refer to a single property or method, provided that all of the objects in the collection are of the same type. For example, we'll retrieve a list of services and put them into the `$service` variable, and then include only the services' names in double quotes:

```
PS C:\> $services = get-service
PS C:\> $var = "Service names are $services.name"
PS C:\> $var
Service names are AeLookupSvc ALG AllUserInstallAgent AppIDSvc Appinfo App
Mgmt AudioEndpointBuilder Audiosrv AxInstSV BDESVC BFE BITS BrokerInfrastr
ucture Browser bthserv CertPropSvc COMSysApp CryptSvc CscService DcomLaunc
h defragsvc DeviceAssociationService DeviceInstall Dhcp Dnscache dot3svc D
PS DsmSvc Eaphost EFS ehRecvr ehSched EventLog EventSystem Fax fdPHost FDR
esPub fhsvc FontCache FontCache3.0.0.0 gpsvc hidserv hkmsvc HomeGroupListe
ner HomeGroupProvider IKEEXT iphlpsvc KeyIso KtmRm LanmanServer LanmanWork
station lltdsvc lmhosts LSM Mcx2Svc MMCSS MpsSvc MSDTC MSiSCSI msiserver M
SSQL$SQLEXPRESS napagent NcaSvc NcdAutoSetup Netlogon Netman netprofm NetT
cpPortSharing NlaSvc nsi p2pimsvc p2psvc Parallels Coherence Service Paral
lels Tools Service PcaSvc PeerDistSvc PerfHost pla PlugPlay PNRPAutoReg PN
RPsvc PolicyAgent Power PrintNotify ProfSvc QWAVE RasAuto RasMan RemoteAcc
ess RemoteRegistry RpcEptMapper RpcLocator RpcSs SamSs SCardSvr Schedule S
CPolicySvc SDRSVC seclogon SENS SensrSvc SessionEnv SharedAccess ShellHWDe
```

We truncated the preceding output a bit to save some space, but we hope you get the idea. Obviously, this might not be the exact output you're looking for, but between this technique and the subexpressions technique we showed you earlier in this section, you should be able to get exactly what you want.

18.6　*Declaring a variable's type*

So far we've only put objects into variables and let PowerShell figure out what types of objects we were using. The fact is that PowerShell doesn't care what kind of objects you put into the box. But you might care.

For example, suppose you have a variable that you expect to contain a number. You plan to do some arithmetic with that number, and you ask a user to input that number. Let's look at an example, which you can type directly into the command line:

```
PS C:\> $number = Read-Host "Enter a number"
Enter a number: 100
PS C:\> $number = $number * 10
PS C:\> $number
1001001001001001001001001001001 00
```

> **TRY IT NOW**　We haven't showed you Read-Host yet—we're saving it for the next chapter—but its operation should be obvious if you follow along with this example.

What the heck? How can 100 multiplied by 10 be 1001001001001001001001001001001001? What crazy new math is that?

If you're sharp-eyed, you may have spotted what's happening. PowerShell didn't treat our input as a number; it treated it as a string. Instead of multiplying 100 by 10, PowerShell *duplicated the string "100" ten times.* The result then is the string 100, listed ten times in a row. Oops.

We can verify that the shell is in fact treating the input as a string:

```
PS C:\> $number = Read-Host "Enter a number"
Enter a number: 100
PS C:\> $number | gm

    TypeName: System.String

Name        MemberType          Definition
----        ----------          ----------
Clone       Method              System.Object Clone()
CompareTo   Method              int CompareTo(System.Object valu...
Contains    Method              bool Contains(string value)
```

Yep, piping $number to Gm confirms that the shell sees it as a System.String, not a System.Int32. There are a couple of ways you could choose to deal with this problem, and we'll show you the easiest one.

First, we'll tell the shell that the $number variable should contain an integer, which will force the shell to try to convert any input to a real number. We do that in the following example by specifying the desired data type, int, in square brackets immediately prior to the variable's first use:

```
PS C:\> [int]$number = Read-Host "Enter a number"
Enter a number: 100
PS C:\> $number | gm
```

⟵ **①** Force variable to [int]

```
   TypeName: System.Int32
```

⟵ **②** Confirm that variable is Int32

```
Name          MemberType  Definition
----          ----------  ----------
CompareTo     Method      int CompareTo(System.Object value), int CompareT...
Equals        Method      bool Equals(System.Object obj), bool Equals(int ...
GetHashCode   Method      int GetHashCode()
GetType       Method      type GetType()
GetTypeCode   Method      System.TypeCode GetTypeCode()
ToString      Method      string ToString(), string ToString(string format...

PS C:\> $number = $number * 10
PS C:\> $number
1000
```

③ Variable was treated as number ⟵

In the previous example, we used [int] to force $number to contain only integers **①**. After entering our input, we piped $number to Gm to confirm that it's indeed an integer, and not a string **②**. At the end, you can see that the variable was treated as a number and real multiplication took place **③**.

Another benefit to using this technique is that the shell will throw an error if it can't convert the input into a number, because $number is only capable of storing integers:

```
PS C:\> [int]$number = Read-Host "Enter a number"
Enter a number: Hello
Cannot convert value "Hello" to type "System.Int32". Error: "Input string
was not in a correct format."
At line:1 char:13
+ [int]$number <<<<  = Read-Host "Enter a number"
    + CategoryInfo          : MetadataError: (:) [], ArgumentTransformati
  onMetadataException
    + FullyQualifiedErrorId : RuntimeException
```

This is a great example of how to prevent problems later on down the line, because you're assured that $number will contain the exact type of data you expect it to.

You can use many different object types in place of [int], but the following list includes some of the ones you'll most commonly use:

- [int]—Integer numbers
- [single] and [double]—Single-precision and double-precision floating numbers (numbers with a decimal portion)
- [string]—A string of characters
- [char]—Exactly one character (as in, [char]$c = 'X')
- [xml]—An XML document; whatever string you assign to this will be parsed to make sure it contains valid XML markup (for example, [xml]$doc = Get-Content MyXML.xml)
- [adsi]—An Active Directory Service Interfaces (ADSI) query; the shell will execute the query and place the resulting object or objects into the variable (such as [adsi]$user = "WinNT:\\MYDOMAIN\Administrator,user")

Specifying an object type for a variable is a great way to prevent certain tricky logic errors in more complex scripts. As the following example shows, once you specify the object type, PowerShell enforces it until you explicitly retype the variable:

```
PS C:\> [int]$x = 5                                        ◄━━❶ Declares $x as integer
PS C:\> $x = 'Hello'
Cannot convert value "Hello" to type "System.Int32". Error: "Input string    ◄━  Creates
was not in a correct format."                                                     error by
At line:1 char:3                                                                  putting
+ $x <<<<  = 'Hello'                                                               string
    + CategoryInfo          : MetadataError: (:) [], ArgumentTransformati     ❷   into $x
    onMetadataException
    + FullyQualifiedErrorId : RuntimeException              ❸ Retypes $x
                                                          ◄━   as string
PS C:\> [string]$x = 'Hello'
PS C:\> $x | gm                                            ❹ Confirms new
                                                          ◄━┘  type of $x
    TypeName: System.String

Name            MemberType              Definition
----            ----------              ----------
Clone           Method                  System.Object Clone()
CompareTo       Method                  int CompareTo(System.Object valu...
```

In the previous example, you can see that we started by declaring $x as an integer ❶, and placing an integer into it. When we tried to put a string into it ❷, PowerShell threw an error because it couldn't convert that particular string into a number. Later we retyped $x as a string, and we were able to put a string into it ❸. We confirmed that by piping the variable to Gm and checking its type name ❹.

18.7 Commands for working with variables

We've started to use variables at this point, without formally declaring our intention to do so. PowerShell doesn't require advanced variable declaration, and you can't force it to make a declaration. (VBScript folks who are looking for something like Option Explicit will be disappointed; PowerShell has something called Set-StrictMode, but it isn't exactly the same thing.) But the shell does include the following commands for working with variables:

- New-Variable
- Set-Variable
- Remove-Variable
- Get-Variable
- Clear-Variable

You don't need to use any of these except perhaps for Remove-Variable, which is useful for permanently deleting a variable (you can also use the Del command within the VARIABLE: drive to delete a variable). You can perform every other function—creating new variables, reading variables, and setting variables—using the ad hoc syntax we've used up to this point in the chapter; using these cmdlets offers no specific advantages in most cases.

If you do decide to use these cmdlets, you'll give your variable name to the cmdlets' -name parameters. This is *only the variable name*—it doesn't include the dollar sign. The one time you might want to use one of these cmdlets is if you're working with something called an *out-of-scope* variable. Messing with out-of-scope variables is a poor practice, and we won't cover out-of-scope variables (or much more on scope) in this book, but you can run help about_scope in the shell to learn more.

18.8   *Variable best practices*

We've mentioned most of these practices already, but this is a good time to quickly review them:

- Keep variable names meaningful, but succinct. Whereas $computername is a great variable name because it's clear and concise, $c is a poor name, because what it contains isn't clear. The variable name $computer_to_query_for_data is a bit long for our tastes. Sure, it's meaningful, but do you want to type that over and over?
- Don't use spaces in variable names. We know you can, but it's ugly syntax.
- If a variable will only contain one kind of object, then declare that when you first use the variable. This can help prevent some confusing logic errors, and if you're working in a commercial script development environment (PrimalScript is the example we're thinking of), the editor software can provide code-hinting features when you tell it what type of object a variable will contain.

18.9   *Common points of confusion*

The biggest single point of confusion we see new students struggle with is the variable name. We hope we've done a good job of explaining it in this chapter, but always remember that the dollar sign *isn't part of the variable's name*. It's a cue to the shell that you want to access the *contents* of a variable; what follows the dollar sign is taken as the variable's name.

The shell has two parsing rules that let it capture the variable name:

- If the character immediately after the dollar sign is a letter, number, or underscore, the variable name consists of all the characters following the dollar sign, up to the next white space (which might be a space, tab, or carriage return).
- If the character immediately after the dollar sign is an opening curly brace, {, the variable name consists of everything after that curly brace up to, but not including, the closing curly brace, }.

18.10   *Lab*

NOTE   For this lab, you'll need any computer running PowerShell v3.

Flip back to chapter 15 and refresh your memory on working with background jobs. Then, at the command line, do the following:

1. Create a background job that queries the Win32_BIOS information from two computers (use "localhost" twice if you only have one computer to experiment with).

2. When the job finishes running, receive the results of the job into a variable.

3. Display the contents of that variable.

4. Export the variable's contents to a CliXML file.

18.11 *Further exploration*

Take a few moments and skim through some of the previous chapters in this book. Given that variables are primarily designed to store something you might use more than once, can you find a use for variables in our topics in previous chapters?

For example, in chapter 13 you learned to create connections to remote computers. What you did in that chapter was create, use, and close a connection more or less in one step; wouldn't it be useful to create the connection, store it in a variable, and use it for several commands? That's only one instance of where variables can come in handy (and we're going to show you how to do that in chapter 20). See if you can find any more examples.

Input and output
19

To this point in the book, we've primarily been relying on PowerShell's native ability to output tables and lists. As you start to combine commands into more complex
scripts, you'll probably want to gain more precise control over what's displayed. You
may also need to prompt a user for input. In this chapter, you'll learn how to collect that input, and how to display whatever output you might desire.

19.1 Prompting for, and displaying, information

How PowerShell displays and prompts for information depends on how it's being
run. You see, PowerShell is built as a kind of under-the-hood engine.

What you interact with is called a *host application*. The command-line console
you see when running PowerShell.exe is often called the *console host*. The graphical
PowerShell ISE is usually called the *ISE host* or the *graphical host*. Other non-
Microsoft applications can host the shell's engine as well. You interact with the hosting application, and it passes your commands through to the engine. The hosting
application displays the results that the engine produces.

Figure 19.1 illustrates the relationship between the engine and the various hosting applications. Each hosting application is responsible for physically displaying
any output the engine produces, and for physically collecting any input the engine
requests. That means PowerShell can display output and collect input in different
ways. In fact, the console host and ISE use different methods for collecting input:
the console host presents a text prompt within the command line, but the ISE produces a pop-up dialog box with a text entry area and an OK button.

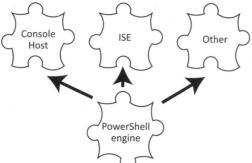

Figure 19.1 Various applications are capable of hosting the PowerShell engine.

We want to point out these differences because it can sometimes be confusing to newcomers. Why would one command behave one way in the command-line window but behave completely differently in the ISE? It's because the way in which you interact with the shell is determined by the hosting application, and not by PowerShell itself. The commands we're about to show you exhibit slightly different behavior depending on where you run them.

19.2 *Read-Host*

PowerShell's `Read-Host` cmdlet is designed to display a text prompt and then collect text input from the user. Because you saw us use this for the first time in the previous chapter, the syntax may seem familiar:

```
PS C:\> read-host "Enter a computer name"
Enter a computer name: SERVER-R2
SERVER-R2
```

This example highlights two important facts about the cmdlet:

- A colon is added to the end of the prompt.
- Whatever the user types is returned as the result of the command (technically, it's placed into the pipeline).

You'll often capture the input into a variable, which looks like this:

```
PS C:\> $computername = read-host "Enter a computer name"
Enter a computer name: SERVER-R2
```

> **TRY IT NOW** Time to start following along. At this point, you should have a valid computer name in the `$computername` variable. Don't use SERVER-R2 unless that's the name of the computer you're working on.

As we mentioned earlier, the PowerShell v2 ISE will display a dialog box, rather than prompting directly within the command line, as shown in figure 19.2. Other hosting applications, including script editors like PowerGUI, PowerShell Plus, or PrimalScript, each have their own way of implementing `Read-Host`. Note that the PowerShell v3 ISE, which uses a simpler two-pane layout than the v2 ISE, will display a command-line prompt much like the regular console window.

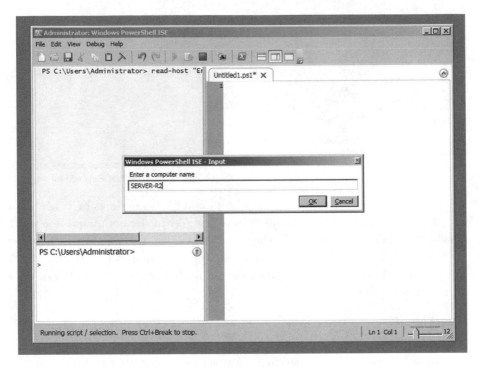

Figure 19.2   The v2 ISE displays a dialog box for Read-Host.

There isn't much else to say about Read-Host: it's a useful cmdlet, but not a particularly exciting one. In fact, after introducing Read-Host in most classes, someone will typically ask us, "Is there a way to always display a graphical input box?" Many administrators want to deploy scripts to their users, and they don't want users to have to enter information into a command-line interface (it isn't "Windows-like," after all). The answer we give is "yes," but it isn't straightforward. The final result is shown in figure 19.3.

To create the graphical input box, you'll have to dive into the .NET Framework itself. Start with the following command:

```
PS C:\> [void][System.Reflection.Assembly]::LoadWithPartialName('Microsoft
➥.VisualBasic')
```

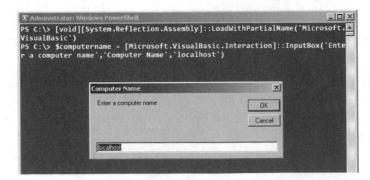

Figure 19.3   Creating a graphical input box in Windows PowerShell

You only have to do this once in a given shell session, but it doesn't hurt to run the command a second time.

This command loads a portion of the .NET Framework, Microsoft.VisualBasic, which PowerShell doesn't automatically load. This portion of the framework contains most of the Visual Basic–centric framework elements, including things like graphical input boxes.

Let's look at what the command is doing:

- The `[void]` part is converting the result of the command into the `void` data type. You learned how to do this kind of conversion with integers in the previous chapter; the `void` data type is a special type that means "throw the result away." We don't want to see the result of this command, so we convert the result to `void`. Another way to do the same thing would be to pipe the result to `Out-Null`.
- Next, we're accessing the `System.Reflection.Assembly` type, which represents our application (which is PowerShell). We've enclosed the type name in square brackets, as if we were declaring a variable to be of that type. But rather than declaring a variable, we're using two colons to access a *static method* of the type. Static methods exist without us having to create an instance of the type.
- The static method we're using is `LoadWithPartialName()`, which accepts the name of the framework component we want to load.

If all of that is as clear as mud, don't worry; you can use the command as is, without needing to understand how it works. Once the right bits of the framework are loaded, you can use them as follows:

```
PS C:\> $computername = [Microsoft.VisualBasic.Interaction]::InputBox('Ente
r a computer name','Computer Name','localhost')
```

In this example, we've used a static method again, this time from the `Microsoft.VisualBasic.Interaction` type, which we loaded into memory with the previous command. Again, if the "static method" stuff doesn't make sense, don't worry—use this command as is.

The three bits you can change are the parameters of the `InputBox()` method:

- The first parameter is the text for your prompt.
- The second parameter is the title for the prompt's dialog box.
- The third parameter, which can be left blank or omitted entirely, is the default value that you want prefilled in the input box.

Using `Read-Host` may be less complicated than following the steps in the previous example, but if you insist on a dialog box, this is how you create one.

19.3 Write-Host

Now that you can collect input, you'll want some way of displaying output. The `Write-Host` cmdlet is one way. It's not always the best way, but it's available to you, and it's important that you understand how it works.

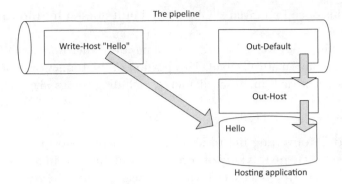

Figure 19.4 `Write-Host` bypasses the pipeline and writes directly to the hosting application's display.

As figure 19.4 illustrates, `Write-Host` runs in the pipeline like any other cmdlet, but it doesn't place anything into the pipeline. Instead, it writes directly to the hosting application's screen. Because it does that, it's able to use alternate foreground and background colors, through its `-foregroundColor` and `-backgroundColor` command-line parameters.

```
PS C:\> write-host "COLORFUL!" -fore yellow -back magenta
COLORFUL!
```

TRY IT NOW You'll want to run this command yourself to see the colorful results.

NOTE Not every application that hosts PowerShell supports alternate text colors, and not every application supports the full set of colors. When you attempt to set colors in such an application, it will usually ignore any colors it doesn't like or can't display. That's one reason we tend to avoid relying on special colors at all.

You should use `Write-Host` only when you need to display a specific message, perhaps using color to draw attention to it. But this isn't the appropriate way to produce normal output from a script or a command.

For example, you should never use `Write-Host` to manually format a table—you can find better ways to produce the output, using techniques that enable PowerShell itself to handle the formatting. We won't dive into those techniques in this book, because they belong more in the realm of heavy-duty scripting and toolmaking. However, you can check out *Learn PowerShell Toolmaking in a Month of Lunches* (Manning, 2012) for full coverage of those output techniques. `Write-Host` is also not the best way to produce error messages, warnings, debugging messages, and so on—again, you can find more specific ways to do those things, and we'll cover those in this chapter. You probably won't use `Write-Host` much, if you're using the shell correctly.

NOTE We often see people using `Write-Host` to display what we call "warm and fuzzy" messages—things like "now connecting to SERVER2," "testing for folder," and so on. Don't. The more appropriate way to display those messages is `Write-Verbose`.

> **Above and beyond**
>
> We'll dive into `Write-Verbose` and the other `Write` cmdlets a bit more in chapter 22. But if you try `Write-Verbose` now, you might be disappointed to discover that it doesn't produce any output. Well, not by default.
>
> If you plan to use `Write` cmdlets, the trick is to turn them on first. For example, set `$VerbosePreference="Continue"` to enable `Write-Verbose`, and `$VerbosePreference="SilentlyContinue"` to suppress its output. You'll find similar "preference" variables for `Write-Debug` (`$DebugPreference`) and `Write-Warning` (`$WarningPreference`).
>
> Chapter 22 will include an even cooler way to use `Write-Verbose`.
>
> It may seem *much* easier to use `Write-Host`, and if you want to, you can. But keep in mind that by using the other cmdlets, such as `Write-Verbose`, you're going to be following PowerShell's own patterns more closely, resulting in a more consistent experience.

19.4 *Write-Output*

Unlike `Write-Host`, `Write-Output` can send objects into the pipeline. Because it isn't writing directly to the display, it doesn't permit you to specify alternative colors or anything. In fact, `Write-Output` (or its alias, `Write`) isn't technically designed to display output at all. As we said, it sends objects into the pipeline—it's the pipeline itself that eventually displays those objects. Figure 19.5 illustrates how this works.

Refer back to chapter 10 for a quick review of how objects go from the pipeline to the screen. Let's look at the basic process:

1 `Write-Output` puts the `String` object `Hello` into the pipeline.
2 Because nothing else is in the pipeline, `Hello` travels to the end of the pipeline, where `Out-Default` always sits.
3 `Out-Default` passes the object to `Out-Host`.

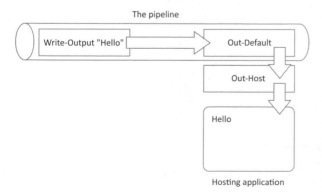

Figure 19.5 `Write-Output` puts objects into the pipeline, which in some cases, eventually results in those objects being displayed.

4 Out-Host asks PowerShell's formatting system to format the object. Because in this example it's a simple String, the formatting system returns the text of the string.

5 Out-Host places the formatted result onto the screen.

The results are similar to what you'd get using Write-Host, but the object took a different path to get there. That path is important, because the pipeline could contain other things. For example, consider the following command (which you're welcome to try):

```
PS C:\> write-output "Hello" | where-object { $_.length -gt 10 }
```

You don't see any output from this command, and figure 19.6 illustrates why. Hello was placed into the pipeline. But before it got to Out-Default, it had to pass through Where-Object, which filtered out anything having a Length property of less than or equal to 10, which in this case included our poor Hello. Our Hello got dropped out of the pipeline, and because there was nothing left in the pipeline for Out-Default, there was nothing to pass to Out-Host, so nothing was displayed.

Contrast that command with the following one:

```
PS C:\> write-host "Hello" | where-object { $_.length -gt 10 }
Hello
```

All we did was replace Write-Output with Write-Host. This time, Hello went directly to the screen, not into the pipeline. Where-Object had no input, and produced no output, so nothing was displayed by Out-Default and Out-Host. But because Hello had been written directly to the screen, we saw it anyway.

Write-Output may seem new, but it turns out you've been using it all along. It's the shell's default cmdlet. When you tell the shell to do something that isn't a command, the shell passes whatever you typed to Write-Output behind the scenes.

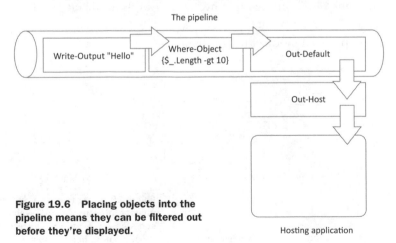

Figure 19.6 Placing objects into the pipeline means they can be filtered out before they're displayed.

19.5 *Other ways to write*

PowerShell has a few other ways to produce output. None of these write to the pipeline as `Write-Output` does; they work a bit more like `Write-Host`. But all of them produce output in a way that can be suppressed.

The shell comes with built-in configuration variables for each of these alternative output methods. When the configuration variable is set to `Continue`, the commands we're about to show you do indeed produce output. When the configuration variable is set to `SilentlyContinue`, the associated output command produces nothing. Table 19.1 contains the list of cmdlets.

Table 19.1 Alternative output cmdlets

Cmdlet	Purpose	Configuration variable
`Write-Warning`	Displays warning text, in yellow by default and preceded by the label "WARNING:"	`$WarningPreference` (Continue by default)
`Write-Verbose`	Displays additional informative text, in yellow by default and preceded by the label "VERBOSE:"	`$VerbosePreference` (SilentlyContinue by default)
`Write-Debug`	Displays debugging text, in yellow by default and preceded by the label "DEBUG:"	`$DebugPreference` (SilentlyContinue by default)
`Write-Error`	Produces an error message	`$ErrorActionPreference` (Continue by default)

`Write-Error` works a bit differently because it writes an error to PowerShell's error stream.

PowerShell also has a `Write-Progress` cmdlet that can display progress bars, but it works entirely differently. Feel free to read its help for more information and for examples; we won't be covering it in this book.

To use any of these cmdlets, first make sure that its associated configuration variable is set to `Continue`. (If it's set to `SilentlyContinue`, which is the default for a couple of them, you won't see any output at all.) Then, use the cmdlet to output a message.

NOTE Some PowerShell hosting applications may display the output from these cmdlets in a different location. In PrimalScript, for example, debugging text is written to a different output pane than the script's main output, allowing the debug text to be more easily separated for analysis. We're not going to dive into debugging in this book, but you can read more about the cmdlet in PowerShell's help system if you're interested.

19.6   *Lab*

NOTE   For this lab, you'll need any computer running PowerShell v3.

Write-Host and Write-Output can be a bit tricky to work with. See how many of these tasks you can complete, and if you get stuck, it's OK to peek at the sample answers available on MoreLunches.com.

1   Use Write-Output to display the result of 100 multiplied by 10.
2   Use Write-Host to display the result of 100 multiplied by 10.
3   Prompt the user to enter a name, and then display that name in yellow text.
4   Prompt the user to enter a name, and then display that name only if it's longer than five characters. Do this all in a single line—don't use a variable.

That's all for this lab. Because these cmdlets are all straightforward, we want you to spend more time experimenting with them on your own. Be sure to do that—we'll offer some ideas in the next section.

TRY IT NOW   After you've completed this lab, try completing review lab 3, which you'll find in appendix A of this book.

19.7   *Further exploration*

Spend some time getting comfortable with all of the cmdlets in this chapter. Make sure you can display verbose output, accept input, and even display a graphical input box. You'll be using the commands from this chapter often from here on out, so you should read their help files and even jot down quick syntax reminders for future reference.

Sessions: remote control with less work

20

In chapter 13, we introduced you to PowerShell's remoting features. In that chapter, you used two primary cmdlets—`Invoke-Command` and `Enter-PSSession`—to access both one-to-many and one-to-one remote control. Those two cmdlets worked by creating a new remoting connection, doing whatever work you specified, and then closing that connection.

There's nothing wrong with that approach, but it can be tiring to have to continually specify computer names, credentials, alternative port numbers, and so on. In this chapter, we'll look at an easier, more reusable way to tackle remoting. You'll also learn about a third way to use remoting that'll also come in handy.

20.1 Making PowerShell remoting a bit easier

Any time you need to connect to a remote computer, using either `Invoke-Command` or `Enter-PSSession`, you have to at least specify the computer's name (or names, if you're invoking a command on multiple computers). Depending on your environment, you may also have to specify alternative credentials, which means being prompted for a password. You might also need to specify alternative ports or authentication mechanisms, depending upon how your organization has configured remoting.

None of that is difficult to specify, but it can be tedious to have to repeat the process again and again. Fortunately, we know of a better way: reusable *sessions*.

20.2 *Creating and using reusable sessions*

A session is a persistent connection between your copy of PowerShell and a remote copy of PowerShell. When the session is active, both your computer and the remote machine devote a small amount of memory and processor time toward maintaining the connection, although there's little network traffic involved in the connection. PowerShell maintains a list of all the sessions you've opened, and you can use those sessions to invoke commands or to enter a remote shell.

To create a new session, use the New-PSSession cmdlet. Specify the computer name (or names), and, if necessary, specify an alternative username, port, authentication mechanism, and so forth. The result will be a session object, which is stored in PowerShell's memory:

```
PS C:\> new-pssession -computername server-r2,server17,dc5
```

To retrieve those sessions, run Get-PSSession:

```
PS C:\> get-pssession
```

Although that works, we prefer to create the sessions and then immediately store them in a variable. For example, Don has three IIS-based web servers that he routinely reconfigures by using Invoke-Command. To make the process easier, he stores those sessions in a specific variable:

```
PS C:\> $iis_servers = new-pssession -comp web1,web2,web3
➥-credential WebAdmin
```

Never forget that those sessions consume resources. If you close the shell, they'll close automatically, but if you're not actively using them, it's a good idea to manually close them even if you're planning to continue using the shell for other tasks.

To close a session, use the Remove-PSSession cmdlet. For example, to close only the IIS sessions, use the following command:

```
PS C:\> $iis_servers | remove-pssession
```

Or, if you want to close all open sessions, use this next command:

```
PS C:\> get-pssession | remove-pssession
```

That was easy enough.

But once you get some sessions up and running, what will you do with them? For the next couple of sections, we'll assume you've created a variable named $sessions that contains at least two sessions. We'll use localhost and SERVER-R2 (you should specify your own computer names). Using localhost isn't cheating: PowerShell starts up a real remoting session with another copy of itself. Keep in mind that this will only work if you've enabled remoting on all computers to which you're connected, so revisit chapter 13 if you haven't enabled remoting.

> **TRY IT NOW**   Start to follow along and run these commands, and be sure to use valid computer names. If you only have one computer, use both its name and localhost.

> **Above and beyond**
>
> There's a cool syntax that allows you to create multiple sessions with one command and have each session assigned to a unique variable (instead of having them all lumped into one variable, as we previously did):
>
> ```
> $s_server1,$s_server2 = new-pssession -computer server-r2,dc01
> ```
>
> This syntax puts the session for SERVER-R2 into $s_server1, and the session for DC01 into $s_server2, which can make it easier to use those sessions independently.
>
> But use caution: we've seen instances where the sessions aren't created in exactly the order you specify, so $s_server1 might end up containing the session for DC01 instead of SERVER-R2. You can display the variable's contents to see which computer it's connected to.

Here's how we'll get our sessions up and running:

```
PS C:\> $sessions = New-PSSession -comp SERVER-R2,localhost
```

Bear in mind that we've already enabled remoting on these computers and that they're all in the same domain. Revisit chapter 13 if you'd like a refresher on how to enable remoting.

20.3   *Using sessions with Enter-PSSession*

As we hope you recall from chapter 13, the Enter-PSSession cmdlet is the one you use to engage a one-to-one remote interactive shell with a single remote computer. Rather than specifying a computer name with the cmdlet, you can specify a single session object. Because our $sessions variable has two session objects, we must specify one of them using an index (which you first learned to do in chapter 18):

```
PS C:\> enter-pssession -session $sessions[0]
[server-r2]: PS C:\Users\Administrator\Documents>
```

You can see that our prompt changed to indicate that we're now controlling a remote computer. Exit-PSSession will return us back to the local prompt, but the session will remain open for additional use:

```
[server-r2]: PS C:\Users\Administrator\Documents> exit-pssession
PS C:\>
```

You might have a tough time remembering which index number goes with which computer. In that case, you can take advantage of the properties of a session object. For example, when we pipe $sessions to Gm, we get the following output:

```
PS C:\> $sessions | gm

    TypeName: System.Management.Automation.Runspaces.PSSession

Name                    MemberType        Definition
----                    ----------        ----------
Equals                  Method            bool Equals(System.Object obj)
GetHashCode             Method            int GetHashCode()
```

```
GetType                  Method          type GetType()
ToString                 Method          string ToString()
ApplicationPrivateData   Property        System.Management.Automation.PSPr...
Availability             Property        System.Management.Automation.Runs...
ComputerName             Property        System.String ComputerName {get;}
ConfigurationName        Property        System.String ConfigurationName {...
Id                       Property        System.Int32 Id {get;}
InstanceId               Property        System.Guid InstanceId {get;}
Name                     Property        System.String Name {get;set;}
Runspace                 Property        System.Management.Automation.Runs...
State                    ScriptProperty  System.Object State {get=$this.Ru...
```

In the preceding output, you can see that the session object has a `ComputerName` property, which means you can filter for that session:

```
PS C:\> enter-pssession -session ($sessions |
➥where { $_.computername -eq 'server-r2' })
[server-r2]: PS C:\Users\Administrator\Documents>
```

That's awkward syntax, though. If you need to use a single session from a variable, and you can't remember which index number is which, it might be easier to forget about using the variable.

Even though you stored your session objects in the variable, they're also still stored in PowerShell's master list of open sessions. That means you can access them by using `Get-PSSession`:

```
PS C:\> enter-pssession -session (get-pssession -computer server-r2)
```

`Get-PSSession` will retrieve the session having the computer named SERVER-R2 and pass it to the `-session` parameter of `Enter-PSSession`.

When we first figured out that technique, we were impressed, but it also led us to dig a bit deeper. We pulled up the full help for `Enter-PSSession` and read more closely about the `-session` parameter. Here's what we looked at:

```
-Session <PSSession>
    Specifies a Windows PowerShell session (PSSession) to use for the
    interactive session. This parameter takes a session object. You ca
    n also use the Name, InstanceID, or ID parameters to specify a PSS
    ession.

    Enter a variable that contains a session object or a command that

    creates or gets a session object, such as a New-PSSession or Get-P
    SSession command. You can also pipe a session object to Enter-PSSe
    ssion. You can submit only one PSSession with this parameter. If y
    ou enter a variable that contains more than one PSSession, the com
    mand fails.
    When you use Exit-PSSession or the EXIT keyword, the interactive s
    ession ends, but the PSSession that you created remains open and a

    vailable for use.
    Required?                 false
    Position?                 1
    Default value
    Accept pipeline input?    true (ByValue, ByPropertyName)
    Accept wildcard characters?  True
```

If you think back to chapter 9, you'll find that pipeline input information near the end of the help interesting. It tells us that the -session parameter can accept a PSSession object from the pipeline. We know that Get-PSSession produces PSSession objects, so the following syntax should also work:

```
PS C:\> Get-PSSession -ComputerName SERVER-R2 | Enter-PSSession
[server-r2]: PS C:\Users\Administrator\Documents>
```

And it does work. We think that's a much more elegant way to retrieve a single session, even if you've stored them all in a variable.

> **TIP** Storing sessions in a variable is fine as a convenience. But keep in mind that PowerShell is already storing a list of all open sessions; having them in a variable is only useful when you want to refer to a bunch of sessions at once, as you'll see in the next section.

20.4 *Using sessions with Invoke-Command*

Sessions show their usefulness with Invoke-Command, which you'll remember you use to send a command (or an entire script) to multiple remote computers in parallel. With our sessions in a $sessions variable, we can easily target them all with the following command:

```
PS C:\> invoke-command -command { get-wmiobject -class win32_process }
➥-session $sessions
```

Notice that we're sending a Get-WmiObject command to the remote computers. We could have chosen to use Get-WmiObject's own -computername parameter, but we didn't do so for the following four reasons:

- Remoting works over a single, predefined port; WMI doesn't. Remoting is therefore easier to use with firewalled computers, because it's easier to make the necessary firewall exceptions. Microsoft's Windows Firewall provides a specific exception for WMI that includes the stateful inspection necessary to make WMI's random port selection (called *endpoint mapping*) work properly, but it can be difficult to manage with some third-party firewall products. With remoting, it's an easy, single port.
- Pulling all of the processes can be labor-intensive. Using the Invoke-Command cmdlet gets each computer to do its own share of the work and sending the results back.
- Remoting operates in parallel, contacting up to 32 computers at once by default. WMI only works sequentially with one computer at a time.
- We can't use our predefined sessions with Get-WmiObject, but we can use them with Invoke-Command.

> **NOTE** The new CIM cmdlets (like Get-CimInstance) in PowerShell v3 don't have a -computerName parameter like Get-WmiObject does. These new cmdlets are designed for you to send via Invoke-Command when you want to run them against a remote computer.

The `-session` parameter of `Invoke-Command` can also be fed with a parenthetical command, much as we've done with computer names in previous chapters. For example, the following sends a command to every session connected to a computer whose name starts with "loc":

```
PS C:\> invoke-command -command { get-wmiobject -class win32_process }
➡-session (get-pssession -comp loc*)
```

You might expect that `Invoke-Command` would be able to receive session objects from the pipeline, as you know `Enter-PSSession` can. But a glance at the full help for `Invoke-Command` shows that it can't do that particular pipeline trick. Too bad, but the preceding example of using a parenthetical expression provides the same functionality without too difficult a syntax.

20.5   *Implicit remoting: importing a session*

Implicit remoting, for us, is one of the coolest and most useful—possibly *the* coolest and *the* most useful—feature a command-line interface has ever had, on any operating system, ever. And unfortunately, it's barely documented in PowerShell. Sure, the necessary commands are well-documented, but how they come together to form this incredible capability isn't mentioned. Fortunately, we have you covered on this one.

Let's review the scenario: You already know that Microsoft is shipping more and more modules and snap-ins with Windows and other products, but sometimes you can't install those modules and snap-ins on your local computer for one reason or another. The ActiveDirectory module, which shipped for the first time with Windows Server 2008 R2, is a perfect example: it only exists on Windows Server 2008 R2 and on Windows 7 machines that have the Remote Server Administration Tools (RSAT) installed. What if your computer is running Windows XP or Windows Vista? Are you out of luck? No. You can use implicit remoting.

Let's look at the entire process in a single example:

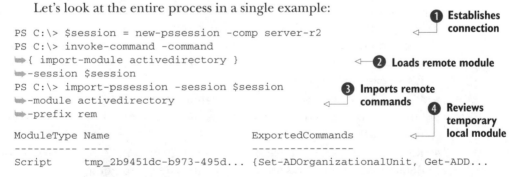

```
PS C:\> $session = new-pssession -comp server-r2
PS C:\> invoke-command -command
➡{ import-module activedirectory }
➡-session $session
PS C:\> import-pssession -session $session
➡-module activedirectory
➡-prefix rem

ModuleType Name                         ExportedCommands
---------- ----                         ----------------
Script     tmp_2b9451dc-b973-495d... {Set-ADOrganizationalUnit, Get-ADD...
```

❶ Establishes connection
❷ Loads remote module
❸ Imports remote commands
❹ Reviews temporary local module

Here's what's happening in that example:

1   We started by establishing a session with a remote computer that has the ActiveDirectory module installed ❶. We'll need that computer to be running PowerShell v2 or later (which Windows Server 2008 R2 and later can do), and we must enable remoting.

2 We tell the remote computer to import its local ActiveDirectory module ❷. That's just one example; we could have chosen to load any module, or even add a PSSnapin, if that's what we needed. Because the session is still open, the module stays loaded on the remote computer.

3 We then tell our computer to import the commands from that remote session ❸. We only want the commands in the ActiveDirectory module, and when they're imported we want a "rem" prefix to be added to each command's noun. That allows us to keep track of the remote commands more easily. It also means the commands won't conflict with any same-named commands already loaded into our shell.

4 PowerShell creates a temporary module on our computer that represents the remote commands ❹. The commands aren't copied over; instead, PowerShell creates shortcuts for them, and those shortcuts point to the remote machine.

Now we can run the ActiveDirectory module commands, or even ask for help. Instead of running `New-ADUser`, we'd run `New-remADUser`, because we added that "rem" prefix to the commands' nouns. The commands will remain available until we either close the shell or close that session with the remote computer. When we open a new shell, we'll have to repeat this process to regain access to the remote commands.

When we run these commands, they don't execute on our local machine. Instead, they're implicitly remoted to the remote computer. It executes them for us and sends the results to our computer.

We can envision a world where we don't ever install administrative tools on our computers again. What a hassle we'd avoid. Today, you need tools that can run on your computer's operating system and talk to whatever remote server you're trying to manage—and getting everything to match up can be impossible. In the future, you won't do that. You'll use implicit remoting. Servers will offer their management features as another service, via Windows PowerShell.

Now for the bad news: the results brought to your computer through implicit remoting are all deserialized, meaning that the objects' properties are copied into an XML file for transmission across the network. The objects you receive this way don't have any methods. In most cases, that's not a problem, but some modules and snap-ins produce objects that you're meant to use in a more programmatic way, and those don't lend themselves to implicit remoting. We hope you'll encounter few (if any) objects with this limitation, as a reliance on methods violates some PowerShell design practices. If you do run into such objects, you won't be able to use them through implicit remoting.

20.6 *Disconnected sessions*

PowerShell v3 introduced two improvements to its remote control capabilities.

First, sessions are much less fragile, meaning they can survive brief network hiccups and other transient interruptions. You get that benefit even if you aren't explicitly using a session object. Even if you've used something like `Enter-PSSession` with its -ComputerName parameter, you're technically still using a session under the hood, so you get the more robust connectivity.

The other new feature in v3 is one you have to explicitly use: disconnected sessions. Say you're sitting on COMPUTER1, logged in as Admin1 (who is a member of the Domain Admins group), and you create a new connection to COMPUTER2:

```
PS C:\> New-PSSession -ComputerName COMPUTER2

Id Name              ComputerName  State
-- ----------------- ------------- -----
 4 Session4          COMPUTER2     Opened
```

You can then disconnect that session. You still do this on COMPUTER1, where you're sitting, and it disengages the connection between the two computers, but it leaves the copy of PowerShell up and running on COMPUTER2. Note that you do this by specifying the session's ID number, which was displayed when you first created the session:

```
PS C:\> Disconnect-PSSession -Id 4

Id Name              ComputerName  State
-- ----------------- ------------- -----
 4 Session4          COMPUTER2     Disconnected
```

This is something you obviously need to think about—you're leaving a copy of Power-Shell running on COMPUTER2. Assigning useful idle timeout periods and so forth becomes important. In earlier versions of PowerShell, a session that you disconnected went away, so you had no cleanup. With v3, it's possible to litter up your environment with running sessions, which means you have to exercise a bit more responsibility.

But here's the cool part: we'll log into another computer, COMPUTER3, as the same Domain Admin named Admin1, and retrieve a list of sessions running on COMPUTER2:

```
PS C:\> Get-PSSession -computerName COMPUTER2

Id Name              ComputerName  State
-- ----------------- ------------- -----
 4 Session4          COMPUTER2     Disconnected
```

Neat, right? You couldn't see this session if you'd logged in as a different user, even as another administrator; you can only see the sessions you created on COMPUTER2. But now, having seen it, you can reconnect it:

```
PS C:\> Get-PSSession -computerName COMPUTER2 | Connect-PSSession

Id Name              ComputerName  State
-- ----------------- ------------- -----
 4 Session4          COMPUTER2     Open
```

Let's spend some time talking about managing these sessions. In PowerShell's WSMan: drive, you'll find a number of settings that can help you keep disconnected sessions under control. You can also centrally configure most of these via Group Policy. The key settings to look for include the following:

- In WSMan:\localhost\Shell:
  - IdleTimeout specifies how long a session can be idle before it's shut down automatically. The default is about 2,000 hours, or about 84 days.
  - MaxConcurrentUsers specifies how many different users can have a session open at once.
  - MaxShellRunTime determines the maximum amount of time a session can be open. The default is, for all practical purposes, infinite. Keep in mind that IdleTimeout can override this if the shell is sitting idle, as opposed to running commands.
  - MaxShellsPerUser sets a limit on how many sessions a single user can have open at once. Multiply this by MaxConcurrentUsers to figure out the maximum possible number of sessions, for all users, on the computer.
- In WSMan:\localhost\Service:
  - MaxConnections sets the upper limit on incoming connections to the entire remoting infrastructure. Even if you allow a larger number of shells per user or a maximum number of users, MaxConnections is the absolute limit on incoming connections.

As an administrator, you obviously have a higher level of responsibility than a plain old user. It's up to you to keep track of your sessions, particularly if you'll be disconnecting and reconnecting. Sensible timeout settings can help ensure that shell sessions don't sit around idling for long stretches of time.

20.7 Lab

NOTE For this lab, you'll need a Windows Server 2008 R2 or Windows Server 2012 computer running PowerShell v3. If you've access only to a client computer (running Windows 7 or Windows 8), you won't be able to complete steps 6 through 9 of this lab.

To complete this lab, you'll want to have two computers: one to remote from, and another to remote to. If you only have one computer, use its computer name to remote to it. You should get a similar experience that way.

TIP In chapter 1, we mentioned a multicomputer virtual environment at CloudShare.com. You'll find other, similar services that offer cloud-based virtual machines. By using CloudShare, we didn't have to set up the Windows OS, because the service had ready-made templates for us to use. You do have to pay a fee for the service, and it isn't available in all countries, but if you can use it, it's a great way to get a lab environment running if you're not able to run one locally.

1 Close all open sessions in your shell.
2 Establish a session to a remote computer. Save the session in a variable named $session.

3 Use the $session variable to establish a one-to-one remote shell session with the remote computer. Display a list of processes, and then exit.

4 Use the $session variable with Invoke-Command to get a list of services from the remote computer.

5 Use Get-PSSession and Invoke-Command to get a list of the 20 most recent Security event log entries from the remote computer.

6 Use Invoke-Command and your $session variable to load the ServerManager module on the remote computer.

7 Import the ServerManager module's commands from the remote computer to your computer. Add the prefix "rem" to the imported commands' nouns.

8 Run the imported Get-WindowsFeature command.

9 Close the session that's in your $session variable.

NOTE Thanks to a new feature in PowerShell v3, you could also accomplish steps 6 and 7 with a single step, by using the Import-Module command. Feel free to review the help for this command and see if you can figure out how to use it to import a module from a remote computer.

20.8 *Further exploration*

Take a quick inventory of your environment: what PowerShell-enabled products do you have? Exchange Server? SharePoint Server? VMware vSphere? System Center Virtual Machine Manager? These and other products all include PowerShell modules or snap-ins, many of which are accessible via PowerShell remoting.

21
You call this scripting?

So far, you could have accomplished everything in this book using PowerShell's command-line interface. You haven't had to write a single script. That's a big deal for us, because we see a lot of administrators initially shying away from scripting, (rightly) perceiving it as a kind of programming, and (correctly) feeling that learning it can sometimes take more time than it's worth. Hopefully, you've seen how much you can accomplish in PowerShell without having to become a programmer.

But at this point, you may also be starting to feel that constantly retyping the same commands, over and over, is going to become pretty tedious. You're right, so in this chapter we're going to dive into PowerShell scripting—but we're still not going to be programming. Instead, we're going to focus on scripts as little more than a way of saving our fingers from unnecessary retyping.

21.1 Not programming, more like batch files

Most Windows administrators have, at one point or another, created a command-line batch file (which usually has a .BAT or .CMD filename extension). These are nothing more than simple text files that you can edit with Windows Notepad, containing a list of commands to be executed in a specific order. Technically, you call those commands a *script*, because like a Hollywood script, they tell the performer (your computer) exactly what to do and say, and in what order to do and say it. But batch files rarely look like programming, in part because the Cmd.exe shell has a very limited language that doesn't permit incredibly complicated scripts.

PowerShell scripts—or *batch files*, if you prefer—work similarly. Simply list the commands that you want run, and the shell will execute those commands in the order specified. You can create a script by simply copying a command from the host window and pasting it into Notepad. Of course, Notepad is a pretty horrible text editor. We expect you'll be happier with the PowerShell ISE, or with a third-party editor like PowerGUI, PrimalScript, or PowerShell Plus.

The ISE, in fact, makes "scripting" practically indistinguishable from using the shell interactively. When using the ISE's Script Editor Pane, you simply type the command or commands you want to run, and then click the Run button in the toolbar to execute those commands. Click Save and you've created a script without having to copy and paste anything at all.

21.2   *Making commands repeatable*

The idea behind PowerShell scripts is, first and foremost, to make it easier to run a given command over and over, without having to manually retype it every time. That being the case, we need to come up with a command that you'll want to run over and over again, and use that as an example throughout this chapter. We want to make this decently complex, so we'll start with something from WMI and add in some filtering, sorting, and other stuff.

At this point, we're going to switch to using the PowerShell ISE instead of the normal console window, because the ISE will make it easier for us to migrate our command into a script. Frankly, the ISE makes it easier to type complex commands, because you get a full-screen editor instead of working on a single line within the console host.

Here's our command:

```
Get-WmiObject -class Win32_LogicalDisk -computername localhost
➥-filter "drivetype=3" |
 Sort-Object -property DeviceID |
 Format-Table -property DeviceID,
 @{label='FreeSpace(MB)';expression={$_.FreeSpace / 1MB -as [int]}},
 @{label='Size(GB';expression={$_.Size / 1GB -as [int]}},
 @{label='%Free';expression={$_.FreeSpace / $_.Size * 100 -as [int]}}
```

> **TIP**   Remember, you can use name instead of label, and either can be abbreviated to a single character, n or l. But it's easy for a lowercase *L* to look like the number 1, so be careful!

Figure 21.1 shows how we've entered this into the ISE. Notice that we selected the two-pane layout by using the toolbar button on the far left of the layout choices. Also notice that we formatted our command so that each physical line ends in either a pipe character or a comma. By doing so, we're forcing the shell to recognize these multiple lines as a single, one-line command. You could do the same thing in the console host, but this formatting is especially effective in the ISE because it makes the command a lot easier to read. Also notice that we've used full cmdlet names and parameter names and that we've specified every parameter name rather than using positional parameters. All of that will make our script easier to read and follow either for someone else, or in the future when we might have forgotten what our original intent was.

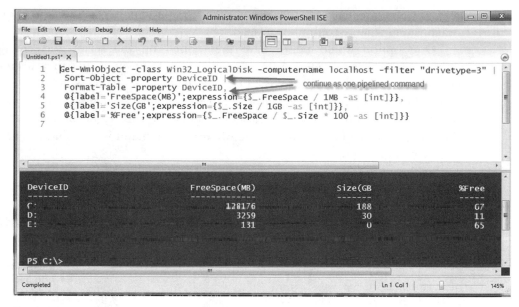

Figure 21.1   Entering and running a command in the ISE

We ran the command by clicking the green Run toolbar icon in the ISE (you could also press F5) to test it, and our output shows that it's working perfectly. Here's a neat trick in the ISE: you can highlight a portion of your command and press F8 to just run the highlighted portion. Because we've formatted the command so that there's one distinct command per physical line, that makes it easy for us to test our command bit by bit. We could highlight and run the first line independently. If we were satisfied with the output, we could highlight the first and second lines, and run them. If it worked as expected, we could run the whole command.

At this point, we can save the command—and we can start calling it a *script* now. We'll save it as Get-DiskInventory.ps1. We like giving scripts cmdlet-style "verb-noun" names. You can see how this script is going to start to look and work a lot like a cmdlet, so it makes sense to give it a cmdlet-style name.

> **TRY IT NOW**   We're assuming that you have already completed chapter 14 and enabled scripting by setting a more permissive execution policy. If you haven't done so, then you should flip back to chapter 17 and complete its lab so that scripts will run in your copy of PowerShell.

21.3   *Parameterizing commands*

When you think about running a command over and over, you might realize that some portion of the command is going to have to change from time to time. For example, suppose you wanted to give Get-DiskInventory.ps1 to some of your colleagues, who might be less experienced in using PowerShell. It's a pretty complex, hard-to-type command, and they might appreciate having it bundled into an easier-to-run script. But, as written, the script only runs against the local computer. You can certainly imagine that some of your colleagues might want to get a disk inventory from one or more remote computers instead.

One option would be to have them open up the script and change the `-computer-name` parameter's value. But it's entirely possible that they wouldn't be comfortable doing so, and there's a chance that they'll change something else and break the script entirely. It would be better to provide a formal way for them to pass in a different computer name (or a set of names). At this stage, you need to identify the things that might need to change when the command is run, and replace those things with variables.

We'll set the computer name variable to a static value for now, so that we can still test the script. Here's our revised script.

Listing 21.1   Get-DiskInventory.ps1, with a parameterized command

```
$computername = 'localhost'                              ← ① Sets new variable
Get-WmiObject -class Win32_LogicalDisk `                      Breaks line
 -computername  $computername `                          ② with backtick
 -filter "drivetype=3" |
 Sort-Object -property DeviceID |                         ③ Uses variable
 Format-Table -property DeviceID,
     @{label='FreeSpace(MB)';expression={$_.FreeSpace / 1MB -as [int]}},
     @{label='Size(GB';expression={$_.Size / 1GB -as [int]}},
     @{label='%Free';expression={$_.FreeSpace / $_.Size * 100 -as [int]}}
```

We've done three things here, two of which are functional and one of which is purely cosmetic:

- We've added a variable, `$computername`, and set it equal to `localhost` ①. We've noticed that most PowerShell commands that accept a computer name use the parameter name `-computername`, and we want to duplicate that convention, which is why we chose the variable name that we did.
- We've replaced the value for the `-computername` parameter with our variable ③. Right now, the script should run exactly the same as it did before (and we tested to make sure it does), because we've put `localhost` into the `$computername` variable.
- We added a backtick after the `-computername` parameter and its value ②. This escapes, or takes away the special meaning of, the carriage return at the end of the line. That tells PowerShell that the next physical line is part of this same command. You don't need to do that when the line ends in a pipe character or a comma, but in order to fit the code within this book, we needed to break the line a bit before the pipe character. This will only work if the backtick character is the last thing on the line!

Once again, we've been careful to run our script and verify that it's still working. We always do that after making any kind of change, to make sure we haven't introduced some random typo or other error.

21.4 Creating a parameterized script

Now that we've identified the elements of the script that might change from time to time, we need to provide a way for someone else to specify new values for those elements. In other words, we need to take that hardcoded $computername variable and turn it into an input parameter.

PowerShell makes this really easy.

Listing 21.2 Get-DiskInventory.ps1, with an input parameter

```
param (
  $computername = 'localhost'                          ◁─❶ Param block
)
Get-WmiObject -class Win32 LogicalDisk -computername $computername `
 -filter "drivetype=3" |
 Sort-Object -property DeviceID |
 Format-Table -property DeviceID,
     @{label='FreeSpace(MB)';expression={$_.FreeSpace / 1MB -as [int]}},
     @{label='Size(GB';expression={$_.Size / 1GB -as [int]}},
     @{label='%Free';expression={$_.FreeSpace / $_.Size * 100 -as [int]}}
```

All we did was add a Param() block around our variable declaration ❶. This defines $computername as a parameter, and specifies that localhost is the default value to be used if the script is run without a computer name being specified. You don't have to provide a default value, but we like to do so when there's a reasonable value that we can think of.

All parameters declared in this fashion are both named and positional, meaning that we can now run the script from the command line in any of these ways:

```
PS C:\> .\Get-DiskInventory.ps1 server-r2
PS C:\> .\Get-DiskInventory.ps1 -computername server-r2
PS C:\> .\Get-DiskInventory.ps1 -comp server-r2
```

In the first instance, we used the parameter positionally, providing a value but not the parameter name. In the second and third instances, we specified the parameter name, but in the third instance we abbreviated that name in keeping with PowerShell's normal rules for parameter name abbreviation. Note that in all three cases, we had to specify a path (.\, which is the current folder) to the script, because the shell won't automatically search the current directory to find the script.

You can specify as many parameters as you need to by separating them with commas. For example, suppose that we wanted to also parameterize the filter criteria. Right now, it's only retrieving logical disks of type 3, which represents fixed disks. We could change that to a parameter, as in the following listing.

Listing 21.3 Get-DiskInventory.ps1, with an additional parameter

```
param (
  $computername = 'localhost',                    Specifying additional
  $drivetype = 3                              ◁─┘   parameter
)
```

```
Get-WmiObject -class Win32_LogicalDisk -computername $computername `
  -filter "drivetype=$drivetype" |
  Sort-Object -property DeviceID |                        Using parameter
  Format-Table -property DeviceID,
      @{label='FreeSpace(MB)';expression={$_.FreeSpace / 1MB -as [int]}},
      @{label='Size(GB';expression={$_.Size / 1GB -as [int]}},
      @{label='%Free';expression={$_.FreeSpace / $_.Size * 100 -as [int]}}
```

Notice that we took advantage of PowerShell's ability to replace variables with their values inside of double quotation marks (you learned about that trick in chapter 18).

We can run this script in any of the three original ways, although we could also omit either parameter if we wanted to use the default value for it. Here are some permutations:

```
PS C:\> .\Get-DiskInventory.ps1 server-r2 3
PS C:\> .\Get-DiskInventory.ps1 -comp server-r2 -drive 3
PS C:\> .\Get-DiskInventory.ps1 server-r2
PS C:\> .\Get-DiskInventory.ps1 -drive 3
```

In the first instance, we specified both parameters positionally, in the order in which they're declared within the `Param()` block. In the second case, we specified abbreviated parameter names for both. The third time, we omitted `-drivetype` entirely, using the default value of 3. In the last instance, we left off `-computername`, using the default value of `localhost`.

21.5   *Documenting your script*

Only a truly mean person would create a useful script and not tell anyone how to use it. Fortunately, PowerShell makes it easy to add help into your script, using comments. You're welcome to add typical programming-style comments to your scripts, but if you're using full cmdlet and parameter names, sometimes your script's operation will be obvious. By using a special comment syntax, however, you can provide help that mimics PowerShell's own help files.

This listing shows what we've added to our script.

Listing 21.4   Adding help to Get-DiskInventory.ps1

```
<#
.SYNOPSIS
Get-DiskInventory retrieves logical disk information from one or
more computers.
.DESCRIPTION
Get-DiskInventory uses WMI to retrieve the Win32_LogicalDisk
instances from one or more computers. It displays each disk's
drive letter, free space, total size, and percentage of free
space.
.PARAMETER computername
The computer name, or names, to query. Default: Localhost.
.PARAMETER drivetype
The drive type to query. See Win32_LogicalDisk documentation
for values. 3 is a fixed disk, and is the default.
```

```
.EXAMPLE
Get-DiskInventory -computername SERVER-R2 -drivetype 3
#>
param (
  $computername = 'localhost',
  $drivetype = 3
)
Get-WmiObject -class Win32_LogicalDisk -computername $computername `
 -filter "drivetype=$drivetype" |
 Sort-Object -property DeviceID |
 Format-Table -property DeviceID,
    @{label='FreeSpace(MB)';expression={$_.FreeSpace / 1MB -as [int]}},
    @{label='Size(GB';expression={$_.Size / 1GB -as [int]}},
    @{label='%Free';expression={$_.FreeSpace / $_.Size * 100 -as [int]}}
```

Normally, PowerShell ignores anything on a line that follows a # symbol, meaning that # designates a line as a comment. We've used the <# #> block comment syntax instead, because we had several lines of comments and didn't want to have to start each line with a separate # character.

Now we can drop to the normal console host and ask for help by running help .\Get-DiskInventory (again, you have to provide a path because this is a script and not a built-in cmdlet). Figure 21.2 shows the results, which proves that PowerShell is reading those comments and creating a standard help display. We can even run help .\Get-DiskInventory -full to get full help, including parameter information and our example. Figure 21.3 shows those results.

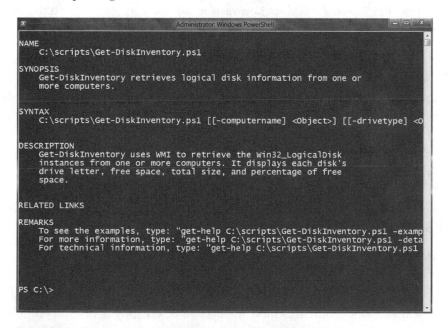

Figure 21.2 Viewing the help by using the normal help command

```
                      Administrator: Windows PowerShell                  _ □ x

NAME
    C:\scripts\Get-DiskInventory.ps1

SYNOPSIS
    Get-DiskInventory retrieves logical disk information from one or
    more computers.

SYNTAX
    C:\scripts\Get-DiskInventory.ps1 [[-computername] <Object>] [[-drivetype]
    <Object>] [<CommonParameters>]


DESCRIPTION
    Get-DiskInventory uses WMI to retrieve the Win32_LogicalDisk
    instances from one or more computers. It displays each disk's
    drive letter, free space, total size, and percentage of free
    space.


PARAMETERS
    -computername <Object>
        The computer name, or names, to query. Default: Localhost.

        Required?                    false
        Position?                    1
        Default value                localhost
        Accept pipeline input?       false
        Accept wildcard characters?  false


    -drivetype <Object>
        The drive type to query. See Win32_LogicalDisk documentation
-- More  --
```

Figure 21.3 Help options like -example, -detailed, and -full are supported for comment-based help.

These special comments, called comment-based help, must appear at the beginning of your script file. There are several keywords in addition to .DESCRIPTION, .SYNOPSIS, and the others we've used. For a full list, run help about_comment_based _help in PowerShell.

21.6 *One script, one pipeline*

We normally tell folks that anything in a script will run exactly as if you manually typed it into the shell, or if you copied the script to the clipboard and pasted it into the shell. That's not entirely true, though.

Consider this simple script:

```
Get-Process
Get-Service
```

Just two commands. But what happens if you were to type those commands into the shell manually, hitting Return after each?

TRY IT NOW You're going to have to run these commands on your own to see the results; they create fairly long output and it won't fit well within this book or even in a screenshot.

When you run the commands individually, you're creating a new pipeline for each command. At the end of each pipeline, PowerShell looks to see what needs to be formatted and creates the tables that you undoubtedly saw. The key here is that *each command runs in a separate pipeline*. Figure 21.4 illustrates this: two completely separate

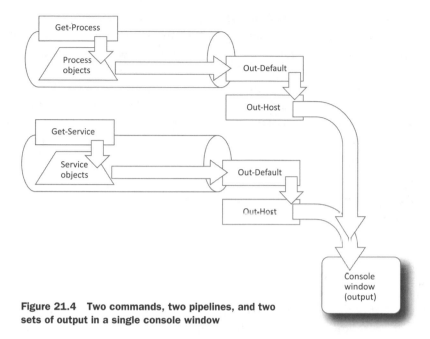

Figure 21.4 Two commands, two pipelines, and two sets of output in a single console window

commands, two individual pipelines, two formatting processes, and two different-looking sets of results.

You may think we're crazy for taking so much time to explain something that probably seems obvious, but it's important. Here's what happens when you run those two commands individually:

1 You run Get-Process.
2 The command places Process objects into the pipeline.
3 The pipeline ends in Out-Default, which picks up the objects.
4 Out-Default passes the objects to Out-Host, which calls on the formatting system to produce text output (you learned about this in chapter 10).
5 The text output appears on the screen.
6 You run Get-Service.
7 The command places Service objects into the pipeline.
8 The pipeline ends in Out-Default, which picks up the objects.
9 Out-Default passes the objects to Out-Host, which calls on the formatting system to produce text output.
10 The text output appears on the screen.

So you're now looking at a screen that contains the results from two commands. We want you to put those two commands into a script file. Name it Test.ps1 or something simple. Before you run the script, though, copy those two commands onto the clipboard. In the ISE, you can highlight both lines of text and press Ctrl-C to get them into the clipboard.

With those commands in the clipboard, go to the PowerShell console host and press Enter. That will paste the commands from the clipboard into the shell. They should execute exactly the same way, because the carriage returns also get pasted. Once again, you're running two distinct commands in two separate pipelines.

Now go back to the ISE and run the script. Different results, right? Why is that?

In PowerShell, every command executes within a single pipeline, and that includes scripts. Within a script, any command that produces pipeline output will be writing to a single pipeline: the one that the script itself is running in. Take a look at figure 21.5.

We'll try to explain what happened:

1 The script runs `Get-Process`.
2 The command places `Process` objects into the pipeline.
3 The script runs `Get-Service`.
4 The command places `Service` objects into the pipeline.
5 The pipeline ends in `Out-Default`, which picks up both kinds of objects.
6 `Out-Default` passes the objects to `Out-Host`, which calls on the formatting system to produce text output.
7 Because the `Process` objects are first, the shell's formatting system selects a format appropriate to processes. That's why they look normal. But then the shell runs into the `Service` objects. It can't produce a whole new table at this point, so it winds up producing a list.
8 The text output appears on the screen.

This different output occurs because the script wrote two kinds of objects to a single pipeline. This is the important difference between putting commands into a script and running them manually: within a script, you only have one pipeline to work with. Normally, your scripts should strive to only output one kind of object, so that Power-Shell can produce sensible text output.

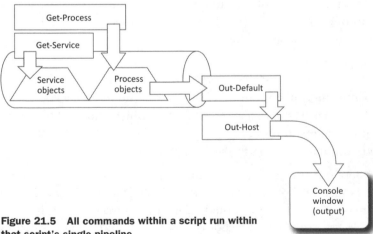

Figure 21.5   **All commands within a script run within that script's single pipeline.**

21.7 A quick look at scope

The last topic we need to visit is *scope*. Scopes are a form of container for certain types of PowerShell elements, primarily aliases, variables, and functions.

The shell itself is the top-level scope and is called the *global scope*. When you run a script, a new scope is created around that script, and it's called the *script scope*. The script scope is subsidiary to the global scope and is said to be a *child* of the global scope, which is the script scope's *parent*. Functions also get their own *private scope*.

Figure 21.6 illustrates these scope relationships, with the global scope containing its children, and those containing their own children, and so forth.

A scope only lasts as long as needed to execute whatever is in the scope. That means the global scope only exists while PowerShell is running, a script scope only exists while that script is running, and so forth. Once whatever it is stops running, the scope vanishes, taking everything inside it with it. PowerShell has some very specific—and sometimes confusing—rules for scoped elements like aliases, variables, and functions, but the main rule is this: If you try to access a scoped element, PowerShell sees if it exists within the current scope. If it doesn't, PowerShell sees if it exists in the current scope's parent. It continues going up the relationship tree until it gets to the global scope.

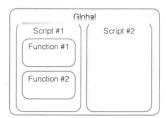

Figure 21.6 Global, script, and function (private) scopes

> **TRY IT NOW** In order to get the proper results, it's important that you follow these steps carefully and precisely.

Let's see this in action. Follow these steps:

1. Close any PowerShell or PowerShell ISE windows you may have open, so that you can start from scratch.
2. Open a new PowerShell window, and a new PowerShell ISE window.
3. In the ISE, create a script that contains one line: `Write $x`
4. Save the script as C:\Scope.ps1.
5. In the regular PowerShell window, run the script with `C:\Scope`. You shouldn't see any output. When the script ran, a new scope was created for it. The `$x` variable didn't exist in that scope, so PowerShell went to the parent scope—the global scope—to see if `$x` existed there. It didn't exist there, either, so PowerShell decided that `$x` was empty, and wrote that (meaning, nothing) as the output.
6. In the normal PowerShell window, run `$x = 4`. Then, run `C:\Scope` again. This time, you should see 4 as the output. The variable `$x` still wasn't defined in the script scope, but PowerShell was able to find it in the global scope, and so the script used that value.
7. In the ISE, add `$x = 10` to the top of the script (before the existing `Write` command), and save the script.

8 In the normal PowerShell window, run `C:\Scope` again. This time, you'll see 10 as output. That's because `$x` was defined within the script scope, and the shell didn't need to look in the global scope. Now run `$x` in the shell. You'll see 4, proving that the value of `$x` within the script scope didn't affect the value of `$x` within the global scope.

One important concept here is that when a scope defines a variable, alias, or function, that scope loses access to any variables, aliases, or functions having the same name in a parent scope. The locally defined element will always be the one PowerShell uses. For example, if you put `New-Alias Dir Get-Service` into a script, then within that script the alias `Dir` will run `Get-Service` instead of the usual `Get-ChildItem`. (In reality, the shell probably won't let you do that, because it protects the built-in aliases from being redefined.) By defining the alias within the script's scope, you prevent the shell from going to the parent scope and finding the normal, default `Dir`. Of course, the script's redefinition of `Dir` will only last for the execution of that script, and the default `Dir` defined in the global scope will remain unaffected.

It's easy to let this scope stuff confuse you. You can avoid confusion by never relying on anything that's in any scope other than the current one. So before you try to access a variable within a script, make sure you've already assigned it a value within that same scope. Parameters in a `Param()` block are one way to do that, and there are many other ways to put values and objects into a variable.

21.8 Lab

NOTE   For this lab, you'll need any computer running PowerShell v3.

The following command is for you to add to a script. You should first identify any elements that should be parameterized, such as the computer name. Your final script should define the parameter, and you should create comment-based help within the script. Run your script to test it, and use the `Help` command to make sure your comment-based help works properly. Don't forget to read the help files referenced within this chapter for more information.

Here's the command:

```
Get-WmiObject Win32_LogicalDisk -comp "localhost" -filter "drivetype=3" |
Where { $_.FreeSpace / $_.Size -lt .1 } |
Select -Property DeviceID,FreeSpace,Size
```

Here's a hint: There are at least two pieces of information that will need to be parameterized. This command is intended to list all drives that have less than a given amount of free disk space. Obviously, you won't always want to target localhost, and you might not want 10% (that is, .1) to be your free space threshold. You could also choose to parameterize the drive type (which is 3, here), but for this lab leave that hardcoded with the value 3.

22

Improving your parameterized script

In the previous chapter, we left you with a pretty cool script that had been parameterized. The idea of a parameterized script is that someone else can run the script without having to worry about, or have to mess with, its contents. They provide input through a designated interface—parameters—and that's all they can change. In this chapter, we're going to take things a bit further.

22.1 Starting point

Just to make sure we're on the same page, let's agree to use listing 22.1 as a starting point. This script features comment-based help, two input parameters, and a command that uses those input parameters. We've made one minor change since the previous chapter: we changed the output to be selected objects, rather than a formatted table.

Listing 22.1   Starting point: Get-DiskInventory.ps1

```
<#
.SYNOPSIS
Get-DiskInventory retrieves logical disk information from one or
more computers.
.DESCRIPTION
Get-DiskInventory uses WMI to retrieve the Win32_LogicalDisk
instances from one or more computers. It displays each disk's
drive letter, free space, total size, and percentage of free
```

```
space.
.PARAMETER computername
The computer name, or names, to query. Default: Localhost.
.PARAMETER drivetype
The drive type to query. See Win32_LogicalDisk documentation
for values. 3 is a fixed disk, and is the default.
.EXAMPLE
Get-DiskInventory -computername SERVER-R2 -drivetype 3
#>
param (
  $computername = 'localhost',
  $drivetype = 3
)
Get-WmiObject -class Win32_LogicalDisk -computername $computername `
 -filter "drivetype=$drivetype" |
 Sort-Object -property DeviceID |
 Select-Object -property DeviceID,
     @{name='FreeSpace(MB)';expression={$_.FreeSpace / 1MB -as [int]}},
     @{name='Size(GB';expression={$_.Size / 1GB -as [int]}},
     @{name='%Free';expression={$_.FreeSpace / $_.Size * 100 -as [int]}}
```

Why did we switch to `Select-Object` instead of `Format-Table`? We generally feel it's a bad idea to write a script that produces preformatted output. After all, if someone needed this data in a CSV file, and the script was outputting formatted tables, that person would be out of luck. With this revision, we can run our script this way to get a formatted table:

```
PS C:\> .\Get-DiskInventory | Format-Table
```

Or we could run it this way to get that CSV file:

```
PS C:\> .\Get-DiskInventory | Export-CSV disks.csv
```

The point is that outputting objects (which `Select-Object` does), as opposed to formatted displays, makes our script more flexible in the long run.

22.2 Getting PowerShell to do the hard work

We're going to turn on some PowerShell magic by adding just one line to our script. This technically turns our script into an "advanced script," which enables a whole slew of useful PowerShell capabilities. Listing 22.2 shows the revision—we've boldfaced the one new line.

> **Listing 22.2   Making Get-DiskInventory.ps1 an advanced script**

```
<#
.SYNOPSIS
Get-DiskInventory retrieves logical disk information from one or
more computers.
.DESCRIPTION
Get-DiskInventory uses WMI to retrieve the Win32_LogicalDisk
instances from one or more computers. It displays each disk's
drive letter, free space, total size, and percentage of free
space.
```

```
.PARAMETER computername
The computer name, or names, to query. Default: Localhost.
.PARAMETER drivetype
The drive type to query. See Win32_LogicalDisk documentation
for values. 3 is a fixed disk, and is the default.
.EXAMPLE
Get-DiskInventory -computername SERVER-R2 -drivetype 3
#>
[CmdletBinding()]
param (
  $computername = 'localhost',
  $drivetype = 3
)
Get-WmiObject -class Win32_LogicalDisk -computername $computername `
 -filter "drivetype=$drivetype" |
 Sort-Object -property DeviceID |
 Select-Object -property DeviceID,
     @{name='FreeSpace(MB)';expression={$_.FreeSpace / 1MB -as [int]}},
     @{name='Size(GB';expression={$_.Size / 1GB -as [int]}},
     @{name='%Free';expression={$_.FreeSpace / $_.Size * 100 -as [int]}}
```

It's important that the `[CmdletBinding()]` directive be the first line in the script after the comment-based help. PowerShell only knows to look for it there. With this one change, the script will continue to run normally, but we've enabled several neat features that we'll explore next.

22.3 *Making parameters mandatory*

We're a little unhappy with our script in its existing form because it provides a default value for the `-ComputerName` parameter—and we're not sure one is really needed. We'd rather prompt for that value than rely on a hardcoded default. Fortunately, PowerShell makes it easy—again, adding just one line will do the trick, as shown in listing 22.3.

Listing 22.3 Giving Get-DiskInventory.ps1 a mandatory parameter

```
<#
.SYNOPSIS
Get-DiskInventory retrieves logical disk information from one or
more computers.
.DESCRIPTION
Get-DiskInventory uses WMI to retrieve the Win32_LogicalDisk
instances from one or more computers. It displays each disk's
drive letter, free space, total size, and percentage of free
space.
.PARAMETER computername
The computer name, or names, to query. Default: Localhost.
.PARAMETER drivetype
The drive type to query. See Win32_LogicalDisk documentation
for values. 3 is a fixed disk, and is the default.
.EXAMPLE
Get-DiskInventory -computername SERVER-R2 -drivetype 3
#>
```

```
[CmdletBinding()]
param (
  [Parameter(Mandatory=$True)]
  [string]$computername,

  [int]$drivetype = 3
)
Get-WmiObject -class Win32_LogicalDisk -computername $computername `
 -filter "drivetype=$drivetype" |
 Sort-Object -property DeviceID |
 Select-Object -property DeviceID,
     @{name='FreeSpace(MB)';expression={$_.FreeSpace / 1MB -as [int]}},
     @{name='Size(GB';expression={$_.Size / 1GB -as [int]}},
     @{name='%Free';expression={$_.FreeSpace / $_.Size * 100 -as [int]}}
```

Above and beyond

When someone runs your script but doesn't provide a mandatory parameter, Power-Shell will prompt them for it. There are two ways to make PowerShell's prompt more meaningful to that user.

First, use a good parameter name. Prompting someone to fill in "comp" isn't as help-ful as prompting them to provide a "computerName," so try to use parameter names that are descriptive and consistent with what other PowerShell commands use.

You can also add a help message:

```
[Parameter(Mandatory=$True,HelpMessage="Enter a computer name to query")
```

Some PowerShell hosts will display that help message as part of the prompt, making it even clearer to the user, but not every host application will use this attribute, so don't be dismayed if you don't see it all the time as you're testing. We like including it anyway, when we're writing something intended to be used by other people. It never hurts. But for brevity, we'll omit `HelpMessage` from our running example in this chapter.

Just that one *decorator*, `[Parameter(Mandatory=$True)]`, will make PowerShell prompt for a computer name if whoever runs this script forgets to provide one. To help Power-Shell even further, we've given both of our parameters a data type: `[string]` for `-computername`, and `[int]` (which means integer) for `-drivetype`.

Adding these kinds of attributes to parameters can become confusing, so let's examine the `Param()` block syntax more closely—look at figure 22.1.

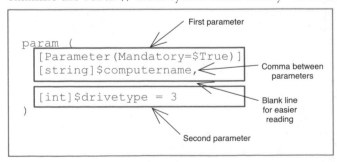

Figure 22.1 Breaking down the `Param()` block syntax

Here are the important things to notice:

- All of the parameters are enclosed within the `Param()` block's parentheses.
- A single parameter can consist of multiple decorators, which can either be strung out on one line, or placed on separate lines as we've done in figure 22.1. We think multiple lines are more readable—but the important bit is that they all go together. Here, the `Mandatory` attribute only modifies `-computerName`—it has no effect at all on `-drivetype`.
- Each parameter name except the last one is followed by a comma.
- For better readability, we also like to put a blank line between each parameter. We think it helps to visually separate them better, making the `Param()` block less confusing.
- We define each parameter as if it were a variable—`$computername` and `$drivetype`—but someone who runs this script will treat them as normal Power-Shell command-line parameters, such as `-computername` and `-drivetype`.

TRY IT NOW Try saving the script in listing 22.3 and running it in the shell. Don't specify a `-computername` parameter and see how PowerShell prompts you for that information.

22.4 *Adding parameter aliases*

Is "computername" the first thing that comes to mind when you think about computer names? Possibly not. We used `-computerName` as our parameter name because it's consistent with the way other PowerShell commands are written. Look at `Get-Service`, `Get-WmiObject`, `Get-Process`, and others, and you'll see a `-computerName` parameter on them all. So we went with that.

But if something like `-hostname` comes more easily to your mind, you can add that as an alternative name, or alias, for the parameter. It's just another decorator, as shown in listing 22.4.

Listing 22.4 Adding a parameter alias to Get-DiskInventory.ps1

```
<#
.SYNOPSIS
Get-DiskInventory retrieves logical disk information from one or
more computers.
.DESCRIPTION
Get-DiskInventory uses WMI to retrieve the Win32_LogicalDisk
instances from one or more computers. It displays each disk's
drive letter, free space, total size, and percentage of free
space.
.PARAMETER computername
The computer name, or names, to query. Default: Localhost.
.PARAMETER drivetype
The drive type to query. See Win32_LogicalDisk documentation
for values. 3 is a fixed disk, and is the default.
.EXAMPLE
Get-DiskInventory -computername SERVER-R2 -drivetype 3
```

```
#>
[CmdletBinding()]
param (
   [Parameter(Mandatory=$True)]
   [Alias('hostname')]
   [string]$computername,

   [int]$drivetype = 3
)
Get-WmiObject -class Win32_LogicalDisk -computername $computername `
 -filter "drivetype=$drivetype" |
 Sort-Object -property DeviceID |
 Select-Object -property DeviceID,
      @{name='FreeSpace(MB)';expression={$_.FreeSpace / 1MB -as [int]}},
      @{name='Size(GB';expression={$_.Size / 1GB -as [int]}},
      @{name='%Free';expression={$_.FreeSpace / $_.Size * 100 -as [int]}}
```

With this minor change, we can now run this:

```
PS C:\> .\Get-DiskInventory -host SERVER2
```

> **NOTE**   Remember, you only have to type enough of a parameter name for
> PowerShell to understand which parameter you meant. In this case, -host was
> enough for PowerShell to identify -hostname. We could also have typed the
> full thing.

Again, this new addition is a part of the -computername parameter—it has no effect on
-drivetype. The -computername parameter's definition now occupies three lines of
text, although we could also have strung everything together on one line:

```
[Parameter(Mandatory=$True)][Alias('hostname')][string]$computername,
```

We just think that's a lot harder to read.

22.5   *Validating parameter input*

Let's play with the -drivetype parameter a little bit. According to the MSDN documentation for the Win32_LogicalDisk WMI class (do a search for the class name, and
one of the top results will be the documentation), drive type 3 is a local hard disk.
Type 2 is a removable disk, which should also have a size and free space measurement.
Drive types 1, 4, 5, and 6 are less interesting (does anyone use RAM drives, type 6, anymore?), and in some cases they might not have an amount of free space (type 5, for
optical disks). So we'd like to prevent anyone from using those types when they run
our script.

  This listing shows the minor change we need to make.

Listing 22.5   Adding parameter validation to Get-DiskInventory.ps1

```
<#
.SYNOPSIS
Get-DiskInventory retrieves logical disk information from one or
more computers.
.DESCRIPTION
```

```
Get-DiskInventory uses WMI to retrieve the Win32_LogicalDisk
instances from one or more computers. It displays each disk's
drive letter, free space, total size, and percentage of free
space.
.PARAMETER computername
The computer name, or names, to query. Default: Localhost.
.PARAMETER drivetype
The drive type to query. See Win32_LogicalDisk documentation
for values. 3 is a fixed disk, and is the default.
.EXAMPLE
Get-DiskInventory -computername SERVER-R2 -drivetype 3
#>
[CmdletBinding()]
param (
  [Parameter(Mandatory=$True)]
  [Alias('hostname')]
  [string]$computername,

  [ValidateSet(2,3)]
  [int]$drivetype = 3
)
Get-WmiObject -class Win32_LogicalDisk -computername $computername `
  -filter "drivetype=$drivetype" |
  Sort-Object -property DeviceID |
  Select-Object -property DeviceID,
      @{name='FreeSpace(MB)';expression={$_.FreeSpace / 1MB -as [int]}},
      @{name='Size(GB';expression={$_.Size / 1GB -as [int]}},
      @{name='%Free';expression={$_.FreeSpace / $_.Size * 100 -as [int]}}
```

This new decorator tells PowerShell that only two values, 2 and 3, are accepted by our -drivetype parameter, and that 3 is the default.

There are a bunch of other validation techniques you can add to a parameter, and when it makes sense to do so, you can add more than one to the same parameter. Run help about_functions_advanced_parameters for a full list—we'll be sticking with ValidateSet() for now. Jeffery also did a great set of blog articles on some of the other "Validate" attributes that might be helpful—you can look it up at http:// jdhitsolutions.com/blog/ (search for "validate").

> **TRY IT NOW** Save this script and run it again—try specifying -drivetype 5 and see what PowerShell does.

22.6 *Adding the warm and fuzzies with verbose output*

In chapter 19, we mentioned how we prefer to use Write-Verbose over Write-Host for producing the step-by-step progress information that some folks like to see their scripts produce. Now's the time for a real example.

We've added a few verbose output messages in this listing.

Listing 22.6 Adding verbose output to Get-DiskInventory.ps1

```
<#
.SYNOPSIS
Get-DiskInventory retrieves logical disk information from one or
```

```
more computers.
.DESCRIPTION
Get-DiskInventory uses WMI to retrieve the Win32_LogicalDisk
instances from one or more computers. It displays each disk's
drive letter, free space, total size, and percentage of free
space.
.PARAMETER computername
The computer name, or names, to query. Default: Localhost.
.PARAMETER drivetype
The drive type to query. See Win32_LogicalDisk documentation
for values. 3 is a fixed disk, and is the default.
.EXAMPLE
Get-DiskInventory -computername SERVER-R2 -drivetype 3
#>
[CmdletBinding()]
param (
  [Parameter(Mandatory=$True)]
  [Alias('hostname')]
  [string]$computername,

  [ValidateSet(2,3)]
  [int]$drivetype = 3
)
Write-Verbose "Connecting to $computername"
Write-Verbose "Looking for drive type $drivetype"
Get-WmiObject -class Win32_LogicalDisk -computername $computername `
 -filter "drivetype=$drivetype" |
 Sort-Object -property DeviceID |
 Select-Object -property DeviceID,
     @{name='FreeSpace(MB)';expression={$_.FreeSpace / 1MB -as [int]}},
     @{name='Size(GB';expression={$_.Size / 1GB -as [int]}},
     @{name='%Free';expression={$_.FreeSpace / $_.Size * 100 -as [int]}}
Write-Verbose "Finished running command"
```

Now try running this script in two ways. This first attempt shouldn't display any of the verbose output:

```
PS C:\> .\Get-DiskInventory -computername localhost
```

Now for a second attempt, where we want the verbose output displayed:

```
PS C:\> .\Get-DiskInventory -computername localhost -verbose
```

> **TRY IT NOW** This is a lot cooler when you see it for yourself—go ahead and run the script as we've shown here, and see the differences for yourself.

How cool is that? When you want verbose output, you can get it—and you don't have to code the -Verbose parameter at all! It comes for free when you add [CmdletBinding()]. And a really neat part is that it will also activate verbose output for every command that your script contains! So any commands you use that are designed to produce verbose output will do so automagically. This technique makes it easy to turn the verbose output on and off, making it a lot more flexible than Write-Host. And you don't have to mess around with the $VerbosePreference variable to make the output show up on screen.

Also, notice in the verbose output how we made use of PowerShell's double quotation mark trick: by including a variable ($computername) within double quotes, the output is able to include the contents of the variable, so we can see what PowerShell is up to.

22.7 Lab

NOTE For this lab, you'll need any computer running PowerShell v3.

This lab is going to require you to recall some of what you learned in chapter 21, because you'll be taking the following command, parameterizing it, and turning it into a script—just like you did for the lab in chapter 21. But this time we also want you to make the -computerName parameter mandatory and give it a hostname alias. Have your script display verbose output before and after it runs this command, too. Remember, you have to parameterize the computer name—but that's the only thing you have to parameterize in this case.

Be sure to run the command as-is before you start modifying it, to make sure it works on your system.

```
get-wmiobject win32_networkadapter -computername localhost |
where { $_.PhysicalAdapter } |
select MACAddress,AdapterType,DeviceID,Name,Speed
```

To reiterate, here's your complete task list:

- Make sure the command runs as-is before modifying it.
- Parameterize the computer name.
- Make the computer name parameter mandatory.
- Give the computer name parameter an alias, hostname.
- Add comment-based help with at least one example of how to use the script.
- Add verbose output before and after the modified command.
- Save the script as Get-PhysicalAdapters.ps1.

23

Advanced remoting configuration

In chapter 13, we did our best to introduce you to PowerShell's remoting technology. We deliberately left a few stones unturned in order to focus on the core technologies and techniques behind remoting, but in this chapter we want to return and cover some of the more advanced and unusual features and scenarios. We'll admit up front that not everything in this chapter will be usable by everyone—but we do think everyone should know about these options, in case a need for them arises in your future.

Also, we'll quickly remind you that this book is focused on PowerShell v3. Revisit chapter 1 if you need help in figuring out which version you're running; much of what we cover in this book won't work in older versions.

23.1 Using other endpoints

As you learned in chapter 13, a single computer can contain multiple *endpoints*, which PowerShell also refers to as *session configurations*. For example, enabling remoting on a 64-bit machine enables an endpoint for 32-bit PowerShell as well as 64-bit PowerShell, with the 64-bit one being the default.

You can see a list of available session configurations on any machine you have Administrator access to:

```
PS C:\> Get-PSSessionConfiguration

Name          : microsoft.powershell
PSVersion     : 3.0
StartupScript :
RunAsUser     :
Permission    : NT AUTHORITY\NETWORK AccessDenied, BUILTIN\Administrators
                AccessAllowed

Name          : microsoft.powershell.workflow
PSVersion     : 3.0
StartupScript :
RunAsUser     :
Permission    : NT AUTHORITY\NETWORK AccessDenied, BUILTIN\Administrators
                AccessAllowed

Name          : microsoft.powershell32
PSVersion     : 3.0
StartupScript :
RunAsUser     :
Permission    : NT AUTHORITY\NETWORK AccessDenied, BUILTIN\Administrators
                AccessAllowed
```

Each endpoint has a name; the one named "Microsoft.PowerShell" is the one that remoting commands like `New-PSSession`, `Enter-PSSession`, `Invoke-Command`, and so forth will use by default. On a 64-bit system, that endpoint is the 64-bit shell; on a 32-bit system, "Microsoft.PowerShell" is a 32-bit shell.

You'll notice that our 64-bit system has an alternative "Microsoft.PowerShell32" endpoint running a 32-bit shell for backward compatibility. To connect to an alternative endpoint, just specify its name to the `-ConfigurationName` parameter of a remoting command:

```
PS C:\> Enter-PSSession -ComputerName DONJONES1D96 -ConfigurationName 'Micr
osoft.PowerShell32'
[DONJONES1D96]: PS C:\Users\donjones\Documents>
```

When might you use an alternative endpoint? Well, if you needed to run a command that relied upon a 32-bit PSSnapin, that might be one reason to explicitly connect to the 32-bit endpoint on a 64-bit machine. You might also have custom endpoints set up, and might need to connect to one in order to perform some specific task.

23.2 Creating custom endpoints

Creating a custom endpoint is a two-step process:

1. You use `New-PSSessionConfigurationFile` to create a new session configuration file, which should have a .PSSC filename extension. This file defines many characteristics of the endpoint, predominantly what commands and capabilities it will include.

2. You use `Register-PSSessionConfiguration` to load the .PSSC file and create the new endpoint within the WinRM service. During registration, you can set numerous operational parameters, such as defining who may connect to the endpoint. You can change those settings later by using `Set-PSSessionConfiguration`, if necessary.

We'll walk through an example that uses custom endpoints for delegated administration, which is possibly one of their coolest features. We'll create an endpoint that members of our domain's HelpDesk group can connect to. Within that endpoint, we'll enable the commands that relate to network adapter management—and only those commands. We don't plan to give our help desk permission to run those commands, just to make the commands visible to them. We'll also configure the endpoint to run commands under an alternative credential that we provide, so the commands will work without our help desk team actually having the necessary permissions themselves.

23.2.1 *Creating the session configuration*

Here's the command we ran—we'll format this nicely for the book, but we actually typed it all on one, long line:

```
PS C:\> New-PSSessionConfigurationFile
  -Path C:\HelpDeskEndpoint.pssc
  -ModulesToImport NetAdapter
  -SessionType RestrictedRemoteServer
  -CompanyName "Our Company"
  -Author "Don Jones"
  -Description "Net adapter commands for use by help desk"
  -PowerShellVersion '3.0'
```

There are a couple of key parameters here, which we've highlighted in bold. We'll explain why we chose the values we did, but we'll leave it up to you to read the help on this command to discover its other options.

- The **-Path** is required, and the filename you provide should end in .PSSC.
- **-ModulesToImport** lists the modules (in this case, just one named NetAdapter) that we want available within this endpoint.
- **-SessionType** RestrictedRemoteServer removes all core PowerShell commands, except for a very short list of necessary ones. Those include Select-Object, Measure-Object, Get-Command, Get-Help, Exit-PSSession, and so on.
- **-PowerShellVersion** defaults to 3.0, but we included it for completeness.

There are also several parameters that start with -Visible, such as -VisibleCmdlets. Normally, when you import a module using -ModulesToImport, every command in the module is made visible to people using the final endpoint, but you can use the -Visible parameters to change that behavior. By listing just the cmdlets, aliases, functions, and providers you want people to see, you're effectively hiding the rest. That's a good way to limit what someone can do with your endpoint. Do be careful when using these visibility parameters, as they can be a bit confusing. For example, if you import a module consisting of both cmdlets and functions, then using -VisibleCmdlets only restricts which of the cmdlets are visible—it will have no effect on the visible functions, meaning they'll all be visible by default.

Note that there's no way to limit the command parameters they can use: PowerShell supports parameter-level restrictions, but to obtain that ability you have to do some heavier-duty coding in Visual Studio, which is beyond what we'll cover in this book. There are some other, advanced tricks you could use, such as creating proxy functions that hide specific parameters, but those are also beyond the scope of this book for beginners.

23.2.2 Registering the session

Having created the session configuration file, here's the command we ran to get it up and running. Again, we'll format this nicely for the book, but we typed it all on one long command line:

```
PS C:\> Register-PSSessionConfiguration
  -Path .\HelpDeskEndpoint.pssc
  -RunAsCredential COMPANY\HelpDeskProxyAdmin
  -ShowSecurityDescriptorUI
  -Name HelpDesk
```

This creates a new endpoint named HelpDesk (as opposed to Microsoft.PowerShell or something else). As shown in figure 23.1, we were prompted for the password for the COMPANY\HelpDeskProxyAdmin account; this is the account that will be used to run all commands within the endpoint. We'll make sure that account has the permissions needed to run the network adapter commands.

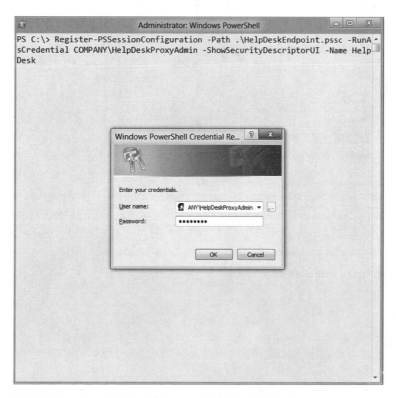

Figure 23.1   Password prompt for our "run as" credential

We had to answer several "are you sure" prompts, which we strongly suggest that you read carefully. This command will stop and restart the WinRM service, for example, which could interrupt other administrators attempting to manage the local machine, so some caution is in order.

As shown in figure 23.2, we were also given a graphical dialog box to specify which users may connect to the endpoint. The dialog box is displayed because we used the `-ShowSecurityDescriptorUI` parameter, rather than specifying the endpoint's permissions in the complex Security Descriptor Definition Language (SDDL), which we're frankly not all that familiar with. This is a case where the GUI is a good thing—we'll add our HelpDesk user group to it, and ensure they have Execute and Read permissions. Execute is the minimum permission needed, given what we plan to have them doing with the endpoint; Read is the only other thing they should need.

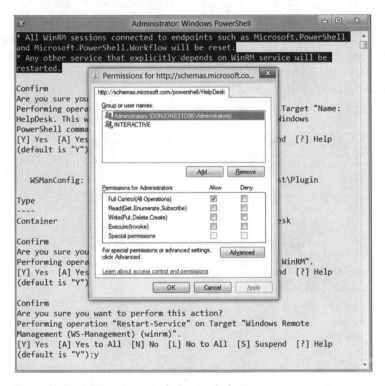

Figure 23.2 Setting the endpoint's permissions

With that, we're done. As you can see from the following (truncated) output, users of our new endpoint have a very limited set of commands to work with:

```
PS C:\> Enter-PSSession -ComputerName DONJONES1D96 -ConfigurationName HelpD
esk
[DONJONES1D96]: PS>Get-Command

Capability      Name                                                ModuleN
                                                                    ame

----------      ----                                                -------
CIM             Disable-NetAdapter                                  NetA...
CIM             Disable-NetAdapterBinding                           NetA...
CIM             Disable-NetAdapterChecksumOffload                   NetA...
CIM             Disable-NetAdapterEncapsulatedPacketTaskOffload     NetA...
CIM             Disable-NetAdapterIPsecOffload                      NetA...
CIM             Disable-NetAdapterLso                               NetA...
CIM             Disable-NetAdapterPowerManagement                  NetA...
CIM             Disable-NetAdapterQos                               NetA...
CIM             Disable-NetAdapterRdma                              NetA...
CIM             Disable-NetAdapterRsc                               NetA...
CIM             Disable-NetAdapterRss                               NetA...
CIM             Disable-NetAdapterSriov                             NetA...
CIM             Disable-NetAdapterVmq                               NetA...
CIM             Enable-NetAdapter                                   NetA...
CIM             Enable-NetAdapterBinding                            NetA...
CIM             Enable-NetAdapterChecksumOffload                    NetA...
CIM             Enable-NetAdapterEncapsulatedPacketTaskOffload      NetA...
CIM             Enable-NetAdapterIPsecOffload                       NetA...
CIM             Enable-NetAdapterLso                                NetA...
CIM             Enable-NetAdapterPowerManagement                   NetA...
CIM             Enable-NetAdapterQos                                NetA...
```

This is a great way to create a very specific set of capabilities for a group of users. They don't even necessarily need to connect to PowerShell from a console session as we did for this test; they might be using a GUI tool that utilizes PowerShell remoting under the hood. Provided that tool only needs these commands, this technique would be a great way to give someone this delegated capability and nothing else.

23.3 Enabling multihop remoting

This is a topic we briefly brought up in chapter 13, but it deserves a bit more depth. Figure 23.3 depicts the "second hop" or "multihop" problem: You start on Computer A, and you create a PSSession connection to Computer B. That's the first hop, and it'll probably work fine. But then you try to ask Computer B to create a second hop, or connection, to Computer C, and the operation fails.

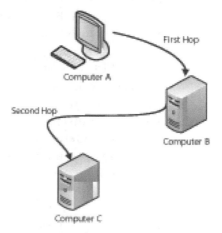

Figure 23.3 Multihop remoting in Windows PowerShell

The problem is related to the way PowerShell delegates your credentials from Computer A to Computer B. Delegation is the process of enabling Computer B to execute tasks as if it were you, thus ensuring that you can do anything you'd normally have permission to do, but nothing more. By default, delegation can only traverse one such hop; Computer B doesn't have permission to delegate your credential on to a third computer, Computer C.

On Windows Vista and later, you can enable this multihop delegation. Two steps are needed:

1 On your computer (Computer A in the example), run `Enable-WSManCredSSP -Role Client -DelegateComputer` *x*. You'll replace *x* with the name of the computer that your credentials may be delegated to. You could specify an individual computer name, but you might also use wildcards. We don't recommend using `*`, as that presents some real security concerns, but you might authorize an entire domain: `*.company.com`, for example.

2 On the server that you're connecting to first (Computer B in the example), run `Enable-WSManCredSSP -Role Server`.

The changes made by the command will be applied to the computers' local security policy; you could also manually make these changes via a Group Policy object, which might make more sense in a large domain environment. Managing this via Group Policy is beyond the scope of this chapter, but you can find more information in the help for `Enable-WSManCredSSP`. Don also authored a *Secrets of PowerShell Remoting* guide (http://PowerShellBooks.com/) that covers the policy-related elements in more detail.

23.4 *Digging deeper into remoting authentication*

We find that folks tend to think of authentication as a one-way process: you want to access some remote machine, and you have to provide it with your credentials before it will let you in. But PowerShell remoting employs *mutual authentication*, which means the remote machine must also prove its identity to you. In other words, if you run `Enter-PSSession -computerName DC01`, the computer named DC01 has to prove it's really DC01 before the connection will complete.

Why? Normally, your computer will resolve a computer name (like DC01) to an IP address using the Domain Name System (DNS). DNS isn't invulnerable to spoofing, so it's not unthinkable that an attacker could get in and modify the entry for DC01 to point to a different IP address—an IP address that the attacker controls. You could unknowingly connect to DC01, wind up on an imposter computer, and then start delegating your credential to it—bad news! Mutual authentication prevents that from happening: if the computer you connect to can't prove it's the one you intended to connect to, then remoting will fail. That's a good thing—you don't want to turn that protection off without careful planning and consideration.

23.4.1 Defaults for mutual authentication

Microsoft expects most PowerShell usage to occur in an Active Directory domain environment. Provided you connect to computers using their real computer names, as listed in Active Directory, the domain will handle the mutual authentication for you. This even happens when you access computers in other, trusting domains. The trick is that you need to provide PowerShell with a computer name that will accomplish both of these requirements:

- The name must resolve to an IP address.
- The name must match the computer's name in the directory.

Providing a computer name from the same domain that you're in, or a fully qualified name (computer and domain name, like DC01.COMPANY.LOC) for a trusting domain, usually accomplishes both of these tasks. But if you need to provide an IP address, or if you need to provide a different name for DNS to work (such as a CNAME alias), then the default mutual authentication won't work. That leaves you with two choices: SSL or TrustedHosts.

23.4.2 Mutual authentication via SSL

For this technique, you'll need to obtain an SSL digital certificate for the destination machine. The certificate must be issued to the same computer name that you'll type to access the computer. That is, if you're running `Enter-PSSession -computerName DC01.COMPANY.LOC -UseSSL -credential COMPANY\Administrator`, then the certificate installed on DC01 must be issued to "dc01.company.loc" or the entire process will fail. Note that the `-credential` parameter is mandatory in this scenario.

After getting your certificate, you need to install it into the Personal certificate store for the computer account—something best accomplished with the Certificates snap-in in the Microsoft Management Console (MMC) GUI. Simply double-clicking a certificate file will usually put it in your user account's Personal store, but that won't work.

With the certificate installed, you'll need to create an HTTPS listener on the computer, telling it to use the newly installed certificate. The step-by-step directions are quite extensive, and because this isn't something a lot of people will probably do, we're not going to cover them all here. Take a look at Don's *Secrets of PowerShell Remoting* guide (it's free) and you'll find step-by-step instructions including screenshots.

23.4.3 Mutual authentication via TrustedHosts

This is a slightly easier technique than using an SSL certificate, and it requires a lot less setup. But it's a bit more dangerous, because it basically shuts off mutual authentication for selected hosts. Before you try it, you need to be able to confidently state, "it is unthinkable that someone could impersonate one of these hosts, or hack their DNS records." For internal computers on your intranet, for example, you might feel pretty confident of that.

Then you just need a way to identify the computers you'll trust without mutual authentication. In a domain, for example, that might be something like "*.COMPANY .COM" for all hosts in the Company.com domain.

This is an instance where you're likely going to want to configure the setting for your entire domain, so we'll give you the Group Policy instructions. You can use these same instructions for a single computer's Local Security Policy.

In any GPO or in the Local Computer Policy editor, follow these steps:

1 Expand Computer Configuration.
2 Expand Administrative Templates.
3 Expand Windows Components.
4 Expand Windows Remote Management.
5 Expand WinRM Client.
6 Double-click Trusted Hosts.
7 Enable the policy and add your trusted hosts lists. Multiple entries can be separated by commas, such as "*.company.com,*.sales.company.com."

NOTE Older versions of Windows might not have the template needed to display these settings in the Local Computer Policy, and older domain controllers might not have them in their Group Policy objects. For those situations, you can change the Trusted Hosts list in PowerShell. Run `help about_remote_troubleshooting` in the shell for instructions.

Now you'll be able to connect to those machines without mutual authentication getting in the way. You must provide a `-Credential` parameter with all remoting commands used to connect to these computers—failure to do so will result in a failed connection attempt.

23.5   *Lab*

NOTE For this lab, you'll need a Windows 8 or Windows Server 2012 computer running PowerShell v3.

Create a remoting endpoint named TestPoint on your local computer. Configure the endpoint so that the SmbShare module is loaded automatically, but so that only the `Get-SmbShare` cmdlet is visible from that module. Also ensure that key cmdlets like `Exit-PSSession` are available, but no other core PowerShell cmdlets can be used. Don't worry about specifying special endpoint permissions or designating a "run as" credential.

Test your endpoint by connecting to it using `Enter-PSSession` (specify localhost as the computer name, and TestPoint as the configuration name). When connected, run `Get-Command` to ensure that only the designated handful of commands can be seen.

Note that this lab might only be possible on Windows 8, Windows Server 2012, and later versions of Windows—the SmbShare module didn't ship with earlier versions of Windows.

Using regular expressions to parse text files

24

Regular expressions are one of those awkward topics. We often have students ask us to explain them, only to realize—halfway through the conversation—that they didn't need regular expressions at all. A *regex*, as a regular expression is sometimes known, is useful in text parsing, which is something you end up doing a lot in Unix and Linux operating systems. In PowerShell, you tend to do less text parsing—and we also find you tend to need regexes less often. That said, we certainly know of times when, in PowerShell, you need to parse some textual content, such as an IIS log file. That's how we'll be covering regular expressions in this chapter: as a tool to parse text files.

Don't get us wrong: there's much more you can do with regular expressions, and we'll cover a few of those at the end of this chapter. But to make sure you have a good expectation up front, let's be clear that we're not going to try to cover regular expressions comprehensively or exhaustively in this book. Regular expressions can get *incredibly* complicated. They're an entire technology unto themselves. We'll get you started, and try to do so in a way that's immediately applicable to many production environments, and then we'll give you some pointers for digging deeper on your own, if that's your need.

Our goal with this chapter is to introduce you to regex syntax in a simplified fashion, and show you how PowerShell can use them. If you want to move on to more complicated expressions on your own, you're welcome to, and you'll know how to use those within the shell.

24.1   *The purpose of regular expressions*

A regular expression is written in a very specific language, and its purpose is to define a text pattern. For example, an IPv4 address consists of one to three digits, a period, one to three more digits, a period, and so forth. A regex can define that pattern, although it would accept an invalid address like 211.193.299.299. That's the difference between recognizing a text pattern and actually checking for the validity of the data.

One of the biggest uses of regular expressions—and the use we'll be covering in this chapter—is to detect specific text patterns within a larger text file, such as a log file. For example, you might write a regex to look for the specific text that represents an HTTP 500 error in a web server log file, or to look for email addresses in an SMTP server log file. In addition to detecting the text pattern, you might use the regex to capture the matched text, enabling you to extract those email addresses from the log file.

24.2   *A regex syntax primer*

The simplest regex is an exact string of text that you want to match. "Don," for example, is technically a regex, and in PowerShell it'll match "DON," "don," "Don," "DoN," and so on—PowerShell's default matching is case-insensitive.

Certain characters, however, have special meaning within a regex, and they enable you to detect patterns of variable text. Here are some examples:

- \w matches "word characters," which means letters, numbers, and underscores, but no punctuation and no whitespace. The regex \won would match "Don", "Ron", and "ton", with the \w standing in for any single letter, number, or underscore.
- \W matches the opposite of \w (so this is one example where PowerShell is sensitive to case), meaning it matches whitespace and punctuation—"non-word characters," in the parlance.
- \d matches any digit from 0 through 9 inclusive.
- \D matches any non-digit.
- \s matches any whitespace character, like a tab, space, or carriage return.
- \S matches any non-whitespace character.
- . (a period) stands in for any single character.
- [abcde] matches any character in that set. The regex d[aeiou]n would match "don" and "dan" but not "doun" or "deen."
- [a-z] matches one or more characters in that range. You can specify multiple ranges as comma-separated lists, such as [a-f,m-z].
- [^abcde] matches one or more characters that are not in that set, meaning the regex d[^aeiou] would match "dns" but not "don".
- ? follows another literal or special character and matches exactly one instance of that character. So, the regex do?n would match "don" but would not match "doon". It would also match "dn" because ? can also match zero instances of the preceding character.

- `*` matches any number of instances of the preceding character. The regex `do*n` would match both "doon" and "don". It would also match "dn" because `*` also matches zero instances of the preceding character.

- `+` matches one or more instances of the preceding character. You'll see this used a lot with parentheses, which create a sort of subexpression. For example, the regex `(dn)+o` would match "dndndndno" because it matches repeating instances of the "dn" subexpression.

- `\` (backslash) is the regex escape character. Use it in front of a character that normally has special meaning in the regex syntax, to make that character a literal. For example, the regex `\.` would match a literal period character, rather than allowing the period to stand in for any single character, as it normally does. To match a literal backslash, escape it with a backslash: `\\`.

- `{2}` matches exactly that many instances of the preceding character. For example, `\d{1}` matches exactly one digit. Use `{2,}` to match two or more, and use `{1,3}` to match at least one, but no more than three.

- `^` matches the beginning of the string. For example, the regex `d.n` would match "don" as well as "pteranodon". But the regex `^d.n` would match "don" but would not match "pteranodon" because the `^` makes the matching occur at the beginning of the string. This is a different use of `^` than in the previous example, where it was used with [square brackets] to indicate a negative match.

- `$` matches the end of the string. For example, the regex `.icks` would match "hicks" and "sticks" (the match would technically be on "ticks" in that example), and would also match "Dickson". But the regex `.icks$` would not match "Dickson" because the `$` indicates that the string should reach its end after the "s".

There you have it—a whirlwind look at the basic regex syntax. As we wrote earlier, there's a lot more where that came from, but this will be enough to get some basic work done. Let's look at some example regular expressions:

- `\d{1,3}\.\d{1,3}\.\d{1,3}\.\d{1,3}` would match the pattern of an IPv4 address, although it'll accept illegal data like "432.567.875.000" as well as legal data like "192.169.15.12".

- `\\\\\w+(\\\w+)+` would match a Universal Naming Convention (UNC) path. All the backslashes make that regex hard to read—which is one reason it's important to test and tweak your regular expressions before you rely on them in a production task.

- `\w{1}\.\w+@company\.com` matches a specific type of email address: first initial, a period, last name, and then "@company.com". For example, "d.jones @company.com" would be a valid match. You do have to be a bit careful with these. For example, "donal**d.jones@company.com**.org" would also be a valid match. We boldfaced the portion of the string that the regex would match—and the regex is fine with there being extra text before and after the matched portion. That's where the `^` and `$` anchors come into play in many situations.

NOTE You'll find more about basic regex syntax by running `help about_regular_expressions` in PowerShell. At the end of this chapter, we'll provide some additional resources for further exploration.

24.3   *Using regex with -Match*

PowerShell includes a comparison operator, -Match, and a case-sensitive cousin, -CMatch, that work with regular expressions. Here are some examples:

```
PS C:\> "don" -match "d[aeiou]n"
True
PS C:\> "dooon" -match "d[aeiou]n"
False
PS C:\> "dooon" -match "d[aeiou]+n"
True
PS C:\> "djinn" -match "d[aeiou]+n"
False
PS C:\> "dean" -match "d[aeiou]n"
False
```

Although it has many uses, we're primarily going to rely on -Match to test regular expressions and make sure they're working properly. As you can see, its left-hand operand is whatever string you're testing, and the right-hand operand is the regular expression. If there's a match, it outputs True; if not, you get False.

TRY IT NOW This is a good time to take a break from reading and try using the -Match operator. Run through some of the examples we gave you in the syntax section earlier, and make sure you're comfortable using the -Match operator in the shell.

24.4   *Using regex with Select-String*

Now we reach the real meat of this chapter. We're going to use some IIS log files as examples, because they're exactly the kind of pure-text file that a regex is designed to deal with. It'd be nice if we could read these logs into PowerShell in a more object-oriented fashion but ... well, we can't. So a regex it is.

TRY IT NOW If you'd like to follow along, we've zipped up our example log files and made them available for download on http://MoreLunches.com. Just look for this book's web page and you'll find the example IIS log files available as a download. We saved the log files in C:\LogFiles for the examples in this chapter; that folder contains three subfolders (WSSVC1, WSSVC2, and WSSVC3), each of which contains one IIS log file.

Let's start by scanning through the log files to look for any $40x$ errors. These are often "file not found" and other errors, and we want to be able to generate a report of the bad files for our organization's web developers. The log files contain a single line for each HTTP request, and each line is broken into space-delimited fields. We have some files that contain "401" and so forth as part of their filename—e.g., "error401.html"—and we don't want those to be included in our results. We'll specify a regex like

\s40[0-9]\s because that specifies a space on either side of the *40x* error code. It should find all errors from 400 through 409 inclusive. Here's our command:

```
PS C:\logfiles> get-childitem -filter *.log -recurse | select-string -pattern
    "\s40[0-9]\s" | format-table Filename,LineNumber,Line -wrap
```

Notice that we changed to the C:\LogFiles directory to run this command. We started by asking PowerShell to get all files matching the *.log filename pattern, and to recurse subdirectories. That will ensure that all three of our log files are included in the output. Then we used Select-String, and gave it our regex as a pattern. The result of the command is a MatchInfo object; we used Format-Table to create a display that includes the filename, the line number, and the line of text that contained our match. This can be easily redirected to a file and given to our web developers.

Next, we want to scan the files for all access by Gecko-based web browsers. Our developers tell us they've been having some problems with customers accessing the sites using those browsers, and they want to see which files in particular are being requested. They think they've narrowed the problem down to browsers running under Windows NT 6.2, meaning we're looking for user-agent strings that look something like this:

```
(Windows+NT+6.2;+WOW64;+rv:11.0)+Gecko
```

Our developers have stressed that the 64-bit thing isn't specific, so they don't want the log results limited to just "WOW64" user-agent strings. We came up with this regex: 6\.2;[\w\W]+\+Gecko—let's break that down:

- 6\.2;—This is "6.2;" and notice that we escaped the period to make it a literal character rather than the single-character wildcard that a period normally indicates.
- [\w\W]+—This is one or more word or non-word characters—in other words, anything.
- \+Gecko—This is a literal +, then "Gecko".

Here's the command to find matching lines from the log files, along with the first couple lines of output:

```
PS C:\logfiles> get-childitem -filter *.log -recurse | select-string -pattern
    "6\.2;[\w\W]+\+Gecko"
W3SVC1\u_ex120420.log:14:2012-04-20 21:45:04 10.211.55.30 GET /MyApp1/
    Testpage.asp - 80 - 10.211.55.29 Mozilla/
    5.0+(Windows+NT+6.2;+WOW64;+rv:11.0)+Gecko/20100101+Firefox/11.0 200 0 0
    1125
W3SVC1\u_ex120420.log:15:2012-04-20 21:45:04 10.211.55.30 GET /TestPage.asp -
    80 - 10.211.55.29 Mozilla/5.0+(Windows+NT+6.2;+WOW64;+rv:11.0)+Gecko/
    20100101+Firefox/11.0 200 0 0 1 109
```

We left the output in its default format this time, rather than sending it to a format cmdlet.

As a final example, let's turn from IIS log files to the Windows Security log. Event log entries include a `Message` property, which contains detailed information about the event. Unfortunately, this information is formatted for easy human reading, not for easy computer-based parsing. We'd like to look for all events with ID 4624, which indicates an account logon (that number may differ between different versions of Windows; our example is from Windows Server 2008 R2). But we only want to see those events related to logons for accounts starting with "WIN", which relates to computer accounts in our domain, and whose account names end in TM20$ through TM40$, which are the specific computers we're interested in. A regex for this might look something like `WIN[\W\w]+TM[234][0-9]\$`—notice how we needed to escape the final dollar sign so that it isn't interpreted as an end-of-string anchor. We needed to include `[\W\w]` (non-word and word characters) because it's possible for our account names to include a hyphen, which wouldn't match the `\w` word character class. Here's our command:

```
PS C:\> get-eventlog -LogName security | where { $_.eventid -eq 4624 } |
    select -ExpandProperty message | select-string -pattern
    "WIN[\W\w]+TM[234][0-9]\$"
```

We started by using `Where-Object` to keep only events with ID 4624. We then expanded the contents of the `Message` property into a plain string, and piped it to `Select-String`. Note that this will output the matching message text; if our goal was to output the entire matching event, we would have taken a different approach:

```
PS C:\> get-eventlog -LogName security | where { $_.eventid -eq 4624 -and
    $_.message -match "WIN[\W\w]+TM[234][0-9]\$" }
```

Here, rather than outputting the contents of the `Message` property, we've simply looked for records where the `Message` property contains text matching our regex—and then output the entire event object. It's all about what you're after in terms of output.

24.5   Lab

NOTE   For this lab, you'll need any computer running PowerShell v3.

Make no mistake about it, regular expressions can make your head spin, so don't try to create complex regexes right off the bat—start simple. Here are a few exercises to ease you into it. Use regular expressions and operators to complete the following:

Get all files in your Windows directory that have a two-digit number as part of the name.

Find all processes running on your computer that are from Microsoft, and display the process ID, name, and company name. Hint: pipe `Get-Process` to `Get-Member` to discover property names.

In the Windows Update log, usually found in C:\Windows, you want to display only the lines where the agent began installing files. You may need to open the file in Notepad to figure out what string you need to select.

24.6 *Further exploration*

You'll find regular expressions used in other places in PowerShell, and many of them involve shell elements that we don't cover in this book. Here are some examples:

- The `Switch` scripting construct includes a parameter that lets it compare a value to one or more regular expressions.
- Advanced scripts and functions (script cmdlets) can utilize a regular expression-based input validation tool to help prevent invalid parameter values.
- The `-Match` operator (which we covered briefly in this chapter) tests for string matches against a regular expression, and—something we didn't share earlier—captures matched strings to an automatic `$matches` collection.

PowerShell utilizes industry-standard regex syntax, and if you're interested in learning more, we recommend *Mastering Regular Expressions* by Jeffrey E.F. Friedl (O'Reilly). There are a gazillion other regex books out there, some of which are specific to Windows and .NET (and thus PowerShell), some of which focus on building a regex for specific situations, and so forth. Browse your favorite online bookstore and see if there are any books that look appealing to you and your specific needs.

We also use a free online regex repository, http://RegExLib.com, which has numerous regex examples for a variety of purposes (phone numbers, email addresses, IP addresses, you name it). We've also found ourselves using http://RegExTester.com, a website that lets you interactively test regular expressions to get them dialed in exactly the way you need.

Additional random tips, tricks, and techniques

We're nearing the end of your "month of lunches," and the next chapter is your final exam, where you'll tackle a complete administrative task from scratch. Before you do, we'd like to share a few extra tips and techniques to round out your education.

25.1 Profiles, prompts, and colors: customizing the shell

Every PowerShell session starts out the same: the same aliases, the same PSDrives, the same colors, and so forth. Why not make the shell a little bit more customized?

25.1.1 PowerShell profiles

We've explained before that there's a difference between a PowerShell hosting application and the PowerShell engine itself. A hosting application, such as the console or the PowerShell ISE, is a way for you to send commands to the PowerShell engine. The engine executes your commands, and the hosting application is responsible for displaying the results. Another thing that the hosting application is responsible for doing is loading and running *profile scripts* each time the shell starts.

These profile scripts can be used to customize the PowerShell environment, by loading snap-ins or modules, changing to a different starting directory, defining functions that you'll want to use, and so forth. For example, here is the profile script that Don uses on his computer:

```
Import-Module ActiveDirectory
Add-PSSnapin SqlServerCmdletSnapin100
cd c:\
```

The profile loads the two shell extensions that Don uses the most, and it changes to the root of his C: drive, which is where Don likes to begin working. You can put any commands you like into your profile.

> **NOTE**   You might think there's no need to load the ActiveDirectory module, because PowerShell will implicitly load it as soon as Don tries to use one of the commands in that module. But that particular module also maps an AD: PSDrive, and Don likes to have that available as soon as the shell starts.

There's no default profile, and the exact profile script that you create will depend a bit upon how you want it to work. Details are available if you run `help about_profiles`, but you mainly need to consider whether or not you'll be working in multiple different hosting applications. For example, we tend to switch back and forth between the regular console and the PowerShell ISE, and we like to have the same profile running for both, so we have to be careful to create the right profile script file in the right location. We also have to be careful about what goes into that profile, because we're using it for both the console and the ISE—some commands that tweak console-specific settings like colors can cause an error when run in the ISE.

Here are the files that the console host tries to load, and the order in which it tries to load them:

1   $pshome/profile.ps1—This will execute for all users of the computer, no matter which host they're using (remember that `$pshome` is predefined within PowerShell and contains the path of the PowerShell installation folder).

2   $pshome/Microsoft.PowerShell_profile.ps1—This will execute for all users of the computer if they're using the console host. If they're using the PowerShell ISE, the $pshome/Microsoft.PowerShellISE_profile.ps1 script will be executed instead.

3   $home/Documents/WindowsPowerShell/profile.ps1—This will execute only for the current user (because it lives under the user's home directory), no matter which host they're using.

4   $home/Documents/WindowsPowerShell/Microsoft.PowerShell_profile.ps1— This will execute for the current user if they're using the console host. If they're using the PowerShell ISE, the $home/Documents/WindowsPowerShell/ Microsoft.PowerShellISE_profile.ps1 script will be executed instead.

If one or more of these scripts doesn't exist, there's no problem. The hosting application will simply skip it and move on to the next one.

On 64-bit systems, there are variations for both 32- and 64-bit scripts, because there are separate 32- and 64-bit versions of PowerShell itself. You won't always want the same commands run in the 64-bit shell as you do in the 32-bit shell. By that we mean that some modules and other extensions are only available for one or the other architecture, so you wouldn't want a 32-bit profile trying to load a 64-bit module into the 32-bit shell, because it won't work.

Note that the documentation in `about_profiles` is different from what we've listed here, and our experience is that the preceding list is correct. Here are a few more points about that list:

- `$pshome` is a built-in PowerShell variable that contains the installation folder for PowerShell itself; on most systems, that's in C:\Windows\System32\WindowsPowerShell\v1.0 (for the 64-bit version of the shell on a 64-bit system).
- `$home` is another built-in variable that points to the current user's profile folder (such as C:\Users\Administrator).
- We've used "Documents" to refer to the Documents folder, but on some versions of Windows it will be "My Documents".
- We've written "no matter which host they're using," but that technically isn't true. It's true of hosting applications (the console and the ISE) written by Microsoft, but there's no way to force the authors of non-Microsoft hosting applications to follow these rules.

Because we want the same shell extensions to load whether we're using the console host or the ISE, we chose to customize $home\Documents\WindowsPowerShell\profile.ps1, because that profile is run for both of the Microsoft-supplied hosting applications.

> **TRY IT NOW** Why don't you try creating one or more profile scripts for yourself? Even if all you put in them is a simple message, such as `Write "It Worked"`, this is a good way to see the different files in action. Remember that you have to close the shell (or ISE) and re-open it to see the profile scripts run.

Keep in mind that profile scripts are scripts and are subject to your shell's current execution policy. If your execution policy is `Restricted`, your profile won't run; if your policy is `AllSigned`, your profile must be signed. Chapter 17 discussed the execution policy and script signing.

25.1.2 *Customizing the prompt*

The PowerShell prompt—the `PS C:\>` that you've seen through much of this book—is generated by a built-in function called `Prompt`. If you want to customize the prompt, you can simply replace that function. Defining a new `Prompt` function is something that can be done in a profile script, so that your change takes effect each time you open the shell.

Here's the default prompt:

```
function prompt
{
    $(if (test-path variable:/PSDebugContext) { '[DBG]: ' }
    else { '' }) + 'PS ' + $(Get-Location) `
    + $(if ($nestedpromptlevel -ge 1) { '>>' }) + '> '
}
```

This prompt first tests to see if the $DebugContext variable is defined in the shell's VARIABLE: drive. If it is, this function adds [DBG]: to the start of the prompt. Otherwise, the prompt is defined as PS along with the current location, which is returned by the `Get-Location` cmdlet. If the shell is in a nested prompt, as defined by the built-in `$nestedpromptlevel` variable, the prompt will have >> added to it.

Here is an alternative prompt function. You could enter this directly into any profile script to make it the standard prompt for your shell sessions.

```
function prompt {
 $time = (Get-Date).ToShortTimeString()
 "$time [$env:COMPUTERNAME]:> "
}
```

This alternative prompt displays the current time, followed by the current computer name (which will be contained within square brackets).

```
6:07 PM [CLIENT01]:>
```

Note that this leverages PowerShell's special behavior with double quotation marks, in which the shell will replace variables (like $time) with their contents.

25.1.3 Tweaking colors

In previous chapters, we've mentioned how stressed-out we can get when a long series of error messages scrolls by in the shell. Don always struggled in English class when he was a kid, and seeing all that red text reminds him of the essays he'd get back from Ms. Hansen, all marked up with a red pen. Yuck. Fortunately, PowerShell gives you the ability to modify most of the default colors it uses.

The default text foreground and background colors can be modified by clicking on the control box in the upper-left corner of PowerShell's window. From there, select Properties, and then select the Colors tab, which is shown in figure 25.1.

Figure 25.1 Configuring the default shell screen colors

Modifying the colors of errors, warnings, and other messages is a bit trickier and requires you to run a command. But you could put this command into your profile, so that it executes each time you open the shell. Here's how to change the error message foreground color to green, which we find a lot more soothing:

```
(Get-Host).PrivateData.ErrorForegroundColor = "green"
```

You can change colors for the following settings:

- `ErrorForegroundColor`
- `ErrorBackgroundColor`
- `WarningForegroundColor`
- `WarningBackgroundColor`
- `DebugForegroundColor`
- `DebugBackgroundColor`
- `VerboseForegroundColor`
- `VerboseBackgroundColor`
- `ProgressForegroundColor`
- `ProgressBackgroundColor`

And here are some of the colors you can choose:

- `Red`
- `Yellow`
- `Black`
- `White`
- `Green`
- `Cyan`
- `Magenta`
- `Blue`

There are also dark versions of most of these colors: `DarkRed`, `DarkYellow`, `DarkGreen`, `DarkCyan`, `DarkBlue`, and so on.

25.2 Operators: -as, -is, -replace, -join, -split, -in, -contains

These additional operators are useful in a variety of situations. They let you work with data types, collections, and strings.

25.2.1 -as and -is

The `-as` operator produces a new object in an attempt to convert an existing object into a different type. For example, if you have a number that contains a decimal (perhaps from the result of a division operation), you can drop the decimal portion by converting, or *casting*, the number to an integer:

```
1000 / 3 -as [int]
```

The object to be converted comes first, then the -as operator, and then, in square brackets, the type you want to convert to. Types can include [string], [xml], [int], [single], [double], [datetime], and others, although those are probably the ones you'll use the most. Technically, this example of converting to an integer will round the fractional number to an integer, rather than just truncating the fractional portion of the number.

The -is operator works similarly: it's designed to return True or False if an object is of a particular type or not. Here are a few one-line examples:

```
123.45 -is [int]
"SERVER-R2" -is [string]
$True -is [bool]
(Get-Date) -is [datetime]
```

> **TRY IT NOW** Try running each of these one-line commands in the shell to see the results.

25.2.2 -replace

The -replace operator is designed to locate all occurrences of one string within another and replace those occurrences with a third string:

```
PS C:\> "192.168.34.12" -replace "34","15"
192.168.15.12
```

The source string comes first, followed by the -replace operator. Then you provide the string you want to search for within the source, followed by a comma and the string you want to use in place of the search string. In the preceding example, we replaced "34" with "15".

25.2.3 -join and -split

The -join and -split operators are designed to convert arrays to delimited lists and vice versa.

For example, suppose you created an array with five elements:

```
PS C:\> $array = "one","two","three","four","five"
PS C:\> $array
one
two
three
four
five
```

This works because PowerShell automatically treats a comma-separated list as an array. Now, let's say you want to join this array together into a pipe-delimited string—you can do that with -join:

```
PS C:\> $array -join "|"
one|two|three|four|five
```

Saving that result into a variable will let you re-use it, or even pipe it out to a file:

```
PS C:\> $string = $array -join "|"
PS C:\> $string
one|two|three|four|five
PS C:\> $string | out-file data.dat
```

The `-split` operator does the opposite: it takes a delimited string and makes an array from it. For example, suppose you have a tab-delimited file containing one line and four columns. Displaying the contents of the file might look like this:

```
PS C:\> gc computers.tdf
Server1 Windows East     Managed
```

Keep in mind that `Gc` is an alias for `Get-Content`.

You can use the `-split` operator to break that into four individual array elements:

```
PS C:\> $array = (gc computers.tdf) -split "`t"
PS C:\> $array
Server1
Windows
East
Managed
```

Notice the use of the escape character, a backtick, and a "t" (`` `t ``) to define the tab character. That had to be in double quotes so that the escape character would be recognized.

The resulting array has four elements, and you can access them individually by using their index numbers:

```
PS C:\> $array[0]
Server1
```

25.2.4   *-contains and -in*

The `-contains` operator causes much confusion for PowerShell newcomers. You'll see folks try to do this:

```
PS C:\> 'this' -contains '*his*'
False
```

In fact, they meant to use the `-like` operator instead:

```
. PS C:\> 'this' -like '*his*'
True
```

The `-like` operator is designed to do wildcard string comparisons. The `-contains` operator is used to test whether or not a given object exists within a collection. For example, create a collection of string objects, and then test to see if a given string is in that collection:

```
PS C:\> $collection = 'abc','def','ghi','jkl'
PS C:\> $collection -contains 'abc'
True
PS C:\> $collection -contains 'xyz'
False
```

The -in operator does the same thing, but it flips the order of the operands so that the collection goes on the right, and the test object on the left:

```
PS C:\> $collection = 'abc','def','ghi','jkl'
PS C:\> 'abc' -in $collection
True
PS C:\> 'xyz' -in $collection
False
```

25.3 *String manipulation*

Suppose you have a string of text, and you need to convert it to all uppercase letters. Or perhaps you need to get the last three characters from the string. How would you do it?

In PowerShell, strings are objects, and they come with a great many methods. Remember that a method is simply a way of telling the object to do something, usually to itself, and that you can discover the available methods by piping the object to Gm:

```
PS C:\> "Hello" | gm

   TypeName: System.String

Name             MemberType   Definition
----             ----------   ----------
Clone            Method       System.Object Clone()
CompareTo        Method       int CompareTo(System.Object value...
Contains         Method       bool Contains(string value)
CopyTo           Method       System.Void CopyTo(int sourceInde...
EndsWith         Method       bool EndsWith(string value), bool...
Equals           Method       bool Equals(System.Object obj), b...
GetEnumerator    Method       System.CharEnumerator GetEnumerat...
GetHashCode      Method       int GetHashCode()
GetType          Method       type GetType()
GetTypeCode      Method       System.TypeCode GetTypeCode()
IndexOf          Method       int IndexOf(char value), int Inde...
IndexOfAny       Method       int IndexOfAny(char[] anyOf), int...
Insert           Method       string Insert(int startIndex, str...
IsNormalized     Method       bool IsNormalized(), bool IsNorma...
LastIndexOf      Method       int LastIndexOf(char value), int ...
LastIndexOfAny   Method       int LastIndexOfAny(char[] anyOf),...
Normalize        Method       string Normalize(), string Normal...
PadLeft          Method       string PadLeft(int totalWidth), s...
PadRight         Method       string PadRight(int totalWidth), ...
Remove           Method       string Remove(int startIndex, int...
Replace          Method       string Replace(char oldChar, char...
Split            Method       string[] Split(Params char[] sepa...
StartsWith       Method       bool StartsWith(string value), bo...
Substring        Method       string Substring(int startIndex),...
ToCharArray      Method       char[] ToCharArray(), char[] ToCh...
ToLower          Method       string ToLower(), string ToLower(...
ToLowerInvariant Method       string ToLowerInvariant()
ToString         Method       string ToString(), string ToStrin...
ToUpper          Method       string ToUpper(), string ToUpper(...
ToUpperInvariant Method       string ToUpperInvariant()
Trim             Method       string Trim(Params char[] trimCha...
TrimEnd          Method       string TrimEnd(Params char[] trim...
TrimStart        Method       string TrimStart(Params char[] tr...
```

```
Chars              ParameterizedProperty char Chars(int index) {get;}
Length             Property              System.Int32 Length {get;}
```

Some of the more useful `String` methods include the following:

- `IndexOf()` tells you the location of a given character within the string.

```
PS C:\> "SERVER-R2".IndexOf("-")
6
```

- `Split()`, `Join()`, and `Replace()` operate similarly to the `-split`, `-join`, and `-replace` operators we described in the previous section. We tend to use the PowerShell operators rather than the `String` methods.

- `ToLower()` and `ToUpper()` convert the case of a string.

```
PS C:\> $computername = "SERVER17"
PS C:\> $computername.tolower()
server17
```

- `Trim()` removes whitespace from both ends of a string; `TrimStart()` and `TrimEnd()` remove whitespace from the beginning or end of a string respectively.

```
PS C:\> $username = "   Don "
PS C:\> $username.Trim()
Don
```

All of these `String` methods are great ways to manipulate and modify `String` objects. Note that all of these methods can be used with a variable that contains a string (as in the `ToLower()` and `Trim()` examples), or they can be used directly with a static string (as in the `IndexOf()` example).

25.4 *Date manipulation*

Like `String` objects, `Date` (or `DateTime`, if you prefer) objects come with a great many methods that allow date and time manipulation and calculation:

```
PS C:\> get-date | gm

    TypeName: System.DateTime

Name                MemberType   Definition
----                ----------   ----------
Add                 Method       System.DateTime Add(System.TimeSpan ...
AddDays             Method       System.DateTime AddDays(double value)
AddHours            Method       System.DateTime AddHours(double value)
AddMilliseconds     Method       System.DateTime AddMilliseconds(doub...
AddMinutes          Method       System.DateTime AddMinutes(double va...
AddMonths           Method       System.DateTime AddMonths(int months)
AddSeconds          Method       System.DateTime AddSeconds(double va...
AddTicks            Method       System.DateTime AddTicks(long value)
AddYears            Method       System.DateTime AddYears(int value)
CompareTo           Method       int CompareTo(System.Object value), ...
Equals              Method       bool Equals(System.Object value), bo...
GetDateTimeFormats  Method       string[] GetDateTimeFormats(), strin...
GetHashCode         Method       int GetHashCode()
GetType             Method       type GetType()
GetTypeCode         Method       System.TypeCode GetTypeCode()
IsDaylightSavingTime Method      bool IsDaylightSavingTime()
```

Subtract	Method	System.TimeSpan Subtract(System.Date...
ToBinary	Method	long ToBinary()
ToFileTime	Method	long ToFileTime()
ToFileTimeUtc	Method	long ToFileTimeUtc()
ToLocalTime	Method	System.DateTime ToLocalTime()
ToLongDateString	Method	string ToLongDateString()
ToLongTimeString	Method	string ToLongTimeString()
ToOADate	Method	double ToOADate()
ToShortDateString	Method	string ToShortDateString()
ToShortTimeString	Method	string ToShortTimeString()
ToString	Method	string ToString(), string ToString(s...
ToUniversalTime	Method	System.DateTime ToUniversalTime()
DisplayHint	NoteProperty	Microsoft.PowerShell.Commands.Displa...
Date	Property	System.DateTime Date {get;}
Day	Property	System.Int32 Day {get;}
DayOfWeek	Property	System.DayOfWeek DayOfWeek {get;}
DayOfYear	Property	System.Int32 DayOfYear {get;}
Hour	Property	System.Int32 Hour {get;}
Kind	Property	System.DateTimeKind Kind {get;}
Millisecond	Property	System.Int32 Millisecond {get;}
Minute	Property	System.Int32 Minute {get;}
Month	Property	System.Int32 Month {get;}
Second	Property	System.Int32 Second {get;}
Ticks	Property	System.Int64 Ticks {get;}
TimeOfDay	Property	System.TimeSpan TimeOfDay {get;}
Year	Property	System.Int32 Year {get;}
DateTime	ScriptProperty	System.Object DateTime {get=if ((& {...

Note that the properties enable you to access just a portion of a DateTime, such as the day, year, or month:

```
PS C:\> (get-date).month
10
```

The methods enable two things: calculations and conversions to other formats. For example, to get the date for 90 days ago, we like to use AddDays() with a negative number:

```
PS C:\> $today = get-date
PS C:\> $90daysago = $today.adddays(-90)
PS C:\> $90daysago

Saturday, July 24, 2012 11:26:08 AM
```

The methods whose names start with "To" are designed to provide dates and times in an alternative format, such as a short date string:

```
PS C:\> $90daysago.toshortdatestring()
7/24/2012
```

These methods all use your computer's current regional settings to determine the correct way of formatting dates and times.

25.5   *Dealing with WMI dates*

WMI tends to store date and time information in difficult-to-use strings. For example, the `Win32_OperatingSystem` class tracks the last time a computer was started, and the date and time information looks like this:

```
PS C:\> get-wmiobject win32_operatingsystem | select lastbootuptime

lastbootuptime
--------------
20101021210207.793534-420
```

PowerShell's designers knew you wouldn't be able to easily use this information, so they added a pair of conversion methods to every WMI object. Pipe any WMI object to Gm and you can see those methods at or near the end:

```
PS C:\> get-wmiobject win32_operatingsystem | gm

    TypeName: System.Management.ManagementObject#root\cimv2\Win32_OperatingS
ystem

Name                                  MemberType    Definition
----                                  ----------    ----------
Reboot                                Method        System.Management...
SetDateTime                           Method        System.Management...
Shutdown                              Method        System.Management...
Win32Shutdown                         Method        System.Management...
Win32ShutdownTracker                  Method        System.Management...
BootDevice                            Property      System.String Boo...
...
PSStatus                              PropertySet   PSStatus {Status,...
ConvertFromDateTime                   ScriptMethod  System.Object Con...
ConvertToDateTime                     ScriptMethod  System.Object Con...
```

We've cut out most of the middle of this output so that you can easily find the `ConvertFromDateTime()` and `ConvertToDateTime()` methods. In this case, what you start with is a WMI date and time, and you want to convert to a normal date and time, so you'd do it like this:

```
PS C:\> $os = get-wmiobject win32_operatingsystem
PS C:\> $os.ConvertToDateTime($os.lastbootuptime)

Thursday, October 20, 2011 9:02:07 PM
```

If you want to make that date and time information part of a normal table, you can use `Select-Object` or `Format-Table` to create custom, calculated columns and properties:

```
PS C:\> get-wmiobject win32_operatingsystem | select BuildNumber,__SERVER,@{
l='LastBootTime';e={$_.ConvertToDateTime($_.LastBootupTime)}}

BuildNumber              __SERVER                 LastBootTime
-----------              --------                 ------------
7600                     SERVER-R2                10/20/2011 9:02:07 PM
```

25.6 *Setting default parameter values*

Most PowerShell commands have at least a few parameters that include default values. For example, run `Dir` by itself and it defaults to the current path, without you having to specify a `-Path` parameter. In PowerShell v3, you can also define your own defaults for any parameter on any command—or even on multiple commands. Your defaults only apply when the command is run without the parameters you specify; you can always override your defaults by specifying the parameter and values when you run the command.

Defaults are stored in a special built-in variable named `$PSDefaultParameterValues`. The variable is empty each time you open a new shell window, and it's meant to be populated with a hashtable (which you could do in a profile script, to have your defaults always in effect).

For example, let's say you want to create a new credential object containing a username and password, and have that credential automatically apply to all commands that have a `-Credential` parameter:

```
PS C:\> $credential = Get-Credential -UserName Administrator -Message "Ente
r Admin credential"
PS C:\> $PSDefaultParameterValues.Add('*:Credential',$credential)
```

Or, you might want to force only the `Invoke-Command` cmdlet to prompt for a credential each time it's run. In this case, rather than assigning a default value, you'd assign a script block that executes the `Get-Credential` command:

```
PS C:\> $PSDefaultParameterValues.Add('Invoke-Command:Credential',{Get-Cred
ential -Message 'Enter administrator credential' -UserName Administrator})
```

You can see that the basic format for the `Add()` method's first argument is `<cmdlet>:<parameter>`, and `<cmdlet>` can accept wildcards like `*`. The second argument for the `Add()` method is either the value you want to make the default, or a script block that executes some other command or commands.

You can always examine `$PSDefaultParameterValues` to see what it contains:

```
PS C:\> $PSDefaultParameterValues

Name                            Value
----                            -----
*:Credential                    System.Management.Automation.PSCredenti
Invoke-Command:Credential       Get-Credential -Message 'Enter administ
```

> **Above and beyond**
>
> PowerShell variables are controlled by something called *scope*. We offered a brief introduction to scope in chapter 21, and it is something that plays into these default parameter values.

> **(continued)**
>
> If you set $PSDefaultParameterValues at the command line, it'll apply to all scripts and commands run within that shell session. But if you set $PSDefaultParameterValues within a script, it'll only apply to things done by that script. That's a useful technique, because it means you can start a script with a bunch of defaults, and they won't apply to other scripts, or to the shell in general.
>
> This concept of "what happens in the script, stays in the script" is the heart of scope. You can read more about scope in the shell's about_scope help file, if you'd like to explore further on your own.

You can learn more about this feature by reading the shell's about_parameters _default_values help file.

25.7   *Playing with script blocks*

Script blocks are a key part of PowerShell, and you've been using them quite a bit:

- The -FilterScript parameter of Where-Object takes a script block.
- The -Process parameter of ForEach-Object takes a script block.
- The hashtable used to create custom properties with Select-Object, or custom columns with Format-Table, accepts a script block as the value of the E or Expression key.
- Default parameter values, as described in the previous section, can be set to a script block.
- Some remoting and job-related commands, including Invoke-Command and Start-Job, accept script blocks on their -ScriptBlock parameter.

So what is a script block? In general, it's anything surrounded by {curly brackets}, with the exception of hash tables, which use curly brackets but are preceded by the @ symbol. You can even enter a script block right from the command line and assign it to a variable. You can then use the call operator, &, to run the block:

```
PS C:\> $block = {
>> get-process | sort -Property vm -Descending | select -first 10 }
>>
PS C:\> &$block

Handles  NPM(K)    PM(K)      WS(K) VM(M)   CPU(s)     Id ProcessName
-------  ------    -----      ----- -----   ------     -- -----------
    680      42    14772      13576  1387     3.84    404 svchost
    454      26    68368      75116   626     1.28   1912 powershell
    396      37   179136      99252   623     8.45   2700 powershell
    497      29    15104       6048   615     0.41   2500 SearchIndexer
    260      20     4088       8328   356     0.08   3044 taskhost
    550      47    16716      13180   344     1.25   1128 svchost
   1091      55    19712      35036   311     1.81   3056 explorer
    454      31    56660      15216   182    45.94   1596 MsMpEng
```

```
  163      17     62808      27132    162      0.94    2692 dwm
  584      29      7752       8832    159      1.27     892 svchost
```

You can do quite a bit more with script blocks, and if you'd like to explore some of the possibilities on your own, read the shell's `about_script_blocks` help file.

25.8 *More tips, tricks, and techniques*

As we said at the outset of this chapter, this has been an overview of some random little things that we needed to show you, but that haven't fit neatly into one of the previous chapters. Of course, you'll continue to pick up little tips and tricks with the shell as you learn more about it, and gain more experience with it.

You can check out our Twitter feeds, too—@jeffhicks and @concentrateddon—where we routinely share little tips and techniques that we discover and find useful. Web sites like PowerShell.com also offer mailing lists that include regular tips. Sometimes, learning bit-by-bit can be an easy way to become more proficient in a technology, so consider these and any other sources you run across as a way to incrementally and continually improve your PowerShell expertise.

26

Using someone else's script

Much as we hope you'll be able to construct your own PowerShell commands and scripts from scratch, we also realize that you'll rely heavily on the internet for examples. Whether you're repurposing examples from someone's blog, or tweaking a script you've found in an online script repository like the PowerShell Code Repository (http://PoshCode.org), being able to re-use someone else's PowerShell script is an important core skill. In this chapter, we'll walk you through the process we use to understand someone else's script and make it our own.

> **THANKS** Credit goes to Christoph Tohermes and Kaia Taylor, who provided us with scripts to use in this chapter. We deliberately asked them for less-than-perfect scripts that don't necessarily reflect all of the best practices we normally like to see. And in some instances we *worsened* their scripts to make this chapter a bit more real-world. We truly appreciate their contribution to this learning exercise!

Note that we've also selected these scripts specifically because they use some advanced PowerShell features that we haven't taught you. Again, we think that's realistic: you're going to run across stuff that looks unfamiliar, and part of this exercise is about how to quickly figure out what the script is doing, even if you aren't fully trained on every technique the script uses.

26.1   *The script*

Listing 26.1 shows the complete script, which is entitled New-WebProject.ps1. This script is designed to work with Microsoft's IIS cmdlets, available in Windows Server 2008 R2 and later when the Web Services role is installed.

Listing 26.1   New-WebProject.ps1

```
param(
  [parameter(Mandatory = $true)]
  [string] $Path,
  [parameter(Mandatory = $true)]
  [string] $Name
  )
$System = [Environment]::GetFolderPath("System")
$script:hostsPath = ([System.IO.Path]::Combine($System, "drivers\etc\"))
➥+"hosts"

function New-localWebsite([string] $sitePath, [string] $siteName)
{
 try
 {
  Import-Module WebAdministration
 }
 catch
 {
  Write-Host "IIS Powershell module is not installed. Please install it
➥ first, by adding the feature"
 }
 Write-Host "AppPool is created with name. " $siteName
 New-WebAppPool -Name $siteName
 Set-ItemProperty IIS:\AppPools\$Name managedRuntimeVersion v4.0
 Write-Host
 if(-not (Test-Path $sitePath))
 {
  New-Item -ItemType Directory $sitePath
 }
 $header = "www."+$siteName+".local"
 $value = "127.0.0.1 " + $header
 New-Website -ApplicationPool $siteName -Name $siteName -Port 80
➥ -PhysicalPath $sitePath -HostHeader ($header)
 Start-Website -Name $siteName
 if(-not (HostsFileContainsEntry($header)))
 {
  AddEntryToHosts -hostEntry $value
 }

}

function AddEntryToHosts([string] $hostEntry)
{
 try
 {
  $writer = New-Object System.IO.StreamWriter($hostsPath, $true)
  $writer.Write([Environment]::NewLine)
  $writer.Write($hostEntry)
```

```
  $writer.Dispose()
 }
catch [System.Exception]
 {
  Write-Error "An Error occured while writing the hosts file"
 }

}

function HostsFileContainsEntry([string] $entry)
{
 try
 {
  $reader = New-Object System.IO.StreamReader($hostsPath + "hosts")
  while(-not($reader.EndOfStream))
  {
   $line = $reader.Readline()
   if($line.Contains($entry))
   {
    return $true
   }
  }
  return $false
 }
 catch [System.Exception]
 {
  Write-Error "An Error occured while reading the host file"
 }
}
```

First up is a parameter block, which you learned to create in chapter 21:

```
param(
  [parameter(Mandatory = $true)]
  [string] $Path,
  [parameter(Mandatory = $true)]
  [string] $Name
  )
```

This parameter block looks a bit different, but it appears to be defining a -Path and a -Name parameter, each of which is mandatory. Fair enough. When you run this, you'll need to provide both pieces of information.

The next couple of lines are a bit more mysterious:

```
$System = [Environment]::GetFolderPath("System")
$script:hostsPath = ([System.IO.Path]::Combine($System, "drivers\etc\"))
➥+"hosts"
```

These don't look like they're doing anything potentially dangerous—words like GetFolderPath don't cause us any alarm. To see what these do, we'll just run them right in the shell.

```
PS C:\> $system = [Environment]::GetFolderPath('System')
PS C:\> $system
C:\Windows\system32
PS C:\> $script:hostsPath = ([System.IO.Path]::Combine($system,"drivers\etc
```

```
\"))+"hosts"
PS C:\> $hostsPath
C:\Windows\system32\drivers\etc\hosts
PS C:\>
```

The $script:hostsPath code is creating a new variable, so you've got that in addition to the new $system variable. These two lines are just setting up a folder path and file path. Make a note of these variables' contents so that you can refer back to them as you progress through the script.

The remainder of the script consists of three functions: New-LocalWebsite, AddEntryToHosts, and HostsFileContainsEntry. A function is like a script within a script: each one represents some packaged bit of functionality that you can call on. You can see that each one defines one or more input parameters, although they don't do so in a Param() block. Instead, they use an alternative parameter declaration technique that's only legal for functions: listing the parameters in parentheses (the same as a Param block) just after the function's name. It's kind of a shortcut.

If you scan through the script, you won't see any of these functions being called from the script itself, so if you were to run this script as-is, nothing would happen. But inside the New-LocalWebsite function, you can see where the HostsFileContainsEntry function is being called:

```
if(-not (HostsFileContainsEntry($header)))
  {
    AddEntryToHosts -hostEntry $value
  }
```

You can also see where AddEntryToHosts is being called by this code. It's all in an if construct. In the shell, you can run help *if* to learn more:

```
PS C:\> help *if*

Name                                Category   Module

----                                --------   ------
diff                                Alias
New-ModuleManifest                  Cmdlet     Microsoft.PowerShell.Core
Test-ModuleManifest                 Cmdlet     Microsoft.PowerShell.Core
Get-AppxPackageManifest             Function   Appx
Get-PfxCertificate                  Cmdlet     Microsoft.PowerShell.S...
Export-Certificate                  Cmdlet     PKI
Export-PfxCertificate               Cmdlet     PKI
Get-Certificate                     Cmdlet     PKI
Get-CertificateNotificationTask     Cmdlet     PKI
Import-Certificate                  Cmdlet     PKI
Import-PfxCertificate               Cmdlet     PKI
New-CertificateNotificationTask     Cmdlet     PKI
New-SelfSignedCertificate           Cmdlet     PKI
Remove-CertificateNotification...   Cmdlet     PKI
Switch-Certificate                  Cmdlet     PKI
Test-Certificate                    Cmdlet     PKI
about_If                            HelpFile
```

Help files are usually listed last, and there's one for about_If. Reading through it, you can learn a bit about how this construct works. In the context of our example script, this is checking to see if HostsFileContainsEntry returns True or False; if it's False, the AddEntryToHosts function is called. This structure suggests that New-LocalWebsite is the "main" function in this script, or the function you'd want to run to make something happen. HostsFileContainsEntry and AddEntryToHosts seem to be utility functions that are called upon as needed by New-LocalWebsite. Let's focus on New-LocalWebsite:

```
function New-localWebsite([string] $sitePath, [string] $siteName)
{
 try
 {
  Import-Module WebAdministration
 }
 catch
 {
  Write-Host "IIS Powershell module is not installed. Please install it
➥ first, by adding the feature"
 }
 Write-Host "AppPool is created with name: " $siteName
 New-WebAppPool -Name $siteName
 Set-ItemProperty IIS:\AppPools\$Name managedRuntimeVersion v4.0
 Write-Host
 if(-not (Test-Path $sitePath))
 {
  New-Item -ItemType Directory $sitePath
 }
 $header = "www."+$siteName+".local"
 $value = "127.0.0.1 " + $header
 New-Website -ApplicationPool $siteName -Name $siteName -Port 80
➥ -PhysicalPath $sitePath -HostHeader ($header)
 Start-Website -Name $siteName
 if(-not (HostsFileContainsEntry($header)))
 {
  AddEntryToHosts -hostEntry $value
 }

}
```

You might not understand that Try construct. A quick search of help (help *try*) reveals the about_try_catch_finally help file, which explains that everything in the Try portion might cause an error. If it does, then the catch portion should execute. Okay, that means the function is going to try to load the WebAdministration module, and if that doesn't work it'll display an error message. Frankly, we think it should probably just exit the function entirely if an error occurs, but it doesn't do that, so if WebAdministration doesn't load, you can expect to see more errors. You should make sure WebAdministration is available before running this!

The Write-Host stuff is useful for helping you track the progress of the script. The next command is New-WebAppPool. Searching help reveals it to be part of the

WebAdministration module, and the command's help file explains what it does. Next, Set-ItemProperty seems to be setting something in the AppPool that was just created.

The plain Write-Host command seems to be there just to put a blank line on the screen. Okay, that's fine. If you look up Test-Path, you'll see that it tests whether a given path, in this case a folder, exists. If not, the script uses New-Item to create that folder.

A variable, $header, is created that turns the $siteName parameter into something like "www.sitename.local," and the $value variable is created to add an IP address. Then the New-WebSite command is run with a variety of parameters—you can read the help on that command to figure out what each parameter does.

Finally, the Start-WebSite command runs. The help file says that will get the website up and running. That's when you get to the HostsFileContainsEntry and AddEntryToHosts commands. Those appear to make sure the new website, as listed in the $value variable, is put into the computer's local HOSTS IP address-to-name lookup file.

26.2 *It's a line-by-line examination*

The process in the previous section is a line-by-line analysis of the script, and that's the process we suggest you follow. As you progress through each line:

- Identify variables, try to figure out what they'll contain, and write that down on a piece of paper. Because variables are often passed to command parameters, having a handy reference of what you think each variable contains will help you predict what each command will do.
- When you run across new commands, read their help and try to understand what they're doing. For Get- commands, try running them—plugging in any values that the script passes in variables to parameters—to see what output is produced.
- When you run across unfamiliar elements, like if or [environment], consider running short code snippets inside a virtual machine to see what those snippets do (using a VM helps protect your production environment). Search for those keywords in help (using wildcards) to learn more.

Above all, don't skip a single line. Don't think to yourself, "Well, I don't know what that does, so I'll just keep going." Stop and find out what each line does, or what you think it'll do. That'll let you figure out where you need to tweak the script to meet your specific needs.

26.3 *Lab*

NOTE For this lab, you'll need any computer running PowerShell v3.

Listing 26.2 shows a complete script. See if you can figure out what it does, and how to use it. Can you predict any errors that this might cause? What might you need to do in order to use this in your environment?

Note that this script should run as-is, but if it doesn't on your system, do you think you can track down the cause of the problem? Keep in mind that you've seen most of these commands, and for the ones you haven't there are the PowerShell help files. Those files' examples include every technique shown in this script.

Listing 26.2   Get-LastOn.ps1

```
function get-LastOn {
<#
.DESCRIPTION
Tell me the most recent event log entries for logon or logoff.
.BUGS
Blank 'computer' column

.EXAMPLE
get-LastOn -computername server1 | Sort-Object time -Descending |
Sort-Object id -unique | format-table -AutoSize -Wrap
ID                  Domain          Computer Time
--                  ------          -------- ----
LOCAL SERVICE    NT AUTHORITY              4/3/2012 11:16:39 AM
NETWORK SERVICE NT AUTHORITY              4/3/2012 11:16:39 AM
SYSTEM           NT AUTHORITY              4/3/2012 11:16:02 AM

Sorting -unique will ensure only one line per user ID, the most recent.
Needs more testing

.EXAMPLE
PS C:\Users\administrator> get-LastOn -computername server1 -newest 10000
 -maxIDs 10000 | Sort-Object time -Descending |

 Sort-Object id -unique | format-table -AutoSize -Wrap

ID                  Domain          Computer Time
--                  ------          -------- ----
Administrator    USS                       4/11/2012 10:44:57 PM
ANONYMOUS LOGON NT AUTHORITY              4/3/2012 8:19:07 AM
LOCAL SERVICE    NT AUTHORITY              10/19/2011 10:17:22 AM
NETWORK SERVICE NT AUTHORITY              4/4/2012 8:24:09 AM
student          WIN7                      4/11/2012 4:16:55 PM
SYSTEM           NT AUTHORITY              10/18/2011 7:53:56 PM
USSDC$           USS                       4/11/2012 9:38:05 AM
WIN7$            USS                       10/19/2011 3:25:30 AM


PS C:\Users\administrator>

.EXAMPLE
get-LastOn -newest 1000 -maxIDs 20
Only examines the last 1000 lines of the event log

.EXAMPLE
get-LastOn -computername server1| Sort-Object time -Descending |
Sort-Object id -unique | format-table -AutoSize -Wrap
#>

param (
        [string]$ComputerName = 'localhost',
        [int]$Newest = 5000,
        [int]$maxIDs = 5,
        [int]$logonEventNum = 4624,
```

```
            [int]$logoffEventNum = 4647
    )

    $eventsAndIDs = Get-EventLog -LogName security -Newest $Newest |
    Where-Object {$_.instanceid -eq $logonEventNum -or
➡$_.instanceid -eq  $logoffEventNum} |
    Select-Object -Last $maxIDs
➡-Property TimeGenerated,Message,ComputerName

    foreach ($event in $eventsAndIDs) {
        $id = ($event |
        parseEventLogMessage |
        where-Object {$_.fieldName -eq "Account Name"}  |
        Select-Object -last 1).fieldValue

        $domain = ($event |
        parseEventLogMessage |
        where-Object {$_.fieldName -eq "Account Domain"}  |
        Select-Object -last 1).fieldValue

        $props = @{'Time'=$event.TimeGenerated;
            'Computer'=$ComputerName;
            'ID'=$id
            'Domain'=$domain}

        $output_obj = New-Object -TypeName PSObject -Property $props
        write-output $output_obj
    }
}

function parseEventLogMessage()
{
    [CmdletBinding()]
    param (
        [parameter(ValueFromPipeline=$True,Mandatory=$True)]
        [string]$Message
    )

    $eachLineArray = $Message -split "`n"

    foreach ($oneLine in $eachLineArray) {
        write-verbose "line:_$oneLine_"
        $fieldName,$fieldValue = $oneLine -split ":", 2
            try {
                $fieldName = $fieldName.trim()
                $fieldValue = $fieldValue.trim()
            }
            catch {
                $fieldName = ""
            }

            if ($fieldName -ne "" -and $fieldValue -ne "" )
            {
            $props = @{'fieldName'="$fieldName";
                    'fieldValue'=$fieldValue}

            $output_obj = New-Object -TypeName PSObject -Property $props
            Write-Output $output_obj
            }
    }
}
Get-LastOn
```

Never the end

We've nearly come to the end of this book, but it's hardly the end of your Power-Shell exploration. There's a lot more in the shell to learn, and based on what you've learned in this book, you'll be able to teach yourself much of it. This short chapter will help point you in the right directions.

27.1   Ideas for further exploration

This book has really focused on the skills and techniques that you need to be an effective PowerShell tool *user*. In other words, you should be able to start accomplishing tasks using all of the thousands of commands that are available for PowerShell, whether your needs relate to Windows, Exchange, SharePoint, or something else.

Your next step would be to start combining commands to create automated, multistep processes, and to do so in a way that produces packaged, ready-to-use tools for other people. We call that *toolmaking*, and it'll be the topic of its own complete book. But even with what you've learned in this book, you can produce parameterized scripts that contain as many commands as you need to complete a task—that's the very beginning of toolmaking.

What else does toolmaking involve?

- PowerShell's simplified scripting language
- Scope
- Functions, and the ability to build multiple tools into a single script file
- Error handling
- Writing help
- Debugging

- Custom formatting views
- Custom type extensions
- Script and manifest modules
- Using databases
- Workflows
- Pipeline troubleshooting
- Complex object hierarchies
- Globalization and localization
- GUI-based PowerShell tools
- Proxy functions
- Constrained remoting and delegated administration
- Using .NET

There's lots more, too. If you get interested enough and have the right background skills, you may even be a part of PowerShell's third audience: software developers. There's a whole set of techniques and technologies around developing for PowerShell, using PowerShell during development, and more. It's a big product!

27.2 *"Now that I've read the book, where do I start?"*

The best thing to do now is to pick a task. Choose something in your production world that you personally find repetitive, and automate it using the shell. You'll almost certainly run across things that you don't know how to do, and that's the perfect place to start learning.

Here are some of the things we've seen other administrators tackle:

- Write a script that changes the password a service uses to log in, and have it target multiple computers that are running that service. (You could do this in a single command.)
- Write a script that automates new user provisioning, including creating user accounts, mailboxes, and home directories. Setting NTFS permissions with PowerShell is tricky, but consider using a tool like Cacls.exe or Xcacls.exe from within your PowerShell script, instead of PowerShell's native (and complex) `Get-ACL` and `Set-ACL` cmdlets.
- Write a script that manages Exchange mailboxes in some way—perhaps getting reports on the largest mailboxes, or creating charge-back reports based on mailbox sizes.
- Automate the provisioning of new websites in IIS, using the WebAdministration module included in Windows Server 2008 R2 and later (which also works with IIS 7 in Windows Server 2008).

The biggest thing to remember is to *not overthink it*. Don once met an administrator who struggled for weeks to write a robust file-copying script in PowerShell so that he could deploy content across a web server farm. "Why not just use Xcopy or Robocopy?" Don asked. The administrator stared at Don for a minute, and then laughed.

He'd gotten so wrapped up in "doing it in PowerShell" that he forgot that PowerShell can use all of the excellent utilities that are already out there.

27.3 *Other resources you'll grow to love*

We spend a lot of time working with, writing about, and teaching PowerShell. Ask our families—sometimes we barely shut up about it long enough to eat dinner. That means we've accumulated a lot of online resources that we use daily, and that we recommend to all of our students. Hopefully they'll provide you with a good starting point as well.

- MoreLunches.com—This should be your first stop, if you haven't already bookmarked it. There you'll find free bonus and companion content for this book, including the lab answers, video demonstrations, bonus articles, and additional recommended resources. You'll also be able to download the longer code listings for this book so that you don't have to type them in manually. Consider bookmarking the site and visiting often to refresh what you've learned in this book.
- http://powershell.com/cs/blogs/donjones/default.aspx—This is Don's PowerShell blog, on the community site Powershell.com
- http://jdhitsolutions.com/blog—This is Jeff's all-purpose scripting and PowerShell blog.
- http://mcpmag.com/Articles/List/Prof-Powershell.aspx—This is Jeff's "Prof. PowerShell" weekly column for MCPMag.com, full of brief lessons and tips.
- http://bit.ly/AskDon—This is a public discussion forum where we answer questions directly. You'll need to register for an account, but once you do, you're welcome to post your PowerShell questions, and we'll do our best to answer. There are also dedicated forums for many domain-specific topics like Exchange, Active Directory, and more, and you should take advantage of the experts who moderate those forums.
- http://ShellHub.com—This is a website that Don maintains. It's a handpicked list of other PowerShell-related online resources, including the blogs we read most, third-party PowerShell tools, and more. Pretty much every URL we've ever recommended to someone is listed here. In the event that any other URL we give you changes, you can hop on ShellHub.com to find an update.

Students often ask if there are any other PowerShell books that we recommend. There are only a few that we keep right on our desks, all of which are listed on http://PowerShellBooks.com, which is kept updated as new books come out. Two of those—*Learn PowerShell Toolmaking in a Month of Lunches* and *PowerShell in Depth* (both available from Manning)—are books we've authored or coauthored, so if you liked this book those ones will probably work well for you also.

Finally, if you'd like some full-length video-based training for PowerShell, visit http://videotraining.interfacett.com for full-length, studio-quality offerings from Don and other PowerShell experts. Keep in mind, though, that MoreLunches.com also hosts free companion video content for each chapter in this book.

PowerShell cheat sheet

28

This is our opportunity to assemble a lot of the little *gotchas* into a single place. If you're ever having trouble remembering what something is or does, flip to this chapter first.

28.1 Punctuation

There's no doubt that PowerShell is full of punctuation, and much of it has a different meaning in the help files than it does in the shell itself. Here's what it all means within the shell:

- ` (backtick)—This is PowerShell's escape character. It removes the special meaning of any character that follows it. For example, a space is normally a separator, which is why `cd c:\Program Files` generates an error. Escaping the space, `cd c:\Program` Files`, removes that special meaning and forces the space to be treated as a literal, so the command works.

- ~ (tilde)—When used as part of a path, this represents the current user's home directory, as defined in the `UserProfile` environment variable.

- ( ) (parentheses)—These are used in a couple of ways:
  - Just as in math, parentheses define an order of execution. PowerShell will execute parenthetical commands first, from the innermost parentheses to the outermost. This is a good way to run a command and have its output feed the parameter of another command: `Get-Service -computerName (Get-Content c:\computernames.txt)`.

- Parentheses also enclose the parameters of a method, and they must be included even if the method doesn't require any parameters: `Change-Start-Mode('Automatic')`, for example, or `Delete()`.

- **[ ] (square brackets)**—These have two main uses in the shell:
  - They contain the index number when you want to refer to a single object within an array or collection: `$services[2]` gets the third object from `$services` (indexes are always zero-based).
  - They contain a data type when you're casting a piece of data as a specific type. For example, `$myresult / 3 -as [int]` casts the result as a whole number (integer), and `[xml]$data = Get-Content data.xml` will read the contents of Data.xml and attempt to parse it as a valid XML document.

- **{ } (curly braces or curly brackets)**—These have three uses:
  - They contain blocks of executable code or commands, called *script blocks*. These are often fed to parameters that expect a script block or a filter block: `Get-Service | Where-Object { $_.Status -eq 'Running' }`.
  - They contain the key-value pairs that make up a new hashtable. The opening brace is always preceded by an @ sign. In the following example, we're using braces both to enclose the hashtable key-value pairs (of which there are two) and to enclose an expression script block, which is the value for the second key, e: `$hashtable = @{l='Label';e={expression}}`.
  - When a variable name contains spaces or other characters normally illegal in a variable name, braces must surround the name: `${My Variable}`.

- **' ' (single quotation marks)**—These contain string values. PowerShell doesn't look for the escape character, nor does it look for variables, inside single quotes.

- **" " (double quotation marks)**—These contain string values. PowerShell looks for escape characters and the $ character inside double quotes. Escape characters are processed, and the characters following a $ symbol (up to the next whitespace) are taken as a variable name and the contents of that variable are substituted. For example, if the variable `$one` contains the value `World`, then `$two = "Hello $one `n"` will contain `Hello World` and a carriage return (`` `n `` is a carriage return).

- **$ (dollar sign)**—This character tells the shell that the following characters, up to the next white space, represent a variable name. This can be tricky when working with cmdlets that manage variables. Supposing that `$one` contains the value two, then `New-Variable -name $one -value 'Hello'` will create a new variable named two, with the value Hello, because the dollar sign tells the shell that you want to use the contents of `$one`. In contrast, `New-Variable -name one -value 'Hello'` would create a new variable `$one`.

- **% (percent sign)**—This is an alias for the `ForEach-Object` cmdlet. It's also the modulus operator, returning the remainder from a division operation.

- ? (question mark)—This is an alias for the `Where-Object` cmdlet.
- > (right angle bracket)—This is a sort of alias for the `Out-File` cmdlet. It's not technically a true alias, but it does provide for Cmd.exe-style file redirection: `dir > files.txt`.
- + - * / % (math operators)—These function as standard arithmetic operators. Note that + is also used for string concatenation.
- - (dash or hyphen)—This precedes both parameter names and many operators, such as `-computerName` or `-eq`. It also separates the verb and noun components of a cmdlet name, as in `Get-Content`, and serves as the subtraction arithmetic operator.
- @ (at sign)—This has four uses in the shell:
  - It precedes a hashtable's opening curly brace (see curly braces, above).
  - When used before parentheses, it encloses a comma-separated list of values that form an array: `$array = @(1,2,3,4)`. Both the @ sign and the parentheses are optional, because the shell will normally treat any comma-separated list as an array anyway.
  - It denotes a *here-string*, which is a block of literal string text. A here-string starts with `@"` and ends with `"@`, and the closing mark must be on the beginning of a new line. Run `help about_quoting_rules` for more information and examples. Here-strings can also be defined using single quotes.
  - It is PowerShell's splat operator. If you construct a hashtable where the keys match parameter names, and those values' keys are the parameters' values, then you can splat the hashtable to a cmdlet. Don wrote an article for Tech-Net Magazine on splatting (http://technet.microsoft.com/en-us/magazine/ gg675931.aspx).
- & (ampersand)—This is PowerShell's invocation operator, instructing the shell to treat something as a command and to run it. For example, `$a = "Dir"` places the string `"Dir"` into the variable $a. Then `& $a` will run the `Dir` command.
- ; (semicolon)—This is used to separate two independent PowerShell commands that are included on a single line: `Dir ; Get-Process` will run `Dir` and then `Get-Process`. The results are sent to a single pipeline, but the results of `Dir` aren't piped to `Get-Process`.
- # (pound sign or hash mark)—This is used as a comment character. Any characters following #, to the next carriage return, are ignored by the shell. The angle brackets, < and >, are used as part of the tags that define a block comment: use <# to start a block comment, and #> to end one. Everything within the block comment will be ignored by the shell.
- = (equal sign)—This is the assignment operator, used to assign a value to a variable: `$one = 1`. It isn't used for quality comparisons; use `-eq` instead. Note that the equal sign can be used in conjunction with a math operator: `$var +=5` will add 5 to whatever is currently in $var.

- | (pipe)—The pipe is used to convey the output of one cmdlet to the input of another. The second cmdlet (the one receiving the output) uses pipeline parameter binding to determine which parameter or parameters will receive the piped-in objects. Chapter 9 has a discussion of this process.
- \ or / (backslash or forward slash)—A forward slash is used as a division operator in mathematical expressions; either the forward slash or backslash can be used as a path separator in file paths: C:\Windows is the same as C:/Windows. The backslash is also used as an escape character in WMI filter criteria and in regular expressions.
- . (period)—The period has three main uses:
  - It's used to indicate that you want to access a member, such as a property or method, or an object: $_.Status will access the Status property of whatever object is in the $_ placeholder
  - It's used to *dot source* a script, meaning that the script will be run within the current scope, and anything defined by that script will remain defined after the script completes: . c:\myscript.ps1
  - Two dots (..) form the range operator, which is discussed later in this chapter. You will also see two dots used to refer to the parent folder in the filesystem, such as in the path ..\
- , (comma)—Outside of quotation marks, the comma separates the items in a list or array: "One",2,"Three",4. It can be used to pass multiple static values to a parameter that can accept them: Get-Process -computername Server1, Server2,Server3.
- : (colon)—The colon (technically, two colons) is used to access static members of a class; this gets into .NET Framework programming concepts. [datetime]::now is an example (although you could achieve that same task by running Get-Date).
- ! (exclamation point)—This is an alias for the -not Boolean operator.

We think the only piece of punctuation on a U.S. keyboard that PowerShell doesn't actively use for something is the caret (^), although those do get used in regular expressions.

28.2 Help file

Punctuation within the help file takes on slightly different meanings:

- [ ]—Square brackets that surround any text indicate that the text is optional. That might include an entire command ([-Name <string>]), or it might indicate that a parameter is positional and that the name is optional ([-Name] <string>). It can also indicate both: that a parameter is optional, and if used, can be used positionally ([[-Name] <string>]). It's always legal to use the parameter name, if you're in any doubt.

- [ ]—Adjacent square brackets indicate that a parameter can accept multiple values (<string[]> instead of <string>).
- < >—Angle brackets surround data types, indicating what kind of value or object a parameter expects: <string>, <int>, <process>, and so forth.

Always take the time to read the full help (add -full to the help command), because it provides maximum detail as well as, in most cases, usage examples.

28.3 Operators

PowerShell doesn't use the traditional comparison operators found in most programming languages. Instead, it uses these:

- -eq—Equality (-ceq for case-sensitive string comparisons)
- -ne—Inequality (-cne for case-sensitive string comparisons)
- -ge—Greater than or equal to (-cge for case-sensitive string comparisons)
- -le—Less than or equal to (-cle for case-sensitive string comparisons)
- -gt—Greater than (-cgt for case-sensitive string comparisons)
- -lt—Less than (-clt for case-sensitive string comparisons)
- -contains—Returns True if the specified collection contains the object specified ($collection -contains $object); -notcontains is the reverse
- -in—Returns True if the specified object is in the specified collection ($object -in $collection); -notin is the reverse

Logical operators are used to combine multiple comparisons:

- -not—Reverses True and False (the ! symbol is an alias for this operator)
- -and—Both subexpressions must be True for the entire expression to be True
- -or—Either subexpression can be True for the entire expression to be True

In addition, there are operators that perform specific functions:

- -join—Joins the elements of an array into a delimited string
- -split—Splits a delimited string into an array
- -replace—Replaces occurrences of one string with another
- -is—Returns True if an item is of the specified type ($one -is [int])
- -as—Casts the item as the specified type ($one -as [int])
- ..—Is a range operator; 1..10 returns ten objects, 1 through 10.
- -f—Is the format operator, replacing placeholders with values: "{0}, {1}" -f "Hello","World"

28.4 Custom property and column syntax

In several chapters, we showed you how to define custom properties using Select-Object, or custom columns and list entries using Format-Table and Format-List respectively. Here's that hashtable syntax.

You do this for each custom property or column:

```
@{label='Column_or_Property_Name';expression={Value_expression}}
```

Both of the keys, `Label` and `Expression`, can be abbreviated as `l` and `e` respectively (be sure to type a lowercase "L" and not the number 1; you could also use n for `Name`, in place of the lowercase "L").

```
@{n='Column_or_Property_Name';e={Value_expression}}
```

Within the expression, the `$_` placeholder can be used to refer to the current object (such as the current table row, or the object to which you're adding a custom property):

```
@{n='ComputerName';e={$_.Name}}
```

Both `Select-Object` and the `Format-` cmdlets look for the n (or name or label or l) key and the e key; the `Format-` cmdlets can also use `width` and `align` (those are for `Format-Table` only) and `formatstring`. Read the help for `Format-Table` for examples.

28.5 *Pipeline parameter input*

In chapter 9 you learned that there are two types of parameter binding: `ByValue` and `ByPropertyName`. `ByValue` occurs first, and `ByPropertyName` only occurs if `ByValue` didn't work.

For `ByValue`, the shell looks at the type of the object that was piped in. You can discover that type name by piping the object to Gm yourself. The shell then looks to see if any of the cmdlet's parameters accept that type of input and are configured to accept pipeline input `ByValue`. It's not possible for a cmdlet to have two parameters binding the same data type in this fashion. In other words, you shouldn't see a cmdlet that has two parameters, each of which accepts <string> input, both of which accept pipeline input `ByValue`.

If `ByValue` doesn't work, the shell switches to `ByPropertyName`. Here, it simply looks at the properties of the piped-in object and attempts to find parameters with the exact same names that can accept pipeline input `ByPropertyName`. If the piped-in object has properties `Name`, `Status`, and `ID`, the shell will look to see if the cmdlet has parameters named `Name`, `Status`, and `ID`. Those parameters must also be tagged as accepting pipeline input `ByPropertyName`, which you can see when reading the full help (add `-full` to the `help` command).

Let's look at how PowerShell does this. For this example, we'll refer to the *first cmdlet* and *second cmdlet*, assuming you have a command that looks something like `Get-Service | Stop-Service` or `Get-Service | Stop-Process`. PowerShell follows this process:

1 What is the `TypeName` of the objects produced by the first cmdlet? You can pipe the results of the cmdlet to `Get-Member` on your own to see this. For multipart type names like `System.Diagnostics.Process`, just remember that last bit: `Process`.

2 Do any parameters of the second cmdlet accept the kind of object produced by the first cmdlet (read the full help for the second cmdlet to determine this:

help <cmdlet name> -full)? If so, do they also accept that input from the pipe-line using the ByValue technique? This is shown in the help file's detailed information for each parameter.

3   If the answer to step 2 is yes, then the entire object produced by the first cmdlet will be attached to the parameter identified in step 2. You're done—do not continue to step 4. But if the answer to step 2 is no, then continue to step 4.

4   Consider the objects produced by the first cmdlet. What properties do those objects have? You can see this, again, by piping the first cmdlet's output to Get-Member.

5   Consider the parameters of the second cmdlet (you'll need to read the full help again). Are there any parameters that (a) have the same name as one of the properties from step 4, and (b) accept pipeline input using the ByPropertyName technique?

6   If there are any parameters meeting the criteria in step 5, then the properties' values will be attached to the same-named parameters, and the second cmdlet will run. If there are no matches between property names and ByPropertyName-enabled parameters, the second cmdlet will run with no pipeline input.

Keep in mind that you can always manually enter parameters and values on any command. Doing so will prevent that parameter from accepting pipeline input in any way, even if it would normally have done so.

28.6   When to use $_

This is probably one of the most confusing things about the shell: when is the $_ placeholder permitted?

This placeholder only works when the shell is explicitly looking for it and is prepared to fill it in with something. Generally speaking, that only happens within a script block that's dealing with pipeline input, in which case the $_ placeholder will contain one pipeline input object at a time. You'll run across this in a few different places:

- In the filtering script block used by Where-Object:

```
Get-Service |3 Where-Object {$_.Status -eq 'Running' }
```

- In the script blocks passed to ForEach-Object, such as the main Process script block typically used with the cmdlet:

```
Get-WmiObject -class Win32_Service -filter "name='mssqlserver'" |
    ForEach-Object -process { $_.ChangeStartMode('Automatic') }
```

- In the Process script block of a filtering function or an advanced function. Our other book, *Learn PowerShell Toolmaking in a Month of Lunches*, discusses these.

- In the expression of a hashtable that's being used to create a custom property or table column. Refer to section 28.4 in this chapter for more details, or read chapters 8, 9, and 10 for a more complete discussion.

In every one of those cases, $_ occurs only within the curly braces of a script block. That's a good rule to remember for figuring out when it's okay to use $_.

appendix
Review labs

This appendix provides three review labs, which you can work on after completing the designated chapters and labs from this book. These reviews are a great way to take a break in your learning process and to reinforce some of the most important things you've learned to that point. As always, you'll find example answers on MoreLunches.com. Just find this book's cover image, click on it, and then go to the Downloads section to download the lab sample solutions file.

Because the instructions for some of these lab tasks are more complex, we've broken them down into discrete task sections. We've also provided you with a list of hints at the start of each lab, to remind you about specific commands, help files, and syntax that you may need to complete the lab.

Review lab 1: chapters 1–6

NOTE To complete this lab, you will need any computer running Power-Shell v3. You should complete the labs in chapters 1 through 6 of this book prior to attempting this review lab.

HINTS:
- `Sort-Object`
- `Select-Object`
- `Import-Module`
- `Export-CSV`
- `Help`
- `Get-ChildItem (Dir)`

TASK 1
Run a command that will display the newest 100 entries from the Application event log. Do not use `Get-WinEvent`.

TASK 2
Write a command line that displays only the five top processes based on virtual memory (VM) usage.

TASK 3

Create a CSV file that contains all services, including only the service names and statuses. Have running services listed *before* stopped services.

TASK 4

Write a command line that changes the startup type of the BITS service to `Manual`.

TASK 5

Display a list of all files named `win*.*` on your computer. Start in the `C:\` folder. Note: you may need to experiment and use some new parameters of a cmdlet in order to complete this task.

TASK 6

Get a directory listing for C:\Program Files. Include all subfolders, and have the directory listing go into a text file named C:\Dir.txt (remember to use the > redirector, or the `Out-File` cmdlet)

TASK 7

Get a list of the most recent 20 entries from the Security event log, and convert the information to XML. Do not create a file on disk: have the XML display in the console window.

Note that the XML may display as a single top-level object, rather than as raw XML data—that's fine. That's just how PowerShell displays XML. You can pipe the XML object to `Format-Custom` to see it expanded out into an object hierarchy, if you like.

TASK 8

Get a list of services, and export the data to a CSV file named C:\services.csv.

TASK 9

Get a list of services. Keep only the services' names, display names, and statuses, and send that information to an HTML file. Have the phrase "Installed Services" displayed in the HTML file before the table of service information.

TASK 10

Create a new alias, named `D`, which runs `Get-ChildItem`. Export just that alias to a file. Now, close the shell and open a new console window. Import that alias into the shell. Make sure you can run `D` and get a directory listing.

TASK 11

Display a list of event logs that are available on your system.

TASK 12

Run a command that will display the current directory that the shell is in.

TASK 13

Run a command that will display the most recent commands that you have run in the shell. Locate the command that you ran for task 11. Using two commands connected by a pipeline, rerun the command from task 11.

In other words, if `Get-Something` is the command that retrieves historical commands, if 5 is the ID number of the command from task 11, and `Do-Something` is the command that runs historical commands, run this:

```
Get-Something -id 5 | Do-Something
```

Of course, those aren't the correct cmdlet names—you'll need to find those. Hint: both commands that you need have the same noun.

Task 14

Run a command that modifies the Security event log to overwrite old events as needed.

Task 15

Use the `New-Item` cmdlet to make a new directory named C:\Review. This is not the same as running `Mkdir`; the `New-Item` cmdlet will need to know what *kind* of new item you want to create. Read the help for the cmdlet.

Task 16

Display the contents of this registry key:

```
HKCU:\Software\Microsoft\Windows\CurrentVersion\Explorer\User Shell Folders
```

Note: "User Shell Folders" is not exactly like a directory. If you change into that "directory," you won't see anything in a directory listing. User Shell Folders is an *item,* and what it contains are *item properties.* There's a cmdlet capable of displaying item properties (although cmdlets use singular nouns, not plural).

Task 17

Find (but please do not run) cmdlets that can...

- Restart a computer
- Shut down a computer
- Remove a computer from a workgroup or domain
- Restore a computer's System Restore checkpoint

Task 18

What command do you think could change a registry value? Hint: it's the same noun as the cmdlet you found for task 16.

Review lab 2: chapters 1–14

NOTE   To complete this lab, you'll need any computer running PowerShell v3. You should complete the labs in chapters 1 through 14 of this book prior to attempting this review lab.

HINTS:

- `Format-Table`
- `Invoke-Command`
- `Get-Content` (or `Type`)

- Parenthetical commands
- @{label='column_header';expression={$_.property}}
- Get-WmiObject
- Where-Object
- -eq -ne -like -notlike

TASK 1

Display a list of running processes in a table that includes only the process names and ID numbers. Don't let the table have a large blank area between the two columns.

TASK 2

Run this:

```
Get-WmiObject -class Win32_UserAccount
```

Now run that same command again, but format the output into a table that has Domain and UserName columns. The UserName column should show the users' Name property, like this:

```
Domain    UserName
=======   ========
COMPANY   DonJ
```

Make sure the second column header says UserName, and not Name.

TASK 3

Have two computers (it's OK to use localhost twice) run this command:

```
Get-PSProvider
```

Use Remoting to do this. Ensure that the output includes the computer names.

TASK 4

Use Notepad to create a file named C:\Computers.txt. In that file, put the following:

```
Localhost
localhost
```

You should have those two names on their own lines in the file—two lines total. Save the file and close Notepad. Then write a command that will list the running services on the computer names in C:\Computers.txt.

TASK 5

Query all instances of Win32_LogicalDisk. Display only those instances that have a DriveType property containing 3 and that have 50 percent or more free disk space. Hint: to calculate free space percentage, it's freespace/size * 100.

Note that the -Filter parameter of Get-WmiObject cannot contain mathematical expressions.

TASK 6

Display a list of all WMI classes in the root\CIMv2 namespace.

TASK 7

Display a list of all `Win32_Service` instances where the `StartMode` is `Auto` and the `State` is not `Running`.

TASK 8

Find a command that can send email messages. What are the mandatory parameters of this command?

TASK 9

Run a command that will display the folder permissions on C:\.

TASK 10

Run a command that will display the permissions on every subfolder of C:\Users. Just the direct subfolders; you don't need to recurse all files and folders. You'll need to pipe one command to another command to achieve this.

TASK 11

Find a command that will start Notepad under a credential other than the one you've used to log into the shell.

TASK 12

Run a command that makes the shell pause, or idle, for 10 seconds.

TASK 13

Can you find a help file (or files) that explains the shell's various *operators?*

TASK 14

Write an informational message to the Application event log. Use a category of 1 and raw data of `100,100`.

TASK 15

Run this command:

```
Get-WmiObject -Class Win32_Processor
```

Study the default output of this command. Now, modify the command so that it displays in a table. The table should include each processor's number of cores, manufacturer, and name. Also include a column called "MaxSpeed" that contains the processor's maximum clock speed.

TASK 16

Run this command:

```
Get-WmiObject -Class Win32_Process
```

Study the default output of this command, and pipe it to `Get-Member` if you want. Now, modify the command so that only processes with a peak working set size greater than 5,000 are displayed.

Review lab 3: chapters 1–19

NOTE   To complete this lab, you'll need any computer running PowerShell v3.

You should complete the labs in chapters 1 through 19 of this book prior to attempting this review lab.

Start by answering the following questions:

1. What command would you use to start a job that runs entirely on your local computer?

2. What command would you use to start a job that was coordinated by your computer, but whose contents were processed by remote computers?

3. Is ${computer name} a legal variable name?

4. How could you display a list of all variables currently defined in the shell?

5. What command could be used to prompt a user for input?

6. What command should be used to produce output that normally displays on the screen, but that could be redirected to various other formats?

Now, complete the following three tasks.

TASK 1

Create a list of running processes. The list should include only process name, ID, VM, and PM columns. Put the list into an HTML-formatted file named C:\Procs.html. Make sure that the HTML file has an embedded title of "Current Processes". Display the file in a web browser and make sure that title appears in the browser window's titlebar.

TASK 2

Create a tab-delimited file named C:\Services.tdf that contains all services on your computer. "`t" (backtick *t* inside double quotes) is PowerShell's escape sequence for a horizontal tab. Include only the services' names, display names, and statuses.

TASK 3

Repeat task 1, modifying your command so that the VM and PM columns of the HTML file display values in megabytes (MB), instead of bytes. The formula to calculate megabytes, displaying the value as a whole number, goes something like $_.VM / 1MB -as [int] for the VM property.

index

MORE TITLES FROM MANNING

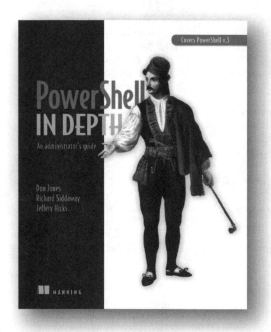

PowerShell in Depth
An administrator's guide
by Don Jones, Richard Siddaway,
 and Jeffery Hicks

ISBN: 978-1-617290-55-8
525 pages
$49.99
December 2012

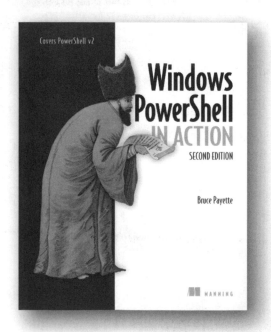

Windows PowerShell in Action
Second Edition
by Bruce Payette

ISBN: 978-1-935182-13-9
1016 pages
$59.99
May 2011

For ordering information go to www.manning.com

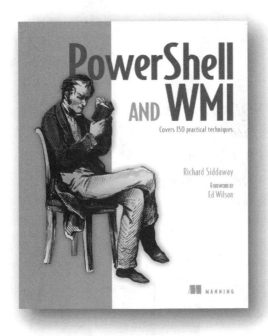

MORE TITLES FROM MANNING

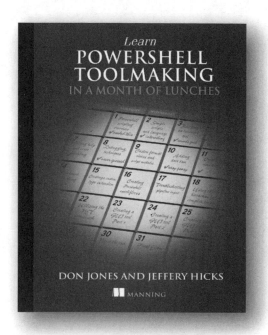